OUR
FAMILY
TIME WITH GOD

OUR
FAMILY
TIME WITH GOD

Family Devotions for Every Day of the Year!

COMPILED BY
HAROLD D. VAUGHAN

Christ *life*
PUBLICATIONS
P.O. Box 399
Vinton, VA 24179

All Scripture quotations are from the King James Version (KJV) of the Bible.

OUR FAMILY TIME WITH GOD

ISBN: 0-942889-15-0
Printed in the United States of America
Copyright © 2006 by Harold D. Vaughan

Christ Life Publications
P.O. Box 399
Vinton, VA 24179
www.christlifemin.org

DEVOTIONAL ORDER

MAY

1-7   Psalm 145 (Ken Varney)
8-15   Obedience (Harold Vaughan)
16-22 Finances (Tom Palmer)
23-29 God's View of Family Living (Jack Palmer)
30-31 Spiritual Warfare (Stanley W. Long, II)

JUNE

1-5   Spiritual Warfare (Stanley W. Long, II)
6-12   Biblical Separation (Tom Palmer)
13-19 The Ten Commandments (Debbie Vaughan)
20-26 The Ten Commandments 2 (Debbie Vaughan)
27   Keep Everyone Working (Jeff Kahl)
28-30 Lessons from History (Tom Palmer)

JULY

1-4   Lessons from History (Tom Palmer)
5-11   Knowing Our God (T.P. Johnston, Jr.)
12-18 Adversity (Harold Vaughan)
19-25 Family Answers to Prayer (Tom Palmer)
26-31 Worship (Jack Palmer)

AUGUST

1   Worship (Jack Palmer)
2-8   Let's Be a Barney (Tom Farrell)
9-15   God-Pleasing Life (Tom Palmer)
16   Revival (Robert Booth)
17-23 Service (Rick Johnson)
24-30 God's Formula for Family Success (Jack Palmer)
31   Resting in God (Stephen Vaughan)

INTRODUCTION

God charged parents in Deuteronomy 6:6-7 with teaching God's Word to their children. "And these words, which I command thee this day, shall be in thine heart: And thou shalt teach them diligently unto thy children, and shalt talk of them when thou sittest in thine house, and when thou walkest by the way, and when thou liest down, and when thou risest up."

Most Christians believe the Bible should be taught in the home. But work schedules and various activities make regular family devotions difficult to prepare and to accomplish.

Our Family Time with God offers a concise, practical teaching for every day of the year. Any head of household can use this volume as a devotional and teaching aid to instruct his family in the things of God.

All contributing authors have worked to instill godly principles in the lives of their own children. We all believe in the truth of Proverbs 22:6. "Train up a child in the way he should go: and when he is old, he will not depart from it."

Bible reading and teaching, praying, and singing should be the norm in our Christian homes. I trust that *Our Family Time with God* will be a tremendous asset to you as you lead your family.

Your Servant for Revival,

Harold Vaughan

ACKNOWLEDGMENTS & AUTHORS

This project would not have been possible apart from the participation of many friends. I want to thank the following for partnering with us by contributing to this book:

Harold and Debbie Vaughan

Harold is a full-time evangelist and founder of Christ Life Ministries (Vinton, VA). C.L.M. sponsors Prayer Advances, produces publications, and sponsors various local church ministries. To learn more about C.L.M., go to www. christlifemin.org. God has blessed Harold and Debbie with three sons.

Tom Palmer

After attending Bible college, Tom Palmer served as assistant pastor and youth pastor with his father, Jack Palmer, at Calvary Independent Baptist Church (Huntingdon, PA). In 1989, he founded the Palmer Revival Ministries (Spring Mills, PA). Married since 1983, he and his wife, Patty, have three children. Through their revival ministry, they minister full time in churches, Christian schools, and Christian camps.

Jack Palmer

Jack Palmer pastored independent Baptist churches for 30 years before founding Victorious Family Living Ministries in 1990. He hosts the Keys to Family Living radio program, conducts family revival meetings in churches, and produces various resources for the family. He and his wife, June, have four children and ten grandchildren. The Palmers live in Spring Mills, Pennsylvania.

T.P. Johnston, Jr.

After his conversion in 1969 and his call to the ministry, T.P. Johnston, Jr., completed Bible college and founded a church in his hometown. In 1994, after he served in that work for more than 18 years, God led him and his wife, Mary, and their four daughters to Smyrna, Georgia, where he serves as senior pastor of Calvary Baptist Church.

ACKNOWLEDGMENTS & AUTHORS (CONTINUED)

Craig M. Scott

Craig M. Scott is senior pastor of Woodside Baptist Church (Denver, CO). Previously, he served as a youth pastor in four independent Baptist churches and has served on various ministry boards. He regularly speaks at conferences, Christian school retreats, revival meetings, youth camps, and Bible conferences. God has blessed him and his wife, Karen, with four children and four grandchildren.

Rick Johnson

Rick Johnson has served as pastor of Friendship Baptist Church (Huntsville, AL) since 1986. He and his wife, Paula, were married in 1979. God has blessed them with seven children.

Tom Farrell

Dr. Tom Farrell has traveled as an evangelist since 1979. From 1974 to 1990, he and his wife, Regina, faithfully served on staff at THE WILDS Christian Camp & Conference Center (Brevard, NC). In 1990, he formed Tom Farrell Ministries. Dr. Farrell serves as vice president of Heart of America Seminary, a ministry of Tri-City Baptist Church. He preaches in local church revivals, area-wide campaigns, Christian colleges, camps; and on many mission fields. God has blessed him and Regina with three children and one grandchild.

Jeff Kahl

Since 2002, Jeff has served as director of Camp CoBeAc (Houghton Lake, MI), a conservative Christian camp serving thousands annually. Jeff is also a frequent youth and family speaker across the country. Prior to his role at Camp CoBeAc, he served as camp director at Northland Camp & Conference Center as well as a vice president and instructor at Northland Baptist Bible College, both in Dunbar, Wisconsin. Jeff and his wife, Carol, have three children.

Stanley W. Long, II

Stanley W. Long, II, serves as associate pastor for Camp Eagle Ministries of Shenandoah Baptist Church (Roanoke, VA). He joined the staff of Shenandoah Baptist in 2000 as the director of Camp Eagle (Fincastle, VA) and has also served as Shenandoah's student ministries pastor. Currently, Stanley serves as the camp director. God has blessed him and his wife, Kelle, with nine children.

Ken Varney

Ken Varney is involved in various ministries, including nursing homes and homeless shelters. He is undergoing chaplain training with Good News Jail Ministry and has served the last 10 years at the Frederick County Jail. He has a bachelor's degree in Theology and is currently pursuing a master's degree. He and his wife, Stacy, home-school their three daughters.

Robert Booth

Robert Booth and his wife, Gina, have been married for 26 years and blessed with 11 children. They reside in Talking Rock, Georgia, and attend Calvary Mountain Baptist Church.

Stephen Vaughan

Stephen is Harold and Debbie Vaughan's youngest son. He is an avid reader and enjoys all kinds of outdoor activities. This is his first contribution to a published volume.

Editing and proofreading by **Adam and Kim Blumer**

Cover design and interior typesetting by **Chris Hartzler**

JANUARY 1
A New Year Brings Opportunity!

Scripture Reading—Matthew 9:29b
"According to your faith be it unto you."

A father showed up late for his son's baseball game. His son was playing third base. "How is it going?" he yelled to his boy.

"Great!" his son responded.

Then the dad noticed the scoreboard. The other team was winning 15 to zero. He yelled back to his son, "The score is 15 to nothing."

"That's right."

"Well, why did you say things are going great?"

His son replied, "We haven't batted yet!" What a fantastic attitude! That boy was looking forward to the opportunity of getting to step up to the plate!

William James said, "The greatest discovery of my generation is that a person can alter his life by altering his attitude of mind." That is what the Bible means when it says as a man "thinketh in his heart, so is he" (Prov. 23:7). Your outlook has a tremendous bearing on your outcome. Negative expectations are usually fulfilled, but God rewards faith-based optimism.

A new year means new opportunities. *Webster's New World Dictionary* defines the word *new* as never existing before. In the coming days, you will encounter things you have never faced before; but God has already been where you are about to go.

The word *new* appears 131 times in the Bible. It speaks of new mercies, a new song, a new spirit, a new birth, a new commandment, and a new covenant. This New Year is a new beginning. New things are in store for you because "if any man be in Christ, he is a new creature: old things are passed away; behold, all things are become new" (2 Cor. 5:17).

You will have challenges and choices over the next 12 months, but you can face the future with confidence. It's your turn to step up to the plate!

PONDER, PRAY, PRAISE: Ponder and discuss the opportunities your family has in store over the next 12 months. Pray in faith and believe God for *great things*. Praise the Lord for opportunities to grow in grace.

—Harold Vaughan

Is There Hope for the Family?

Scripture Reading—Psalm 42
Give special attention to verses 5 and 11.

Many are wondering if there's hope for the family because of the decline of family values in our 21st century society. Fifty years ago, no one would have been able to conceive of the devastation to family life that's now common in America. In a 1999 issue of *Time Magazine*, an article titled "Beyond the Year 2000" states the following:

> We are fast becoming a homeless race. We are born in hospitals, raised in daycare, married in church, vacation at resorts, entertain friends in restaurants, die in hospitals, and are buried from the funeral parlor. To thousands of families, home is simply a place where family members resort for a minimum of sleep, a quick bite to eat, and wait their turn to use a family car.

What a sad commentary on our way of life! If we listened to historians, sociologists, and media, we would wonder if the family, as we've known it, is on the way out. Thank God, we don't get our information from those voices. The Bible is our source of encouragement and direction.

In today's Scripture, we hear the cry of the spiritually desperate (vv. 1-2), downhearted (v. 6), and disillusioned (vv. 9-10). And that could well describe many of God's people these days. But in the midst of it all, the psalmist knows where to find hope—"Hope thou in God" (vv. 5, 11). With the divorce rate in excess of 50 percent, the future of the family doesn't look good. We must keep looking up because God is our only hope.

This week, we'll be looking at biblical reasons there's hope for the family, even during these difficult days. Yes, we need God to revive our families. He's more than ready to do His work if we'll submit to Him.

PRAYER TIME: Pray this verse. "Wilt thou not *revive us again*: that thy people may rejoice in thee?" (Ps. 85:6, emphasis added). Whenever we see revival, we always find rejoicing!

—*Jack Palmer*

GOD IS OUR ONLY HOPE!

Scripture Reading—2 Chronicles 14:11
"And Asa cried unto the Lord his God, and said,
Lord, it is nothing with thee to help, whether with many, or with them
that have no power: help us, O Lord our God; for we rest on thee,
and in thy name we go against this multitude.
O Lord, thou art our God; *let not man prevail against thee"*
(emphasis added).

When folks say there's no hope for the family, they're forgetting that God is still God! When King Asa faced a humanly impossible situation, he knew there was hope as long as God was on His throne. God is greater than any situation we'll ever face.

Never forget, the family was God's idea. "And the Lord God said, It is not good that the man should be alone; I will make him an help meet for him" (Gen. 2:18). From the beginning, Satan has attacked the family because he knows it's near and dear to God's heart. If anyone wants you to think there's no hope for the family, it's Satan. When a family has trouble, Satan does whatever he can to make things look impossible. He wants husbands and wives to give up on each other. He encourages parents to think they're failures. He wants to destroy our hope, joy, and peace.

In Romans 15:13, the apostle Paul writes, "Now the God of *hope* fill you with all *joy* and *peace* in believing, that ye may abound in *hope*, through the power of the Holy Ghost" (emphasis added). Herein is our hope—that God by His Spirit can fill our lives with hope because He's the God of hope. He's the God of the impossible! "With men this is impossible; *but with God all things are possible*" (Matt. 19:26b, emphasis added). No situation lies beyond God's hope. Remember, when God's going to do something wonderful, He begins with a difficulty. When He's going to do something exceptionally wonderful, He begins with an impossibility!

BELIEVING PRAYER: Consider a family situation that appears hopeless. Pray and trust God to work a miracle in that situation.

—*Jack Palmer*

JANUARY 4
GOD'S WORD
IS STILL TRUE!

Scripture Reading—John 17:17
*"Sanctify them through thy truth: **thy word is truth**" (emphasis added).*

"What is truth?" is the question many are asking these days. Embracing relativism, they believe there's no such thing as absolute truth. "What's truth to you is truth, and what's truth to someone else is truth to him." Many also believe that no one has the right to impose his idea of truth on someone else. It's up to each person to decide for himself.

In Judges 17:6b, we read, "Every man did that which was right in his own eyes." No wonder there's so much confusion, even in the Church! As we study reasons we believe there's hope for the family, we find great comfort and strength in the fact that there's absolute truth, and it's found in God's Word. Times may change, but God's Word doesn't (Ps. 119:89).

A famous trapper from the North Country shared his secrets with a young man who wanted to be a great trapper, too. The trapper told the young man that if he did exactly what he said, he could be as good as the trapper. At the end of the trapping season, the famous trapper met the young man again, eager to hear about his results. Much to his surprise, he discovered that the young man had done poorly. The trapper asked the young man if he'd followed his directions. "No, I found a better way," the young man replied. No wonder he failed!

We all want strong families, and God gives us all we need in His Word. The Bible is still the greatest book ever written. In its pages, God tells us how to live life; but we keep turning to our "better ways." Then we wonder why we struggle and fail. If we would get back to the Bible and do things God's way, we'd see God's blessing on our families. Yes, there's hope for the family because *God's Word is still truth.*

APPLICATION: Read Ephesians 5:18–6:4. Discuss how God expects us to live if we want His blessing.

—*Jack Palmer*

JANUARY 5
GOD STILL
ANSWERS PRAYER!

Scripture Reading—Jeremiah 33:3
*"Call unto me, and **I will answer thee**, and shew thee great and mighty things, which thou knowest not" (emphasis added).*

We must never forget that *as long as God still answers prayer*, there's hope for the family. In fact, prayer is one of the greatest needs of the family. Many Christian families are struggling with major issues. Marriages are unstable. Children are rebellious. Finances are tight. Parents are neglectful. Families face conflicts over decisions they must make. And in the midst of it all, God says, "Call unto me!" Why is it that the thing we need most is often the thing we neglect?

When we're on our knees before God in prayer, there's not a question that cannot be answered, a problem that cannot be solved, a need that cannot be met, a battle that cannot be won, an obstacle that cannot be overcome, a sin that cannot be forgiven, or a conflict that cannot be resolved. That's how powerful prayer is!

A poor widow lived in a city with her two children, one of whom was a cripple. One day the widow saw a sign for special meetings in a church nearby. She and her children decided to go and were wonderfully saved!

She and her children began praying every day about their needs. Finally, when they had nothing left to eat, she gathered her children for prayer and told God about their desperate condition. That day, a letter arrived from out of the country. The letter was from a friend of her late husband. The man had spent months trying to locate her.

Inside the envelope was a large amount of money. Her need was met! Was it coincidence that the money arrived that day? No, God honored their faith and prayers and provided when they needed it most.

ACTION POINT: Read and discuss the prayer of the apostles in Acts 4:23-31. How did God answer their prayer?

—*Jack Palmer*

JANUARY 6
FAITH STILL PLEASES GOD!

Scripture Reading—Hebrews 11:1, 6

*"Now faith is the substance of things hoped for, the evidence of things not seen. . . . But **without faith it is impossible to please him**: for he that cometh to God must believe that he is, and that he is a rewarder of them that diligently seek him."*

If it's impossible to please God *without* faith, then it's possible to please Him *by* faith. Sometimes we see families in such serious trouble that we assume they're beyond help. Such was the case of the man who brought his demon-possessed son to Jesus for deliverance. Jesus told the man, "If thou canst *believe, all things are possible to him that believeth*" (Mark 9:23b, emphasis added). The gentleman said tearfully, "Lord, *I believe*; help thou mine unbelief" (v. 24b, emphasis added). The disciples were unable to help. After Jesus set the boy free, they asked why they were powerless. Jesus replied, "This kind [of faith] can come forth by nothing, but by prayer and fasting" (v. 29b).

A special friend of ours went home to be with the Lord. Talking to his widow, we discovered something we never knew. For many years, her alcoholic husband had caused misery in their marriage. Her friends advised her to leave him. Because she was a Christian, she refused but remained faithful and trusted the Lord. Eventually, he was saved, and their final years were wonderful. At the end of her testimony, she said, "I'm so glad that I chose to trust God!"

Hers was not an easy decision, and she faced a difficult life for many years. *But faith still pleases God!* And God still honors genuine faith. And that means there's hope for the family.

The Bible is a book about faith. When life isn't going well, trusting God can be difficult. But faith develops best in tough situations. If God is testing your faith as a family, make the choice to trust Him and to allow Him to strengthen your faith.

ASSIGNMENT: Read John 4:46-54. What happened to the nobleman's family because of his faith?

—Jack Palmer

JANUARY 7
OBEDIENCE STILL BRINGS BLESSING!

Scripture Reading—Isaiah 1:19-20
*"If ye be **willing and obedient**, ye shall eat the good of the land: But if ye refuse and rebel, ye shall be devoured with the sword: for the mouth of the Lord hath spoken it" (emphasis added).*

Willing obedience always produces blessing. In Deuteronomy 6, while preparing His people to enter the Promised Land, God commanded them to obey His Word if they wanted His blessing. In verse 3a, He says, "Hear therefore, O Israel, and *observe to do it*; that it may be well with thee, and that ye may increase mightily, as the Lord God of thy fathers hath promised thee" (emphasis added). At the close of the chapter, the parents told their children why obeying God's Word was so important. "And the Lord commanded us *to do all these statutes*, to fear the Lord our God, *for our good always*, that he might preserve us alive, as it is at this day. And it shall be our righteousness, if we *observe to do all these commandments* before the Lord our God, as he hath commanded us" (vv. 24-25, emphasis added).

A father taught his son the value of instant obedience. One day, while they were hiking in the mountains, the father said with urgency, "Son, drop to the ground immediately!" The youngster didn't understand his dad's command but obeyed. Instantly, the father shot a rattlesnake coiled on a rock behind the boy's head. Had the boy delayed, the dangerous snake may have bitten him. Because the boy obeyed, his life was spared.

Obedience is doing what we're told immediately with the right heart attitude. When God tells a family what to do and they obey without question, even if the obedience is hard or if they don't understand, God will bless. The problem is that many families know what to do but don't do it. Then they wonder why God isn't blessing. Because God still blesses obedience, there's hope for the family.

DO THIS NOW: Read Jeremiah 29:17-19. Discuss what God says about the danger of not hearing and obeying what He says.

—Jack Palmer

JANUARY 8
THE DEVIL IS STILL A DEFEATED ENEMY!

Scripture Reading—James 4:7
*"Submit yourselves therefore to God. Resist the devil, **and he will flee from you**" (emphasis added).*

Today, we consider one more reason there's hope for the family. If anyone wants our families to fail, it's Satan. He hates to see Christian families successfully living for the Lord. He hates to see husbands and wives content and happy in their relationship. He hates to see Christian parents training their children for God. He hates to observe children being respectful and obedient to their parents. He hates witnessing family worship and Christian service. Is it any wonder he attacks Christian families so hard?

There's one fact Satan doesn't want us to know—that he's still a defeated enemy. In Scripture, Satan lost every encounter he had with God or Christ. First John 4:4 says, "Ye are of God, little children, and have overcome them: because *greater is he that is in you, than he that is in the world*" (emphasis added). Satan knows that God is greater than him, but he doesn't want us to believe that. Romans 8:37 reminds us that "we are *more than conquerors* through him that loved us" (emphasis added). Satan gets the victory in Christian homes because we permit him to. Because Christ is in us and because we're more than conquerors, we can claim victory over Satan, too.

When Satan confronted Jesus in the wilderness (Luke 4:1-13), Jesus was victorious over him three times because He used the "sword of the Spirit, which is the word of God" (Eph. 6:17). He countered each attack with the words "it is written" or "it is said" (Luke 4:4, 8, 12). If we know and believe God's Word, we can stand our ground against Satan, counter his attack, and experience victory.

We should rejoice that Satan is still a defeated enemy because that means there's still hope for the family.

DISCUSSION: Share ways you as a family can be better prepared to "withstand in the evil day, and having done all, to stand" (Eph. 6:13).

—Jack Palmer

JANUARY 9
THE LEATHER POUCH

Scripture Reading—Proverbs 4:20-27

Several years ago, I found a small leather pouch on my desk with a note that said, "Give this to me when I kill my first deer." It was signed by my son Tim who was not old enough to go deer hunting.

I put the pouch away, making a mental note to have it with me during Tim's first deer season. That season came in 2004. As we headed out on opening day, I secretly hung the pouch around my neck under my hunting clothes.

That was a tough deer season. In fact, we hunted in cold and rain. Over a period of several days, Tim and I sat approximately 18 hours together in a tree stand with no results. On the final day of the season, we went to our stand, knowing that we had to head home by 11 to go to a meeting where I was going to preach. I told Tim we would get down at 10:50.

Our morning was uneventful; we never saw hide or hoof of a deer. I kept quietly asking God to give Tim a chance. Does God answer prayers about deer hunting? Of course, He does. At 10:40, Tim whispered, "Dad, there's a deer."

I positioned Tim with my rifle, and he carefully took aim. The rifle cracked, and the deer leaped into the air and started to run. Moments later, we stood over the beautiful whitetail doe Tim had taken, just 10 minutes before our season ended.

As father and son, we paused to enjoy this thrilling moment. I unzipped my coat and unbuttoned my shirt. Tim was pleasantly surprised when I took off his leather pouch and hung it around his neck. Later, he put the casing from the bullet he shot inside the pouch. The casing was not only a personal treasure but also a reminder of a special experience a 12-year-old boy shared with his dad.

EXERCISE: Ask each family member to share a favorite memory of an experience with one of the parents.

—Tom Palmer

JANUARY 10
WITH MINE OWN HAND

Scripture Reading—2 Thessalonians 3:16-18
"Now the Lord of peace himself give you peace always by all means.
The Lord be with you all. The salutation of Paul with mine own hand,
which is the token in every epistle: so I write.
The grace of our Lord Jesus Christ be with you all.
Amen."

The apostle Paul was a letter writer. A large portion of the New Testament is comprised of letters Paul wrote either to churches or to individuals. These letters represent Paul's heart to the ones he loved intensely in the Lord. Sometimes he warned them and offered correction. On other occasions, he instructed them and offered counsel. He used other times to encourage and to express appreciation. In each letter, Paul shared a part of himself with pen and paper.

As a father, I've enjoyed writing letters to my children. When Julie turned 16, I started writing "Dearest Daughter" letters. I wrote some letters on special occasions like her graduation from high school or her departure to college. I've written letters when I knew she was struggling and needed encouragement.

In some of my letters, I've dealt with topics like modesty, money, jobs, and friendships. In each, I've shared my heart along with the truths of God's Word in a way she could apply to her heart and life. I've also provided a keepsake I trust will be a lifelong treasure after I, as her father, am gone. I have put my counsel and experiences down on paper for one of my children to cherish for a lifetime.

By the way, I also enjoy getting letters from my children. In my office is a wooden box with the word "Dad" at the top. Within is a collection of notes and letters from my children. I will keep these treasures for a lifetime.

ASSIGNMENT: Give each family member a piece of paper and an envelope. Exchange names and ask each family member to write a note to another family member during the next week.

—Tom Palmer

HANDING OUT HIGH-FIVES

Scripture Reading
Proverbs 13:12—*"Hope deferred maketh the heart sick: but when the desire cometh, it is a tree of life."*
Proverbs 13:19—*"The desire accomplished is sweet to the soul: but it is abomination to fools to depart from evil."*

It was a pleasant fall evening in archery season as I settled into my tree stand on the edge of a soybean field. It wasn't long before the deer started moving in abundance as they made their way to feed. Clutching my bow, I watched two large bucks in particular as they began feeding.

Suddenly, I heard a sound in the brush behind me. Turning, I saw my 13-year-old son Andrew making his way toward me. My first thought was, *Now what does he want?*

I signaled to him to be quiet as he approached my tree. "I think I got one," he said before he updated me on the events of the last 15 minutes.

Gathering my gear, I joined him on the ground. Moments later, we were on the trail and soon we found what we were looking for—his deer. Without a word, I turned and raised my right hand. He did the same, and we shared a super high-five.

Over the years, high-fives have become a way for me and my son to say, "We did it!" without using words. When the two of us beat a five-man team of junior high boys in basketball, we did a high-five. When we rappelled to the bottom of a large, stone cliff, we did another high-five. After a thrilling horse ride or a challenging canoe trip, a high-five seemed like the right thing to do.

Dads and their sons need high-fives often. They need to face challenges, to solve problems, and to experience thrills together. High-fives have a way of keeping fathers and sons close. No, I don't just mean a closeness with their hands but with their hearts.

ASSIGNMENT: It's your turn, Dad. Plan a "High-Five Event" for you and your boy.

—*Tom Palmer*

JANUARY 12
LOVING LIKE A BROTHER

Scripture Reading
1 Thessalonians 4:9—*"But as touching brotherly love*
ye need not that I write unto you:
for ye yourselves are taught of God
to love one another."
Hebrews 13:1—*"Let brotherly love*
continue."

My brothers and I always had a dream. For years, we talked about maybe getting together for a big game hunt out west. Finally, our opportunity came, and we met for a week in Wyoming to hunt antelope. We each took a nice antelope buck, we hiked in a canyon, we rode horses, we rounded up cattle on a ranch, and we stayed in a log cabin in the mountains. We also ate like kings, laughed like clowns, and spent a lot of time sharing about our families and ministries. It was hard to say goodbye. Even as my brothers pulled out of the ranch and headed back to Arkansas, I knew we would never have an experience like the one we had just shared.

Not long after Brad and Scott left, I had a talk with my own boys. I told them about the unique blessing of sharing my life with my brothers and offered them the following challenge: Live your lives together as brothers so 15 or 20 years from now, you will be able to enjoy an experience together like my brothers and I did.

It's so sad when brothers and sisters grow up with resentment and bitterness toward each other. I know that children in the same family have their occasional squabbles. However, if they are willing to resolve conflicts and to show genuine love, they will develop a relationship that will be a great blessing. Brothers and sisters can be not only part of the same family but also best friends for life. That's what "let brotherly love continue" means.

DO THIS NOW: Let your brothers and sisters know you're thankful for them. Your note or phone call would be special.

—*Tom Palmer*

JANUARY 13
SAYING "I LOVE YOU"

Scripture Reading
Proverbs 19:26—*"He that wasteth his father, and chaseth away his mother, is a son that causeth shame, and bringeth reproach."*
John 13:34— *"A new commandment I give unto you, That ye love one another; as I have loved you, that ye also love one another."*

Few words in the English language have greater impact than the phrase, "I love you." To say "I love you" is to say, "You are special, and you mean the world to me." These words are especially meaningful when parents and children share them with each other. This verbal expression of love has the unique ability of drawing a family together and of keeping a family together with incredible strength.

Years ago, I was driving home late at night from a preaching engagement. It was necessary for me to travel through a town where my parents were attending a week of meetings. I knew the motel where they were staying and pulled into the parking lot. Not knowing their room number, I drove around until I found their van. Their room was dark, so I knew they had already gone to bed. Parking, I wrote a note that said, "I am thankful for you, and I love you." After signing my name, I placed the note under one of their van's windshield wipers. As I drove away, I was grateful for another opportunity to tell my parents how much they meant to me.

I dread the thought of causing shame and bringing reproach to my parents. For that reason, I will never be too old or too big to give them a hug and to say, "I love you." As a father, I now understand what a blessing it is when my children tell me that they love me. Someone has said that talk is cheap; however, when someone speaks the words "I love you" from a genuine heart of love, they are priceless. Nobody ever gets too far away who continues to say, "I love you."

ASSIGNMENT: Whether you are an adult or a child, look for a way to say "I love you" to your parents A.S.A.P.

—*Tom Palmer*

JANUARY 14
A DATE FOR ALMOST NOTHING

Scripture Reading—Proverbs 5:18
"Let thy fountain be blessed: and rejoice with the wife of thy youth."

Most married couples enjoyed going on dates before they were married. Time and money seemed to be of no concern whatsoever. Then they got married. Now time and money are two reasons special outings together are a thing of the past. Once my wife and I tried something that cost us almost nothing but a couple of hours. Here's what we did:

- •• We put on comfortable shoes and went to a mall so we could walk together.
- • In a clothing store, we each picked a shirt for the other person. The person put the shirt on and modeled it.
- • In a card shop, we split up, and each picked a "mushy" card. We exchanged cards, read them, put them back, and left the store.
- • We walked through the food court and tried all the free samples. We turned around and went through the food court again, taking more of the free samples.
- • We found a photo booth and had hilarious portraits taken just for a few dollars.
- • We took Gospel tracts and shared them with several people we saw sitting in the mall.
- • Each time we saw a man wearing a ball hat backwards, we paused to give each other a kiss.

About two hours later, we left the mall and went home. During our time, we hardly spent any money. We exercised together, laughed a lot, witnessed to others, and even added a romantic touch. While returning home, we remembered a basic principle about marriage relationships. A little time and money have a wonderful way of providing one of the greatest ingredients of a strong marriage relationship—togetherness. You don't need a week-long cruise or a $200 dinner outing to spend time together. A little creativity works fine, and you'll love it.

HUSBAND'S ACTION POINT: Now, Sir Hubby, get with it and plan the next date with your Sweetie!

—Tom Palmer

JANUARY 15
MOTHER APPRECIATION DAY

Scripture Reading—Proverbs 31:28
"Her children arise up,
and call her blessed; her husband also,
and he praiseth her."

We did it as a total surprise. The children and I planned a special day for Mom just to let her know how thankful we were for her. We prepared special decorations and "thank you" signs and secretly arranged them for Mom. I got her up and took her for a walk to get coffee while the children decorated and got everything ready. I even got flowers to put on the table. We'd prepared special gift bags and planned to share them each hour throughout the day. Each one contained something special that my wife enjoyed like a candle or a snack.

Our meal that day was all for her. We chose the menu with her favorites, and we fixed the meal, served it, and cleaned up while she relaxed and enjoyed the food. It was one of those special family times when we enjoyed sharing love and appreciation with someone special to us.

Mothers have a thankless job. In a given year, they prepare more than 1,000 meals, wash hundreds of loads of laundry, and clean a house they didn't get dirty. They give dozens of rides to lessons, practices, and activities; and it seems like they do a million other things nobody notices, all to make home a special place.

Dads and kids need to show their appreciation. That's why Mother Appreciation Day is so important. Those notes, gifts, smiles, hugs, and acts of kindness are more meaningful to Mom than a check for $100,000. Unfortunately, most families are inclined to think that Mom is just doing her job. Yes, she is, but we dare not take her for granted. A spirit of gratitude is one of the best ways to rekindle your love for each other as a family.

SECRET ASSIGNMENT: Okay, Dad, you and your kids should begin planning her special day. Keep the day a secret and let her know she's the greatest. By the way, kids, Dad would enjoy his special day sometime, too.

—Tom Palmer

JANUARY 16
THE VALUE OF TIME

Scripture Reading—Ephesians 5:15-16
"See then that ye walk circumspectly,
not as fools, but as wise, redeeming the time,
because the days are evil."

At the end of your life, you will answer the question, "What will you leave your children?" What should your children expect from their parents as an inheritance? Will they treasure things that rust and depreciate more than the memory of a long-practiced family tradition? Will they embrace money and property more than the tribute of family character?

Right now, decide what you value most in life. If it's gold and silver, all you will leave your children is gold and silver. If it's family, character, and example, then you will leave something that is prized far above earthly riches—something no one can value in dollars and cents.

Statistics reveal that many families spend too little time together. While they devote much time to retirement portfolios and to life's ambitions, they fail to develop a memory portfolio that highlights the importance of family.

It is important that Christian families spend time together at church, time in the Word, and time at home working on special projects together. Time together is something we all need to make time for. When we measure the value of all things, we will treasure the gift of time more than anything else.

At the end of our lives, we will value time most of all! Is your family spending time together? Or is work, friends, hobbies, and other pursuits stealing God's precious gift of time? Life is too short not to prioritize how we spend it.

Many have argued about whether families should spend quantity time or quality time together. Friend, most of us measure quality of time in terms of quantity. It's about time we start thinking about how we spend it.

APPLICATION: Do something special today. Spend time playing a game or reading a book. Look through a photo album and remember the good times you spent together as a family.

—Jeff Kahl

ALERTNESS TO SATAN'S DEVICES

Scripture Reading—Judges 7:4-7
"And the Lord said unto Gideon,
The people are yet too many; bring them down unto the water,
and I will try them for thee there: and it shall be,
that of whom I say unto thee, This shall go with thee,
the same shall go with thee" (v. 4a).

God called Gideon to deliver Israel from the Midianites. Twenty-two thousand fearful soldiers had already retreated, and only 10,000 remained. But God told Gideon he still had too many men and gave him a plan to thin the ranks. Gideon led the men to a stream for a drink. Those who knelt on all fours and put their lips to the water "as a dog lappeth" (v. 5) were separated on one side. Gideon grouped those who cupped water in their hands, pulling it to their mouths, on the other side.

This was a test. Those who cupped water in their hands were cautious and aware of their surroundings. No doubt they looked around to see if there was a trap. God wanted Gideon to have men who were both watchful and courageous.

Satan is a deceiver. "Be not deceived" is a phrase the New Testament repeats many times. A liar, Satan tempts us to believe lies.

Satan is a discourager. He tries to intimidate us with fear. Fear, in turn, robs us of courage. When we become discouraged, we lose our drive.

Satan is a divider. We must guard against his tactic of sowing discord among family members and friends. I believe Winston Churchill said, "If the current generation goes to war with the previous generation, we are sure to lose the future generation." Division and discord are satanic strategies that cause huge problems.

Only 300 men passed God's test. God would use these few to conquer a huge army. We must be alert to satanic devices.

DISCUSSION: Talk about satanic schemes we must guard against.

—Harold Vaughan

JANUARY 18
BOLD WITNESSES

Scripture Reading—Judges 7:2-3
"And the Lord said unto Gideon,
The people that are with thee are too many for me to give the Midianites
into their hands, lest Israel vaunt themselves against me, saying,
Mine own hand hath saved me.
Now therefore go to, proclaim in the ears of the people, saying,
Whosoever is fearful and afraid,
let him return and depart early from mount Gilead.
And there returned of the people twenty and two thousand; and there
remained ten thousand."

Boldness is a key ingredient for success in the Christian life. When the Lord decided to whittle down Gideon's band, He did it by eliminating the fearful. Gideon announced that anyone who was fearful could leave. Instantly, 22,000 men walked off the field. Two-thirds of the soldiers left. We must overcome timidity, shyness, and cowardice in order to serve the Lord effectively.

"The wicked flee when no man pursueth: but the righteous are bold as a lion" (Prov. 28:1). The lion is the king of the jungle because he's fearless. God wants His people to be courageous. Boldness is a byproduct of the Holy Spirit. In the Book of Acts, the disciples spoke the word of God with boldness after they were filled with the Holy Spirit. These same disciples had denied the Lord at the crucifixion, but now they bravely and powerfully preached the Gospel. An unworldly power had possessed these men and transformed them into mighty witnesses.

Unsaved men, women, boys, and girls are headed for eternal destruction. It's our job to give them the good news. God calls every Christian to be a missionary wherever he lives. R.A. Torrey said, "It's impossible to witness to the wrong person." Are you bold in your witness for Christ?

EXERCISE: Take a breath and hold it. Now exhale. Take another breath and hold it. Exhale. That didn't take long; but in those brief seconds, 10 people passed into eternity, unprepared to meet God. Ask God to fill you with His Spirit and to make you fearless in your witness.

—Harold Vaughan

CAN GOD USE SOMEONE LIKE ME?
Scripture Reading—Judges 6:1-13

Because of their sins, the Israelites were oppressed by the Midianites. In their bondage, the Israelites cried out to the Lord for deliverance. God put His hand on Gideon, whom He chose to liberate His covenant people. Gideon was an unlikely man who did extraordinary things.

The Lord met Gideon while he was threshing wheat by the winepress. Why was Gideon at the winepress with his wheat? Because he feared the Midianites were going to steal his crop. Do you get the picture? God chose one who lacked the qualities of greatness that normally accompany mighty exploits. The Lord specializes in using weak things to confound the powerful (1 Cor. 1:27).

God chose Gideon. The angel of the Lord appeared to Gideon. Bible scholars tell us the "angel of the Lord" refers to Christ. Here we find an appearance of Jesus in the Old Testament. When God selects weak vessels to perform mighty deeds, He is guaranteed to get the credit! God uncovered His plan by selecting one who was hiding his wheat.

God called Gideon. "And the Lord looked upon him, and said, Go in this thy might, and thou shalt save Israel from the hand of the Midianites: have not I sent thee?" (Judg. 6:14) Upon hearing these words, Gideon made excuses. "Oh my Lord, wherewith shall I save Israel? behold, my family is poor in Manasseh, and I am the least in my father's house" (v. 15b). Because his family was insignificant and because he was insecure, Gideon reasoned, surely he was not the man for the job.

God confirmed Gideon. "And the Lord said unto him, Surely I will be with thee, and thou shalt smite the Midianites as one man" (v. 16). Gideon needed assurance, so God verified His call by speaking directly to Gideon and by giving him a vision of victory.

PRINCIPLES TO CONSIDER: God uses unlikely people to do extraordinary things. You are here for a special purpose. Background, lack of finances, and inexperience are not hindrances to fulfilling your mission. What mission has the Lord laid on your heart?

—Harold Vaughan

JANUARY 20
FINISH THE TASK

Scripture Reading—Judges 7:7-22
"So Gideon, and the hundred men . . . blew the trumpets,
and brake the pitchers that were in their hands.
And the three companies . . . cried,
The sword of the Lord, and of Gideon" (vv. 19-20).

Gideon defeated Israel's enemy with 300 soldiers and an unusual plan. God instructed Gideon and his band to take trumpets and lamps and to surround the Midianites, who were camping in the valley. As darkness fell, Israel surrounded the camp. When Gideon blew his trumpet, his companions blew their trumpets. Gideon lit his lamp, and the others did likewise. When the Midianites heard 300 trumpets and saw 300 lights, they thought they were surrounded by a huge army. God's hand turned against the Midianites, and they started killing each other. Gideon and his men blew the trumpets and held up the lamps. God took care of the rest.

A handful of Midianites managed to escape from the field of slaughter. "And Gideon came to Jordan, and passed over, he, and the three hundred men that were with him, faint, yet pursuing them" (Judg. 8:4). By following God's plan, Gideon didn't lose a single man! The Lord gave Gideon a job, and he was determined to complete it. Though he and his men were exhausted, they chased the few remaining Midianites. These loyal men were "faint" yet still pursuing.

Persistence is a key ingredient to success. We measure a man's character not by wealth or achievement but by what discourages him. Those who make strides in life are the ones who persevere. Hurdles don't stop them; hindrances don't dishearten them. Regardless of circumstances, they press on! The Book of Proverbs says if we "faint in the day of adversity . . . [our] strength is small" (24:10). It's important to see the job through to the end.

"And let us not be weary in well doing: for in due season we shall reap, if we faint not" (Gal. 6:9).

CITE BIBLE EXAMPLES: List Bible characters whom God rewarded because they persevered. What obstacles did they overcome?

—Harold Vaughan

JANUARY 21
SURRENDER TO CHRIST
Scripture Reading—Judges 6:25
"And it came to pass the same night, that the Lord said unto him, Take thy father's young bullock, even the second bullock of seven years old, and throw down the altar of Baal that thy father hath, and cut down the grove that is by it."

God called Gideon to full consecration on the night after he had a face-to-face encounter with Christ. Gideon came from a family of idol worshipers. The Lord told him to tear down the altar of Baal. This instruction was quite a challenge for a man who was afraid the Midianites might steal his wheat! But God's calling is accompanied by His enabling. God enables us for the task He calls us to fulfill. Gideon obeyed and threw down the altar of Baal. He had to make a clean break with false religion.

The idols Gideon smashed were statues or images representing false gods. "Thou shalt have no other gods before me" (Ex. 20:3) was God's command through Moses.

Unearthing ruins in Mexico, archeologists found idols of every size, shape, and description. They were made of glass, gold, silver, and bronze. This ancient civilization was totally given over to idolatry, prompting archeologists to name the site "The City of the Gods."

We who live in western culture are prone to think idolatry is confined to pagan religion and primitive cultures. An idol, however, can be any object of excessive attachment—anything that takes God's place, including a person, a habit, or a job. God deserves full allegiance from His creation, and whatever comes between us and God is our god. Spurgeon said, "Idolatry is the greatest insult the creature can offer the Creator." Nothing could be worse than putting something or someone in God's place.

Gideon dedicated himself fully to the Lord. The best day in our lives is when we run up the white flag of surrender to the lordship of Christ. He alone is worthy of our devotion.

INVITATION: "I Have Decided to Follow Jesus" is a great song. Read through the verses, discuss them, and sing the song.

—Harold Vaughan

JANUARY 22
THE VIRTUE OF VIRTUES

Scripture Reading—Judges 8:22-23

"Then the men of Israel said unto Gideon, Rule thou over us, both thou, and thy son, and thy son's son also: for thou hast delivered us from the hand of Midian. And Gideon said unto them, I will not rule over you, neither shall my son rule over you: the Lord shall rule over you."

God used Gideon to deliver the nation. Afterwards, his countrymen wanted to make him king. They were ready to declare Gideon and his descendants the royal family, but Gideon remembered where he'd been when the Lord called him—threshing wheat by the winepress. He was hiding because he was afraid his wheat would be stolen. He recognized that God's hand had brought them the victory. Without hesitation, Gideon declined the offer to rule. He remained meek and gave God the glory.

John Bunyan penned the following words:

He that is down, need fear no fall;
He that is low no pride;
He that is humble ever shall
Have God to be his guide.

Humility is a foundational virtue, a platform from which other good qualities may be built. A humble man receives the desire and power to do right—"[God] giveth grace to the humble" (1 Pet. 5:5b). As a small seed is capable of producing much fruit, humility is the beginning point for countless graces. Psalm 34:18 says, "The Lord is nigh unto them that are of a broken heart; and saveth such as be of a contrite spirit [lowly attitude]." The gateway to spiritual prosperity is a humble spirit.

In addition to giving birth to other virtues, humility is a shield to vice. The humble heart is protected from many snares. "Nothing sets a person so much out of the devil's reach as humility," Jonathan Edwards said. Pride is the oldest, deadliest sin in the world.

POINTS TO PONDER: How many Bible verses about humility can you list? What do these verses teach us about humility?

—Harold Vaughan

JANUARY 23
THE MOST IMPORTANT DECISION

Scripture Reading—Romans 12:2

"And be not conformed to this world: but be ye transformed by the renewing of your mind, that ye may prove what is that good, and acceptable, and perfect, will of God."

"Okay, class. Let's begin today's lesson with a quiz. This quiz is to help us determine the most important decision you will make in life, other than the decision to be saved. On your paper are listed six important decisions you will make as you grow up. You should put them in order of importance, listing which is most important and which is least important."

After receiving the quiz paper, you see the following:

A. Where you will go to college

B. What your occupation will be

C. Where you will live

D. Whom you will marry

E. What kind of car you will drive

F. What you will name your dog

"All right, family. You are the students in the classroom. Take your quiz. You may discuss your answers with each other before giving your final decision. Are you finished? Good, let's see how you did."

Though this quiz may seem simple, I'm going to surprise you with your grade. You see, if you chose any of the decisions as the most important, you missed all six and failed the quiz. Yes, it was a trick quiz, but I'm making a point.

At least five choices were major decisions (the dog's name is no big deal). However, there's a greater decision you must make, and you must make it before the others. You can't properly make decisions as a person or as a family until you've first decided that you will know and do God's will no matter what. This decision is called surrender. It's a decision to yield my will to God's will so His will is the most important priority in my life. Until that's settled, nothing else is going to be important.

ACTION POINT: Ask each family member to define "God's will" in his own words.

—*Tom Palmer*

JANUARY 24
GOD'S WILL
FOR ME

Scripture Reading—Ephesians 5:17
"Wherefore be ye not unwise, but understanding
what the will of the Lord is."

We may describe God's will for an individual's life as three-dimensional. We can illustrate this relationship by drawing a circle and writing your name inside. Now we draw three more circles around the original circle.

The outer circle represents God's **universal** will for everyone. God's will for every human who will ever live on planet Earth is that he would be saved. God is "not willing that any should perish, but that all should come to repentance" (2 Pet. 3:9). He "will have all men to be saved, and to come unto the knowledge of the truth" (1 Tim. 2:4). God has no greater desire in His heart than that sinners would be saved from their sin.

The second circle represents God's **general** will for every Christian. This will is based on God's revealed will in His Word. Christians should live by the basic biblical principles of holiness, godliness, and practical Christian living (for examples, see 1 Thess. 4:3, 5:18).

Finally, the inner ring represents God's **personal** will for each Christian. Here His will is specific and custom-fits each believer, expressing God's desire for the individual's life. In Psalm 143:10a, David prayed, "Teach me to do thy will; for thou art my God." In this prayer, he asked God to make His will clear as it applied to David's life. God has a perfect plan—or an agenda, we might say—for each of His children. It's crucial for each believer to know and to follow that plan for his life.

To be out of God's will or to miss His will for your life is tragic. God's will must determine your direction in this life and your destination in eternity. God's will is best.

ASSIGNMENT: From Scripture, make a list of five qualities God desires for every Christian. Determine whether you're living according to God's will.

—Tom Palmer

JANUARY 25
OUR EXAMPLE IS JESUS
Scripture Reading—Philippians 2:5-8

When we consider living a life according to God's will, we have no greater example than the Lord Jesus Christ. He was God, yet as a man He humbly submitted Himself to the will of the Father. His example teaches us the following important truths:

1. God's will means **DOING**—After the woman at the well brought the city to see and to hear Jesus, He said, "My meat is to do the will of him that sent me, and to finish his work" (John 4:34b). The pursuit of God's will requires obedience. We can never accomplish God's will without action.

2. God's will means **SEEKING**—Jesus said, "I seek not mine own will, but the will of the Father which hath sent me" (John 5:30b). He was able to know the Father's will because He desired to know what it was. You will never know God's will for your life until you truly want to know what it is.

3. God's will means **YIELDING**—When Jesus was in the Garden of Gethsemane, He expressed His attitude with the following statement to His Father: "Not as I will, but as thou wilt" (Matt. 26:39b). Surrender enabled Jesus to do God's will with no strings attached. You cannot know God's will until you first have no will of your own.

4. God's will means **FINISHING**—In John 17:4b, Jesus said, "I have finished the work which thou gavest me to do." When Jesus cried out from the cross, His final words were, "It is finished"! You cannot experience God's fullest blessing until you're willing to go all the way to do God's will.

No one in history has touched the world like Jesus did. He made His impact because the will of His Father reigned supreme. Nothing else mattered to Him. Likewise, nothing should be more important to us.

READ AND DISCUSS: See what 1 John 2:6 says about our walk. Whom should we imitate?

—*Tom Palmer*

JANUARY 26
WHO'S IN THE
DRIVER'S SEAT?

Scripture Reading—Proverbs 3:5-6
"Trust in the Lord with all thine heart; and lean not unto thine own understanding. In all thy ways acknowledge him, and he shall direct thy paths."

We had finished lunch in the camp dining room and were going back to the trailer where we were staying. As we climbed into the van, I asked my toddler-age son, Andrew, if he would like to drive. He quickly agreed and climbed onto my lap.

As we headed down the gravel road through the woods, I took my hands off the steering wheel, and he took the wheel with his little hands. In a moment, we were in a crisis! Ahead was the ditch, the hedgerow, and even a tree.

Andrew couldn't stay on the road for anything. To make things more exciting, I stepped on the accelerator, and the van lunged forward. I hit the brakes just before we had a collision. Andrew laughed, screamed, and threw his hands into the air.

I put the van into reverse and backed up. Meanwhile, my wife and daughter were laughing uncontrollably in the backseats.

Each time we almost had another collision, I included a fun "lecture" about good driving. After the third incident, Andrew took his hands off the steering wheel and blurted, "I can't do it. You'll have to drive." A moment later, we were safely home.

What does "acknowledge him" mean? In toddler language, it means, "I can't do it. You'll have to drive." It's the acknowledgment that I can't get where I'm supposed to go by myself. I must have God's hand guiding me.

Could it be that many times we've gotten on the wrong half of Proverbs 3:6? We try so hard to direct our own paths when all God wants is for us to simply acknowledge Him. He just wants us to stay on our half of the verse.

EXERCISE: Blindfold one of your children and see how well he can follow directions without seeing where he's going. Discuss "trusting."

—*Tom Palmer*

JANUARY 27
WHEN THE BIBLE
IS YOUR LIGHT

Scripture Reading—Psalm 119:105
"Thy word is a lamp
unto my feet, and a light
unto my path."

Imagine living in the days before electricity. Imagine no streetlights, headlights, floodlights, or flashlights. When the sky grew dark at night, it became pitch black. Unless the sky glowed with moonlight, no one had a way of knowing where he was going.

The only way to see the path was with a lamp, which one carried or strapped to his ankle. This lamp became the light that made the path visible. What's so interesting is that the light usually shined for only a short distance. The bearer of the light couldn't see a mile or even 100 yards ahead; he saw only a few steps. Yet if he allowed the lamp to lighten his path, he could get where he wanted to go.

The Bible describes itself as a "lamp unto my feet." In other words, God's Word is one of the ways God guides us to follow His will. By the way, God's Word *is* His will; the will of God will never contradict His Word. Some folks speak of knowing God's will, but what they say contradicts God's Word. Mark it down. If what you assume to be God's will is in violation of His truth, it isn't God's will.

In the Bible, we find principles, examples, illustrations, and direct commands that clearly show us what God desires. A careful study of God's Word is a great blessing in knowing God's will. The Bible becomes like a directional arrow and like a stop sign warning us of danger.

When you are facing a decision, go to the Word of God and allow God to "instruct thee and teach thee in the way which thou shalt go" (Ps. 32:8). Even in our modern day of electricity, we need a good light to show us the path.

ASSIGNMENT: List several Bible principles that are helpful when you need to make a decision.

—Tom Palmer

JANUARY 28
DON'T PICK
THE LOCK

Scripture Reading—Psalm 37:23
"The steps of a good man are ordered by the Lord:
and he delighteth in his way."

My dad was trying to finish a paint job. If he could get it done, he hoped to go away that weekend. Suddenly a gust of wind blew the ladder over, causing the paint to spill all over the porch. Was the event just a coincidence?

My brother was considering going back to his college for an alumni basketball game. He prayed about whether to go. The week before the game, he was playing pickup basketball when he tore his Achilles tendon. Was his injury just an accident?

Some people, even Christians, assume life "just happens." Resting on fate or chance, they wait to see what will happen. To children of God who are walking with God, however, the events of life are not coincidences or accidents. God is in control of everything. You see, not only are the "steps of a good man . . . ordered by the Lord." God orders the stops, too. He uses divinely directed circumstances to lead His children.

God opens and closes doors by directing or permitting certain events to occur. My father and brother came to know what God wanted them to do because of circumstances God allowed to impact their lives.

One word of caution is essential. Circumstances aren't always the Lord's leading. They are God's leading only when they are blended with the leading of God's Word and godly counsel.

Sometimes God creates a situation and uses it to open a new door of opportunity. When God leads this way, we can rejoice that He's at work to order our steps. Someone once said, "Try the doorknob. Just don't pick the lock." If the door of circumstance opens, step through it; but don't force a situation God doesn't allow to develop.

APPLICATION: Read Acts 16:6-10. See how God closed two doors to open another one.

—*Tom Palmer*

JANUARY 29
WHO MAKES
THE FINAL CALL

Scripture Reading—Colossians 3:15
"And let the peace of God
rule in your hearts,
to the which also ye are called
in one body; and be ye thankful."

The crowd is on its feet. Millions of people around the world are glued to their TVs. It's game seven of the World Series. With the score tied and two outs, the runner takes his lead off second base. The pitch is delivered. *Crack!* It's a hit into center field. As the center fielder rushes to pick up the bouncing ball, the runner rounds third base and heads for home. The throw comes home. The runner slides into a cloud of dust. The catcher makes the tag. And who does everybody look at?

Anyone who knows anything about baseball knows that at that moment, everybody is looking at the umpire. Why? Because this one man must make the call. His call of "safe" or "out" may determine who will be world champions.

The word *rule* means to be like an umpire. In other words, we must allow the "peace of God" to make the final call when we're determining His will. When God has given clear leading through His Word, through godly counsel, and through circumstances, the peace of God is still what must seal the decision. If God's peace is there, we should do it! If God's peace isn't there, we shouldn't dare!

Often in my life God gave His peace as confirmation of His leading. It was such a blessing to rest assured that I was doing God's will. Though I may not have understood what God was doing—or even how He would do it—I knew I could trust the Lord's leading.

Chaos and confusion never accompany God's leading. God doesn't play "hard to get" or tease us with His will. When He's leading, He will make His wishes clear and will give the peaceful assurance that we are doing His will.

DO THIS NOW: Take turns giving "six words or less" definitions of "peace."

—Tom Palmer

JANUARY 30
PASS
IT ON!

Scripture Reading—Psalm 78:1-8

O ne of the most exciting events in track and field is the relay race. Not only exciting, the sport requires a great deal of teamwork and precise timing. Four runners are on each relay team, and the race begins with one of the fastest. Hopefully, he will give his team a good start. The middle runners are usually not the strongest, but the last one is the real speedster.

Each team member runs a certain distance and stays within defined boundaries. The key to a successful relay is the baton handoff from one runner to the next. Runners spend many hours perfecting the handoff, and every split second counts. The handoff must be done with great precision because it has won or lost many a relay.

Today's Scripture passage describes the passing on of faith from one generation to another. In fact, it makes reference to four succeeding generations: "our fathers" (v. 3), our generation (v. 4), our children (v. 5), and "their children" (v. 6). The progression is like a spiritual relay. Our generation is responsible to pass on the faith to the next generation so when we finish our part of the race, they are prepared to carry on for God.

God's purpose for your family is to raise up the next godly generation. The only way to be successful is to faithfully communicate God's Word to family members each day. Verse 7 describes three results of this education: (1) They will see God as their only hope, even in a hopeless world. (2) They will be unable to forget all that God has done. (3) They will learn the value of obedience to Him.

As you run your "race" for God, endeavor to be faithful in passing on a vital, living faith to those following behind you. Remember, they must carry the torch to the next generation.

ACTION POINT: Share with your family your spiritual goals for passing on the faith and for raising up the next godly generation.

—Jack Palmer

NO TURNING BACK!

Scripture Reading—Psalm 78:9-11, 40-42, 56-58
"The children of Ephraim, being armed, and carrying bows, turned back in the day of battle. They kept not the covenant of God, and refused to walk in his law" (vv. 9-10).

Did you hear the story of the general? As his troops were preparing to go to battle, he gave them the order never to retreat. They encountered the enemy, the battle began, and immediately one platoon turned and ran for the hills. After the battle and the regathering of troops, the general reprimanded the lieutenant for retreating. The lieutenant replied, "We didn't retreat. I just ordered them to about-face and charge!"

That may be a humorous story, but one of the most serious offenses a soldier can commit is running from the battle and abandoning his comrades. A soldier who is guilty of this offense will be severely punished.

In today's Scripture, we read three times that God's people, Israel, "turned back." Psalm 78 is an historical account of God's blessing upon His people. Over and over, we read of how good God was to them; but repeatedly, they turned their backs on Him. Lest we become too hard on Israel, we must not forget that we, too, can be guilty of the same sins.

When I was a teen, I remember singing, "I have decided to follow Jesus, *no turning back, no turning back.*" It's easy to make promises, commitments, and vows to God and not keep them. We may be sincere in what we promise; but for some reason, we don't follow through. We turn back! In the Christian life, this behavior is a serious offense. In Ecclesiastes 5:4-5, God says we are better not to make a promise than to make it and not follow through. Turning back grieves God's heart and results in serious consequences for us. Don't be guilty of turning back!

EXERCISE: Have you made promises, commitments, or vows to God but have since turned your back on them? If so, ask God for forgiveness and recommit yourself to faithfulness.

—*Jack Palmer*

FEBRUARY 1
LEST WE FORGET

Scripture Reading—Psalm 78:10-11

*"They kept not the covenant of God, and refused to walk in his law;
And forgat his works, and his wonders that he had shewed them"
(emphasis added).*

I enjoy deer hunting. During my recent archery season, the weather had been warm until a cold front caused the temperature to drop significantly. I knew I needed to wear warmer clothes to withstand the cold.

One of the most important requirements for deer hunting in our state is to properly display a legal hunting license on the back of one's coat. In my haste to get to the woods, *I forgot* to change my license from one coat to the other. I didn't realize my mistake until I returned home hours later. A sick feeling washed over me when I imagined meeting the game warden. His first question would have been, "Where's your hunting license?"

Psalm 106:13-15 says, "They *soon forgat* his works; they waited not for his counsel: But lusted exceedingly in the wilderness, and tempted God in the desert. And he gave them their request; but sent leanness into their soul" (emphasis added). Israel had a bad memory. So quickly they forgot God's goodness to them. Their forgetfulness was the first step toward spiritual poverty.

Forgetting my hunting license is minor compared to forgetting what God has done for us. How gracious and good He is to us each day! His greatest blessing is our salvation—and that's only the beginning. He has given us health and strength, food and clothing, a home, family and friends, a church, the Bible, prayer—and the list is endless. You'd think we would never forget, but we do. And each time we forget, we take a dangerous step toward spiritual poverty. The answer is to live in a constant spirit of gratitude and to praise God for who He is and for all He has done for us.

DO THIS NOW: With your family, make a list of great things God has done for you that you never want to forget.

—Jack Palmer

FEBRUARY 2
BREAD FROM HEAVEN
Scripture Reading—Exodus 15:14-22; Psalm 78:23-25

Bread is one of the most common elements of a well-balanced diet. Throughout the centuries, bread has been called "the staff of life." Even when people had little to eat, they usually had bread of some kind. In the olden days, housewives usually set aside a day each week to make bread. And was it good! A warm piece of homemade bread, spread with fresh-churned butter and jelly—why, it doesn't get any better than that! Bread not only tastes good but is also good for us.

When the Israelites were in the wilderness, they complained to God about their food supply. God graciously provided "bread from heaven," which they called "manna" (Ex. 16:15; John 6:31). In manna was everything they needed to sustain their lives. God told them to take only enough for each day. For the Sabbath day, they gathered twice as much as the day before. If they failed to believe God and took more than they needed, the manna spoiled (Ex. 16:20).

In Psalm 78:19b, the Israelites asked, "Can God furnish a table in the wilderness?" What they were really asking was whether God could take care of them. Of course, He could; and they lacked nothing.

We often ask the same question. Philippians 4:19 assures us that God will "supply *all your need* according to his riches in glory by Christ Jesus" (emphasis added). What needs are your family members concerned about? Remember, no need is too small or too big for God to meet. When He says "all your need," that's exactly what He means. Your extremity is merely God's opportunity. God is at His best when things are at their worst. If He provided "bread from heaven" to care for the children of Israel, surely He will take care of you.

ASSIGNMENT: Make a list of needs your family members are trusting God to meet. Commit yourselves to trust Him to meet those needs.

—*Jack Palmer*

All Smoke and No Fire

Scripture Reading—Psalm 78:36-37

"Nevertheless they did flatter him with their mouth, and they lied unto him with their tongues. For their heart was not right with him, neither were they stedfast in his covenant" (emphasis added).

Talk is cheap! It's easy to say the right thing and live the wrong way. We can compliment a person to his face but tear him apart behind his back. We can quote Scripture on Sunday but live an ungodly life during the week. We can be sweet to our spouse in public but be as mean as a snake at home. We can praise God during a church service but take His name in vain at work. James 3:10 says, "Out of the same mouth proceedeth blessing and cursing. My brethren, these things ought not so to be." It's too easy to be "all smoke and no fire"!

In Mark 7:6b, Jesus said, "This people honoureth me with their lips, but their heart is far from me." Try to imagine the pain Jesus felt when He spoke those words. He knew the people were saying all the right things, but their lives didn't match their words. That's hypocrisy!

An actor is trained to act like someone he isn't. He dresses and talks like the character. But when he steps off the stage, he's someone else. Some Christians act the same way. When they are around other believers, they play their roles to perfection. But when they live in the world, no one would suspect they know the Lord.

When professing Christians talk big but live little, they are all smoke and no fire! God requires us to live up to our profession. When we do, God is pleased; and others see a clear testimony of a genuine Christian. Let's not be guilty of grieving the Lord and confusing others.

APPLICATION: What activities in your life make God unhappy and hurt your testimony for Him? Be willing to let Him change those areas so you will be consistent.

—Jack Palmer

FEBRUARY 4
A DECEITFUL BOW

Scripture Reading—Psalm 78:56-64

Several years ago, I went on a bow hunt with men from my church at a wildlife refuge near our home in New York. While getting our equipment ready, I carelessly laid my bow down on a razor-sharp broadhead and heard a sickening *twang*. The string on my recurve had been cut. I saw my great day going up in smoke until I remembered that I had a spare string in my pack. We didn't get any deer, but we had a great time.

While reading Psalm 78, I noticed that verse 57 describes "a deceitful bow." In studying the verse more closely, I discovered that the word *deceitful* means unstrung or no string. The term means "a slack bow." I thought about the many years I have bow-hunted and of the many lessons God has taught me. I've learned that a bow with no string gives (1) no **pleasure**. What fun would it be to go to the woods with a bow minus a string? (2) It has no **purpose**. What can you do with a stringless bow? Maybe you could use it to stake up your tomatoes. (3) It has no **power**. The string transfers power of the bow to the arrow. And (4) it gets no **prize**. A hunter with no string on his bow will never bring home the venison.

It's interesting that God describes Israel as "a deceitful bow." Because of the problems described in today's text, the Israelites experienced no pleasure, no purpose, no power, and no prize. God was unhappy and withdrew His blessing from them. As a result, they suffered severe consequences.

When we get out of fellowship with God, we, too, are much like Israel. God will take no **pleasure** in us. He will not be able to use us for His **purpose**, we will lose His **power**, and we will receive no **prize**. May God enable you and your family to learn the lesson of the "deceitful bow."

ACTION POINT: As a family, share some problems that can make you like a "deceitful bow."

—*Jack Palmer*

FEBRUARY 5
GOD IS FAITHFUL!
Scripture Reading—Psalm 78:42-55, 65-72

The 72 verses of Psalm 78 remind us of Israel's unfaithfulness. They turned their backs on God and refused to walk in His ways. They repeatedly forgot what God had done for them. They sinned against Him, defied Him, and even spoke against Him. They doubted Him. They lusted. They lied to Him. They provoked and grieved Him. There wasn't much more they could have done to break God's heart. In Deuteronomy 7:6, God said, "For thou art *an holy people* unto the Lord thy God: the Lord thy God hath chosen thee to be a special people unto himself, *above all people* that are upon the face of the earth" (emphasis added). Israel held a special place in God's heart, but they were unfaithful.

Of course, they paid a price for their rebellion and sin. But through all of their unfaithfulness, God was faithful. Was God good to them because they deserved it? Of course not. He was good to them because He is God! In His mercy, He did not give them what they deserved. And in His grace, He gave them what they could never have deserved.

Are you always faithful to God? Remember, if you are a born-again Christian, you, too, are special to God. You have every reason to be faithful as you consider all God has done for you. But if you are like most Christians, you struggle with being faithful. God expects you to be faithful. "Moreover it is required in stewards, that a man be found *faithful*" (1 Cor. 4:2, emphasis added).

What if you aren't faithful? Will your faithlessness change God? Not at all! Second Timothy 2:13 says, "If we believe not, yet he abideth *faithful*: he cannot deny himself" (emphasis added). One of God's wonderful attributes is His faithfulness. He cannot change. Just because God remains faithful is no excuse for you to be unfaithful. Be *faithful*. God is counting on you.

TALK IT OVER: Discuss ways God has been faithful to your family.

—*Jack Palmer*

FEBRUARY 6
THE LORD IS MY SHEPHERD
Scripture Reading—Psalm 23

Psalm 23 offers some of the most comforting verses in Scripture. This psalm is the testimony of a shepherd who truly knew the Great Shepherd. Having cared for sheep, David saw himself as a sheep who needed God's care and concern. For David, knowing the Lord as his own Shepherd was a great comfort in times of need.

Listen to the story of a young shepherd boy. One day someone shared the Gospel with him, using Psalm 23:1 as a key verse. That person instructed him to remember the verse by using the five fingers on one hand. Starting with his thumb, he learned to say the verse while pointing to each finger. When he came to the ring finger and the word *my*, he was told to grasp the ring finger with his other hand, holding it securely. As a result of learning the verse, the lad trusted Christ as his Savior and Shepherd.

Later, while caring for his sheep, the shepherd boy became trapped in a blizzard. Unable to find shelter, the boy was left to the mercy of the bitter cold and the snow. When he didn't return, a search party discovered his lifeless body.

Those who found him noticed that one of the boy's frozen hands tightly gripped the ring finger of his other hand. The blessing came when they realized that even in "the valley of the shadow of death" the Lord had truly been with him. This simple thought from Psalm 23 had comforted the boy during his final moments.

Do you and your family know the Great Shepherd? Can each member of your family truly say, "The Lord is *my* shepherd"? If not, come to Him as a lost sheep and let Him take you into His care. Then you, like David, will be able to say, "I will dwell in the house of the Lord for ever."

ACTION POINT: Read John 10:27-28. Note what the Good Shepherd gives.

—Tom Palmer

THE MOST FAMOUS VERSE
Scripture Reading—John 3:14-18

Probably the most famous Bible verse is John 3:16. This verse is an excellent explanation of God's love for the world. Within it we find an in-depth look at the heart of God for mankind and note three truths about the love of God.

"For God so loved the world, that he gave his only begotten Son, that whosoever believeth in him should not perish, but have everlasting life."

The Expression of God's Love— God didn't just say to the world, "I love you." He proved His love when "he gave his only begotten Son" as evidence of His love. Someone wisely said that you can give without loving, but you cannot love without giving. Genuine love has something to give to those who are loved. God granted His love gift in the Person of his Son. Jesus came into the world "that we might live through him" (1 John 4:9).

The Extent of God's Love—God's love is an unconditional love that has a far-reaching impact. The word *whosoever* is an all-inclusive word that means "everybody" and "anybody." No boundary confines God's love to a certain geographical location or to a certain race. God does not limit His love to those who are lovable or lovely. He extends the same love to a murderer on death row that he extends to a newborn in a nursery.

The Experience of God's Love—When someone chooses to believe in Him, Jesus Christ, he receives "the gift of God [that] is eternal life through Jesus Christ our Lord" (Rom 6:23). This gift means that a soul will not perish in eternal hell but will have everlasting life in heaven. The love of God makes spiritual life a living reality, both in this life and throughout eternity.

John 3:16 is more than a famous verse; it's the Gospel contained in a single package. Don't just memorize it; make sure you experience it.

ACTION POINT: Ask each family member to write a "love letter" to God, thanking Him for His love. Read your letters to God.

—Tom Palmer

FEBRUARY 8
TOGETHER
FOR GOOD

Scripture Reading—Romans 8:28
"And we know that all things work together for good
to them that love God,
to them who are the called
according to his purpose."

If we aren't careful, we may be guilty of quoting only part of this verse, leaving out several key thoughts we must not neglect. It's easy to claim that "all things work together for good," but we must understand that this promise is conditional. God gave it to those who love Him and to those who are allowing Him to accomplish His purposes in their lives.

A fact of life is that bad things *do* happen to good people; however, good people are able to see bad things as good things only when God works out His purposes in their lives. God has a purpose in everything He allows to touch the life of a child of God. We can see even an apparent accident as a divinely controlled incident. God doesn't make mistakes!

Have you ever prayed, "Lord, just get me out of this situation"? Why not pray, "Lord, what can I get out of this situation?" Now your focus has become not only deliverance from the problem but also development of the purpose God has for your life. It's not always easy to see the good because we often view difficulty from a human perspective. Yet we *can* see good when, from a divine perspective, we begin to see the good God will bring about.

We must never assume that Romans 8:28 is a blanket statement that any old body at any old time can apply to any old thing. Rather we have a message of encouragement that brings hope to those who experience bad things in life. As you yield to God's purposes, He will make the good He is seeking to produce in your life evident. You can trust a God who cannot and will not make a mistake.

ACTION POINT: Recall a time when God brought good out of a bad situation. What lessons did your family learn?

—*Tom Palmer*

A Heart Not Troubled
Scripture Reading—John 14:1-6

Our Scripture text is often a favorite at funerals. To those who are going through "the valley of the shadow of death," this passage brings comfort and a sense of peace. When Jesus spoke, He emphasized three truths that are part of this peace.

First, He spoke of a **prepared place.** The disciples had a hard time accepting the fact that Jesus was going to leave them. Yet, as Jesus explained, His Father's house was the place He was preparing for them. We know this place is heaven. It is the hope of heaven that brings peace to a child of God who encounters death.

Second, Jesus spoke of a **prepared people.** He was going to prepare a house for those who were prepared to come. Going to heaven is a matter of personal choice. Heaven is not a possibility for those who reject Christ.

Third, Jesus spoke of a **prepared plan**. He made it clear that He was the Way, the Truth, and the Life. Some people would have us believe that there are many paths to heaven. Of course, that's not what the Bible says. Others say it doesn't matter how you go as long as you're sincere. That's not biblical either, for it's possible to be sincerely wrong!

No one enjoys a trip to the cemetery. When loved ones gather at the graveside to say their final goodbyes, they face a troubling time; however, those who know the Lord find the peaceful assurance that together they will be with the Lord forever.

Not long after speaking these words, Jesus left His disciples. Yet He left His peace to comfort them. "Peace I leave with you, my peace I give unto you: not as the world giveth, give I unto you. Let not your heart be troubled, neither let it be afraid" (John 14:27). Knowing Him provided the guarantee that they would be together again someday.

ACTION POINT: List five people you know who are already in heaven. Take time to discuss why you want to see them again.

—Tom Palmer

FEBRUARY 10
GOD MADE
IT GOOD

Scripture Reading—Genesis 1:1-5, 29-31

A little poem goes something like this:

First he was a polliwog beginning to begin.
Then he was a frog with his tail tucked in.
Then he was a monkey swinging from a tree.
Now he is a professor with a Ph.D.

Thankfully, the Bible clearly says that man did not come into existence because of some silly coincidence. As a matter of fact, so-called evolution might be better called "devilution" because it deliberately leaves God out. To try to explain the beginning of all things without God is impossible. Only four words into the first chapter of the Bible, we find the name "God."

Genesis 1 is a chapter about God. Verse one tells us that God (the Father) created the heaven and the earth. Verse two speaks of God (the Spirit) moving upon the face of the waters. In verse three, God (the Son) begins the creation process by creating light.

In this wonderful chapter, we discover that God first formed then filled the earth. God separated light from darkness and dry land from water. He created plant life, then animal life. He created various creatures to fill the skies, to inhabit the seas, and to cover the earth. Finally, He created man in His own image. He told man to have dominion over the earth, to be fruitful, to multiply, and to replenish the earth.

As God was creating, He blessed His creation; and when creation was completed, it was very good. Too bad, Mr. Darwin—you are wrong! The Bible tells us how it all began. God did it, and He gets all the praise.

ACTION POINT: Invite young children to draw a chart or picture to illustrate the days of creation.

—Tom Palmer

FEBRUARY 11
I WILL GIVE YOU REST

Scripture Reading—Matthew 11:28-30

Life can be hard to take sometimes. We live in a fast-paced, hurry-up, on-the-go society that is overdosed on adrenaline and is typically all stressed up (or out) with nowhere to go. People try to survive on power naps and fast food while bankrupt of joy, peace, and a purpose for living. Stress factors like change, conflict, criticism, concern, and crisis have drained many folks of their energy and enthusiasm about life. It's time for the yoke.

In this special passage of Scripture, Jesus offers His yoke to those who "labour and are heavy laden." Those who "labour" are those who faint from weariness while those who are "heavy laden" are those who endure what is placed upon them. It may seem odd that Jesus offers a yoke to those who are already excessively burdened.

When we imagine a yoke, we picture an ox with a heavy piece of equipment around his neck; Jesus, however, had something else in mind. A yoke placed upon several animals was a tool that enabled them to work together by sharing the load. When Jesus said, "Take my yoke upon you, and learn of me," He offered to come alongside so He might share our load. A shared load is a lighter load, one that is easier to bear. Interestingly, Jesus promised not to remove the load but to share it.

Are you bearing a heavy burden today? It may be a health need. It may be a financial difficulty or a family crisis. I can't guarantee you immediate healing, provision, or resolution; but I can assure you that you don't need to carry your burden alone. "Cast thy burden upon the Lord" (Ps. 55:22a). Cast "all your care upon him" (1 Pet. 5:7). Truly His "yoke is easy," and His "burden is light."

ACTION POINT: In prayer, tell God what burdens you today. Thank Him for sharing the load with you.

—Tom Palmer

FEBRUARY 12
HEAVEN—ABSOLUTELY OUT OF THIS WORLD

Scripture Reading—Revelation 21:1-4, 22:1-5

Several years ago, I prepared a message I planned to preach in a Sunday night church service. I invited to the service a local funeral director I'd worked for after college. While preaching the message, I was making the point that nothing will be associated with death in heaven. My explanation went something like this: "In heaven there will be no funeral homes, no caskets, no funeral coaches, no cemeteries, no tombstones."

Then I nearly got into big trouble. I continued, "And there will be no funeral directors." Glancing at my funeral director friend, I quickly added, "Unless they are saved funeral directors." Wow, that was a close call!

What do you think will be special about heaven? I must confess that in some ways I struggle to comprehend the structural beauty of heaven. Heaven will be beautiful, but I have a limited ability to comprehend streets of gold and foundations of precious stones.

The "river of life" and the "tree of life" sound fascinating, but again, I don't know a lot about them. On the other hand, I'm thrilled with the thought that there will be no sorrow, suffering, sin, or Satan in heaven. I can't wait to meet and fellowship with the sons of God (21:7), the saved of God (21:24), and the servants of God (22:3).

One blessing, however, will stand above all other wonderful blessings of heaven. Jesus will be there, and we will be with Him (1 Thess. 4:17). We will see Him (Rev. 22:4), and we will be like Him (1 John 3:2).

As a child, I used to sing, "I'm going to heaven, and I can't wait." There's still a lot I don't know about heaven. Yet even with what I do know, I'm certain that heaven will be absolutely out of this world!

ACTION POINT: Ask each family member to list one thing he wants to see or do in heaven.

—Tom Palmer

FEBRUARY 13
A Joy-Filled Home

My wife and I attended a conference dealing with the family. Questionnaires were distributed to all the participants. One question on the children's survey asked, "How would you describe your home? (1) Very Happy (2) Happy (3) Not So Happy (4) Miserable." Of the close to 200 children who received the questionnaire, only two described their home as a "very happy" place. I was shocked! From that point until the end of the conference, I could hardly wait to ask my children that question. We can work at making our homes happy places.

Following God's order for the family eliminates a lot of tension and discord. When we work together instead of against each other, life goes more smoothly. God has given fathers, mothers, and children specific instructions. Parents should nurture and train their sons and daughters. Likewise, children should honor and obey their moms and dads. Everyone is obligated to esteem others better than himself. The law of love is simply doing to others as we would want them to do to us; no wonder they call it "The Golden Rule." *It's priceless!* As we follow God's blueprint for the home, a blessed atmosphere emerges. Peace, encouragement, harmony, and love result when family members follow God's instructions.

What is the root cause of arguments and disagreements? Proverbs 13:10a says, "Only by pride cometh contention." The source of all relational conflict is pride. Strife between parents and children and between siblings and spouses can always be traced to the culprit of pride. Humble people are easy to live with. "Likewise, ye younger, submit yourselves unto the elder. Yea, all of you be subject one to another, and be clothed with humility" (1 Pet. 5:5a). What a prescription for a happy home!

APPLICATION TIME: Read 1 Peter 5:5 aloud. Discuss it. Then ask each family member, "How would you describe our home? (1) Very Happy (2) Happy (3) Not So Happy (4) Miserable." Ask each family member what could be done to make your home a happier place.

—Harold Vaughan

FEBRUARY 14
JOY FROM
THE WORD

Scripture Reading—Jeremiah 15:16
"Thy word was unto me
the joy and rejoicing of mine heart."

Jeremiah, the weeping prophet, grieved over the sins of his people. Often God called upon him to bear the news of judgment to his sinning countrymen, but Jeremiah wasn't weeping all the time. He had bright spots along the way. One joy of his life was the Word of God.

The Bible serves many functions. It is a sword to cut, a fire to burn, a rod to chasten, bread to feed, water to quench, a lamp to lighten, and a source of great joy.

Jeremiah said, "Thy words were found, and I did eat them; and thy word was unto me the joy and rejoicing of mine heart: for I am called by thy name, O Lord God of hosts" (Jer. 15:16). This prophet feasted on God's words. He took in the Word, and it became part of him. God's Word was his source of joy.

The Old Testament reveals God's character. The Psalms show the heart of God. In Proverbs, we find God's wisdom; and the New Testament gives us an understanding of Christ and the Christian life. Everything that pertains to life and godliness can be found in the pages of this book.

But sadly, the worst dust storm in history would probably take place if Christians opened their Bibles! The reason many come away cold from Bible reading is because they don't warm by the fires of meditation. We need to dwell on God's words until they make an impression.

George Mueller, who experienced many answers to prayer, read through the Bible twice every year. A closed Bible is not a good luck charm. But an open Bible can be the source of great joy to an open heart. Perhaps you've heard this little chorus: "The B-I-B-L-E. Yes, that's the book for me."

CHORUS: If you know this little song, sing it!

—Harold Vaughan

FEBRUARY 15
JOY IN GIVING

Scripture Reading—2 Corinthians 9:7
"Every man according as he purposeth in his heart,
so let him give; not grudgingly, or of necessity:
for God loveth a cheerful giver."

It's a privilege and blessing to give. Giving is an opportunity, not an obligation. We are free, not forced, to give. We don't *have* to give. We *get* to give! God loves a *cheerful giver*. That means He loves a hilarious giver.

I once attended a church that broke into applause when offering time came. Not knowing what this response meant, I asked the pastor about it after the service. He had taught his flock that God loves people who give cheerfully and hilariously. As an expression of joy and hilarity, the congregation applauded and cheered when time came to give.

Jesus said, "It is more blessed to give than to receive" (Acts 20:35b). Everyone likes to receive gifts from others. Do you like to receive presents on your birthday? Do you look forward to Christmas and to gifts under the tree? Are you one who sneaks around, peeling back the wrapping, to see what's in the box? Of course, you enjoy receiving gifts! Gifts are a blessing, but Jesus said, "It is more blessed to give"!

The Lord has freely given us all things to enjoy. He chose to give; He did not have to give. God willingly gave His Son to save us from sin. He offered the ultimate sacrifice.

Learning the joy of giving is a mark of spiritual maturity. It reflects the generous character of God. God is a Giver. As we grow in His likeness, we become givers as well. One reason God gives to us is so we can give to others. It is fulfilling to know we have helped someone. We are blessed to be a blessing!

CONSIDERATION: Do you know someone who is currently in need? Could you help a neighbor by mowing the grass or raking leaves? Do you know an elderly person who needs assistance? Start giving and enjoy it because "it is more blessed to give than to receive"!

—Harold Vaughan

FEBRUARY 16
JOY IN
THE LORD

B illy Sunday said, "If you have lost the cup of joy in your religion, there's a leak in your Christianity someplace." Joy should be a distinguishing feature of Christians.

Mary commented, "My soul doth magnify the Lord, and my spirit hath *rejoiced in God* my Saviour" (Luke 1:46b-47, emphasis added). Her spirit *rejoiced in God*. God Himself is the source of our joy. "Let them also that love thy name be joyful *in thee*" (Ps. 5:11b, emphasis added). These verses say nothing about being joyful in circumstances, prosperity, or great benefits. The greatest joy is found in God Himself. To be precise, the joy *of* the Lord is found *in* the Lord. "My soul shall be *joyful in my God*; for he hath clothed me with the garments of salvation" (Isa. 61:10, emphasis added). We can find many Scriptures that plainly state that God is the spring of our joy. Nehemiah said, "The joy of the Lord is your strength" (Neh. 8:10b).

George Mueller said the first order of business every day wasn't breakfast, prayer, or even Bible reading. It was finding his joy in the Lord. We've all heard how he prayed in millions of dollars to support his orphanages. The Lord provided miraculously time and time again for his needs. However, Mr. Mueller's first concern was liberating his soul so it was overflowing with joy.

Do you remember where Peter was at Jesus' crucifixion? He was warming himself at the enemy's fire. He boldy denied he knew Christ, as Jesus was about to die on the tree. But after Pentecost, we never find Peter warming himself at someone else's fire. Once the Spirit of God filled him, he had a fire within himself!

God wants us to experience His joy. In his epistle, Peter wrote, "Whom having not seen, ye love . . . though now ye see him not . . . ye rejoice with joy unspeakable and full of glory" (1 Pet. 1:8).

SONG TIME: Think of a chorus or song that talks about the joy of the Lord. Sing the song with all your heart.

—Harold Vaughan

FEBRUARY 17
THREE CHEERS FROM JESUS!

Hip! Hip! Hooray! Hip! Hip! Hooray! Hip! Hip! Hooray!

We often use these words to honor people or to celebrate an event. Sometimes people say things like, "Three cheers for so and so." Then they shout the chorus: "Hip! Hip! Hooray!"

On three occasions, the Lord Jesus encouraged His followers with words of cheer.

"Be of good cheer; thy sins be forgiven thee" (Matt. 9:2b). Sweeter words have never been spoken! Jesus spoke these words to a sick man as he lay on his bed. Jesus said that our sins are blotted out; they are gone. The word *Gospel* means "good news." The best news a person could receive is hearing that his sins are covered. If our sins are forgiven, we can be of good cheer!

"Be of good cheer; it is I; be not afraid" (Matt. 14:27b). The ship was tossing to and fro on the stormy sea. The disciples were scared. When they saw Jesus walking on the water, they were terrified and thought he was a ghost. "But straightway Jesus spake unto them, saying, Be of good cheer; it is I; be not afraid." David had many enemies, yet he had learned to say, "What time I am afraid, I will trust in thee" (Ps. 56:3). If we believe the Bible, then we know Jesus is with us and will keep us safe from all harm. We can be of good cheer, too!

"Be of good cheer; I have overcome the world" (John 16:33b). Jesus told His disciples that trouble was coming. Then He gave the following reassuring words: "Be of good cheer; I have overcome the world." The word *cheer* means "to have courage." No matter what we're facing, we can take heart in knowing that Jesus has triumphed over the world. Surely we can take courage in Him.

As God's children, we are blessed to have three cheers *from* Jesus!

PRAYER: "Thank you, Lord, for giving us courage, confidence, and a covering for our sins!"

—Harold Vaughan

GOD'S GREATEST RESOURCE—PRAYER

Scripture Reading—Luke 18:1
*"And he spake a parable unto them to this end, **that men ought always to pray**, and not to faint" (emphasis added).*

Of all the resources God has provided for us to be successful in the Christian life, none is of greater value than prayer. Every revival in history has been born out of prayer, bathed in prayer, and blessed through prayer.

To the family that aspires to be godly, prayer must be a priority. Consider these vital facts about the importance of prayer.

1.   Prayer is our response of **obedience to God**. In 1 Thessalonians 5:17, God commands us to "pray without ceasing." Each time we obey God's commandments, we experience blessing (Isa. 1:19). A praying family is a blessed family.

2.   Prayer is our admission of our **need for God**. First Chronicles 4:10 records the prayer of Jabez. In it we hear the heart cry of one who desperately needs God. We are never in a better position than when we cry out to God in our need.

3.   Prayer enlists the **power of God**. When Asa, King of Judah, was outnumbered by the mighty Ethiopians, he called upon the almighty power of God for victory in the battle. He prayed, "It is nothing with thee to help, whether with many, or with them that have no power: help us, O Lord our God; for we rest on thee" (2 Chron. 14:11). No battle we face as a family will be too big for our Almighty God.

4.   Second Chronicles 14:12 implies that prayer displays the **glory of God**. The battle was won, and God did it! Every answer to prayer is an opportunity for God to display His glory.

What part does prayer play in your family? Is it an indispensable part of your family life?

ACTION POINT: Make a family prayer journal for recording dates and requests. When God answers, record the date and how God displayed His glory.

—Jack Palmer

FEBRUARY 19
THE PROBLEM WITH PRAYER

Scripture Reading—1 Samuel 12:23
"Moreover as for me, God forbid that I should sin against the Lord in
ceasing to pray for you: but I will teach you the good and the right
way" (emphasis added).

Yesterday, we considered the **priority of prayer**. Before your family can experience an effective prayer life, you must realize that God's greatest resource is prayer. If we fail to use that resource, we've already failed. Today, we want to focus on one of the **problems of prayer**.

A few years ago, a survey among Christian families in fundamental, Bible-believing churches revealed disturbing findings. One survey question was, "Do you and your spouse have a daily, consistent, meaningful prayer time together?"

The results were shocking and revealing. Only one percent of the couples were able to say "yes." That means 99 out of 100 answered "no." If we want to identify why many families are struggling with major issues in their lives, prayer is a great place to start! The most basic problem with prayer is simply that *we don't pray*. James 4:2b tells us, "Ye have not, because ye ask not." Dr. John R. Rice said that all of our failures are prayer failures.

Mom and Dad, you need to have a committed prayer time for your family's needs. Satan has his sights on your family, and he desires to destroy you. Only as you surround your family with the protective power of prayer can you hope to survive his assault. Dad, as you daily lead your family in prayer, remember that you're training them to understand the value and power of prayer by your example. Your children need to hear you pray for them and learn *how* you pray for them. You also need to pray *with* them, allowing them to participate in your family prayer time.

Don't allow your family to be in the 99 percent of families who fail to pray. Today's verse indicates that **prayerlessness is sin.**

APPLICATION: If God has convicted you about your prayer failure, confess your sin to God and commit yourself to be a praying family.

—Jack Palmer

FEBRUARY 20
MOTIVES
IN PRAYER

Scripture Reading—James 4:3
*"Ye ask, and receive not, because **ye ask amiss**,*
that ye may consume it upon your lusts"
(emphasis added).

God is concerned about *what* we do, but He's more concerned about *why* we do it. Our motives in prayer are important. So many typical prayers these days are selfish. Perhaps the selfishness is due, in part, to a misunderstanding of Psalm 37:4, which says, "Delight thyself also in the Lord; and he shall give thee the desires of thine heart." To some folks, the verse means that if we ask God for what we want, He'll give it to us. The verse actually means that when God's desires become ours, He can give us our desires.

Another problem is that we pray for the wrong reasons. D.L. Moody was conducting meetings when a lady approached him about praying for her husband's salvation. He asked her why she wanted her husband saved.

"If you had to live with him like I do," she said, "you'd want him to get saved, too!"

When Moody said he didn't have time for her request, she was offended that this great man of God treated her with such disinterest. That night, Moody preached about motives in prayer, stating that our highest motivation should always be glorifying God.

The woman was convicted and confessed her selfishness to the Lord. After the meeting, she asked Moody to forgive her, stating that she wanted her husband to get saved so God would be glorified. He said, "Let's pray right now for your husband's salvation!" The next night, her husband came to the meeting and trusted Christ as his Savior.

When God answers a prayer request, you should be quick to say, "Look what God did!" That way, you'll always be sure of giving Him the glory.

ACTION POINT: Read 2 Chronicles 20:1-30. Note the ways God was glorified in answering Jehoshaphat's prayers.

—Jack Palmer

FEBRUARY 21
PRAYING
IN FAITH

Scripture Reading—James 1:6-7
"But let him ask in faith, nothing wavering.
For he that wavereth is like a wave of the sea driven with the wind and
tossed. For let not that man think that he shall receive any thing
of the Lord" (emphasis added).

The essence of prayer is faith. Everything about prayer hinges on our ability to believe God. James describes someone who prays and doesn't believe God as a "double minded man" (1:8). To be "double minded" means to try to go in two directions at the same time—an impossibility. In the same verse, he says the double-minded man is "unstable in all his ways." Another serious problem with prayer is **praying without faith**.

George Mueller, that great man of faith, was traveling to a speaking engagement when his ship was enveloped in a dense fog. The captain could do nothing but hold the ship steady and wait for the fog to lift. After a couple of days, when the foggy conditions remained unchanged, Mueller went to the captain. He asked to pray that God would remove the fog so he could reach his destination on time. The captain was hesitant but consented.

Mueller prayed first, reminding God that he'd never been late for an engagement, and asked God to lift the fog. The captain began to pray, but Mueller interrupted him. "Sir, don't bother," he said. "You don't believe God can, and I believe He already has!" To the captain's surprise, when they went on deck, the fog was gone. God had again honored the great faith of George Mueller.

Romans 14:23b says, "Whatsoever is not of faith is sin." One of the most overlooked sins of God's people is unbelief. We can talk all we want about faith and about how wonderful trusting God is. But if we pray without faith, our prayers are in vain.

ASSIGNMENT: Read the story of the prophet Elijah in 1 Kings 18. Observe how he prayed in faith. God answered his prayer.

—Jack Palmer

FEBRUARY 22
PRAYING WITH
A CLEAN HEART

Scripture Reading—Psalm 66:18
"If I regard iniquity in my heart,
the Lord will not hear me"
(emphasis added).

Today, we want to address another problem with prayer—*praying with a sinful heart.* An important aspect of prayer is coming before God spiritually clean. That means allowing God to search our hearts and to reveal any sin we need to confess. How easily we overlook sin in our lives! We're concerned about those "big sins" like cursing, being immoral, or committing murder while we excuse what we call "little sins." Those are bad attitudes, unkind words, and critical spirits. But in God's eyes, there's no distinction between sins—*sin is sin!* And every sin is an offense to a holy God.

In operating rooms, doctors make every effort to maintain a sterile environment. Surgery is often a life-and-death situation, and infection can cause serious complications or even death to the patient. A surgeon was in the middle of a serious operation when he asked his assistant for a certain instrument. One of the assistant's responsibilities was to examine each instrument and to ensure it was clean. Carelessly, she handed the doctor a dirty instrument. When he realized her mistake, he threw the instrument across the room. "Don't you ever hand me an unclean instrument again!" he shouted.

Clean instruments are important in an operating room but even more critical in the prayer room. When we pray, we deal with issues that affect not only this life but also eternity. Isaiah wrote, "But your iniquities have separated between you and your God, and your sins have hid his face from you, *that he will not hear*" (59:2, emphasis added). God will not bless and use a "dirty instrument." When we pray, we need to be sure our hearts are spiritually clean by confessing and forsaking every known sin so God can hear and answer.

ACTION POINT: Read Proverbs 28:13. Discuss the importance of dealing with sin in your life.

—Jack Palmer

FEBRUARY 23
HITTING THE TARGET

Scripture Reading—Philippians 4:6
"Be careful for nothing; but in every thing by prayer and supplication
*with thanksgiving **let your requests be made known unto God***
(emphasis added).

Those who aim at nothing usually hit it! That fact is true not only on the rifle or archery range but also in prayer. In Luke 18:1-8, Jesus tells a story that illustrates important aspects about effective prayer. The story is about a widow who was unfairly treated. She went to a judge in her city and made a specific request. "Avenge me of mine adversary" (v. 3b). In only five words, she clearly stated her case. She didn't use a lot of fancy words; she went right to the point.

In Matthew 14, when Peter stepped out of the boat and walked on the water toward Jesus, he became fearful when he saw the storm raging around him. "Lord, save me!" he cried. His prayer wasn't fancy, but it was right on target!

Years ago, at Charles Spurgeon's church in London, a young seminary student was invited to lead in prayer. To make the best impression, he began praying in the most glowing terms about "Gawd"—that was his fancy way of saying "God"—and all "Gawd" could do. Finally, Spurgeon could tolerate the prayer no longer. Putting his hand on the young man's shoulder, he said, "Son, call Him 'Father' and ask Him for something!" Spurgeon understood the importance of praying specifically.

When the Bible tells us to "let . . . [our] requests be made known unto God" (Phil. 4:6), that's exactly what it means. Too often we pray in generalities and wonder why we never see answers to prayer. Learn to be specific in your prayer and expect specific answers from God. That's how God delights to answer prayer. Philippians 4:19 says, "But my God shall supply all your need according to his riches in glory by Christ Jesus." That's hitting the target!

APPLICATION: As a family, choose a special need and pray specifically about it. Wait patiently and see how God specifically answers that request.

—Jack Palmer

FEBRUARY 24
PRAYER AND THE WILL OF GOD

Scripture Reading—Matthew 26:39

*"And he went a little further, and fell on his face, and prayed, saying, O my Father, if it be possible, let this cup pass from me: nevertheless **not as I will, but as thou wilt**" (emphasis added).*

As Jesus anticipated the cross and the agony of paying for the sins of the world (2 Cor. 5:21), He prayed. In His prayer, He asked the Father that if there was another way to provide salvation for lost sinners would He do it? That was His specific request; however, He concluded by submitting to His Father's will. Yesterday, we learned that our prayers must be specific. We must also be willing to submit to God's will.

One of my Bible school teachers told an interesting story about his grandmother. A godly lady, she spent much time in prayer. On her kitchen table, she kept two books: her prayer book and the Sears and Roebuck catalog. On the Sears order form was a check box. If the customer checked the box, Sears personnel would provide a substitute if they couldn't supply what the customer had ordered. She never checked that box because she knew what she wanted. But once, just for the fun of it, she checked the box to see what would happen. At just that time, Sears was out of the item she had ordered. To her surprise, when her order arrived, she discovered that Sears always substitutes something of better quality. From then on, she always checked that box first!

My teacher explained that when we pray and submit to God's will, we're saying, "God, if you can't supply what I order, please substitute something else." God always substitutes what we prayed for with something better (see Isa. 55:8-9).

In Romans 12:2, we read that God's will is "good, and acceptable, and perfect." We never need to fear God's will.

MEDITATION: Read Matthew 26:36-46. Meditate on Jesus' prayer in the Garden of Gethsemane.

—*Jack Palmer*

FEBRUARY 25
GROWING UP

Scripture Reading—Luke 2:52
"And Jesus increased in wisdom
and stature, and in favour
with God and man."

Jesus was both 100 percent God and 100 percent man. As a human, He grew in four ways: First, He matured in wisdom, which is intellectual growth. Second, He grew physically. Third, He grew in favor with God, which is spiritual development. Fourth, He grew in favor with man, which is social maturity. Living things grow, and the Lord Jesus provides an example or pattern for us. I understand this verse describes Jesus when He was only 12 years old. He was maturing intellectually, physically, spiritually, and socially.

We are young only once, but we can stay immature indefinitely! As we grow older, we must grow up. Maturity means we become responsible for our actions, attitudes, and behavior. Simply put, we do things without being told what to do. As we mature, we look for ways to assist and to help others. We gain favor with people by behaving maturely. Our lives become a blessing to those around us. Like Jesus, we grow in favor with men.

On the other hand, rebellion is a refusal to grow up. It is a revolt against maturity. We can model ourselves after Jesus, and He can empower us to mature early in life.

Our forefathers never heard the word *teenager*. When children turned 13, parents considered them young adults and expected them to behave like adults. The concept of adolescence came into existence around 1950. During that period, standards became relaxed, and expectations for young people were lowered. When young people misbehaved, parents commonly said, "Why don't you grow up?" That was another way of saying, "Stop acting like a baby and act your age."

Jesus was subject to His parents and was "about my [His] Father's business" (Luke 2:49) early in life. We can be about our Father's business, too!

CONSIDER: Read Luke 2:52 again and talk about the four areas of growth.

—Harold Vaughan

FEBRUARY 26
DON'T FORGET GOD!

Scripture Reading—Ecclesiastes 12:1a
*"Remember now thy Creator
in the days of thy youth."*

Remember now. Yesterday is gone, and tomorrow may never come; therefore, today is the time on which we must focus. The Bible tells us to redeem the time, our most valuable resource. That means we must *rescue time from loss* or *buy back* time by using it for the glory of God. Our journey through life is brief at best. *Now* is the time to remember our Creator.

Remember our Creator. We are not an accident. God created us for a purpose. This verse reminds us that we are God's creation. Psalm 100:3 echoes this thought. "Know ye that the Lord he is God: it is he that hath made us, and not we ourselves; we are his people, and the sheep of his pasture." Creators design their inventions for a specific reason. The Bible says we are "the sheep of His pasture" (Ps. 100:3). Because we were created by God and for God, we owe our existence to Him.

Remember God in our youth. Youth is a time of preparation. During this phase, God is training us. We need to prepare for life with education and training for our occupation. Patterns we formed in childhood tend to stick with us throughout our lives. Remembering God when we are young prepares us not to forget God as we grow older.

But we are also preparing for eternity. Life on this planet is temporary, and we're going to live forever somewhere. Saved people go to heaven when they die and give account for their lives on earth. We are accountable for how we live on earth. "For we must all appear before the judgment seat of Christ; that every one may receive the things done in his body, according to that he hath done, whether it be good or bad" (2 Cor. 5:10).

DISCUSSION TIME: "So teach us to number our days, that we may apply our hearts unto wisdom" (Ps. 90:12). What does the phrase "teach us to number our days" mean?

—Harold Vaughan

FEBRUARY 27
STRENGTH THROUGH THE CROSS

Scripture Reading—1 Corinthians 1:18
"For the preaching of the cross is to them that perish foolishness;
but unto us which are saved
it is the power of God."

Alexander Solzhenitsyn, the Russian dissident, worked 12 hours a day at hard labor. He had lost his family, and doctors in the gulag told him he was dying of cancer. One day he thought, *There is no use going on. I'm soon going to die anyway.* Ignoring the guards, he dropped his shovel, sat down, and rested his head in his hands.

Sensing a presence beside him, he glanced up and saw an old man he'd never seen before and would never see again. The man took a stick and drew a cross in the sand. The simple act reminded Solzhenitsyn that there is a Power in the world greater than any empire or government, a Power that could bring new life to his situation. Picking up his shovel, he went back to work. A year later, Solzhenitsyn was unexpectedly released from prison.

Solzhenitsyn found strength and hope through the Christ of Calvary. With renewed vision, he overcame terrible circumstances, including cancer.

To believers, the preaching of the Cross is the power of God. The word *power* comes from the Greek word from which we get our word *dynamite.* The *power of God* is powerful! Jesus told His disciples, "But ye shall receive *power*, after that the Holy Ghost is come upon you: and ye shall be witnesses unto me" (Acts 1:8a, emphasis added). God gives "dynamite power" to His Spirit-filled witnesses so the Gospel can explode in the hearts of men. The preaching of the cross is powerful because by it men find forgiveness of sins, inspiration to persevere, and purpose in life. Of all people who have ever lived, Jesus Christ has had the greatest impact. His life and death have transformed more lives than all others put together.

CELEBRATE: Sing all the stanzas of that great hymn "There Is Power in the Blood."

—*Harold Vaughan*

FEBRUARY 28
WHO'S IN CHARGE?

Scripture Reading—2 Kings 22:1-2
*"Josiah was eight years old when he began to reign,
and he reigned thirty and one years in Jerusalem. . . . And he did that
which was right in the sight of the Lord, and walked in all the way of
David his father, and turned not aside
to the right hand or to the left."*

Think of it, a king at age eight! How many eight-year-olds do you know who would make good kings? Josiah made a fantastic king because he walked in the footsteps of David his father.

During the Middle Ages, kings lived in castles. Do you know who else lived in the castle? The royal family, soldiers, servants, cooks, the cupbearer, the joker, the dungeon keeper, and many others. The job of the king was to rule, so he sat on his throne and ruled all the subjects inside his castle. He was in charge. Occupying the throne meant he had authority over everyone in his kingdom.

Your body is similar to a castle. Inside you is a Thinker, a Chooser, and a Feeler. These are the subjects in your kingdom. You think with your brain, choose with your will, and feel through your emotions. Someone is going to be in charge. Whoever occupies the throne of your heart will rule your castle.

You were born with King SELF in charge of your castle. King SELF is a tyrant who wants everything for himself. When he's in control, all kinds of ugly things can happen. The only way for King JESUS to take control is by your dethroning King SELF.

Someone will be in charge of your castle—SELF or JESUS. You can yield your members to Him. When He is on the throne of your heart, good things happen. Jesus is the LORD, and LORD means Boss, Ruler, or King. Jesus is kind and gracious. He came to impart His life to you. Will you yield yourself completely to Him?

CONSIDER: How does Romans 6:13 relate to this topic?

—Harold Vaughan

FEBRUARY 29
SAVING TRUST

In 1859, Charles Blondin, the French acrobat, walked across a tightrope suspended across the Niagara River just above the falls. Thousands watched him push a bag of cement in a wheelbarrow along the wire, over 150 feet above the raging waters.

Blondin challenged a nearby reporter. "Do you believe I can do anything on a tightrope?"

"Oh yes, Mr. Blondin," the reporter said. "After what I've seen today, I believe it. You can do anything." The reporter, however, melted into the crowd when Blondin invited him to put his trust to the test and to get into the wheelbarrow.

Another man took the challenge, and onlookers placed bets on the outcome. The man entered the wheelbarrow, and Blondin began pushing him across the wire. But when they were halfway across the 550-yard journey of trust, someone with a heavy bet against Blondin's success cut one of the guide ropes.

The tightrope pitched crazily from side to side. Blondin fought for his balance, only seconds from death. If the rim of the wheelbarrow came off the wire, they would both be pitched into the churning water. Blondin ordered, "Stand up! Stand up and grab my shoulders."

The man in the wheelbarrow was paralyzed.

"Let go and stand up!" Blondin cried. "Do it or die!"

Somehow, the man stood up and stepped out of the swaying wheelbarrow.

"Your arms," Blondin said. "Put them round my neck! Now your legs . . . around my waist!"

Again, the man obeyed, clinging to Blondin. The wheelbarrow fell, disappearing into the frothy turmoil below. Using his years of experience, the aerialist stayed on the wire until the pitching had subsided. Then inch by inch, Blondin made his way across, carrying the man like a child. Finally, he deposited the man safely on the other side.

THOUGHT: Jesus is the only safe passage to eternal life. Have you put your trust in Him alone to save you?

—*Harold Vaughan*

THE BOY WHO PROVIDED SUPPER

Scripture Reading—John 6:4-14

"And Jesus took the loaves; and when he had given thanks, he distributed to the disciples, and the disciples to them that were set down; and likewise of the fishes as much as they would" (v. 11).

The feeding of the 5,000 was unlike any other miracle Jesus had done. He displayed the power of God by feeding a host of people with just five loaves and two fish. However, a small boy helped make this miracle possible. Pause and look again at the verses. Can you find the boy's name? Even if you look hard, you won't find it. He is one of those "no names" in Scripture. Verse nine tells us that he was just "a lad."

Look again. Can you find out how old he was? Again, the Bible doesn't say. Was he four, seven, or ten years old? We know only that he was a boy. How old does a boy or a girl need to be to do something worthwhile for the Lord? Probably the best answer is not a number of years. Rather, youngsters are old enough to serve the Lord when they realize that He desires to use them and when they are willing to let the Lord work through them.

Here is the key thought: **Nobodies become somebodies when they make themselves available to the Lord.** Usefulness to God is an issue of attitude, not age!

I am one, and only one,
I cannot do everything, but I can do something,
What I can do, I ought to do,
What I ought to do,
By the grace of God, I will do!

God is not looking for celebrities to do His work. He is looking for volunteers—moms, dads, teenagers, boys and girls—who are willing and available to be part of His work. Whether providing a meal or preaching a sermon, serving God is a privilege to those who desire to be used of God.

ASSIGNMENT: List boys and girls in the Bible who did something special for God.

—Tom Palmer

MARCH 2
LUNCHES GET SACKED!
Scripture Reading—Matthew 14:15-21

I feel sorry for sack lunches. Moms work so lovingly to prepare them, but we don't treat them very well. Anyone who looks around the lunch room will see that lunch is hard on sack lunches. Dissatisfaction with lunch meat in a sandwich can result in a slam dunk in the trash can. Other lunches get eaten but only with a grumble and a gripe between bites. Still others are swapped and exchanged like inexpensive stock on Wall Street. A banana for a cupcake is a great deal if you don't like bananas!

The five loaves and two fish a boy brought to Jesus became one of the most famous lunches in history. It was just a simple, packed lunch of bread and fish a mother placed into the hands of a boy running excitedly out the door. Yet the boy placed the lunch into the hands of Jesus. That's what made the lunch extra special.

The boy could have thrown his lunch away. He could have kept it all for himself, or he could have given away only part of it. He could have bargained to see what he would get for it. But he chose to give it all to Jesus, and he still got to partake of the food, along with thousands of other hungry people who needed to be fed.

The simple lesson is this: **Nothing becomes something when it becomes usable to the Lord.** The lunch's value was determined by the hands in which it was placed. Jesus took the lunch, and "looking up to heaven, he blessed, and brake, and gave the loaves to his disciples, and the disciples to the multitude. And they did all eat, and were filled" (vv. 19-20).

Only God can take so little and make so much. The lunch blessed many because a child placed it into the hands of the Lord.

APPLICATION: From the Bible, make a list of "little things" God used for His glory.

—Tom Palmer

MARCH 3
THE PAPER MISSIONARY

Scripture Reading

Isaiah 55:11—*"So shall my word be that goeth forth out of my mouth: it shall not return unto me void, but it shall accomplish that which I please, and it shall prosper in the thing whereto I sent it."*

Hebrews 4:12—*"For the word of God is quick, and powerful, and sharper than any twoedged sword, piercing even to the dividing asunder of soul and spirit, and of the joints and marrow, and is a discerner of the thoughts and intents of the heart."*

Late on a Saturday night, my wife, my daughter, and I got off a subway in upper Manhattan. Along with a group of teens, my family was returning to the church where we were staying. Because we were 10 stories underground, we entered an elevator to ride up to street level. The elevator operator was a miserable, angry-looking man; and we rode in uncomfortable silence.

When we reached the top, we quickly exited. But Julie, a little girl in elementary school, turned back and gave the man a Gospel tract. He received it kindly and broke into a big smile. As Julie joined us, we glanced again to see the smiling man sitting in the elevator and holding the Gospel tract.

I suppose we'll never see that man again—at least not here on earth. The blessing, however, lies in the fact that we may see him again in heaven someday. The Gospel tract, offered by a cute little girl, contained enough truth to help that man spend eternity in heaven.

Gospel tracts are like paper missionaries. Though just a simple booklet or pamphlet, a tract presents the message of the Gospel to its reader. Like sowing seed, a tract places truth in the heart and mind of someone who needs the Lord. Only in heaven will we see the results. And for what it's worth, children are usually effective at distributing paper missionaries. Most folks have a difficult time refusing anything from a child.

ASSIGNMENT: Get tracts from your church. Instruct each family member to pass out one tract in the coming week.

—*Tom Palmer*

FRONT-PORCH EVANGELISM
Scripture Reading—Matthew 5:13-16
"Let your light so shine before men,
that they may see your good works,
and glorify your Father which is in heaven" (v. 16).

As a family, we've never allowed our children to celebrate Halloween or to go trick-or-treating. We've discovered, however, that this annual event provides a wonderful opportunity to present the Gospel to boys and girls in our neighborhood. As the big night approaches, we select a Gospel tract. Usually we choose a tract that is well-illustrated with pictures or comic book-style illustrations. We make plans to be home on trick-or-treating night and turn on the porch light during the designated hours.

When someone comes to our door, our children place a tract, instead of candy, in the child's bag. More than once I've watched a child dash off the porch, calling to his parents, "They gave me a comic book!"

Within an hour or two, our front porch has become a platform from which as many as 150 youngsters have received the Gospel. On one occasion, we used a puppet show to draw attention. Cars stopped, and children got out. We gave them the Gospel, too. In so doing, we allowed the light of Christ to shine brightly in our neighborhood not only in the darkness of a fall evening but also in the spiritual darkness of sin that fills the hearts of men and women, boys and girls.

Few Christian families would consider their front porch to be a platform for evangelism. They may not see their living room or backyard as a mission field. But the place you call home can become a lighthouse, shining the way to God.

Some neighbors may never accept your invitation to attend church. But your home may be a more comfortable setting, making them more open to the Gospel. Treat them to a Gospel presentation that could change their lives.

THINK ABOUT IT: What event (like a game, a picnic, or a holiday) could provide an opportunity for you to share the Gospel at your house?

—Tom Palmer

MARCH 5
GO MAD!

Scripture Reading—Philippians 2:5-12

"Let this mind be in you, which was also in Christ Jesus: Who, being in the form of God, thought it not robbery to be equal with God: But made himself of no reputation, and took upon him the form of a servant, and was made in the likeness of men" (vv. 5-7).

Years ago, I heard a radio preacher describe something he did with his teens each morning before they left for school. After gathering at the front door, the family prayed, committing the day to the Lord. After saying goodbye, as the kids headed out the door, the preacher called, "Go MAD!" When I heard his testimony, I thought, *I know teenagers can be a little crazy, but they sure don't need encouragement!*

The radio pastor explained that the three letters in the word *MAD* stood for "Make a Difference." The pastor challenged his children to make their lives count for something—or for someone—in the day ahead.

Someone has said that three kinds of people live in this world—those who watch things happen, those who wonder what happened, and those who make things happen. Most of us probably fit into the first two categories, but Jesus was a "difference maker."

Every time He met someone, that person went away different. The Gospels record the life of a Man who changed people. Jesus didn't simply meet people—He changed them.

In most situations, our self-centered world gives little or no thought to others. Christians should be different. In reality, we were saved to save others; we were changed to change others; and we were blessed to bless others. God did a work *in* our lives so He could ultimately do a work *through* our lives.

As Christian men and women, teenagers, and children, we would do well to occasionally ask ourselves, "Whose life is different because of me?" If you're having a difficult time answering that question, determine that with God's help you will "Go MAD!"

TEST YOUR KNOWLEDGE: Identify several people in Scripture whose lives were different after they met Jesus.

—*Tom Palmer*

MARCH 6
DO GOOD

Scripture Reading—Galatians 6:10
"As we have therefore opportunity, let us do good unto all men,
especially unto them who are of the household of faith."

Do all the good you can, by all the means you can,
In all the ways you can, in all the places you can,
At all the times you can, to all the people you can,
As long as ever you can.
—John Wesley

Two kinds of people comprise our society: selfish people and selfless people. Selfish people are getters; selfless people are givers. Selfish people live to be served; selfless people live to serve. Selfish people live for self; selfless people live for others. Can you guess which people are more satisfied and happy?

Years ago, a national chain of auto repair centers used the promotional slogan, "What can we do for you today?" Wisely, they communicated a desire to take good care of their customers.

Likewise, families experience a blessing when they look for ways to care for others. Consider, for example, an elderly neighbor couple who are homebound due to health problems. Mom can fix a meal. The girls can help clean. Dad can run errands. The boys can mow the lawn. In so doing, the whole family gets involved in serving those in need.

Helping others takes time, effort, and money; but the greatest blessings come from *being* a blessing. As children grow old enough, they can experience the thrill of bringing a smile to someone's face. A picture colored with crayons, a bouquet of flowers, or a plate of cookies can be a great way to say, "You are special." Being others-conscious instead of self-conscious is a great way to approach life. Living for others, however, doesn't just happen; it's a choice. Make the right choice and live for others.

BIBLE READING: Acts 10:38 says, "How God anointed Jesus of Nazareth with the Holy Ghost and with power: who went about doing good, and healing all that were oppressed of the devil; for God was with him." What did Jesus do as He traveled?

—*Tom Palmer*

MARCH 7
CRAYONS DO
THE JOB

Scripture Reading
Hebrews 6:10—*"For God is not unrighteous to forget your work
and labour of love, which ye have shewed toward his name,
in that ye have ministered to the saints, and do minister."
1 Thessalonians 1:3*—*"Remembering without ceasing
your work of faith, and labour of love, and patience of hope
in our Lord Jesus Christ, in the sight of God
and our Father."*

Julie and Andrew, our two oldest children, were barely school-age when I asked them to help me with a project. I was scheduled to speak the next day at a senior citizens' center for a weekly Bible study. Wanting a special gift for each of the elderly people, I asked my children to help.

They took a box of crayons to the back porch. From the driveway, they gathered a bag of stones and colored the stones using crayons. Some stones were a solid color. Some had stripes. Patriotic stones were red, white, and blue. Others were multicolored with various designs.

After several hours of work, my children gave me a bag of stones for the Bible study. The next day, after finishing my lesson at the center, I explained that my children had a special gift for everyone. As my children distributed their colored stones, the smiles and thank-yous indicated that the colored stones were a real blessing. Some stones probably ended up on windowsills or dressers, but each one was special. I imagined how these elderly folks would be blessed in the days ahead simply by glancing at these little tokens of kindness.

Can God use crayons and stones? I think so. In a world of bigness, little things matter to God. He does not overlook a little blessing just because it's "little." We make a big mistake when we assume little things don't matter. God can use our talents, even if all we do is color stones with crayons.

ACTION POINT: Who in your family likes to color with crayons? Find stones, a coloring book, or some drawing paper and get busy.

—*Tom Palmer*

MARCH 8
Kindness in
Your Family

Scripture Reading—Ephesians 4:32
"And be ye kind one to another, tenderhearted, forgiving one another,
even as God for Christ's sake hath forgiven you."

Often we are kinder to strangers, acquaintances, and friends than we are to our own flesh and blood. This lack of kindness is a sin against God and our family members.

One of the greatest hindrances to kindness is time. God's Word speaks of "the kindness of thy youth, the love of thine espousals" (Jer. 2:2). Often a husband and wife are kind in their early years and gradually lose that kindness as the years go by.

In Ephesians 4:32, the word *kind* means "that which is easy and gracious." It's a disposition of one's spirit. An unkind person is one who is rough, coarse, and demanding.

We should especially practice kindness in our homes. The words *kindly affectioned* in Romans 12:10 convey the idea of a fondness toward those related to us. It is the norm for a believer to cherish and to be kind to his family.

However, something happens to our hearts as time passes. We lose our tenderness. Kindness and a tender heart are related—"And be ye kind one to another, tenderhearted" (Eph. 4:32a).

Because of life's struggles and the depravity of our own hearts, a neglected heart sometimes becomes an unkind heart as the seasons of life pass. Rather than becoming more tenderhearted, we become unfeeling, tough, and harsh. Those who are kind, easy, and gracious bring great blessing to those with whom they associate. This truth is especially magnified in family relationships. Thomas Moore said, "The ordinary acts we practice every day at home are of more importance to the soul than their simplicity might suggest."

Being unkind is a sin. Would you confess your lack of kindness to God and to those in your family you might have hurt? It has been said, "Be kind to everyone you meet, because everyone is having a tough time."

THOUGHT: When you think of kindness, what person comes to mind?

—Rick Johnson

MARCH 9
WHAT HAPPENS WHEN KINDNESS IS IN A FAMILY?

Scripture Reading—Proverbs 19:22a
"The desire of a man is his kindness."

My wife and I are close friends with an older, married couple who are gracious and kind to each other. After leaving their home one day, my wife said, "When we grow old, I want us to be like them." She referred not to their financial condition but to the graciousness with which they treated each other.

Kindness benefits a family in three ways. First, kindness encourages family members to spend time with each other. "The desire of a man is his kindness" (Prov. 19:22a). If you could pick between two people—one who was crusty, brusque, and quick to react; and one who was kind, tender, and gracious—who would you choose?

Second, kind people include others and share freely with them. Kindness isn't passive but proactive.

Finally, kindness is thoughtful in the smallest matters. James E. Amos, personal valet to President Theodore Roosevelt, included a powerful illustration of this truth in his book, *Theodore Roosevelt, Hero to His Valet:*

> My wife one time asked the President about a bobwhite. She had never seen one and he described it to her fully. Some time later, the telephone in our cottage rang. My wife answered it and it was Mr. Roosevelt himself. He had called her, he said, to tell her that there was a bobwhite outside her window and that if she would look out she might see it. Little things like that were so characteristic of him.

The kind "small things" we do for others are actually the "big things" they remember years later. If you want to improve your family relationships, learn to be kind.

ACTION POINT: What small deeds of kindness could your family members remember about you someday? How have you been unkind and need to change?

—Rick Johnson

MARCH 10
Kindness and the Grace of God

Scripture Reading—Luke 6:35
*"But love ye your enemies, and do good, and lend, hoping for nothing
again; and your reward shall be great, and ye shall be the children of the
Highest: for he is kind unto the unthankful and to the evil."*

We have a natural tendency to treat people as they've treated us; however, kindness doesn't require recipients to be deserving or worthy. Kindness and grace are interrelated (see Luke 6:35). Where you find one, you will find the other.

Kindness means being good to others even when they are undeserving. If we require others to behave in a certain way before we will be kind to them, we will never be consistently kind.

I have often been undeserving of my wife's kindness. On many occasions, my children have given me a break when I didn't deserve one. Surely I can do the same for them. The Bible says that God "is kind unto the unthankful and to the evil" (Luke 6:35).

We don't need to conjure feelings of kindness; kindness is an expression of God's grace in our lives, and the source of kindness is God Himself. Thus a godly man is a kind man because he reflects the heart of God. The Bible says "the Lord is gracious" (1 Pet. 2:3).

The opposite of kindness is roughness, harshness, and severity. Godly leaders don't drive others but lead them in graciousness and kindness (see 2 Chron. 10:7).

Though God offers kindness through His grace, we are responsible to put it on. Colossians 3:12 says, "Put on therefore, as the elect of God, holy and beloved, bowels of mercies, kindness, humbleness of mind, meekness, longsuffering." We become kind by allowing God's grace to live through our words, actions, and attitudes. We can carry grace into our homes and transform the atmosphere there. Instead of reciprocating the treatment we receive, we can offer grace and kindness.

THINK ABOUT IT: What kind, undeserving deed did a family member do for you recently?

—Rick Johnson

MARCH 11
HOW IS KINDNESS EXPRESSED IN A FAMILY?

Scripture Reading—Proverbs 15:1
"A soft answer turneth away wrath: but grievous words stir up anger."

Over time friction will wear down a machine and destroy it. The same is true in any relationship. Kindness is the oil that reduces the friction in relationships. Kindness isn't charisma or a personality trait; it's grace in action. Kindness can defuse an abrasive person—"A soft answer turneth away wrath: but grievous words stir up anger." (Prov. 15:1)

My friend Tim is always gracious to me. His kind spirit challenges me to be like him during tense situations. Another friend Price always says good things about others. These men model Christlikeness through their kind spirits and gentle words.

An unkind person is reactive and demanding. Our abrasive qualities are most apparent to those with whom we spend most of our time—our families. Sadly, they often bear the brunt of our unkind words.

Several years ago, those conducting a survey asked teens to list qualities they would like to change in their fathers. The number-one response was, "I wish my father would admit when he was wrong." Perhaps the primary way we express kindness is in our words, especially in the tone of our voice. Though Joseph's brothers were undeserving, he spoke kind words to them in grace (Gen. 50:21).

A principle of kindness ruled the virtuous woman's speech (Prov. 31:26). It isn't enough to speak the truth; we should speak with graciousness and kindness.

When people react to us, they frequently do so not because of what we say but because of how we say it. Kindness is especially important for fathers. Fathers communicate more to their children by their spirits than by the words they use. Kind words are also important for mothers as they establish the atmosphere in the home throughout the day.

THINK ABOUT IT: What kind things have people said to you lately? Who has the kindest tone of voice in your family?

—Rick Johnson

WORDS THAT WOUND THE HEART— PART 1

Scripture Reading—Proverbs 12:18
"There is that speaketh like the piercings of a sword:
but the tongue of the wise is health."

Most of us have no idea how much we talk. It is said that, in a single day, some use enough words to fill a 50-page book. In one year's time, the average person's words fill 132 books, each containing 400 pages.

Our words have incredible power. They have power to hurt or to heal. Proverbs 12:18 says, "There is that speaketh like the piercings of a sword: but the tongue of the wise is health." Some use words that cut and wound the souls of others.

In preparation for a message, I asked several people to recall deeply hurtful words someone had said to them. In each case, they remembered a specific childhood incident involving a family member, a coach, or a teacher.

Something that motivates others is the words they hear from those they respect. Words can carry enormous weight. Approval or disapproval from the right person can last a lifetime. Proverbs 18:21a says, "Death and life are in the power of the tongue."

God compares words to a sharp sword (Ps. 57:4), poison (Rom. 3:13-14), a tree of life (Prov. 15:4), deep waters (Prov. 18:4), and a fire (James 3:5). Oh, how powerful our words are! Words can follow us throughout our lives, scarring our souls and our destinies. "You'll always be a failure." "You'll never be a decent person." "I can never trust you again."

In contrast, words can motivate others to noble deeds. After a service, a boy named Billy approached evangelist Dr. John R. Rice. Placing his hand on the boy's head, Dr. Rice said, "Son, you would make a fine preacher." The boy, W.A. Criswell, later became the well-known pastor of the First Baptist Church in Dallas, Texas.

ACTION POINT: Your words make a difference—for good or for bad. What kind of words are you speaking? Throughout the day, be aware of your words and of the effect they have on others.

—Rick Johnson

MARCH 13
WORDS THAT WOUND THE HEART—
PART 2

Scripture Reading—James 3:8
"But the tongue can no man tame; it is an unruly evil,
full of deadly poison."

Our mouths are like a dispensary at a pharmacist's bench. They can pour out poison or medicine depending on the words we speak. Poisonous words can wound the heart, some wounding us deeper than others. We must be careful to deal with them properly and not to dispense them to others.

Lies wound the heart. The most important quality we can have is a commitment to the truth. The Bible is filled with warnings against lying (see Prov. 6:16-19, 18:8, 25:18; and Eph. 4:25). Those lies reflect the character of Satan (Gen. 3:4; John 8:44). God wants our words to be marked with the simplicity of truth (Matt. 5:37). It has been wisely observed, "If you always tell the truth, you don't have to remember what you said the last time."

Truth spoken without love wounds hearts. God places a premium on truth; however, speaking truth alone is insufficient (see Eph. 4:15). This verse mentions truth before love, but that doesn't diminish our responsibility to guard the way we speak the truth. God doesn't give us permission to speak truth without thought to how we present it. Keith Miller said, "Love without truth is hypocrisy, but truth without love is brutality."

Jesus' words were gracious. "And all bare him witness, and wondered at the gracious words which proceeded out of his mouth" (Luke 4:22a). He not only spoke the truth, but He did so graciously.

Sarcasm is often hyperbole intended to motivate, but it often hurts instead. A lack of kindness in our speech makes us focus on the messenger rather than on the message. It has been said, "When a man speaks, his words convey his thoughts, and his tone conveys his mood." In your desire to help and to correct, be careful to rebuke from a heart of tenderness, love, and kindness. "The words of a wise man's mouth are gracious" (Ecc. 10:12a).

THINK ABOUT IT: When did someone's words wound your heart?

—*Rick Johnson*

MARCH 14
WORDS THAT WOUND THE HEART— PART 3

Scripture Reading—Proverbs 18:8
"The words of a talebearer are as wounds,
and they go down into the innermost
parts of the belly."

Some words stay with us for a long time, perhaps even a lifetime, because of the wound they inflict on the heart. Many speak like a loose cannon without regard for appropriateness, timing, or kindness. Though they speak the truth, sometimes the truth is neither helpful nor necessary and shouldn't be spoken at all.

Sadly, our families often receive the brunt of our careless words. My wife's life verse is Psalm 19:14. "Let the words of my mouth, and the meditation of my heart, be acceptable in thy sight, O Lord, my strength, and my redeemer." Every believer should pray this prayer. God's Word clearly warns against careless speaking. (See Prov. 10:19, 13:3, 15:2, 17:27, 21:23, 29:11; and Ecc. 5:2-3.) Take time to read these instructive and convicting verses.

The Lord will hold us accountable for careless words. "But I say unto you, That every idle word that men shall speak, they shall give account thereof in the day of judgment" (Matt. 12:36). I believe one reason for such stern accountability is because of how damaging careless words can be.

Angry words wound us. Words and anger are often linked in God's Word (see Gen. 30:1-2; 1 Sam. 17:28; 2 Sam. 12:5; Luke 15:28-29; and James 1:19). When we're angry, we don't realize the volume and intensity of our voices, words, and tones. Regrettably, we often fail to realize how deeply we've hurt those to whom we've spoken in anger.

Destructive words wound us. Some words lead to destruction (Prov. 18:7), but encouraging words should characterize the Christian (Isa. 50:4; Eph. 4:29). We should repent of hurtful words by making restitution and seeking forgiveness. Psalm 141:3 is another appropriate prayer. "Set a watch, O Lord, before my mouth; keep the door of my lips."

THINK ABOUT IT: When was a time you spoke carelessly and foolishly?

—Rick Johnson

MARCH 15
DON'T MISS GOD'S GLORY

Scripture Reading—1 Corinthians 10:31
"Whether therefore ye eat, or drink, or whatsoever ye do,
do all to the glory of God."

The pages of *National Geographic* give us glimpses into the beauty and vastness of this great world. With each picture, we can grab, in imaginative detail, the wonder and awe of the creative nature of our God. While appreciating the skills of explorers, photographers, and editors, we realize these men and women fail to grasp the spiritual significance of their discoveries. The magazine never gives credit to God, and its contributors never seem moved by His genius design.

We can observe God's greatness regularly by observing nature during a walk, by enjoying the fragrance of a blooming flower, by eating fresh vegetables from our garden, and by welcoming a new baby into the world. We should praise God for what He allows us to see and experience every day.

Selfish men see man as the center of his own universe. Their faulty view distorts their image of God, preventing them from recognizing His unique greatness. The world dethrones God by ignoring Him. By ignoring Him, they belittle Him. By belittling Him, they worship themselves and serve "the creature more than the Creator" (Rom. 1:25).

We should value God, recognizing that He is credible, reliable, and powerful in His dealings with men without exception. Our God is profoundly interested in us and in directing our lives. By showing us His greatness, He has shown us His ability to guide us throughout life. The psalmist said, "The steps of a good man are ordered by the Lord" (Ps. 37:23a). "To God be the glory!" should be our cry.

While *National Geographic* is enamored with man's achievements, we should recognize that God is the "author and finisher of our faith" (Heb. 12:2), the Sustainer of our lives, and He who is worthy of our worship.

APPLICATION: Take a moment and prayerfully express gratitude to God for who He is and what He has done and is doing in your life. Find a verse that reflects God's greatness and memorize it.

—Jeff Kahl

MARCH 16
HOLY DAY
OR HOLIDAY

Scripture Reading—Exodus 20:8-11
On Mount Sinai, God gave Moses the Ten Commandments.
These Ten Commandments became the foundation of God's law that
showed His people the difference between right and wrong.
These commandments weren't optional; rather,
they stated exactly what God required of His people.

In the first four commandments, God told His people about their relationship with Him. The fourth commandment set aside a special day each week for the Lord. On this day of rest and refreshment, God wanted His people to meet with Him. God said the day was to be holy because He is holy.

In the 21st century, many fail to understand the significance of this day. Someone has said that our great-grandfathers called the Lord's Day the "Holy Sabbath," our grandfathers called it the "Sabbath," our fathers called it "Sunday," and our generation calls it the "weekend." We see evidence of this decline in the fact that Sunday is "Funday" for so many people. Tragically, many have left little of the Lord in the Lord's Day.

More tragic is the fact that our view of God's day is a direct indication of our view of Him. Those who are casual and careless about God's day are typically casual and careless about God Himself. They don't care much about His day because they care little about Him.

When the Lord's Day becomes a day for shopping, eating out, traveling, and playing sports, God quickly gets eliminated from our thoughts and efforts. Ask yourself what's more important—the worship service at 11 or the kickoff at 1? Do you care more about the Sunday sermon or about Sunday dinner? Which do you enjoy most—going to church or going to the mall?

A godly family must place great importance on the Lord's Day. Without this emphasis, a weakened relationship with God will cause family members to drift away from God.

APPLICATION: Take time to review the first four commandments, noting the significance of each.

—*Tom Palmer*

MARCH 17
THE PRIORITY
OF WORSHIP

Scripture Reading

Psalm 5:7—*"But as for me, I will come into thy house in the multitude of thy mercy: and in thy fear will I worship toward thy holy temple."*
Psalm 69:13—*"But as for me, my prayer is unto thee, O Lord, in an acceptable time: O God, in the multitude of thy mercy hear me, in the truth of thy salvation."*

Years ago, Ann Landers published letters in which her readers described their church services. Several were especially interesting.

A reader from Alabama wrote, "Protestant worship services are mostly selling tickets to ball games, tapes, pictures, records, and signing petitions on political issues. There is very little spirituality. And the music is a disgrace. No hymns anymore, just modern junk."

Someone from Florida wrote, "There is very little worshiping and meditation in our church. No time for it. Too busy congratulating couples on new babies, wedding anniversaries, engagements and leaning on parishioners to shell out more money. I pray at home."

We might assume that these letters reflect members of main-line denominational churches. For the most part, that may be true. However, these members aren't the only ones who've lost the concept of an atmosphere of worship where folks meet with God.

Worship demands a consciousness of God that focuses everything on Him. When we leave a genuine worship service, we should have a sense of being overwhelmed by God and by His greatness. Here's a good test: What does your family talk about on the way home from church? Your answer will indicate whether your family goes to church to meet with God. If their talk is about the donuts, the softball trophy, or the next political election, your family may have missed the point in going to church.

Worship begins with God. If He's not the center of our attention at church, we should hardly say that we've been to a worship service.

ACTION POINT: As a family, discuss the atmosphere of Sunday morning worship at your church.

—*Tom Palmer*

MARCH 18
GOD MUST
BE THERE

Scripture Reading—Ephesians 2:21-22
*"In whom all the building fitly framed together groweth unto an holy
temple in the Lord: In whom ye also are builded together
for an habitation of God through the Spirit."*

The pastor of a big church in Washington D.C. was sitting in his office
on a Sunday morning when a visitor called. "Will the president be in
attendance this morning?" the visitor asked.

"I can't tell you if the president will be here," replied the pastor, "but God
will be here, and that's a good enough reason to come." In a unique way, the
pastor had exposed the motive of someone who wanted to come to church
only to see the president.

When you go to church, who do you want to see? A friend or members
of your family? Do you find yourself looking around, seeing who might be
impressed by your presence? How sad that when we go to church, we're often
more conscious of others than we are of God. Church should be a time for
getting in touch and staying in touch with God.

Francois Fenelon was the court preacher for King Louis XIV of France in
the 17th century. One Sunday, when the king and his attendants arrived at
the chapel for the regular service, no one was there except the preacher. King
Louis demanded, "What does this mean?"

Fenelon replied, "I had published that you would not come to church
today in order that Your Majesty might see who serves God in truth and who
flatters the king."

Amazingly, some folks would see church as special only if a president or
king were in attendance. Church is special, however, because God is there in
the Person of the Holy Spirit. If God's presence isn't there, then services will
be no different than those of many churches that do not even know God.

TALK ABOUT IT: As a family, discuss how services at your church would
change if Jesus sat on the platform.

—Tom Palmer

MARCH 19
WHAT SHOULD
WE DO AT CHURCH?
Scripture Reading—Acts 2:41-47

Three basic parts should comprise the time we spend in church. Each of them should draw us closer to God as we get to know Him better.

1. First is **praising**. Acts 2:46-47 tells us that showing "gladness" and "praising God" were activities of early believers when they met for worship. Typically, they participated in these activities through music. Music dominates the part of the service when we worship God in song. The whole congregation sings songs, and the choir or other individuals or groups present songs as special music. If the music has a message about God and is presented in a godly style, it draws our attention to the Lord.

2. Second is **praying**. During this part of the service, we talk to God. Acts 2:42 tells us that prayers were also a part of the gatherings of believers. "And they continued stedfastly in the apostles' doctrine and fellowship, and in breaking of bread, and in prayers." When we talk to God, we bring our needs and requests to Him, asking Him to answer according to His will. Prayer has a unique way of bringing believers together, whether one person leads the prayer or many meet in a prayer meeting. Talking to God is always a special time.

3. Third is **preaching**. In Acts 2:41, we read that many "gladly received" God's Word. Verse 42 tells us that they continued learning doctrine. Preaching is when we hear from God and His Word. Each believer must listen to and learn God's truth, whether in a Sunday school class, a youth meeting, or a preaching service.

As you prepare for church this Sunday, be aware of how these basic parts of the service will help you meet with God as a family. Our time in church will be more meaningful if we understand why we're there.

ACTION POINT: Discuss how each person can be more involved in each part of the service.

—*Tom Palmer*

A MIND TO LEARN

Scripture Reading—Ezra 7:10
"For Ezra had prepared his heart to seek the law of the Lord, and to do it,
and to teach in Israel statutes and judgments."

Years ago, I visited an old country church in Madisonville, Pennsylvania. On the auditorium wall hung an antiquated sign with the following message:

Our Aim
1. Every member present every Sunday
2. On time
3. With his own Bible
4. A liberal offering
5. A studied lesson
6. And a mind to learn

I copied the message into my Bible as a reminder of the importance of preparing my heart when I go to church. As a preacher, I've been fascinated by folks who walk out of the service saying, "I got nothing out of the sermon," while others make life-changing decisions. I'm convinced that the key is a prepared heart. The best seed must have good soil that is prepared and ready to receive it.

Several tips will help your family prepare to learn on Sunday morning. Ask God to speak to you (Ps. 81:10, 85:8, 119:18). Make sure each family member brings a Bible and has it open during the message. Instruct children to take notes as soon as they are able to write. Limit distractions. Tell everyone to sit up and look at the preacher. On the way home, ask each family member to share something he learned from the message. On Saturday night, go to bed early; this step will enable everyone to stay awake.

Don't allow yourself to "Come as you are and leave as you were"—as one of my preacher friends said. Allow church to be a place of learning and growing in the things of God.

DISCUSSION: What does Matthew 5:6 say about hunger and thirst? Compare your physical appetites to your spiritual appetites.

—Tom Palmer

MARCH 21
GETTING READY
FOR CHURCH
Scripture Reading—Hebrews 10:22-25

Why are so many families late for church? And why are those on time hurried, stressed, irritable, pushed, aggravated, pressured, scrambling about, and—well, you're getting the idea, aren't you? For many families, just the thought of Sunday morning causes frustration. Frustration comes from getting up late, from missing shoes, from spilled cartons of milk, from lost lesson books, from misplaced keys, and—of course—from lots of squabbling on the way to church. Again, I ask the question. Why?

We may find the answer in when we start getting ready. If we wait until Sunday morning to start getting ready for church, we're already in trouble. By sleeping in (since there's no work or school), we communicate that Sunday isn't as important as other days of the week. Many tasks we must get done for Sunday could be completed on Saturday. Ironing outfits, gathering Bibles, preparing breakfast, giving the children baths, putting gas in the car, setting the table for dinner—these are tasks we can complete before that final hour before we leave for church.

Getting ready for church begins with attitude. It's amazing that families who are late for church are never late for school or work. If they were consistently late, the kids would get detention, and Dad would get fired. Except for rare occasions that can't be helped, lateness is an excuse. The reason is carelessness about the Lord's Day and the Lord's house.

Dedication and discipline enable families to treat the Lord's Day like the most important day of the week. We have no excuse for arriving at church in a frenzy, wishing we could skip the idea because of all the hassle we must go through. Changes begin with choices. Choose to get ready for church early.

ACTION POINT: Ask each family member to make a list of tasks he could do on Saturday to help prepare for Sunday morning.

—Tom Palmer

MARCH 22
Revival

Scripture Reading
Psalm 85:6—*"Wilt thou not **revive** us again:
that thy people may rejoice in thee?" (emphasis added).*
Psalm 138:7—*"Though I walk in the midst of trouble,
thou wilt revive me: thou shalt stretch forth thine
hand against the wrath of mine enemies,
and thy right hand shall save me."*

A man died in his sleep. His wife asked the barber to shave her husband's face prior to his burial. Taking a candle, the barber climbed the stairs to the bedroom and found the body. He placed the candle on the man's chest so he could see while shaving the man's face. He finished the man's face nearest to where he stood and needed to get to other side, but the bed had been shoved tightly against the wall. Weighing his options, the barber decided the best solution was to remove his shoes and to crawl over the corpse so he could see. As he crawled across the man's body, he absently placed his knee in the man's midsection. When he rested his weight on the midsection, the dead man rose and blew out the candle.

Startled, the barber ran downstairs and dashed out of the house in his stocking feet. "He's alive! He's alive!" he shouted. Upstairs, family members found the extinguished candle lying on the bed and the barber's shoes lying on the floor. Figuring out what had happened, they went to the terrified barber and said, "The man isn't alive. He had wind, but he didn't have breath."

The word *revive* means "to breathe life into." It describes the refreshing, life-giving breath of God. Unfortunately, it's possible for us to go through the motions and to do right things apart from God's power. Yes, we may have *wind* but not have *breath*!

Perhaps your heart has grown cool toward the things of God. Maybe your Christian life has become mechanical. David and his associates needed a fresh touch. He prayed for revival, and so can we!

INVITATION: Sing the hymn "Breathe on Me, Breath of God." Pray as the Lord leads.

—*Harold Vaughan*

MARCH 23
The Continuation of Revival

Scripture Reading—Psalm 85:6

*"Wilt thou not revive us **again**: that thy people may rejoice in thee?" (emphasis added)*

Spiritual vitality is not a onetime shot. The word *again* indicates that what has happened before needs to happen over and over again. God has moved in the past, and we need Him to move among us once more.

As we read church history, we discover that God periodically brings a neglected truth to the forefront. Like a fresh spring, the illuminated truth gives life to thirsty souls. People are refreshed and invigorated when they feast on the recovered truth. God's presence and power energize His people, and God's kingdom is expanded. If not for these seasons of rejuvenation, the entire Christian enterprise would have collapsed long ago.

The word *revive* means to give life again. Because our hearts are "prone to wander," we stand in need of a reviving work from time to time. Our needy hearts need the ever-flowing grace of God to meet our deepest needs. Like branches on a vine, we must abide in the true vine if we are to bring forth fruit.

God will complete the good work He started in us (Phil. 1:6). As we cooperate with Him, we grow in grace and go from glory to glory. The purpose of a wake-up call is to keep us awake, not to put us back to sleep! The purpose of revival is to set us on the path of spiritual progress.

Paul admonished Timothy to "stir up the gift of God" (2 Tim. 1:6). The gift was there, but it needed to be rekindled. Yesterday's manna won't meet today's needs. The old hymn says,

Revive us again—
Fill each heart with Thy love;
May each soul be rekindled
With fire from above.

SONG TIME: Sing "Revive Us Again."

—Harold Vaughan

THE OBJECT OF REVIVAL

Scripture Reading—Psalm 85:6

*"Wilt thou not revive **us** again: that thy people
may rejoice in thee?" (emphasis added)*

One man prayed, "Lord, turn me upside down. Lord, turn me upside down, because what's on the top should be on the bottom, and what's on the bottom should be on the top. Lord, turn me upside down!" This candid prayer demonstrates that this man realized his life was out of order.

Note the psalmist is praying for himself and for those who are close to him. "Wilt thou not revive *us*?" (emphasis added). We are the object of revival. God does not revive nations, denominations, or churches. He revives individual Christians. Of course, when a group of people receive a fresh touch of grace, it has positive effects on the whole. But the point here is that we need a fresh encounter with God. In verse 4, David prayed, "Turn *us*, O God of our salvation, and cause thine anger toward us to cease" (emphasis added). He didn't pray for the heathen or the compromisers; he prayed for himself and for his comrades.

Revival is God's pointing His finger right at me! This kind of experience is intensely personal, painful, and powerful. In chapter 6, when Isaiah the prophet saw the Lord, he said, "Woe is me." The clear vision of God brought the recognition of unclean lips in him and in others. God sent the seraphim to cleanse Isaiah's mouth with the live coal from off the altar.

There is a time to pray for a broad, sweeping move of God. This is certainly appropriate and right. But God desires a revived man to pray for revival on a larger scale.

Someone asked Alan Redpath, "Do you think we are out of touch with our generation?" To which he responded, "No, our problem is that we are out of touch with God!" What about you? Do you stand in need of spiritual cleansing? God is ready to revive His people.

PRAYER: "Lord, search us, break us, melt us, and revive us. Amen."

—Harold Vaughan

MARCH 25
THE RESULT
OF REVIVAL

Scripture Reading—Psalm 85:6
"Wilt thou not revive us again:
that thy people may rejoice in thee?"

Rejoicing is the result of revival. I'm not in favor of feel-good religion, but there's nothing wrong with feeling good! God wants His people to *rejoice* in Him. Our God is a supremely happy God. "In thy presence is fulness of joy" (Ps. 16:11).

Dealing with sin is a dirty business. In Bible times, a silversmith put silver ore in a big pot and turned up the heat until the ore melted. Scum rose to the surface on the liquefied metal. With ladle in hand, the smith skimmed the scum off. If he failed to do so, impurities settled back into the fabric of the metal as it cooled.

Purifying silver required a process of heating the ore successive times. Each time, the heat became hotter than the time before, and a different type of impurity surfaced. Seven times, the smith reheated the silver until the ore was so pure he could see the reflection of his face in the liquefied silver.

As we deal honestly with sin before God, He cleanses us; and we reflect His glory. It's good to be clean in God's sight. What a blessing to feel the blood applied, as the old hymn says! Intense pain comes with conviction, but intense joy is the outcome of God's reviving touch.

Throughout the Bible, Scriptures tell us and even command us to *rejoice.* The rejoicing that honors God is the type of joy that finds its source in God Himself. When we get our hearts clear with God and man, we can rejoice in Him.

God's grace is "greater than all our sin"! Look up! Clean up! Pack up! Soon we're going up! God's mercy is plentiful. His will is for His people to rejoice, and the byproduct of revival is rejoicing.

ACTION POINT: Which Bible verses can you quote about rejoicing? Look up several Scripture references on joy and rejoicing.

—*Harold Vaughan*

MARCH 26
WHAT IS GOD'S GLORY?
Scripture Reading—Psalm 19:1-6

Perhaps one of the most glorious events in our nation is the inauguration of the president of the United States. Gathered on such an occasion are dignitaries of every stripe. Crowds of citizens gather, bands play, prayers are prayed, and songs are sung as we observe the swearing in of our president every four years.

This event is a glorious one because it embodies truth about what has made the United States a great nation. Here, after an election, the most powerful nation on earth changes leadership without a single shot being fired!

What an immeasurably glorious sight must be the vision of the God of heaven! But what do we mean when we speak of "God's glory" or of the glory of anything? Authors have written volumes, seeking to define God's glory adequately. God is such a great God that no description can suffice. Examining God's Word, we learn that we can express "God's glory" as the external demonstration of an inward quality. God is glorious because of who God is.

The glory of a winning team of athletes is not in the beauty of their uniforms, in the impressiveness of their home stadium, or in the enthusiasm of the cheering squad. The glory of the winning athletes lies in the internal quality that brought them to the place of victory. It is long hours of hard practice, careful planning, and skillful plays worked out in detail and learned through discipline. It is the interaction as athletes work together.

"Glory" is only an outward manifestation of what's true inside. People may try to look glorious, but the appearance is not true glory unless there is that inner working of quality behind it.

God is all-glorious. Everything within Him and about Him is above and beyond all else. His glory demands our worship, and part of His glory is that such a One would desire it.

SELAH: As you ponder the glory of God as revealed in creation (Ps. 19), consider whether He receives from your life the worship that is rightfully His.

—*T.P. Johnston, Jr.*

MARCH 27
IMAGES
OF GLORY

Scripture Reading
1 Corinthians 11:15a—"But if a woman have long hair,
it is a glory to her."
1 Peter 3:3—"Whose adorning let it not be that outward adorning
of plaiting the hair, and of wearing of gold,
or of putting on of apparel."

God says that a woman's hair is her glory. Yet He clearly says in 1 Peter 3 that a woman's true beauty is not the arrangement of her hair or her outward appearance. It is the inner person of the heart. A truly beautiful woman is not one with the right hair style, though God says her hair "is a glory to her." True beauty derives from a right relationship with the Lord. That is, a truly beautiful woman is one who has invested as much in her spiritual life as she has in arranging her outward appearance.

God also says that "the woman is the glory of the man" (1 Cor. 11:7). The Bible does not say that women shouldn't pay attention to how they look. What it says is that a woman's true beauty is an inner beauty that comes from a right relationship with God, with her husband, and with those around her—even though her hair is her glory.

Many men and women try to achieve glory by looking glorious, but that glory doesn't exist if they have nothing internal to back it up. Our society places great emphasis on the outward appearance, and often certain people will look glorious to us. They may look appealing and important. But as we get to know them, we will realize that they have nothing inside to back up their glorious appearance. True glory comes from within, and that fact is certainly true of the glory of God.

SELAH: Ask family members to list qualities of God that reveal His glory. Take time to thank God for who He is in Himself and for the qualities that make Him so glorious.

—*T.P. Johnston, Jr.*

MARCH 28
GLORIOUS
LIGHT

Scripture Reading—Ezekiel 1:28
"As the appearance of the bow that is in the cloud in the day of rain,
so was the appearance of the brightness round about.
This was the appearance of the likeness of the glory of the Lord.
And when I saw it, I fell upon my face,
and I heard a voice of one that spake."

Have you ever experienced pain from looking at the sun? Eye specialists say that looking directly at the sun causes permanent eye damage, even blindness. Full sunshine on a cloudless day is beautiful. Even then, however, we do not experience complete light. There is still some measure of darkness.

Our God often describes His glory in terms of light. First Timothy 6:15-16 says, "Which in his times he shall shew, who is the blessed and only Potentate, the King of kings, and Lord of lords; who only hath immortality, [notice this] *dwelling in the light which no man can approach unto*; whom no man hath seen, nor can see: to whom be honour and power everlasting. Amen" (emphasis added).

God is so glorious that if we were to think of Him in terms of light, He would be unapproachable. We could not come into His presence if He didn't allow us. John explains this truth in 1 John 1:5. "This then is the message which we have heard of him, and declare unto you, that God is light, and *in him is no darkness at all*" (emphasis added). No darkness at all! Consider that truth in view of how we shield our eyes from "full" sunshine that provides only partial light, as bright as it is!

Ezekiel saw a vision of God—like the appearance of a rainbow in a cloud on a rainy day. This was the likeness of the glory of the Lord. The Lamb of God, our Lord Jesus, will be the Light of heaven.

SELAH: Discuss the greatness of God's glorious light. He will someday change our bodies so we will be able to behold Him.

—T.P. Johnston, Jr.

MARCH 29
GLORY IN CREATION

Scripture Reading—Romans 1:20-21

*"For the invisible things of him from the creation of the world are clearly
seen, being understood by the things that are made,
even his eternal power and Godhead; so that they are without excuse:
Because that, when they knew God, they glorified him not as God,
neither were thankful; but became vain in their imaginations,
and their foolish heart was darkened."*

According to astronomers, we can see more than 3,000 stars in the night
sky with the naked eye. Sophisticated telescopes allow us to view some
two billion stars just in our galaxy, and scientists estimate the existence of one
million galaxies beyond our own. The Bible says God calls each star by name.
That thought is staggering, and *staggering* is a good word to describe God's
glory.

Plentiful stars aren't the only indication of God's glory in His creation.
Consider the nearly six billion people who inhabit planet Earth, each having
a distinct set of fingerprints. What a glorious God who can create such
wonders!

Such wonders make the statement "It all happened by chance" seem even
more ridiculous. It would be like a builder giving a tour of a newly constructed
home and remarking, "Oh, by the way, we just had the lumber and
materials hauled onto the lot. We threw a stick of dynamite into the pile.
After the explosion, there was this house!"

In Romans 1, God tells us that He doesn't believe in atheists. Every
human being is accountable to God because everyone, just by looking at
nature, recognizes the existence of a Creator. The Bible says that those who
deny the existence of a Creator, who say the creation of the world happened
by chance, are deliberately denying the truth God has made available to them
about His glory.

SELAH: As a family, discuss why people try to explain away all the evidence
God has given us of His glory.

—*T.P. Johnston, Jr.*

MARCH 30
WHEN GOD
SHOWS UP

At different times and places in history, God chose to reveal His glory in specific ways. In Exodus 40, for example, God gave instructions for constructing the Tabernacle, a sort of mobile chapel for worship. The Tabernacle was designed so the Israelites could take it down and carry it with them in their wilderness wanderings. When the Tabernacle was completed, the presence of God came down in a cloud of fire and a pillar of smoke.

Later, when the Temple, a more permanent place of worship, was completed, the Lord manifested His glory again (1 Kings 8).

Many years later, the glory of God came forth in the Person of God's Son, the Lord Jesus Christ. John 1:14 says, "And the Word was made flesh, and dwelt among us, [notice this] (and we beheld his glory, the glory as of the only begotten of the Father,) full of grace and truth." God's glory was veiled in Jesus. Many knew Jesus was God, but they saw only hints of God's glory when Jesus performed miracles. Finally, on the Mount of Transfiguration, Jesus allowed some of His veiled glory to "leak out" for Peter, James, and John to see.

The glory of God was present in the Tabernacle, in the Temple, and in the Person of the Lord Jesus. Did you know that God's glory is present today in a specific place on planet Earth? Ephesians 3:20-21 says, "Now unto him that is able to do exceeding abundantly above all that we ask or think, according to the power that worketh in us, unto him be glory in the church by Christ Jesus throughout all ages, world without end. Amen."

That's right! If we know Jesus Christ, God's glory resides in you and me. The Scriptures tell us that God has chosen to display His glory in your life and in mine.

SELAH: Thank the Lord today for the amazing privilege of being one in whom His glory dwells!

—*T.P. Johnston, Jr.*

MARCH 31
GLORY
PRIVILEGES

Scripture Reading
1 Corinthians 6:19-20—*"What? know ye not that your body is the temple of the Holy Ghost which is in you, which ye have of God, and ye are not your own? For ye are bought with a price: therefore glorify God in your body, and in your spirit, which are God's."*
1 Corinthians 7:23—*"Ye are bought with a price; be not ye the servants of men."*

If we are saved through the precious blood of Christ, God has chosen us to experience the same special place of honor as the Temple in Jerusalem. People came from all over the world to see the Temple of God and of Jerusalem—not just because it was an architectural marvel but because people somehow knew it was a glorious place. Many knew it was the place of God's dwelling on earth, the place of His presence on earth. You and I are no less important in God's plan.

Believe it or not, you and I are God's dwelling place on earth!

That is a sobering thought. Think about the places where we sometimes take the glory of God with us. Think about what we allow the glory of God to witness in our relationships with others, even with those we love. You and I are the residence of God's glory on earth right now.

It is important to understand that the dwelling place of God's glory on earth isn't just in the stars in the heavens or in the intricacies of His creation on earth. God demonstrates His glory in your life and in mine. At least, that's what God intends. God wants us to live our lives in such a way that when others see us, they will see His glory. How are you doing with that responsibility?

SELAH: Consider the various areas of your life. Ask the Holy Spirit to speak to you about how you are glorifying—or failing to glorify—God in each area.

—*T.P. Johnston, Jr.*

APRIL 1
IT'S IN
THE WORKS

Scripture Reading—Psalm 9:1
"I will praise thee, O Lord, with my whole heart;
I will shew forth all thy marvellous works."

As we come to appreciate something of the glory of God, the only proper response is that we will tell others about Him. We may bear witness in any of the following ways: by singing hymns, by witnessing to others orally, and by allowing the Lord to work in our lives so others see something different in us—something that could have come only from God.

It's impossible to grit our teeth and to work up such a demonstration of God's glory in our lives. Rather this demonstration comes automatically as we spend time in His presence, learning more about Him from His Word and through prayer. If we don't allow God to work in our lives in these ways, we prevent the means by which He desires to manifest His glory that He placed in us at salvation.

When others observe us as we praise God in the midst of trying circumstances, exhibiting godly choices when irritations and difficult relationships confront us, we increase God's glory.

Many Christians struggle with knowing God's will for their lives. Yet if they would make glorifying God the focus of their lives, His will would fall into place step by step. First Corinthians 10:31 exhorts us, "Whether therefore ye eat, or drink, or whatsoever ye do, do all to the glory of God." If our focus is on glorifying God in everything—even the small things of life—it will be impossible for us to miss God's will!

Perhaps the most exciting benefit of glorifying God is that when we glorify Him, we become more like Him. Second Corinthians 3:18 says, "But we all, with open face beholding as in a glass the glory of the Lord, are changed into the same image from glory to glory, even as by the Spirit of the Lord."

SELAH: What is there about your life that you can explain only by God's working in you?

—*T.P. Johnston, Jr.*

APRIL 2
BE YE HOLY—
AND REPENT

Scripture Reading—Psalm 51:1-10

David was guilty! He was in the wrong place, at the wrong time, with the wrong person, and doing the wrong thing. Second Samuel 11:27 says that "the thing that David had done displeased the Lord." His adultery with Bathsheba and the murder of her husband, Uriah, were secret sins; but God knew about them. Nathan the prophet exposed the scandal in the palace when he confronted David about his sin. Under God's conviction, David declared in 2 Samuel 12:13, "I have sinned against the Lord."

Nathan followed David's simple confession by saying, "The Lord also hath put away thy sin" (v. 13). David could and would be clean before God again. Some people are afraid to confess their sin to God because they fear they're letting God in on a secret. For this reason, they allow their life to remain contaminated and corrupted by unconfessed sin. David's sins were severe, but he refused to blame, defend, or explain them away.

Human beings hate to admit wrongdoing. Just watch the typical toddler try to talk his way out of something he did wrong. He didn't touch the birthday cake—or so he says. Yet there's icing all over his face. He didn't write on the wall, he says, but there's marker on his hand. The evidence is obvious, but fallen human nature causes us to struggle with being honest about our sin.

David was a man who enjoyed God. Just read the Psalms. Yet in Psalm 51, he didn't enjoy God. He was guilty of sin, and he knew it. Rather than making excuses, he sought in this prayer to be holy, as pure as God is, by agreeing with God about his sin. Needless to say, David soon knew the excitement and enjoyment of the God he'd known before.

APPLICATION: Read 1 John 1:8-10. What two events occur when we say we have no sin?

—*Tom Palmer*

APRIL 3
BE YE HOLY—
AND RESOLVE

Scripture Reading—Daniel 1:3-8

No significant change in life can occur without a choice. Right choices are key in going the right direction in life. In Daniel 1, we read about Hebrew young men God placed in a "cultural pressure cooker." The Babylonians had taken them away from their homeland and placed them in an anti-God society that sought to disconnect them from their God. This disconnect occurred initially by the change of their language, of their names, and of their diet. Daniel had to make a choice. He could do as he was told and "go with the flow," or he could maintain standards of purity in his life. Thankfully, he made the right choice.

When Daniel "purposed in his heart that he would not defile himself" (v. 8), he made a choice that would significantly impact his life. To eat of the king's meat and drink of his wine would be a direct violation of the Jewish dietary laws. Daniel decided that his life would remain pure.

I believe so few Christians live holy lives because they don't *want* to live holy lives. They have not chosen to live holy lives; therefore, when impurity confronts them, they constantly struggle. Let's face it. If you wait until your TV is on and until you're surfing channels to decide what your family will watch, it's too late. You must decide to be pure long before you push the power button. Actually, you must decide before you open the box or plug in the TV. The TV is just one example that illustrates the impact right choices can make. Holy living begins with a choice to live a holy life.

Daniel's choice may seem risky, but God loves choices that require us to be pure and to do right. When Daniel honored God, God honored Daniel. Purity paid off for Daniel, and God blessed him.

ACTION POINT: Read Daniel 1:15-17. Note the specific blessings Daniel experienced.

—*Tom Palmer*

APRIL 4
BE YE HOLY—
AND REQUEST

Scripture Reading—1 Chronicles 4:9-10

Author Bruce Wilkinson didn't intend *The Prayer of Jabez* to be a spiritual good luck charm as it has become to so many. Rather, the Bible records for us a sincere prayer with specific requests by a man who wanted to be blessed of God. Notice, if you will, the fourth request in this simple prayer list: "And that thou wouldest keep me from evil" (v. 10). The best part is that "God granted him that which he requested" (v. 10). Here is the prayer of a man who desired to live a pure and holy life, and God granted his desire in answer to prayer. God truly answered the prayer of a man who wanted to be holy.

Often our prayers are limited. Of course, many times, "ye [we] have not, because ye [we] ask not" (James 4:2). Yet even when we pray, we sometimes easily forget about spiritual prayer requests. Much of our praying centers on the physical and material needs in our lives. It would be good, however, to add Jabez's request to our list. Parents should pray Jabez's prayer for each member of their family. Teens and children should pray his prayer for their own lives.

By praying, we enlist God's assistance. God desires that we live holy lives and be kept from evil. This is His will. When we pray about holy living, we pray according to God's will. He loves to answer those prayers.

Ask God to protect your eyes and ears because they provide input into the mind. Pray for the protection of your mind because we become what we think about. Ask for God's help with your words, attitudes, and reactions because these are areas where becoming sinful is easy. As God answers these prayers, your life will become blessed by the holy lifestyle God desires.

APPLICATION: Recite the Lord's Prayer as a family. Make note of the requests about protection from sin.

—Tom Palmer

APRIL 5
BE YE HOLY—
AND RESIST

Scripture Reading—Matthew 4:1-11

We can describe dealing with the devil as a battle. The devil, the arch-enemy of all that is God, has declared war on those who would go God's way. His weapons are powerful, and his tactics are deceitful. He never plays by the rules. One of his goals is to defeat and to destroy the efforts of any child of God who would seek to live a holy life.

In our text, Jesus was involved in hand-to-hand conflict with the devil. Notice that Jesus didn't try outsmarting the devil. He didn't rely on intellect, logic, or a good argument to defeat His enemy. Rather, He simply quoted Scripture.

Satan tempted Jesus with self-sufficiency (v. 3), with self-preservation (vv. 5-6), and finally with self-fulfillment (vv. 8-9). The basis of these temptations was the desire for a self-centered life—which is basically the root of all sin. Each temptation presented Jesus with an opportunity to yield to the devil.

What's amazing is to watch what happened as Jesus began using God's Word. Ephesians 6:17 describes the Word of God as the "sword of the Spirit," the one offensive weapon God gives to those who battle Satan's temptations. Three times Jesus refers to the Old Testament Book of Deuteronomy. One of my teachers in Bible college said, "Jesus took the machine gun of Scripture and mowed the devil down." It was the power of God's Word that enabled the Lord Jesus to win this victory over His enemy, the devil.

For this reason, Christians need a working knowledge of the Word. Sin may keep them from God's Word, but God's Word will keep them from sin! (Ps. 119:9, 11). An Army Ranger with a cap gun or a Marine with a squirt gun will soon become casualties of war. So the Christian who lacks an effective weapon will be overwhelmed by the assault of Satan and will easily be defeated.

ACTION POINT: Find verses in Deuteronomy 6 and 8 that Jesus quoted.

—Tom Palmer

APRIL 6
BE YE HOLY—
AND RUN

Scripture Reading—Genesis 39:7-12
"And she caught him by his garment, saying, Lie with me: and he left his garment in her hand, and fled, and got him out" (v. 12).

Let's pretend your family is taking a hike while on vacation in the Rocky Mountains. Suddenly, you hear a growl from a nearby ledge. As gravel breaks loose and tumbles down the steep incline, each family member turns to see a mountain lion crouching and ready to pounce. The big cat is motionless except for the twitching of his long tail. His piercing eyes stare, and his curling lips expose razor-sharp teeth. Occasionally, he allows the rumble of a deep growl.

Suddenly, four-year-old little brother steps toward the ledge with his hand out. "Here, Kitty, Kitty!" Simultaneously, teen big brother blurts, "I tought I taw a puddy tat" as everyone bursts into laughter. Right? I don't think so!

Of course, this is just a hypothetical situation, but I can tell you what would have happened if it were real. Your family would have sprinted, dashed, and raced for safety. Even Mom and Dad, who were never track stars to begin with, would have moved quickly. Why? Because danger was threatening the family. A hasty escape was necessary to spare the family from harm.

Interestingly, the Bible says, "Be sober, be vigilant; because your adversary the devil, as a roaring lion, walketh about, seeking whom he may devour" (1 Pet. 5:8). Yes, sometimes we should resist, but other times we should run. Sometimes the best thing we can do when evil confronts us is to make a hasty escape.

Mrs. Potiphar grabbed Joseph's coat, but she never touched his character. There's nothing cowardly about running from sin. When dealing with our adversary, the devil, running may mark the difference between a victim and a victor. Those who linger usually lose. Get up and get out before it's too late!

ACTION POINT: Read a father's advice to his children in Proverbs 4:14-15.

—Tom Palmer

APRIL 7
BE YE HOLY—
AND REMOVE
Scripture Reading—2 Kings 23:3-8

Your home will never be a holy place if impurity occupies a place in it. The Spirit-filled home is the kind of place where God is present and where the Lord Jesus would feel comfortable. For these reasons, the practice of spiritual housecleaning is essential. We must be willing to remove anything from our lives that would disgrace the presence of God, grieve the Holy Spirit, or offend the Lord Jesus.

As a youth pastor, I introduced the "Sin Bin" to my teens following a youth retreat where many of our teens met with God. I painted a large box black and placed it in our youth room. For two weeks, our teens did some spiritual housecleaning. They brought in immodest clothing and ungodly music, books, magazines, and games. These were items they wore, listened to, looked at, or used to decorate their bedrooms—all the while knowing these items were unholy. They broke the items, tore them up, and eventually burned them publicly. As the "trash" burned, our teens sang the hymn "To God Be the Glory." For many, this event signified a great change in their lives. They were taking a major step toward living a holy life.

It's a great mistake to let impurity accumulate in our lives. We may put it in a box or a bottom drawer. We may hide it under our bed, but it's still there. A simple prayer, a trash bag, and a box of matches may be our turning point spiritually. Unfortunately, many Christians still cherish things that occupied their lives before they were saved. These items limit God's blessing and provide a constant temptation to return to the ways of the past.

APPLICATION: Bring your family together for a time of spiritual housecleaning. Ask the Spirit of God to guide you, get a trash bag, and take a walk through your house. Clean house and finish with a burning. Your family will never forget it.

—*Tom Palmer*

APRIL 8
BE YE HOLY—
AND REPLACE

Scripture Reading—1 Kings 18:25-30

Some assume that holy living is all negative. They falsely conclude that a holy way of life is a list of all the activities we can't do. Yet there's another dimension of holy living we cannot overlook. The principle of replacement means we not only "put off" but also "put on" (Eph. 4:22-24).

In Luke 11, Jesus told the story of a man who had an unclean spirit (vv. 24-26). The unclean spirit departed but eventually returned to find the "house" still unoccupied. Jesus said that the unclean spirit—actually a demon—returned with seven like himself, and "the last state of that man is worse than the first" (v. 26). The basic application is this: The good will overcome the bad, the right will crowd out the wrong, and holiness will replace impurity.

A teen who destroys a secular music collection must replace it with sacred music. The family that eliminates the TV must develop new ways to fill their home with wholesome activity. The man who discontinues the input of lustful mental images must memorize and meditate on God's Word. Doing spiritual housecleaning is a wonderful spiritual step, but we must not stop there. We must aggressively pursue putting quality replacements into our lives.

In Ephesus, believers publicly burned items used in pagan worship (Acts 19:18-19). The next verse says that the Word of God "mightily grew . . . and prevailed." The city became better not just because pagan worship was gone but because the worship of God had come. When Elijah repaired the altar of God, he put the altar of God in the place of the altar of Baal. At that point, the nation of Israel was ready to again acknowledge that God was truly God. The nation was again a holy nation.

EXERCISE: List three items that will keep your family focused on God and will cause you to think more of Him.

—*Tom Palmer*

ENCOURAGED IN THE BATTLE
Scripture Reading—Judges 6:1-10

Do you ever get discouraged? Sure you do. We all do. Children fight with their playmates. Mothers get overwhelmed by housework. Fathers work hard at their jobs, but someone else gets the promotion. A pastor plans special meetings, but church attendance is small. Life is full of discouragements.

In our text, Israel disobeyed God, so God used the Midianites to punish them. The Israelites hid in caves for their protection and planted their crops in the spring. But at harvest time, the Midianites took all their food. Discouraged, Israel cried out to God for help. "And Israel was greatly impoverished because of the Midianites; and the children of Israel cried unto the Lord" (v. 6).

We must remember that their disobedience brought discouragement upon themselves. "And I said unto you, I am the Lord your God; fear not the gods of the Amorites, in whose land ye dwell: but ye have not obeyed my voice" (v. 10). Sometimes we create our own discouraging situations. Instead of studying, a student watches TV and fails his test. His discouragement is his own fault.

Sometimes events we can't control discourage us. You plant your garden, and everything is fine until a late spring frost kills your vegetables. The frost wasn't your fault, but you're discouraged.

The Bible says a lot about discouragement because God knows how easily we can get down. Yes, we live in a world of discouraged people, and the battles of life are taking their toll on Christian families. Unfortunately, many believers aren't handling trials biblically. Discouraged, they're ready to give up.

But giving up isn't the answer. According to God's Word, we can and must overcome discouragement. Only when we learn to cry out to God during discouraging times will we gain the victory. God is our greatest Encourager. His Word and prayer are two of our greatest assets. We must use them!

ACTION POINT: As a family, discuss events that cause discouragement. How can family members encourage each other when discouraging times come?

—Jack Palmer

APRIL 10
ARE YOU DOWNHEARTED?
Scripture Reading—Judges 6:11-16

Isn't it amazing how God comes to our aid even when we've been unfaithful to Him? God's people were in a mess of their own making. God allowed trouble by way of the Midianites so the Israelites would return to Him. Now He was going to give them a way out.

Discouragement usually comes at the worst time and from the most unexpected source, prompting us to do the most unpredictable things. Yet discouragement teaches us the most valuable lessons about ourselves, about others, and about God.

In out text, God sent His angel to inform Gideon that he would be God's instrument of deliverance, calling Gideon a "mighty man of valour" (v. 12). Can you imagine Gideon's shock? *You've gotta be kidding!* he probably thought. He was hiding from the Midianites, afraid they would take his wheat (v. 11); God assured him of the following important truths:

1. God was sending him (v. 14).
2. God would be with him (v. 16).

God's words should have encouraged Gideon, but they didn't. In verses 17-24, we discover how God convinced Gideon that he was God's man. In reverent response, Gideon built an altar to the Lord and called it "Jehovah-shalom" (The Lord Our Peace).

When we are discouraged, nothing can provide peace like the awareness of God's presence. In Exodus 33:14b, when Moses was discouraged because of Israel's rebellion, God said, "My *presence* shall go with thee, and I will give thee rest" (emphasis added). Isaiah wrote, "Fear thou not; for *I am with thee*: be not dismayed; for I am thy God" (41:10a, emphasis added). God's presence grants peace and dispels fear in spite of the most discouraging circumstances. Don't be downhearted!

ACTION POINT: When you are discouraged, don't complain. Cry out to God, claim His presence, and allow His peace to encourage your troubled heart.

—*Jack Palmer*

APRIL 11
GOD HAS A PURPOSE

Scripture Reading
Judges 6:16—*"And the Lord said unto him [Gideon], Surely I will be with thee, and* **thou shalt smite the Midianites as one man** *" (emphasis added).*
Romans 8:28—*"And we know that* **all things work together for good** *to them that love God, to them who are the called according to his purpose" (emphasis added).*

During discouraging times, we must not only rely on the presence of God but also understand the purpose of God. When the apostle Paul was discouraged because of his "thorn in the flesh," he pleaded with God three times to remove it. Instead, God assured Paul that his physical weakness was God's opportunity to demonstrate His grace and to show His power (2 Cor. 12:7-10). Only after Paul understood God's purpose was he able to rejoice in his problem.

Recently, my wife and I made a delicious coffeecake for guests. She carefully measured the ingredients and placed them on the counter. My job was to stir the cake batter. As I did my part, I realized I wouldn't care to eat two sticks of butter, a cup of sugar, two raw eggs, a spoon of vanilla, two cups of flour, or a pint of sour cream. By themselves, those ingredients weren't appetizing. But after I stirred the ingredients together, placed them in a pan, and baked them in the oven, they created a delicious cake.

By themselves, the events in Gideon's life weren't good—he was discouraged—but they were part of God's plan and purpose. As God put them all together, He accomplished His purpose. Perhaps the difficulties you're going through, in themselves, aren't good either. *But God has a purpose.* Allow Him to work circumstances together with other events. The result will be for your good and for His glory.

TALK IT OVER: Share experiences that seemed bad at the time but turned out to be good in the end—all because God had a purpose.

—Jack Palmer

APRIL 12
GOD HAS THE POWER

Scripture Reading

Judges 7:7a—*"And the Lord said unto Gideon, By the* **three hundred** **men** *that lapped will I save you, and deliver the Midianites into thine hand" (emphasis added).*

Judges 7:22a—*"And the* **three hundred** *blew the trumpets, and the Lord set every man's sword against his fellow, even throughout all the host: and the host fled" (emphasis added).*

A familiar song says, "Little is much when God is in it!" When God revealed His plan to Gideon and word spread that help was needed, 32,000 men responded. But God told Gideon he had too many men (Judg. 7:2). If the Israelites successfully defeated the Midianites, they would take the glory for themselves. When Gideon told those who were afraid to go home, 22,000 left (v. 3). With only 10,000 left, God tested them again at the creek (v. 4). This time, only 300 remained (v. 6). Imagine how discouraged Gideon must have felt. How could they face the host of Midian with so few soldiers?

God was about to prove that victory depended not on the power of Gideon's men but on how powerful God is. One man who is totally yielded to God is more powerful than a whole army. Remember the story of David and Goliath in 1 Samuel 17? Israel's army was discouraged because they were powerless against the Philistines. But David, by God's power, won the victory for God's glory.

Amid the battles we fight as Christian families, we can become discouraged when the enemy seems strong compared to our weakness. Often we lose the battle because we doubt God and give up. But every difficulty we face is an opportunity for God to reveal His power.

Though Gideon struggled with discouragement, God encouraged him with an incredible demonstration of His power. When discouragement threatens to defeat you, let God prove Himself.

REJOICE: During family prayer time, honestly admit your inability and rejoice in God's ability. When you can't, He can!

—*Jack Palmer*

APRIL 13
DON'T GET CAUGHT
UNDER A JUNIPER TREE
Scripture Reading—1 Kings 19:1-4

In today's Scripture, we read a prayer God never answered. In chapter 18, when Elijah called upon God at Mount Carmel, God answered by sending fire to prove to unbelieving Israel that He was Jehovah God. After Elijah's great victory over the prophets of Baal, Queen Jezebel threatened to kill him. He became so discouraged that he asked God to take his life. Thank God, He didn't answer that prayer.

Have you ever been so discouraged that you didn't want to keep living? If so, you're not alone. In fact, that's one of the main reasons people commit suicide. We will all experience discouragement at one time or another. The question is, how do we handle it?

Recently, I spoke to a discouraged young preacher who had filled the pulpit for a church that lacked a pastor. At the close of the service, a man tore the young preacher and his message apart. The man was out of order and had no business saying what he did.

Though many commented on how wonderful the message was and on how it ministered to them, all the young preacher could remember was the unkind way the man had treated him. Satan used the bad experience to discourage this fine, young man and to hinder his ministry. The young preacher needed encouragement, and God graciously allowed me to provide it.

What if you find someone under a juniper tree? Should you ignore him? Should you criticize him? Should you "preach" at him? I heard about a little girl who was crying over her broken doll. An older lady tried to help the little girl. Later, a friend asked the older lady if she had fixed the doll. "No," the older lady replied. "I just sat down and cried with her." Sometimes just letting someone know you understand is the greatest form of encouragement.

ASSIGNMENT: Find someone who is discouraged. Ask God to let you be his encourager.

—Jack Palmer

APRIL 14
ELIJAH'S
PROBLEM

Scripture Reading—1 Kings 19:1-8

Elijah had a serious problem. When someone gets so discouraged that he doesn't want to live, you know his problems have brought him to his lowest point. Though God had wonderfully proved Himself on Mount Carmel, people and problems had so distorted Elijah's perspective that he lost heart. Queen Jezebel was the person, and her threat on his life was the problem (1 Kings 19:1-2). I'd say the situation was pretty serious! And Elijah thought so, too.

Notice his response. (1) **He took his eyes off the Lord.** This is the first step toward discouragement. Remember Peter? Jesus came walking on the water in the midst of the storm. Stepping out of the boat, Peter began walking toward Jesus. But as soon as he took his eyes off the Lord, he sank. He lost his perspective (Matt. 14:22-31). (2) **He focused on people and problems.** No, it was not a good situation. Elijah's life was in danger. As soon as he focused on his problems, he became discouraged. (3) **He saw the problem instead of God's purpose.** When all Elijah could see was his problems, he lost sight of God's purpose. God always has a purpose He wants to accomplish in our lives. (4) **He resorted to self-pity.** A "pity party" is no good for anyone. If you want to get discouraged, self-pity is a great place to start! (5) **He sank into despair.** All Elijah wanted to do was to die. Discouragement causes a downward spiral.

Have you seen Elijah's pattern in your life when you get discouraged? If so, don't let people and problems distort your view of God. Keep your focus on Him through prayer and Bible study. Ask God to fulfill His purpose in your life. Cancel the "pity party." No one wants to come anyhow. Let God lift you above your circumstances. Yes, Elijah had a problem. Let his example encourage you when you get discouraged.

APPLICATION: As a family, make a commitment. Refuse to allow people and problems to distort your view of God.

—*Jack Palmer*

God's Solution

Scripture Reading
1 Peter 5:7—"Casting all your care upon him; for he careth for you"
(emphasis added).
Psalm 55:22—"Cast thy burden upon the Lord, and he shall sustain thee: he shall never suffer the righteous to be moved" (emphasis added).
*Philippians 4:6-7—"Be careful for nothing; but in every thing by prayer and supplication with thanksgiving **let your requests be made known unto God**. And the peace of God, which passeth all understanding, shall keep your hearts and minds through Christ Jesus" (emphasis added).*

We've seen how people and problems discouraged Gideon and Elijah. Discouragement is a serious problem each Christian must deal with at some time. We don't want to be discouraged, but our human nature makes life difficult in the midst of trials.

Does God have a solution? He sure does! How did God encourage Elijah when he was at his lowest point? We find God's solution in 1 Kings 19.

First, **God spoke to him** (vv. 5, 7, 9). If there's ever a time when we need to hear from God, it's when we're discouraged. You may experience times when you're so discouraged, all you have left is the Bible. When that happens, you still have all you need. Count on God to speak to you.

Second, **God provided for him** (vv. 5-7). God is so practical! Elijah needed rest and refreshment. Exhaustion and weakness often cause discouragement. Consider your life. What do you need? Whatever it is, God is willing and able to meet your need.

Third, **God understood him** (v. 7b). "The journey is too great for thee." Some of our worst discouragement arises from the feeling that no one understands. Remember, God always understands!

Finally, **God directed him** (vv. 9-18). When you lack direction, you get discouraged. Elijah thought he was all alone. By giving him direction, God lifted his burden. Perhaps you're discouraged because you aren't sure what to do next. Let God give you direction, and He will lift your burden, too.

LOOK TO GOD: When you're discouraged, don't depend on human solutions. Only God can provide the encouragement you need.

—Jack Palmer

APRIL 16
WHEN I GROW UP

Scripture Reading—Hebrews 13:17
"Obey them that have the rule over you, and submit yourselves: for they watch for your souls, as they that must give account, that they may do it with joy, and not with grief: for that is unprofitable for you."

What do you want to be when you grow up? "Daddy, I want to be a cowboy! No, I want to be a policeman. A preacher! A *cowboy* preacher! I want to be . . ."

Do you want to be a daddy or a mommy someday? Do you want to have children? What kind of children? Good children? Obedient children? Children who love God?

Do you want to be a godly person when you grow up? I have four children. All of them are serving the Lord and want to please God. My daughter and sons didn't decide to serve the Lord all of a sudden. They had to learn some important biblical principles in order to become godly in their later years.

Parents must apply an important biblical principle during a child's early years if he is going to be godly in his later years.

Having worked with thousands of young people through the years, I can say that the ones who learned this principle as children are living for God later in life. The ones who didn't learn this principle are not living for God later in life.

What is this principle? It is the principle of authority. This means that I understand the reason and importance of having various authorities in my life.

What is an authority? An authority is someone who has the right and power to tell me what to do. This is a person or an institution that can command me, direct me, rule me, and judge me. I have to answer to this authority if I want to have peace and direction in my life.

QUESTIONS TO PONDER: Who are the authorities in my life right now? Why does God put authorities over me? What should my attitude be toward my authorities?

—*Craig M. Scott*

APRIL 17
WHY DOES GOD PLACE AUTHORITIES IN MY LIFE?

Come with me to the inner city of a huge metropolis. We're looking for a teenage runaway. She ran away about one year ago, and her parents received word that she is living on the streets. It is wintertime and very cold. We look everywhere for her. Suddenly, we see cardboard boxes placed next to the huge heating vents of a commercial building for warmth.

Inside one of these boxes, we find a sickly woman lying on a pile of rags. She is shivering. Her hair is falling out, her face is full of scars, and some of her teeth are missing. She appears to be in her late thirties. The smell is horrible.

No, it's not her. Not our daughter, her parents say.

From the box, we hear a faint sound. *Mommy! Daddy! Is that you?*

We can't believe our ears, much less our eyes.

Is that you, honey?

Oh yes! It's me. Please help me.

The parents notice that their daughter is sick. She has very little time left to live unless she comes home and receives medical treatment. Faint words drift from her mouth. *Mommy and Daddy, I need you. I can't make it without you. I'm so sorry for not obeying you. I'm so sorry for running away! I need God.*

Have you ever heard of Hymenaeus and Alexander? What did Paul say these men would learn as a result of getting out from under the protection of God's authority?

"Of whom is Hymenaeus and Alexander; whom I have delivered unto Satan, that they may learn not to blaspheme [mock God; speak evil of God]" (1 Tim. 1:20).

QUESTIONS TO DISCUSS: What did this young girl learn as a result of getting out from under her authority? Do you think she learned that the purpose of authority in her life is that of protection instead of domination?

REMEMBER THIS: The purpose of authority is not to dominate your life. It is to protect you from Satan's influence.

—Craig M. Scott

WHO ARE MY AUTHORITIES?

Scripture Reading—Ephesians 6:1
"Children, obey your parents in the Lord: for this is right."

Do you remember a time when Jesus was doing something for God but Mary and Joseph asked Him to do something different? How did Jesus respond to His parents?

Luke 2:51a says, "And he went down with them, and came to Nazareth, and was subject unto them."

Notice what the next verse says about Jesus.

Luke 2:52 says, "And Jesus increased in wisdom and stature, and in favour with God and man."

"Jesus increased [grew] in wisdom and stature [character]." Why? He understood that God, the Father, had given Him earthly parents as His authorities. Jesus learned to put His own separate plans aside and obey them.

Remember this—an authority is one who has the God-given right and power to tell you what to do. This is a person or an institution that can command you, direct you, rule you, and judge you.

If I want to grow in wisdom and character, I must learn to willingly yield my rights to God by obeying my authorities.

Think about it. Who in your life has the right and power to tell you what to do?

How about in your home? In the government (police, laws)? In your church (elders, pastors)? How about in your school? Do you have a job? Does your boss have the power to tell you what to do? What do you think would happen if you didn't obey your boss?

QUESTIONS TO PONDER: Have you learned to put your own separate plans and goals aside in order to obey your God-given authorities? Do you realize that in order for you to grow in wisdom and character, you need to willingly place yourself under the authorities God has placed in your life?

ASSIGNMENT: Look up the following verses and see what God says about the various authorities in your life: Romans 13:1-4; Ephesians 5:21-28; Ephesians 6:1-4; Titus 2:9-10; Hebrews 13:17.

—Craig M. Scott

APRIL 19
HOW'S YOUR
FAITH?

Through the years, young people have asked me many questions. Here are a couple commonly asked questions. How would you answer these?

"I'm facing a major decision in my life. Where do I go to college?"

"A certain girl has come into my life. Should I pursue a relationship with her?"

In Matthew 8:5-10, Jesus and His disciples were entering into Capernaum. A very important military leader, a centurion, told Jesus that his servant was sick and about to die. Jesus replied, "I will come and heal him."

The centurion said to Jesus, "Lord, I am not worthy that thou shouldest come under my roof: but speak the word only, and my servant shall be healed. For I am a man under authority, having soldiers under me: and I say to this man, Go, and he goeth; and to another, Come, and he cometh; and to my servant, Do this, and he doeth it."

How did Jesus respond to this man? Verse 10 says, "When Jesus heard it, he marvelled, and said to them that followed, Verily I say unto you, I have not found so great faith, no, not in Israel."

Why did Jesus say that this man's faith was so great? This man didn't need physical evidence; he believed Jesus could heal at a distance. Also, this man understood the principle of authority.

QUESTIONS TO PONDER: What is your answer to the questions at the beginning? Generally, my answer is, "This decision isn't totally up to you. You are protected from making the final decision on these issues. Trust in God! Have great faith to trust God to work through your authorities. Let your father make the decision for you. If you don't have a father, let your mother make the decision for you. Trust God to work through your authorities!" Will you allow God to strengthen your faith by willingly placing yourself under the various authorities God has placed in your life?

—*Craig M. Scott*

APRIL 20
YOUR FUTURE MATE

Our four children are in the ministry and have a passion for serving the Lord. My wife and I realized the importance of our children finding the right mates. After all, they'll spend the rest of their lives with their mates. We were concerned that they not get emotionally attached to a girlfriend or a boyfriend who would discourage them from being all that they could be for God.

We decided that our children would never turn down an opportunity to develop a relationship with the opposite sex. Simultaneously, we decided that our children would never pursue an opportunity to develop a relationship with the opposite sex. That was our job as their God-given authorities. Their responsibility before God was to follow the command God had given to children in Ephesians 6:1-3 to obey and honor their parents.

Here's how this situation played out. When a fellow wanted to take my daughter to an Artist Series at her college, she told him, "You need to ask my father."

She called me, and I asked her questions about his character and motives. Sometimes I asked others about his character and motives. Then I asked her to give me a "thumbs up" or "thumbs down."

When the guy called, I asked him the following questions. "Where do you want to take her? What are your intentions?" I explained to him that my goal as her father was that her first kiss be at the marriage altar. I asked him to treat her like a lady and to be pure.

Sometimes I said something like, "Listen to me. If you touchee my girl, I will breakee your face!" He got the point.

With my boys, they talked with me and their mom before pursuing a relationship with a girl. Then I asked them to call the girl's father and to ask for permission.

QUESTIONS TO PONDER: Do you really believe Ephesians 6:1-3? Read it together. Will you allow God to protect your future by placing yourself under the authority of your parents?

—*Craig M. Scott*

WHAT ABOUT MY
SPIRITUAL LEADERS?

In 2 Kings 2, we read that Elisha, the man of God, was leaving Jericho on his way to Bethel. A group of young people mocked him and called him names, showing disrespect for the man of God.

What happened? Did God let these disrespectful children go unpunished? Second Kings 2:24 says, "And he turned back, and looked on them, and cursed them in the name of the Lord. And there came forth two she bears out of the wood, and tare forty and two children of them."

God sent two mama bears to kill these children. Why? Because they did not respect the spiritual authority God had placed over them.

Should we ever rebuke an elder? Paul answers this question in his letter to Timothy. "Rebuke not an elder, but intreat him as a father" (1 Tim. 5:1a).

This verse says we shouldn't treat a spiritual leader harshly. Instead, we should make sure we approach him in respect.

"Intreat him as a father." This phrase carries the idea of saying, "Please. Yes, sir! Yes, ma'am!" It means looking authorities in the eye when they speak to us. It means giving them the best seats, showing them dignity and respect, and obeying them with the right attitude of humility. It means not talking back to them or treating them with disrespect of any kind.

If your authorities tell you, "Lights out!" God is telling you, "Lights out!"

If your authorities tell you when to be home, God is telling you when to be home.

If your authorities tell you, "Don't chew gum on the bus!" obey your authorities.

QUESTIONS TO PONDER: Will you willingly place yourself under the spiritual authorities God has placed over you?

ASSIGNMENT: Read and discuss 2 Kings 2:23-24; 1 Timothy 5:1; and Hebrews 13:17.

—*Craig M. Scott*

WHAT IF MY AUTHORITIES ARE WRONG?

A young lady in my youth group in California made an important, life-changing decision. In fact, it was one of the most important decisions a young person can make after becoming a Christian. She decided to obey the authorities God had placed over her. She was going to demonstrate faith by trusting God to work through her authorities.

But she had a problem; her father wasn't born again. In fact, he was heavily into drug trafficking, and she was his runner. He would give her a sack of drugs, and she would deliver it to his customers. By doing so, she was participating in his illegal activities.

"Pastor, what do I do?" she asked me. "I've decided to obey the God-given authorities in my life, and that includes my unsaved father."

I explained to her that if she had a new spirit of obedience and submission to her unsaved father, he would see the difference in her, and it would make him thirsty for Jesus (Matt. 5:13-16).

Three passages of Scripture came to my mind. First, in Acts 4:18-20, government authorities told the disciples not to preach the Gospel. Second, in Daniel 6:12-16, the king commanded Daniel to worship him instead of God. Third, in Daniel 1:8-15, the king commanded Daniel and the other Jewish children to submit to his diet. The diet included alcohol and meats forbidden in Scriptures.

What did the disciples do? What did Daniel do? Here's the principle: Always obey the higher authority (God) and learn to respectfully appeal to your human authorities.

What would you tell this young lady? What did I tell this young lady? I told her to look at the life of Daniel and to apply the same approach to her father that Daniel did to his authority.

ASSIGNMENT: Read and discuss Daniel 1:12-15 in light of the counsel to this young lady.

—*Craig M. Scott*

APRIL 23
LOYALTY IN
THE SWAMP

Scripture Reading—Acts 23:12-22

*"And when Paul's sister's son heard of their lying in wait, he went . . .
and told Paul. Then Paul called one of the centurions unto him, and said,
Bring this young man unto the chief captain: for he hath a certain thing
to tell him. So he took him, and brought him to the chief captain,
and said, Paul the prisoner . . . prayed me to bring this young man unto
thee, who hath something to say unto thee" (vv. 16-18).*

A peaceful calm settled over the swamp as evening engulfed the marshy wetland. A pair of Canadian geese had built their nest, and the female goose sat quietly on the eggs she had laid only weeks before. When a mother raccoon approached, hoping to steal some eggs for her young, a fierce battle ensued. The geese drove the raccoon away, but the mother goose broke her wing during the battle. The next night, the raccoon returned. Again, the geese drove the raccoon away, but this time the female goose broke her other wing. On the third night, the raccoon attacked again, this time killing the mother goose before her mate could fight off their attacker. The next day, the eggs hatched, and the gander took on the role of caring for his young alone.

Loyalty means sticking by those we care about when life gets tough. In Acts 23, the apostle Paul's nephew risked his life to save his uncle. In the opening story, the mother goose lost her life trying to save her eggs.

Being loyal isn't always easy. Loyalty can require risks and danger—even the threat of personal safety. Yet loyalty is a tremendous blessing to the recipients of our devotion. When trials come, we must chose to stand for our God, for our family, for our friends, or for the cause of Christ. When the going gets tough, pressures will test our loyalty. Only with courage and commitment can we stand by those we love.

ACTION POINT: Look up Matthew 26:56. Note how the disciples responded to Jesus' betrayal.

—*Tom Palmer*

APRIL 24
OBEDIENCE IN
THE NEST

Scripture Reading—Luke 2:41-52

"And he [Jesus] went down with them, and came to Nazareth, and was subject unto them: but his mother kept all these sayings in her heart. And Jesus increased in wisdom and stature, and in favour with God and man"
(vv. 51-52).

For the wood duck, obedience is a matter of life and death. A duckling who doesn't obey will die.

Wood ducks lay their eggs in a hollow tree, sometimes using a tree hole 40 feet above ground. A female wood duck lays one egg each day for 11 days. As hatching time approaches, she communicates to her unhatched ducklings, and they respond with "cheeping" sounds. It is important for them to learn the voice of their mother.

The mother signals to her babies when hatching time has come. The babies use a small "egg tooth," a small bump on the end of their bill, to break their egg open. Though the mother lays her eggs over 11 days, the babies hatch within minutes.

Within 24 hours, the mother duck flies to the base of the tree and calls to her young to join her. Unable to fly, the ducklings must jump to the ground, landing on the forest floor with their mother. If a duckling has not learned the voice of his mother or chooses not to come when she calls, he will be left alone in the nest to starve to death or to be eaten by a predator.

The duckling who obeys his parents discovers that they will provide direction, protection, and provision until he is old enough to strike out on his own. Young people must learn as Jesus did (v. 51)—and as wood ducklings do—that obedience is the key to a safe and happy life. Obedience is part of God's plan in nature and in our homes. Children need to obey their parents.

ACTION POINT: Get a book about birds and do a more in-depth study about the wood duck.

—*Tom Palmer*

APRIL 25
UNDERGROUND
ORDERLINESS

Scripture Reading—Genesis 41:37-49

Let's pretend we're on our hands and knees, crawling across the forest floor. Suddenly, we see a flash of brown and white chipmunk fur disappear down a hole in the ground.

It's a tight squeeze, but we follow him to see where he goes. Making our way through the underground burrow, we're amazed to find a series of rooms. Chipmunks usually have between three and six of these underground rooms that make up their home. As we stick our head through the door of each room—wow, it's tight—we discover that each room has a special purpose.

We find bedrooms, a nursery, storage rooms—even a waste room filled with dry grass and materials a chipmunk can remove once they are saturated. Another tunnel leads back to the surface and to a listening post where the chipmunk listens for danger before leaving his burrow. Our brief underground tour reveals that chipmunks have learned how to be orderly.

The chipmunk is orderly because his existence depends on it. His primary task is making sure he has enough food for winter. In his underground home, he has a place for everything; and everything must be in its place. The chipmunk must store his supply of nuts, corn, wheat kernels, and sunflower seeds in such a way that they will not spoil. He must remove waste so he won't be overcrowded and lose storage space. Through it all, he must be sure that no predator can detect his home.

Orderliness is a quality that helps the chipmunk survive and helps us keep our homes from becoming chaotic. Keeping our home organized and clean maintains a pleasant atmosphere for all to enjoy. It eliminates frustration when items are lost, misplaced, or damaged. It enables us to appreciate and enjoy the good things God has provided.

ACTION POINT: Take some time to describe the purpose of each room in your house. Determine ways you can take better care of each room.

—*Tom Palmer*

APRIL 26
INITIATIVE AT
THE PICNIC
Scripture Reading—2 Kings 5:1-5, 13-14

Some people watch things happen. Others wonder what happened. Then some make things happen—that's what initiative is all about. Initiative means doing what I can to make a difference. When I think of initiative, I can't help thinking of Roger the raccoon.

Roger came to us as an orphaned baby. His mother had been killed, leaving four baby raccoons in a nest in a farmer's barn. When he came to us, his eyes were closed, and he couldn't walk. We fed him first with an eye dropper and then a baby bottle. Roger wasn't a baby for long!

One day, we sat down at the backyard picnic table for a family picnic. Roger was playing in a nearby flowerbed when he got a sniff of our plate of chicken. In a flash, he was on the table. People were yelling, glasses and containers were spilling, and food was flying as Roger pounced on the plate of chicken.

Snarling and snapping, he let us know that we should leave him alone while he decided which piece of chicken he wanted. Choosing a drumstick, he bounded off the table and returned to the flowerbed to enjoy his prize. As I said, some people—or animals, in this case—make things happen!

Initiative is a wonderful quality to have unless you're a raccoon inviting himself to a picnic. Naaman's little maid saw her master suffering greatly and determined to do something to change his condition. Because of her initiative, Naaman's life was spared, and his leprosy was cured. Ultimately, God did His work, but He used a maid whose name isn't even recorded in the Bible. Making a difference requires commitment to be all I can be for God.

ACTION POINT: Ask your family to think of someone in need. What could your family do this week to make a difference in that person's life?

—Tom Palmer

APRIL 27
DILIGENCE ON THE POND

Scripture Reading—1 Samuel 1:24-28, 2:18, 3:1

Have you ever heard the phrase "busy as a beaver"? The phrase is true because beavers work tirelessly to build dams, to gather food, and to care for their young. An entire wilderness can be transformed by the masterful architecture of a couple beavers.

Once in Wyoming, five unmated pairs of beavers were released in a new area. Within one year, they had chosen mates, established their territories, and built 55 dams. Usually a pair of beavers needs just one dam, but in this case the beavers had prepared 10 extra dams where their offspring could raise their families. Once the beaver builds his dam and a pond is formed, he improves the habitat for other animals.

God has specially equipped the beaver for his work. His sharp teeth are ideal for cutting, enabling him to cut down trees needed in building. For example, a beaver can take down a five-inch aspen in less than three minutes. Beavers have been known to take down trees as high as 110 feet tall.

The beaver's flat tail is also an essential tool. It functions as a rudder when he's swimming. He uses his tail for balance while he's cutting trees, and he smacks the water with it to send a message of warning that can be heard up to half a mile away.

With these tools, the beaver can prepare a pond, build a safe and secure lodge for his family, and gather food to supply for his family's nourishment.

Just as God equipped the beaver with special tools for work, He has done the same for us. Though everyone is different, each person has special talents or abilities that enable him to do special tasks for God. Diligence means taking those gifts and doing the job God wants us to do for Him.

DISCUSSION: Ask each family member to describe a talent he has. Discuss how family members can use these talents for God.

—Tom Palmer

APRIL 28
Alertness in the Meadow

Scripture Reading—Genesis 39:7-12

"And it came to pass after these things, that his master's wife cast her eyes upon Joseph; and she said, Lie with me. But he refused" (vv. 7-8a).

The bull elk is one of the most awesome and majestic animals in North America. This giant member of the deer family rules the mountains and meadows of much of the western part of our country. One of the outstanding qualities of this great animal is his constant awareness of what's going on around him. He constantly pays attention to any form of danger that could threaten him.

Several members of our family had the opportunity to observe a big bull elk in the mountains of Wyoming. The bull was rolling in a wallow, which is nothing more than a mud hole. His body was soaking wet and caked with mud. Nearby, a small herd of cow elk was grazing in a meadow.

My son had an elk bugle, a specially designed call that imitates a bull elk. Once we were hidden in the rocks overlooking the meadow, Tim sounded a shrill call. The bull bounded out of his mud hole and ventured into the meadow with the cows, staring our direction. Occasionally, he turned to make sure his cows stayed close. Yet every time he heard the bugle, he spun around to see where the call came from. In his mind, he must have assumed another bull might be approaching to take some of the cows from his herd.

Recognizing the threat of a possible intruder or attacker, he soon moved his herd toward the timber to safety. Had he not been paying attention, he would have become vulnerable. The approach of an enemy would have been possible.

Often believers are careless about impending danger. They forget to be alert, putting themselves in danger. If Joseph hadn't sensed danger, he would have become caught in a trap of Satan, and sin would have harmed his life greatly.

DO THIS NOW: In Proverbs 4:14-15, read the warning of a father to his son.

—Tom Palmer

APRIL 29
DECISIVENESS
ON THE TRAIL
Scripture Reading—Daniel 1:8-16

A fox hunt was underway, and a pack of hunting dogs quickly picked up the scent of a red fox. The dogs aggressively followed the trail while hunters were not far behind in hopes of catching their prey. This sly old fox, however, had a bag of tricks that would make him tough to catch.

First, the fox cleverly used a shallow stream. He waded through the water for a long distance then jumped onto the bank, forcing the dogs to spend time trying to find his scent again. Then he crossed a cow pasture. His scent was clouded by the scent of the cows, and the dogs were confused as they tried to follow the fox underfoot of the grazing animals. Occasionally, the fox doubled back on his own trail.

At a precise location, he left the trail and hid himself, watching the unsuspecting dogs go by as they followed his original trail. Finding a hollow log, the fox entered on one end and came out the other. Too large to go through the log, the dogs again sought to regain the trail.

Since it was wintertime, he pulled one more sly move. Approaching the banks of a frozen pond, the light-footed fox made his way across thin ice. The dogs, being much heavier, endeavored to follow him only to break through the ice. While they recovered, the red fox escaped for good.

Evaluating situations and responding properly is part of decisiveness. The fox must be a quick thinker, and he must make right choices. Daniel was a man who made good decisions. Realizing the king's menu would defile him, he determined to follow another plan of action. God honored Daniel's decision, and he was able to protect himself and honor his God.

ASSIGNMENT: Ask each child to pretend he is a wild animal trying to escape hunters. How might you flee hunters? Would your plan work?

—Tom Palmer

SOULS FOR CHRIST

Scripture Reading—Acts 1:8b

"Ye shall be witnesses unto me . . . unto the uttermost part of the earth."

After Hurricane Katrina struck our southern coastline with unusual force and fury, the United States launched certainly one of the greatest search and rescue operations in American history. Seeing the hungry, the wounded, and the displaced without food, direction, or a safe place to go, millions responded with kindness, generosity, and a determination to relieve the pain caused by such a massive tragedy.

When the world saw footage of thousands of hurting people, many were moved to action. A unified commitment to help came from all corners of the world. A similar dedication should equally move us to rescue those living without hope, without direction, and—most of all—without Christ. Though hurricanes wreak physical destruction, the aftermath of spiritual unbelief is even more devastating. Every community around the world suffers an untold number of unstable homes, wrecked relationships, ruined lives, and broken dreams. While a storm's devastation is generally confined to a specific geographical location, sin affects the entire world.

We should reach out to neighbors and friends living near us. We need to be actively winning souls for Christ. While sending clothes, food, and money to the needy is commendable, we need to share the Gospel with the unbelievers we come in contact with regularly.

Jesus often told those He helped, "Shew how great things God hath done unto thee" (Luke 8:39). Jesus was "moved with compassion" (Matt 9:36) when He saw people living separate lives from Him. Without Him, their future would be filled with dismay—their eternity filled with disaster. You can make a difference by having the same compassion Jesus modeled for us. Go and win souls!

ACTION PLAN: Pray for a lost friend, relative, or neighbor right now. Commit to get involved in your church's soul-winning program. Plan a dinner with an unbeliever and share your salvation testimony.

—Jeff Kahl

I Will Extol

Scripture Reading—Psalm 145:1a
"I will extol thee, my God,
O king."

Read Psalm 145. You will discover that the words *will* and *shall* appear frequently. In this psalm, the Lord has chosen to place the phrase "I will" at the top of the list of "wills." The Lord has given us this psalm to show us that our "will" has an effect on the "will" of others.

During a recent family vacation, I was looking for a psalm to share during our morning devotional time. The Lord directed me to Psalm 145. I was excited to share this psalm with my family because of the psalmist's desire to lift up and honor the name of the Lord.

The first "I will" of this psalm is found in verse one. "I will extol thee, my God, O king." The phrase "I will" shows intention on the part of the individual. Notice the psalmist does not say, "God, please help me" or "I'm going to try." The psalmist had a plan and an intention—to praise his God and King.

It's great to have a plan and an intention about something; but my seven-year-old asked an important question. "What does 'extol' mean?" It means to raise on high, to lift up, or to exalt. When we speak honorably of God, we interpret and accept this act as extolling Him.

Extolling, exalting, or speaking honorably about God should always be linked to His character. The Lord God is glorious—"Be thou exalted, O God, above the heavens; let thy glory be above all the earth" (Ps. 57:5). The Lord is holy—"Exalt ye the Lord our God, and worship at his footstool; for he is holy" (Ps. 99:5). In Psalm 145:5, the psalmist extols God by declaring His majesty, His honor, and His works. Let it be our intention and purpose to open our mouths and to lift up the name, character, and works of our great God.

THOUGHT: Make a daily commitment to say, "I will extol thee, my God, O king."

—Ken Varney

I WILL BLESS

Scripture Reading—Psalm 145:1b-2a
"I will bless thy name for ever and ever. Every day will I bless thee."

The idea of man blessing God seems contrary to what most of us understand about the word *blessing*. Generally, blessing is something God gives to man. After all, God's blessings have been around since Eden. The Hebrew word for "bless" is used 330 times in the Old Testament—almost always as something God gave to others. From our perspective, blessing as in the blessing of our Heavenly Father is something all of God's children desire.

The whole of creation depends on God's blessing for its continued existence and function. This is the God-to-man benefit of blessing. Yet the man-to-God blessing is an act of adoration mingled with praise and thanksgiving. The psalmist David understood that God was infinitely happy in the enjoyment of Himself and had no need of David's services. Yet God was pleased to receive the honor due Him through David's blessing. Likewise, He will receive blessing from all who render it with the right heart.

The psalmist had a premeditated action—"I will bless. . . . Every day will I bless thee [God]." Blessing God must be our daily work. Matthew Henry wrote, "No day must pass, though ever so busy a day, though ever so sorrowful a day, without praising God. We should reckon it the most needful of our daily activities and the most delightful of our daily comforts. God is every day blessing us, doing well for us; there is therefore reason that we should be every day blessing him, speaking well of him."

The psalmist resolved to continue in the discipline of blessing God every day of his life. Furthermore, he determined to render blessing to God throughout all eternity.

QUOTE:
Through all eternity to thee
A joyful song I'll raise;
But O, eternity's too short
To utter all thy praise! —Adam Clark

—Ken Varney

I WILL PRAISE

Scripture Reading—Psalm 145:2b
"I will praise thy name for ever and ever."

Raising three daughters has been one of the greatest joys of my life. In their younger years, before they discovered that their dad didn't know everything, they believed I could do no wrong. With great pride and boasting, they told others about my achievements. If fact, I believe they received great joy from boasting in their father.

Similarly, boasting in our Savior should be a mark of the Christian life. The Hebrew for "praise" is *halal*. It means to praise, celebrate, glory, sing, and boast. The word *halal* is the source of the word *hallelujah*, a Hebrew expression of praise and boasting of God that now appears in virtually every language of mankind. Certainly our great Christian hymns would be greatly impoverished if the term *hallelujah* were suddenly removed from our language of praise.

David desired to praise the name of his God and King forever. "I will praise thy name for ever and ever" (Ps. 145:2b). In fact, all of eternity could not possibly exhaust his boasting in the greatness of God.

Charles Spurgeon noted that though God could search him, he was utterly lost in the realm of searching God's greatness. Yet what we *do* know about God gives us an endless supply of praise.

Unfortunately, whether through work, chores, play, or other activities, the world seeks to distract us from the continual praise of God. During this struggle is where discipline, determination, and desire come into play. "I will praise" is the intention of someone sold out for God. Those who make praise their constant work on earth shall have it as their everlasting bliss in heaven!

QUOTE:
My God, I'll praise thee while I live,
And praise thee when I die,
And praise thee when I rise again,
And to all eternity. —Charles Spurgeon

—Ken Varney

MAY 4
I WILL DECLARE

Scripture Reading—Psalm 145:6
"And men shall speak of the might of thy terrible acts:
and I will declare thy greatness."

Psalm 145 speaks of extolling, blessing, and praising. We can view these actions primarily as communication mankind gives to God; however, a declaration is communication men give to other men. When one makes praising and adoring the Lord his daily practice, consequences will be associated with that declaration. The consequence of God-ward devotion is man-ward witness. The psalmist David, because his devotion to God was so full of the Spirit of God, could not help but proclaim the greatness of God to others.

Declaring the greatness of God is not just for here and now. "One generation shall praise thy works to another, and shall declare thy mighty acts" (v. 4). Each family has a godly heritage that begins at some point. Perhaps your father and mother are first-generation Christians, or possibly you come from a long line of believers. Whatever the case may be, our generation has the responsibility to proclaim the greatness of our God to the next.

There is much to declare! Along with declaring God's greatness, David said he would speak of God's "mighty acts," His "glorious honour," His "majesty," and His "wondrous works" (vv. 4-5). If we wrote commentaries on God's attributes alone, it would be enough to fill up most libraries.

Witnessing to others of the greatness of God, particularly His greatness in creation and in redemption through Jesus Christ, isn't something we should feel like we *have* to do but something we *get* to do. It should be our daily intention to "declare thy [God's] greatness" (v. 6).

QUOTE: "There is a hallowed tradition of praise; each generation should hand on the praise of God as a precious legacy to the next one. Train up your sons and daughters to praise your God, so that, when your voice is silent in death, another voice, like your own, may continue the strain." —Charles Spurgeon

—Ken Varney

Men Shall Speak

Scripture Reading—Psalm 145:6a
"And men shall speak of the might
of thy terrible acts."

Psalm 145 begins with David stating that "I will extol," "I will bless," "I will praise," and "I will declare." He was purposeful in his speech toward his God. As a result of David's great praises of God, we discover a wonderful transition in the psalm. After "I will," we find the statement "men shall." This is a result of David's life of verbal and utter commitment to speak aloud of the greatness of his God. Others caught his vision and began imitating David by doing the same thing.

"We must have discipline, determination, and desire to live a life focused on eternity."

What a magnificent opportunity we have as individuals and families to do the same. My wife and I have spoken many times about the fact that God does not always let us look behind the veil, so to speak, to see how our actions have impacted others. One man put it this way, "Every action of our lives touches on some chord that will vibrate in eternity." Everything we do will reap some kind of consequences, whether good or bad.

David's actions so impacted those around him that they began to sound the same praises he had. This was one time when David was able to see the spiritual results of his actions. "And men shall speak of the might of thy terrible acts: and I will declare thy greatness. They shall abundantly utter the memory of thy great goodness, and shall sing of thy righteousness" (vv. 6-7).

How can we live our lives like the psalmist? Is it possible for us to see the same results? The answer is yes! We must have discipline, determination, and desire to live a life focused on eternity. We need to have the same resolve David did. We need to rise above the mediocrity we see around us.

ACTION POINT: Seek the blessing of seeing others sing praises to God because they first saw your family's deep devotion to the Lord.

—Ken Varney

MAY 6
GOD WILL

Scripture Reading—Psalm 145:19a
"He will fulfil the desire of them that fear him."

Psalm 145:14-20 is the focus of today's devotional. What great hope we have in the Lord our God, who has promised much on our behalf through His Son Jesus Christ. Psalm 145 lists many of these promises. By making the statement, "He will," David wants us to know that God intends to carry out something on our behalf. The best part of "God will" is that it will come to pass.

As part of my personal study of this psalm, I looked at the phrase "He will" and also "God will" in an exhaustive Bible concordance. I was amazed at the number of times these two phrases appeared. One thing is certain—God is intentional and determined to bring about His will on earth and in us.

It is necessary to survey the following promises God has made on our behalf, as described in Psalm 145:14-20:

He will uphold all who fall.

He will raise up those who are bowed down.

He will give us food in due season.

He will satisfy the desire of all living things.

He will be near those who call upon Him in truth.

He will fulfill the desire of those who fear Him.

He will hear our cry.

He will save us.

He will preserve all who love Him.

Many of these statements also appear in the New Testament. It is fitting to ask, "What shall we then say to these things? If God be for us, who can be against us? He that spared not his own Son, but delivered him up for us all, how shall he not with him also freely give us all things?" (Rom. 8:31-32)

THANKSGIVING: We can give thanks to God for many blessings. We should be thankful that when God decrees something, He will bring it to pass.

—*Ken Varney*

MAY 7
OPEN THOU
MY LIPS
Scripture Reading—Psalm 51

Read Psalm 51 in its entirety. The most difficult part of hearing God's Word is responding to it. Without a response, we have only gained knowledge. We need to apply the things we have learned to our lives and implement them in our walk with the Lord. David was called the "Sweet Psalmist" of Israel. Yet he experienced a time in his life when his witness to the grace and glory of God ceased. In fact, he couldn't open his mouth and say anything. He had not applied God's Word, which he knew well, to his own life.

David had committed sins concerning the lust of the flesh (not going to war as kings were accustomed to do, 2 Sam. 11:1), the lust of the eyes (committing adultery with Bathsheba, 2 Sam. 11:4), and the pride of life (ordering Uriah be put to death, 2 Sam. 11:14-21). We must understand, as David did, that sin always has consequences. Sometimes these consequences last a short time; and sometimes, like the price of David's sin, they can last a lifetime.

David knew his witness for God was in jeopardy. He was willing to accept the consequences of his sin but somehow had to come out of the situation with a renewed zeal to exalt his Lord. David did the only thing he could do. He cried out to the Lord for mercy, purging, cleansing, a clean heart, a right spirit, a restored joy, and a renewed walk with the Spirit of God.

David had great sin in his life; but after confessing and repenting from it, he cried out to God, "O Lord, open thou my lips; and my mouth shall shew forth thy praise" (Ps. 51:15). Like David, we may need to deal with sin in our lives before we can renew the witness of Jesus Christ to others.

ACTION POINT: Take a personal inventory. Has sin damaged your witness for God? As a family, take time to develop a plan for being more faithful witnesses of the goodness of God.

—*Ken Varney*

MAY 8
COMPLETE OBEDIENCE

Scripture Reading—1 Samuel 15:13b
"*I have performed the commandment
of the Lord.*"

These were Saul's words to Samuel. The problem is, they weren't true. God had sent Saul to destroy the Amalekites. Saul wiped out the vast majority of the enemy, but he and his army were only partially obedient. Going against God's clear command, they spared the king and the best of the cattle. They disobeyed even though they had specific instructions to spare nothing.

Obedience is instantly doing *all* God tells me to do with the right heart attitude. If we are to obey God, we must do everything God tells us. Saul obeyed most but not all of what God had told him to do. Partial obedience is total disobedience in the sight of God. Saul lost the kingdom because he was only partially obedient.

Total obedience isn't just for pastors and missionaries. Jesus said, "Go ye therefore, and teach all nations, baptizing them in the name of the Father, and of the Son, and of the Holy Ghost: teaching them to observe *all* things whatsoever I have commanded you" (Matt. 28:19-20a, emphasis added). In matters of obedience, the Lord expects us to act on *all* we have been commanded.

When I was small, my mother told me to take out the trash. I was watching cartoons at the time. When a commercial came on the TV, I jumped to my feet and took the kitchen trash out. When Mom returned, I informed her that I had taken out the trash. She asked, "Did you take the trash from the bedrooms, living room, and bathroom?"

"No," I said, "but I did get the trash from the kitchen!"

Like Saul who boasted he had obeyed the commandment of the Lord, I did part but not *all* Mom had told me to do.

Whether Dad, Mom, or the Lord, obedience is doing all we're told to do.

POINTS TO PONDER: Has anything come to your mind that calls for follow-through on your part? Do you have tasks you need to complete?

—*Harold Vaughan*

MAY 9
INSTANT OBEDIENCE

Scripture Reading—Mark 1:18
"And straightway they forsook their nets, and followed him."

Someone has defined *obedience* as instantly doing all God tells us to do with the right heart attitude. When Jesus called Simon and Andrew, they immediately left their nets and followed Him. They didn't hesitate, quibble, or delay. They dropped those stinking fish nets and took off!

"I made haste, and delayed not to keep thy commandments" (Ps. 119:60). When God directs you, *obey!* D.L. Moody was crossing a busy street when an unconfessed sin came to mind. Instantly, he knelt in the bustling traffic and confessed his sin to God. He didn't wait until he'd reached the safety of the other side before he made things right with God.

Elisabeth Elliot said, "Obedience is immediate. Delayed obedience is disobedience, and disobedience is sin." We should pray about certain things, but there are other things on which we *must act*. We don't need to pray about obeying God's clearly revealed will. We shouldn't pray about following the Lord in believer's baptism after we've been saved, about supporting a local church, about abstaining from evil, and about doing a host of other things God has commanded. In fact, it's sin to pray about doing what God has told us to do instead of doing what He has commanded.

At a conference, I wrote down the names of two people God had prompted me to witness to. That night, I put that piece of paper in my Bible. I'm ashamed to admit that the paper stayed in my Bible for one year before I acted on it. Though I ultimately witnessed to those people, my delay was disobedience.

Have you put off doing things you know God wants you to do? Are there people you need to talk to, witness to, exhort, or befriend?

STEPS OF ACTION: Give a blank sheet of paper to each family member. Ask each member to list specific acts of delayed obedience that are disobedience in the sight of God. Share lists with one another. Pray and ask for God's forgiveness. Discuss strategies for following through in obedience.

—Harold Vaughan

New Testament Obedience

Scripture Reading—1 John 2:17b
"He that doeth the will of God abideth for ever."

A lot of people think of obedience as an Old Testament doctrine, but the New Testament says, "He that doeth the will of God abideth for ever."

How does the New Testament spell "love"? Jesus said, "If ye love me, keep my commandments" (John 14:15). Actions speak louder than words. It's not just the words from our lips but the direction of our lives that shows our love for God. "He that saith, I know him, and keepeth not his commandments, is a liar, and the truth is not in him" (1 John 2:4). Not only your profession of faith but also the practice of your life proves your true spiritual character.

Obedience is mentioned throughout the New Testament. Romans 1:5 speaks of "obedience to the faith." Romans 15:18 speaks of making "the Gentiles obedient, by word and deed." Colossians 3:20 says, "Children, obey your parents in all things: for this is well pleasing unto the Lord."

Obedience is a trait of saved people. God's children may stumble and fall, but in their hearts, they desire to please their Heavenly Father. The people of God are imperfect, but their lives are characterized by obedience. Likewise, there's no better way to describe the lost than the Bible does—the children of disobedience. Unsaved people are disobedient to God.

Christianity isn't something to be believed; it's Someone to obey, namely the Lord Jesus Christ! Jesus said, "And why call ye me, Lord, Lord, and do not the things which I say?" (Luke 6:46). If we call Jesus our Lord (Master, Ruler), then we will do everything He tells us to do. God's grace empowers us to do His will by giving us the desire and power to obey. Not only does obedience bring blessing; it's God's blessing that makes obedience possible!

SOMETHING TO CONSIDER: Can you think of other New Testament Scriptures that mention obedience?

—*Harold Vaughan*

OBEDIENCE BRINGS BLESSING!

God also required obedience during Old Testament times. He said to His covenant people, "If ye will *obey* my voice indeed, and keep my covenant, then ye shall be a peculiar treasure unto me" (Ex. 19:5, emphasis added). If we've read the Old Testament, we know it's loaded with commandments; and commandments are to be obeyed.

When Moses came down from Mount Sinai, he had the Ten Commandments, not the Ten Suggestions! God gave him not only the Ten Commandments but also instructions for building the tabernacle. God told him to build the tabernacle according to the pattern God had showed him on the mount. The instructions included the dimensions, the materials, and all the details for the construction of the tabernacle.

Moses, along with the children of Israel, "did according to all that the Lord commanded" (Ex. 39:32). We find that saying or its equivalent at least 18 times in the last two chapters of Exodus. Israel fully obeyed God's command, and God's glory filled the tabernacle! God's presence so overshadowed the place that men had to bow in reverence before the glory cloud. The glow of God came when they had done all God showed them!

Obedience brings blessing! God always responds positively to the obedience of His people. "Behold, I set before you this day a blessing and a curse; a blessing, if ye obey the commandments of the Lord your God, which I command you this day" (Deut. 11:26-27).

Disobedience brings conflict, guilt, unbelief, fear, frustration, torment, worry, and doubt. God has established the principle of reaping and sowing. If we want to reap blessing, we must sow obedience and faith. Sowing disobedience always yields a bitter harvest. Whatever we sow determines what we will reap.

This principle, found in the Old Testament, has an application for us today. If we want to be blessed by God, we must obey all God tells us to do.

CELEBRATE OBEDIENCE: Think of someone in the Bible who obeyed God's voice and was blessed as a result. Find a hymnbook and sing all the stanzas of "Trust and Obey."

—*Harold Vaughan*

OBEDIENCE IS ACTIVE!

Scripture Reading—1 Samuel 15:22

"And Samuel said, Hath the Lord as great delight in burnt offerings and sacrifices, as in obeying the voice of the Lord? Behold, to obey is better than sacrifice, and to hearken than the fat of rams."

*Obedience is **doing** all God tells me to do with the right heart attitude.*

Do you know that little chorus? "Obedience is the very best way to show that you believe." The truth is that obedience isn't the very best way; it's the *only* way to show that we believe!

The call to obey is a call to action. How often do we look for a feeling before we act? We don't need to wait for an emotional prompting before we *do* what God has commanded us to do. Obedience is when we activate our will and act on the things we should.

Many Christians look for a feeling or experience, but God is looking for obedience. There's more to obedience than knowing and believing the truth; it is doing. One of the greatest mistakes we can make is thinking that because we know about a certain thing, we assume we have the experience of it. Understanding is one thing, but implementation is another.

Someone surveyed the high school students from five leading industrialized countries. The Americans thought they were the best students in the world; the Japanese thought they were the worst. When surveyors tabulated the results, they discovered that American students, who *thought* they were the best students, actually scored the worst. Furthermore, the Japanese, who thought they were the worst students, actually scored the best!

The Laodiceans said they were rich and increased with goods, in need of nothing. But God's evaluation was somewhat different! He said they were poor, blind, miserable, and naked. Thinking we're a certain way doesn't mean we are that way. Thinking we're obedient in our heads doesn't guarantee we're obedient in real life. There's more to obedience than thinking. Obedience involves action. Obedience is doing. Obedience is doing *all* God tells me to do.

TABLE TALK: Obedience is not knowing, believing, or thinking. It is doing. What do you need to do in order to be fully obedient to God?

—Harold Vaughan

MAY 13
OBEDIENCE

Scripture Reading—1 Samuel 15:22a
"And Samuel said . . .
Behold, to obey
is better than sacrifice."

God told Saul to utterly destroy the Amalekites. Saul started out well enough with more than 200,000 soldiers. God's instructions were specific. Saul was to destroy everything and everyone, but he made a few exceptions to what God had commanded. He spared King Agag and the best of the cattle. In essence, Saul was saying he knew better than God, and his way was just as good.

In Bible times, the custom of conquering kings was to take the captured king alive, bring him home, put him on a chariot, and parade him through the streets as a defeated and deposed king. The citizens then hailed their king as a great military strategist. Do you think Saul wanted the praise of men more than simple obedience to the Lord? Pride is at the root of all disobedience. The prophet Samuel said to Saul, "To obey is better than sacrifice." No amount of religious sacrifice will offset disobedience!

Disobedience cost Saul the kingdom. He rejected God's command, and God rejected him. The Lord spoke to Samuel and told him what Saul had done. When Samuel went out the next day to deliver God's message to Saul, Saul said, "Blessed be thou of the Lord: I have performed the commandment of the Lord" (1 Sam. 15:13b). Samuel replied, "What meaneth then this bleating of the sheep in mine ears, and the lowing of the oxen which I hear?" (v. 14b). The forbidden spoils witnessed against the disobedient king.

Then Saul in pride attempted to cover his own hide by shifting the blame to the people. If that wasn't bad enough, he put a religious spin on it when he said they had spared the animals to sacrifice to the Lord.

God exalted Saul when he was humble in his own sight. But when pride rose in his heart, it destroyed him. God desires and deserves total obedience.

POINTS TO PONDER: Read 1 Samuel 15 and see the destructive effects of pride and disobedience.

—Harold Vaughan

MAY 14
OBEYING WITH THE PROPER ATTITUDE

Obedience is doing all God tells me
*to do with the **right heart attitude**.*

Our family was attending church when we witnessed a teenager throwing a fit. I mean, he was totally out of control. My 11-year-old son said afterwards, "If that's what being a teenager is all about, I'm going to skip that part." Praise the Lord, he *did* skip that part!

Our attitude is important. Going through the motions without a proper spirit is unacceptable. One evening, my mom asked me take out the trash. I jumped up from the couch and stormed from room to room, gathering trash. The coffee table was loaded with old magazines—they looked like trash to me! Grabbing them, I stuffed them into my trash container. In my fit of rage, I even took a pile of old shoes from my mother's closet. My actions were above and beyond the instructions she'd given to me. After going through the entire house, I had a sizeable load. Outside I went with trash, magazines, and closet items! I obeyed instantly and completely but regrettably not with the right heart attitude.

True obedience is about attitudes as well as actions. Our frame of mind is just as important as the performance of the task. Because I had a bad attitude, I was disobedient even though I had done what my mom told me. To obey reluctantly and angrily is not obedience!

Outward conformity without the right heart is unacceptable. Going through the motions isn't enough. It's not enough to give our tithe in the offering plate if our hearts are full of greed. Of what value is it if we never miss a church service yet have a cold war with our brother or sister in Christ? Man looks on the outward appearance, but God looks on the heart. He sees our inner motives as well as our actions. He not only observes our deeds but also knows our inner thoughts.

PRAYER: "Lord, I want to obey You completely, instantly, and with the proper attitude. Amen."

—*Harold Vaughan*

THE NECESSITY OF OBEDIENCE

Scripture Reading—1 Samuel 15:22b
"To obey is better than sacrifice."

In the Bible, we find three categories of content: facts, promises, and commandments. Bible facts are to be believed, Bible promises are to be claimed, and Bible commandments are to be obeyed. I read nowhere in Scripture where men are free to claim the promises while ignoring the commands. Obedience is not optional.

Obedience was required in Paradise. "And the Lord God *commanded* the man, saying, Of every tree of the garden thou mayest freely eat: But of the tree of the knowledge of good and evil, thou shalt not eat of it: for in the day that thou eatest thereof thou shalt surely die" (Gen 2:16-17, emphasis added). We see that obedience was the one condition of man's abiding in Eden. Andrew Murray called obedience the virtue of Paradise. It was the one thing the Creator asked of Adam and Eve.

Notice that God did not highly recommend, strongly suggests, or even ask; He *commanded* the man. God warned the first couple that disobedience would bring certain death—"Thou shalt surely die." This is the only barrier that separates man from God. It wasn't merely unbelief that caused the fall; it was disobedience!

When Adam and Eve sinned, death was the result; and spiritual death was the immediate consequence. They were banished from Paradise. Their innocent natures had been corrupted. They were sinners, and all their offspring would be sinners as well.

Physical death and suffering followed in the wake of that disobedience. Death means separation. When someone dies, his spirit is separated from his body. Spiritual death means man is separated from God. This is why we must be born again. It was our forefather's sin that plunged the entire race into death and misery.

POINTS TO PONDER: Talk through the consequences of Adam and Eve's disobedience. What are the consequences when we disobey?

—Harold Vaughan

MAY 16
It's Mine

Scripture Reading—Psalm 24:1
"The earth is the Lord's, and the fulness thereof; the world,
and they that dwell therein."

Children enter the world with an inborn sense of possessiveness, beginning with a baby bottle or pacifier. Try to take a pacifier from a typical 12-month-old, and you may be in for a real scrap. As they grow older, this attitude continues with toys, food, or money. Maybe you've read a few of the "Rules of a Toddler."

If it's yours, it's mine!

If you have it, it's mine!

If I can't have it, it's mine!

If it's the last one, it's mine!

Human nature has a tendency to claim ownership and to maintain that ownership when challenged. Unfortunately, most teens and adults have a hard time outgrowing this self-centered approach to life.

For this reason, we must understand the Bible principle of ownership. According to Colossians 1:16b, "All things were created by him [God], and for him [God]." James 1:17 tells us that "every good gift and every perfect gift is from above, and cometh down from the Father of lights." If we took God out of the picture, we would have nothing.

As young people mature, they must understand from Scripture that God owns everything. This principle of ownership determines the basis of control. Since God owns it all, He should control it all; we need to experience the process of yielding control. Yielding occurs when we say, "God, You own it. Thank You for letting me have it. I give it back to You. Do with it as You choose."

EXERCISE: Ask family members to list (on paper) five prized possessions. As a family, thank God for each possession and yield control to God.

—Tom Palmer

MAY 17
GENUINE SECURITY

Scripture Reading—Proverbs 11:28
"He that trusteth in his riches shall fall:
but the righteous shall flourish as a branch."

Insecurity makes us vulnerable and places our lives at risk. Why do parents place a newborn in an approved car seat before they leave the hospital? They want to keep the child safe should circumstances beyond their control place the child in harm's way.

Insecurities result from unexpected change. Financial planners help people build a portfolio that will be safe regardless of what happens on Wall Street or in Washington. Employees seek job security because they don't want to be another statistic of the rising unemployment rate. The reality is that many changes occur in our economy and in the job market that we cannot control.

Proverbs 29:25b says, "Whoso putteth his trust in the Lord shall be safe." In an ever–changing world, Christian families must realize that only a few things will never change. One is our relationship to the living Word—Jesus Christ (Heb. 13:8). The other is our relationship to the written Word—the Bible (Ps. 119:89).

We experience true security when we trust something no one can take away from us. Our jobs may change. Our health may change. But our God will never change, and we can trust Him to provide during times of need.

When my wife and I were newlyweds, we invested in a financial plan that would supposedly provide significant interest and return. But when we withdrew the money months later, we received only about $25 in return for our investment. Upon inquiring, we learned that several hundred dollars of earned interest had been consumed by various fees. We learned the hard way that only an unchanging God can provide security in a changing world.

BIBLE READING: Read Proverbs 23:4-5. To what does God compare fleeting riches?

—Tom Palmer

MAY 18
LEAVING IT
ALL BEHIND

Scripture Reading—Matthew 6:19-20

"Lay not up for yourselves treasures upon earth, where moth and rust doth
corrupt, and where thieves break through and steal:
But lay up for yourselves treasures in heaven,
where neither moth nor rust doth corrupt,
and where thieves do not break through nor steal."

Have you ever watched a funeral procession slowly make its way to a cemetery? The funeral director sits in the lead car. Then comes the funeral coach followed by the minister and the family vehicles. The lineup then includes vehicles of friends and acquaintances.

Have you ever seen a moving truck in the procession? Of course not. There's no need for a moving van or cargo trailer when someone goes to the grave.

The explanation is simple. When people step out of this life—when death takes them from this world—they take nothing with them. After the death of a wealthy man, someone asked, "How much did he leave?" The answer? "He left it all." That's right. When we die, we leave everything behind. No matter how much we accumulate or accomplish in this world, we cannot take any possessions from this world to the next.

A simple test helps us determine which things in this life will have value in the next. You can determine the true value of anything by evaluating what it will be worth to you in 1,000 years. Unfortunately, many things that occupy our lives aren't going to be of much value in eternity.

Someone has said, "Someday, all I will have is what I gave to God." As families, we must carefully evaluate the value system we are establishing in our homes. To live only for the "here and now" will leave us bankrupt in the "then and there."

APPLICATION: Pass a $20 bill around to each family member. Ask each person to suggest a way the money could be worth something in 1,000 years.

—*Tom Palmer*

MAY 19
BEWARE OF
COVETOUSNESS!
Scripture Reading—Luke 12:15-21

Covetousness, an uncontrollable desire for more, results when getting and having become a passion. "How much does it take to satisfy a rich man?" someone once asked. The answer? "Just a little bit more." Rich people, however, are not the only ones who can covet. Poor people can be covetous too because covetousness is based not on our bank accounts but on the attitudes of our hearts.

In our text, Jesus told the story of a rich man. No doubt the man had worked hard for his possessions, but he had made three false assumptions.

1. He assumed that goods would satisfy his soul.
2. He assumed that his goods would last for many years.
3. He assumed that he would live long enough to enjoy his goods.

What a shock when God informed the man that he had only hours to live before he would stand before God! His passion for possessions had been intense, but now they would be nothing to him.

What a man is, Jesus taught, is more important than what a man has. In other words, having what we want isn't nearly as important as being what God wants. Unfortunately, many Christian families are driven by a desire for things that are newer and nicer, bigger and better. But "dream houses," for example, are not a necessity. Covetousness feeds a lust for more than we need to meet our family's basic necessities. Before long, a family becomes consumed with building a house that will last only during this lifetime but forgets about building a home that will last for eternity.

Jesus issued a warning. When we ignore His warnings, we face the potential for imminent catastrophe. The catastrophe is even greater when we discover that we have only a few hours to live and that our time on earth has been wasted. I'm sure the rich man knows that now.

BIBLE READING: Do a deeper study of covetousness by looking up the following verses: Proverbs 15:27; 28:16, 20, 22.

—Tom Palmer

MAY 20
LET US BE CONTENT

Scripture Reading—Philippians 4:11-12
"Not that I speak in respect of want: for I have learned,
in whatsoever state I am, therewith to be content.
I know both how to be abased, and I know how to abound:
every where and in all things I am instructed
both to be full and to be hungry, both
to abound and to suffer need."

The opposite of covetousness is contentment. A covetous person always wants more while a content person is always satisfied with what he has. Interestingly, if someone isn't content with what he has, he will never be content with what he wants.

Advertisers are not dumb! Understanding how easily people become dissatisfied, they prepare advertising to feed discontentment. They show people with beautiful complexions and impressive, new cars. Of course, they are smiling because their faces are attractive and their cars are awesome.

Typical people like you and me look in the mirror or in the garage, but we don't smile. Without realizing it, we've become ungrateful and dissatisfied with God's provision for us. Those wrinkles and dents (the dents in the car, of course) have a way of short-circuiting God's blessing in our lives. Advertisers know they can make a lot of money if they can make us think they have a way to get rid of wrinkles and dents.

Contentment is an attitude of acceptance and appreciation for the things God has given to us. When we are satisfied with God's gifts, we can be at peace because we know our possessions are from Him. Content people are rarely driven to have more and are usually happy and pleasant people to be around. They always have a testimony of praise and thanksgiving. They've realized that what they have is more than they deserve—especially when they consider life without the Lord.

PRAYER TIME: Ask each family member to praise God for three things he is thankful for.

—Tom Palmer

SPENDING MY MONEY

Scripture Reading
James 4:15—*"For that ye ought to say, If the Lord will,*
we shall live, and do this, or that."
1 Timothy 6:10—*"For the love of money is the root of all evil: which*
while some coveted after, they had erred from the faith,
and pierced themselves through with many sorrows."

Many people assume that as long as they have money, they can spend it how they want. But spending habits should be different for a Christian family. A family that is surrendered to God's will in all things realizes God's control over wallets and credit cards. We must spend money carefully and prayerfully so we are doing God's will.

Sometimes we foolishly spend money without knowing what's best. When we buy things on sale, we still spend money. Even a good bargain costs us something. Have we considered that most products are overrated to make them appear more attractive? Have we considered that we often buy things we don't really need? Have we considered that there may be a better time or place to buy an item? You see, thinking is a big part of buying. Good money management makes our brains a bigger part of purchasing than our wallets!

Consider these suggestions before making a purchase:

1. Prayer—Talk to God about a purchase even while you are in the showroom or in the fitting room.

2. Permission—Be sure God has given you the green light to spend money that ultimately belongs to Him.

3. Patience—If necessary, be willing to wait so you make the right purchase and get the best and most for your money.

When moms and dads approach buying from God's perspective, they will set a godly example for their children and teens. Young people will also learn the benefits and blessings of handling money God's way.

EXERCISE: On paper, rough out your basic family budget. Show the budget to your children so they can understand how you spend money for the family.

—*Tom Palmer*

GIVE, AND IT SHALL BE GIVEN

Scripture Reading—Luke 6:38
"Give, and it shall be given unto you;
good measure, pressed down,
and shaken together, and running over,
shall men give into your bosom.
For with the same measure that ye mete
withal it shall be measured
to you again."

As Christmas approached, our family chose a special project for giving to missions. Our children were young at the time, but we shared that we wanted each person to give. We prayed about the project and determined the time when we would "pass the plate." At the set time, we gathered together, each bringing his own "offering" to the Lord. Everyone, including the children, was generous. As we shared, however, God impressed on them to give more. One of the boys left the room only to return a moment later with more money from his wallet. As we totaled our giving, we were excited to see what God had provided through our family.

A few days later, someone gave an unexpected monetary gift to our family with a portion designated for each child. We were thrilled to discover that the amount equaled or exceeded what the children had given to missions. No one knew these gifts were coming, so we hadn't worked a deal with God. Needless to say, the experience was a great blessing and an important lesson.

Truly you can't out-give God. Our self-centered lifestyles cling to all that is our own; however, even young children experience a wonderful thrill when they learn this truth about God.

In 2 Corinthians 9:7, we read about three types of givers. **Sad** givers give *grudgingly,* and **mad** givers give *of necessity.* But **glad** givers give *cheerfully.* Truly "it is more blessed to give than to receive" (Acts 20:35), but you will never experience the blessing without an open heart, an open hand, and an open wallet.

APPLICATION: As a family, pick your project and "pass the plate."

—*Tom Palmer*

MAY 23
GOD'S VIEW OF THE FAMILY

Scripture Reading—Psalms 127-128
"Thy wife shall be as a fruitful vine by the sides of thine house: thy children like olive plants round about thy table" (128:3).

*Read these chapters daily this week
to see the family from God's perspective.*

Our response to everything in life depends on how we view it. This fact is especially true of the family. Everyone has ideas about family life. The government, the media, the judicial system, educators, entertainers, TV producers—they all promote their views of the family. Many of these influences are strongly and negatively affecting our families. One need only look around to see the devastation. Is it any wonder many have distorted views about family life? To get the proper perspective on family living, we must go to God's Word and see family from God's point of view.

Have you ever looked through the wrong end of a pair of binoculars? Everything appears small and so far away—a completely wrong picture. But when you look through the right end, everything comes into focus. Things that appeared far away and hard to see are suddenly up close, larger, and clearer.

Many today are trying to see God *through* the family, but that perception makes God appear far away and out of focus. We must look at the family *through* God. Remember, God created the family. Who knows more about family living than God? Christian bookstores are full of books about family living. Some are good; some aren't so good. The greatest book ever written to families is still God's Word.

This week, we'll be looking at the family from God's perspective through His Word. Hopefully, this study will help your family keep a proper focus.

EXERCISE: Ask family members to look through the wrong end of a pair of binoculars. Let them share their thoughts. Turn the binoculars around and ask them to look again. Talk about the different view and discuss how perception relates to our views about the family.

—*Jack Palmer*

The Priority of the Family
Scripture Reading—Psalms 127-128
"Except the Lord build the house, *they labour in vain that build it:
except the Lord keep the city, the watchman waketh but in vain"*
(127:1, emphasis added).

When seeking a proper view of the family, we must understand the *priority of the family* or why the family is so important to God. Psalm 127:1 says that the family is so important to God that we're wasting our time unless we allow Him to build it. Let's look at three reasons the family is God's priority.

First, **God created the family**. In Genesis 2:18b, after declaring everything He'd created to be good, God said, "It is not good that the man should be alone; I will make him an help meet for him." Though alone in the Garden of Eden, Adam wasn't lonely. He had wonderful fellowship with God, but God knew he was incomplete. He created a woman (v. 22), Eve, and brought her to Adam, creating the first family. God's uniting of Adam and Eve shows the importance of family to God!

Second, **the family is the foundation of society**. Genesis 1:28a says, "And God blessed them, and God said unto them, Be fruitful, and multiply, and replenish [fill] the earth, and subdue it." As a result, humanity came into existence. During the flood, all humans except Noah and his family were destroyed. God told Noah and his family to "replenish the earth" (Gen. 9:1). In both instances, God used one family to populate the earth. God's choosing to use the family in this way shows its importance to Him!

Third, **the family is the heart of the Church**. In 1 Timothy, where God gives requirements for spiritual leadership in the Church, the family plays a major role (3:2, 4, 5, 11-12). Before a man is qualified to lead in the Church, he must be a proven spiritual leader to his family. The Church can never be stronger than its families. That fact makes the family important to God!

POINT TO PONDER: There's no question the family is important to God. How important is your family to you?

—Jack Palmer

THE PEOPLE OF THE FAMILY

Scripture Reading—Psalms 127-128

Can you imagine this modern-day attempt to define the family? "A family is any group of people living together with a mutual commitment to each other's happiness." How offensive that definition is to a Christian family seeking to honor God! But that definition shows how the world views the family. No wonder we who want to please God must embrace His view of family. The world's view of the family is all-inclusive (broad) while God's view is exclusive (narrow).

If the above definition is correct, that means an unmarried couple that lives together constitutes a family. But God describes that type of live-in relationship as fornication. According to this definition, married people who leave their spouses and live with someone else also constitute a family. Again, God's Word calls this lifestyle "adultery." By this definition, two men or two women who live together as "domestic partners" are also a family. The Bible clearly defines their behavior as "sodomy." What a contrast to God's view of the family!

Reading Psalms 127 and 128, we see that God's view of the family is confined to specific people—the husband or father (127:4, 5; 128:4), the wife or mother (127:3; 128:3), and any children God chooses to give them (127:3, 4; 128:3, 6). From God's perspective, a family consists of one man and one woman who are legally married and any children God allows them to have. Psalm 128:6, which speaks of grandparents and grandchildren, describes three generations of family. Do you see the difference between the world's definition of the family and God's?

In a world of constantly changing family values, may we as Christian families never be moved from seeing the family from God's point of view. Our protection lies in solidly based, biblical values. The world's view may change, but God's won't!

POINT TO PONDER: Review your family heritage. Thank God that your family reflects God's view of the family.

—Jack Palmer

MAY 26
THE PRODUCT
OF THE FAMILY

Scripture Reading—Psalms 127-128
Particularly notice what these verses say about children.

Examining the family from God's perspective, we have an imperative to consider what He says about children, the product of the family. An improper view of children is damaging to the parent-child relationship. Too many parents see their children as burdens instead of blessings. They force their children to build their lives around their goals and ambitions rather than devoting themselves to the training of their children for God. Godly parents must see their children as their most valued earthly treasure. Every investment in the life of a child is eternal because the only thing we can take to heaven with us is our family.

This week's Scripture passage says wonderful things about God's view of children. First, "children are an heritage of the Lord" (127:3). As God's gift to the family, we must cherish them. Do you value your children? Verse three also describes children as God's "reward." As such, we must accept them as God's gifts. Each is unique, and we must accept him just the way God made him. Psalm 127:4 describes children as "arrows" which need a dynamic (a force to send them on their way) and a direction (where they need to go). Godly parents have the responsibility to provide that for them. Children are also something God intends parents to enjoy (127:5). Psalm 128:3 describes them as "olive plants," which means they are tender and easily influenced. Godly parents must protect their children from harmful influences.

How do you see your children? When you see them from God's perspective, that outlook will have a dynamic effect on how you treat them. See them as a trust from the Lord. Your children really belong to Him, but He has entrusted them to you to develop for Him. Be faithful! (1 Cor. 4:2)

DISCUSSION: Talk with your family about God's view of children. Ask them to evaluate your performance as a parent. Be prepared for anything and learn from what they share.

—Jack Palmer

MAY 27
THE PLEASURE OF THE FAMILY
Scripture Reading—Psalms 127-128

For many families, even Christian ones, family life isn't a pleasure. The home is filled with tension and strife, arguments and disagreements. Some families experience times of both shouting and silence because family members have withdrawn from each other in anger. The Bible, on the other hand, teaches the importance of resolving conflicts. Ephesians 4:26 says, "Be ye angry, and sin not: let not the sun go down upon your wrath." Many young couples begin their married lives with lofty dreams only to see them turned into nightmares. Is such failure what God intends for the Christian family? Absolutely not!

Why are these problems characteristic of so many families today? Could it be because many believers have failed to consider God's view of the family? God wants Christian couples to enjoy their married lives together. He wants them to enjoy raising their children for Him. He wants homes to be places where families love being together.

In our study of Psalms 127 and 128, God reveals some of the pleasures He wants us to experience in our families.

1. The Pleasure of Children (127:5)
2. The Pleasure of Parenting (127:5)
3. The Pleasure of Obedience (128:1)
4. The Pleasure of Labor (128:2)
5. The Pleasure of Fearing God (128:4)
6. The Pleasure of Grandchildren (128:6)
7. The Pleasure of Grand Parenting (128:6)

Your family should be a source of pleasure not only to you but also to God. Enjoying your family life together will make God happy.

ASSIGNMENT: Use the above list to evaluate your family. Do you really enjoy each other? Are you bringing pleasure to God? If not, search your heart and confess known sin to God. If you need to restore a relationship with another family member, do so right away. God is displeased by prolonged, fractured relationships in the home. He promises to forgive.

—Jack Palmer

MAY 28
GOD'S PURPOSE
FOR THE FAMILY
Scripture Reading—Psalm 78:1-8; 127; 128

Today, I want you to see the purpose of your family existence. Young people meet, discover an attraction to each other, begin courting, fall in love, get engaged, and marry. Suddenly, life becomes real. They must have a job to provide an income, a place to live, food to eat, clothes to wear, a car to drive, money to pay bills—and suddenly children arrive. But most parents never stop to ask themselves, "Why are we doing this?"

According to Psalm 78:1-8, God's purpose for the family is *to raise up the next generation for God* (vv. 6-7). These verses represent four generations. Each generation has the responsibility to prepare the next generation to know God, to love God, to worship God, to obey God, and to glorify God. When the older generation steps off the scene, the younger generation should be ready to take their place. But statistics show that average Christian families lose their children for the Lord in less than one and a half generations. Sadly, many families are failing to fulfill God's purpose for them.

In Psalm 78:4-6, God presents His plan for accomplishing His purpose. We parents have the job of passing along a vital, living faith in the Lord to our children. We're like runners in a relay race. We carry the baton a distance and hand it to the next person. The process continues until the race is over and hopefully the runner has won.

According to verse seven, if we succeed in passing on our faith, those who follow us will be a generation that (1) has hope in God, (2) is always mindful of what God has done for them, and (3) has a steadfast spirit toward God. Do those words describe what you want your family to be? Remember, God is counting on us to fulfill His purpose for our families.

ACTION POINT: With your family, list ways you're carrying out God's purpose and plan for your family. Explain your goals. This information will help family members be more understanding and appreciative of your commitment.

—Jack Palmer

The Problem
with the Family

Scripture Reading—Psalms 127-128
Do not allow the daily repetition to create a casual attitude
toward these wonderful chapters.

Most family problems result from people not getting along with each other. Hurts and misunderstandings cause family members to withdraw or to react harshly. Conflicts can come from words, actions, or attitudes. Some problems are never resolved and become a source of bitterness. Brothers and sisters can be selfish and unkind to each other. Husbands and wives can be inconsiderate and intolerant of each other's faults. Parents and children can have serious conflicts. Our tendency is to blame the other person and say, "It's not my fault!"

But God commands us to take personal responsibility. James 5:16a says, "Confess *your faults* one to another, and pray one for another, that ye may be healed" (emphasis added). It's easier to tell the other person where he was wrong. It takes a humble, tender heart to confess your fault to someone else.

Nine words are so important to solving family conflicts. They are "I was wrong," "Please forgive me," and "I forgive you." If parents had spoken these words in brokenness and humility, many a family would have been spared a divorce and a destroyed family. Consider the words of Ephesians 4:32. "And be ye kind one to another, tenderhearted, *forgiving one another*, even as God for Christ's sake hath forgiven you" (emphasis added). We all need to be forgiven and to be forgivers!

When we really understand God's view of the family, we will have a sincere desire to resolve family problems His way. The world says, "Tell them off," "Get even," "Make them pay for what they did to you." But God says, "Be humble, honest, loving, and forgiving."

APPLICATION: Do you have a problem with another family member? If so, will you seek to resolve the problem God's way? You will be blessed, and God will be honored.

—Jack Palmer

MAY 30
THREE AGAINST ONE—IS THAT FAIR?

Scripture Reading—Romans 8:37
"Nay, in all these things we are more than conquerors through him that loved us."

When children are divided for a game and one team has more players than the other, someone inevitably shouts, "That's not fair!" When numbers seem to be lopsided, we automatically assume some injustice or disadvantage.

At first glance, because of the enemies who oppose us, we may be tempted to say the same thing about being a Christian. Those enemies are the sin nature (characterized by self-centered desires), Satan (who wants to steal God's glory), and the world system (that tries to conform us to its mold). All of these enemies combined stand *no chance* to defeat our Savior and His finished work on the cross. When we surrendered to Christ, we became "more than conquerors" (Rom. 8:37) with Him.

Our sin nature is powerless and defeated through Christ. Rom. 6:6 says, "Knowing this, that our old man is crucified with him, that the body of sin might be destroyed, that henceforth we should not serve sin." We do not become sinless, but through Christ we have the power to say "no" to sin during temptation. Those who are without Christ cannot say "no" because they are slaves to sin. But we can because we are "servants to God" (Rom. 6:22). *Now that's victory!*

Satan is a defeated foe! (Rev. 12:9-12). Before salvation, we had Satan's characteristics (John 8:44); but after salvation our characteristics become Christlike. Those characteristics are evidence of our salvation. Therefore, Satan lost his power over the Christian. *Now that's victory!*

Finally, the world is a defeated foe! (1 John 5:4-5). The world and all its ways have no more dominion over the Christian when he walks with the Lord. *Now that's victory!*

Three against one! There's no hope for these enemies when we choose Christ! Praise God!

PRAISE: Thank God in prayer for the victory we have in Christ. Close by singing "Victory in Jesus."

—Stanley W. Long, II

MAY 31
ENLISTING IN GOD'S ARMY—
DETERMINE TO BE A WARRIOR

Scripture Reading—2 Timothy 2:3-4

"Thou therefore endure hardness, as a good soldier of Jesus Christ. No man that warreth entangleth himself with the affairs of this life; that he may please him who hath chosen him to be a soldier."

When someone receives Jesus Christ as Lord and Savior, he enlists in God's army. In other words, every Christian is a soldier of the cross. Therefore, like a well-trained soldier, the Christian must determine to be prepared, disciplined, and fit to accomplish the objectives of his Commanding Officer. In 2 Timothy 2:3-4, Paul uses the analogy of a soldier to describe the privilege and duty a Christian has to his commander.

First, Christianity is not a life of ease. Paul encourages Timothy to "endure hardness." Our old sin nature wants everything easy, but the Christian must determine to endure the hardness of this world because we no longer fit in with it. Our goals, desires, and even citizenship (Eph. 2:19) are not of this world. The great thing is that, as we endure this hardness, God gives us joy, fulfillment, and even peace.

Second, Christianity is a life of disciplined freedom. Receiving Christ as Lord gives us freedom from the bondage of sin, from Satan, and from the world. We are free to serve God! When we entangle ourselves "with the affairs of this life," we give up our freedom in Christ and are no longer effective in the spiritual war.

Third, Christianity is a privilege to please the God who has chosen us. All of us like to please those we love. When we understand that God demonstrated His love for us (Rom. 5:8), we will desire to please Him because of our love and admiration for Him. He has chosen us by dying for us, and we say "yes" to Him when we receive Him. This choosing becomes a partnership and a team. As we engage in battle, He never leaves nor forsakes us (Heb. 13:5). What a privilege!

DISCUSSION: Discuss things that can entangle us in the Christian life.

—*Stanley W. Long, II*

JUNE 1
A Good Soldier Develops Trained Sight

Scripture Reading—Romans 13:11-12
*"And that, knowing the time, that now it is high time to awake out of
sleep: for now is our salvation nearer than when we believed.
The night is far spent, the day is at hand:
let us therefore cast off the works of darkness,
and let us put on the armour of light."*

A soldier who desires to live a life of victory and to keep from being overtaken by the enemy must develop "trained sight." When finishing his first letter to the church at Corinth, Paul said in 1 Corinthians 16:13, "Watch ye, stand fast in the faith, quit you like men, be strong." The thought here is to stay "alert" or "wide awake." In other words, we must be keenly aware of our surroundings in order to recognize the attacks of the enemy.

God's creation can teach us many lessons about walking with Him. The deer is a great illustration of how we believers should be keenly aware of our surroundings. When a deer, especially a five-year-old buck, is feeding and moving through the woods, he keeps a keen eye on everything around him. He is especially alert to predators who may seek his harm; if he senses the slightest danger, he's out of there. His eyes constantly scan his surroundings to ensure the enemy is not approaching, but every hunter knows when he is most vulnerable. During mating season, that usually cautious buck lets down his guard. He becomes distracted and chases after does. He falls for the temptations of his flesh, regardless of danger he knows is present.

Christians often fall for the enemy's tactics because they let their guard down. They stop being alert to temptation.

Are your eyes wide open to the temptations around you? Do you recognize the tactics of the enemy when he seeks to entrap you?

ACTION POINT: List ways our spiritual enemies attack us. This exercise will help us be alert to the temptations around us.

—Stanley W. Long, II

JUNE 2
A GOOD SOLDIER DEVELOPS TACTICAL STABILITY

Scripture Reading—Galatians 5:1
"Stand fast therefore in the liberty
wherewith Christ hath made us free,
and be not entangled again with the yoke of bondage."

One of the most famous soldiers in American history is General Thomas "Stonewall" Jackson. He received his nickname, "Stonewall," during the American Civil War on July 21, 1861, at the battle of First Manassas, also known as Bull Run. During the battle, Jackson's brigade held a hill in spite of heavy enemy attack. A fellow Confederate general, trying to rally his men, pointed to Jackson's soldiers and cried, "There is Jackson standing like a stone wall! Let us determine to die here, and we will conquer." From then on, Jackson was known as General "Stonewall" Jackson.

Look at 1 Corinthians 16:13a, "Watch ye, stand fast [firm] in the faith." In order for a Christian to be a good soldier of the Lord Jesus Christ, he must develop "tactical stability." During the Civil War, the army that held the high ground was most likely to win the battle. We Christians hold the "high ground" when we build our lives on the firm foundation of the Lord Jesus Christ, standing on the principles of God's Word.

Notice in 1 Corinthians 16:13 Paul tells us to "stand fast in *the* faith" (emphasis added). Here "*the* faith" refers to the principles and doctrines of God's Holy Word. Building on God's Word ensures that we will be able to stand when the enemy attacks or when trials of life confront us. Ephesians 4:14 says, "That we henceforth be no more children, tossed to and fro, and carried about with every wind of doctrine, by the sleight of men, and cunning craftiness, whereby they lie in wait to deceive." Let us determine to live and die on God's Word, which will provide the stability to conquer! Are you building on its firm foundation?

ACTION POINT: Find and discuss other verses that speak of standing firm for the Lord Jesus Christ.

—Stanley W. Long, II

JUNE 3
A GOOD SOLDIER DEVELOPS
A TENACIOUS SPIRIT

Scripture Reading—Psalm 31:24
"Be of good courage, and he shall strengthen your heart,
all ye that hope in the Lord."

When I was a child, several bullies lived in my neighborhood. Each had his own ways of intimidating, but all had one thing in common— they ruled by fear! If you gave them any hint that they could intimidate you through cowardly tactics, they knew they could control you. But if you were courageous and didn't give in to their demands, they realized they had no control over you.

A victorious principle needed in the good Christian soldier's life is the development of a "tenacious spirit." The word *tenacious* means "not easily pulled apart, tough; persistent to maintain to something valued or worthwhile." Paul wrote in 1 Corinthians 16:13, "Watch ye, stand fast in the faith, *quit you like men*, be strong" (emphasis added). At first glance, this verse sounds funny, especially if you're a female; but the thought Paul conveys is that of "maturity" or that of being "courageous." In other words, if we're going to be good Christian soldiers, we must develop courage that doesn't let go in the face of fear.

Enemies of the cross of Christ try to rule Christians through fear and intimidation. Satan knows he can control us if he can make us fearful to share the Gospel with a friend, to stand up for the Bible in our school or workplace, or to pray in public. He will use our neighbors, friends, and family if he can keep us from being courageous for the Lord Jesus. He knows that when we're courageous, we'll be bold for Christ. We'll be tools in God's hand to advance His kingdom. Proverbs 28:1 says, "The wicked flee when no man pursueth: but the righteous are bold as a lion." When we practice righteousness, we can be bold and courageous for God. Don't let fear make you let go of God!

ACTION POINT: Talk about ways the enemy tries to intimidate us. Ask God for courage to face these fears.

—Stanley W. Long, II

JUNE 4
A Good Soldier Develops Transcendent Strength

Scripture Reading—Philippians 4:13
"I can do all things through Christ
which strengtheneth me."

"It's a bird. It's a plane. No, it's Superman!" Everybody loves the idea of a superhero! That's someone who has superhuman strength and uses good to triumph over evil. If only there were someone like that . . .

Did you realize that the Lord has equipped every Christian with extraordinary strength? We're not referring to the strength that can stop a steaming locomotive or enable us to leap over the tallest building in a single bound. The Bible describes the kind of strength that's available to every Christian.

As soldiers of the cross, we need to develop "transcendent strength." The word *transcendent* means superior or extraordinary. First Corinthians 16:13 says, "Watch ye, stand fast in the faith, quit you like men, be strong." Jesus calls every believer to be strong in the Christian walk.

Does God expect us to start working out physically by lifting weights? Not at all! We will never find spiritual strength in our own flesh and power. Christ not only calls us to be strong but also gives us the ability to be strong. The idea here is to live our lives through the superior or extraordinary strength of the Holy Spirit. To be effective soldiers for Christ, we must realize that our strength comes from Him. Paul put it this way in Ephesians 6:10. "Finally, my brethren, be strong in the Lord, and in the power of his might."

Every soldier wants to use the most powerful weapon in battle. The only way we can wield God's strength and power is to surrender our own. When we understand that we *cannot* live the Christian life in our strength and abilities, we are in a position to access the extraordinary strength the Holy Spirit provides. *We* can't live the Christian life, but *God* can through us. Are you frustrated trying to live the Christian life? Surrender now to God's strength!

DISCUSSION: Discuss ways God gives strength.

—*Stanley W. Long, II*

JUNE 5
A GOOD SOLDIER DEVELOPS TOTAL SELFLESSNESS

Scripture Reading—1 Corinthians 16:14
"Let all your things be done with charity."

You've heard the saying, "Look out for A—Number 1!" In other words, "Look out for yourself." All people have one thing in common: they're selfish, self-centered, and self-serving. This is the attitude of the sin nature. We're our own worst enemy with our selfish desires, wants, and ambitions; with the "me, myself, and I" mentality.

Thanks be to God that He rendered this aspect of the sin nature powerless at the cross of Christ. Once we receive Jesus as our Lord and Savior, the Holy Spirit indwells us, giving us the enabling power to serve through love! The Holy Spirit gives and motivates this love, and serving others is the demonstration of this God-produced love. We cannot manufacture this love through our own strength, and this love is evidence that we are truly children of God. Our question becomes, "Whom should we serve?"

Serve the One and Only—Jesus Christ. In Mark 12:30, Jesus said, "And thou shalt love the Lord thy God with all thy heart, and with all thy soul, and with all thy mind, and with all thy strength: this is the first commandment." We demonstrate our love for Him by our service to Him!

Serve One Another—Fellow Believers. What distinguishes the Christian from someone without Christ is his love for others. John 13:35 says, "By this shall all men know that ye are my disciples, if ye have love one to another."

Serve All Others—When Christ reigns in our lives, we will have a desire to serve those without Christ in hopes that we may see them receive the Lord. The natural man hates those who oppose him, but the Holy Spirit enables the Christian to love those who oppose him. Christ is the ultimate example of a servant (Phil. 2:1-8). When He is in charge of our lives, serving will be our outflow.

DISCUSSION: Discuss ways you may serve Jesus, fellow believers, and those outside the faith.

—Stanley W. Long, II

JUNE 6
SEPARATION IS OLD-FASHIONED
Scripture Reading—Leviticus 22:1-3

Few subjects raise the blood pressure of Bible-believing Christians like the subject of separation. Unfortunately, many discussions of the subject have become more of a debate. When we mention words like *convictions* and *standards*, folks are quick to put on their spiritual boxing gloves, expecting another round of controversy. Terms like *legalism, license,* and *liberty* are spiritual hot potatoes that have a way of heating up even the best of so-called "sharing" among brothers and sisters in Christ. Now we have included "degrees" of separation, which simply complicate an already confusing issue. We need to rediscover basic scriptural principles regarding biblical separation.

Separation is an old-fashioned issue and God's way of differentiating between the holy and the unholy. Separation has both negative and positive dimensions. We need to be separated *from* something and *to* something. Many Christians are afraid of the word *different* because to be different means not to be like everyone else.

Try this experiment. Ask a family member to stand and face one wall in the room where you are now gathered. Instruct him to list five things he sees. Then ask the family member to face the opposite wall in the room. Again, instruct him to list five things he sees.

Did the family member see the same things when facing opposite directions? Of course not. He saw different things because of a new direction. A change took place, and things appeared differently, depending on which direction he was facing. A change that makes a difference is not necessarily a bad thing. Second Corinthians 5:17 says, "Therefore if any man be in Christ, *he is a new creature*: old things are passed away; behold, all things are become new" (emphasis added). Once "all things are become new," separation is not a big problem because it makes us distinctly different as Christians.

ACTION POINT: Make a list of things that should be different once a person has become a Christian.

—*Tom Palmer*

JUNE 7
MEASUREMENT
OF SEPARATION
Scripture Reading—1 John 2:15-17

We determine biblical separation not by **how far I am from the world** but by **how close I am to God.** Unfortunately, many people assume separation carries a negative impact. They fail to understand that the primary goal of separation is not to avoid worldliness but to develop godliness. James 4:8a says, "Draw nigh to God, and he will draw nigh to you." Nearness to God produces *likeness* to God.

One great enemy of godliness is what I call the "invisible yardstick." Churches, schools, and families are quick to declare that they refuse to be worldly. As we hold up the invisible yardstick, we show how far we are from the world. If we don't look like, act like, talk like, and think like the world, then we certainly aren't worldly, right? That way of thinking, however, has one simple flaw.

As time goes by, the world continues to drift farther from God. As the world moves, unfortunately the Church also moves. That's why the Church now stands in places where the world once stood. I'll use an example to prove my point.

Not long ago, many Christian families would have had nothing to do with a Hollywood movie theater. Preachers preached against going to the movies, and Christians simply wouldn't go. Today, some Christian families think nothing of buying or renting the same kind of movies and showing no sense of shame because of the crude and lewd nature of what they are watching.

In our generation, the world is becoming very "churchy," and Church is becoming very worldly. Sometimes it's hard to tell the difference between the two. Again, we should determine our spiritually not by how far we are from the world but by how close we are to God.

APPLICATION: First John 2:16 says, "For all that is in the world, the lust of the flesh, and the lust of the eyes, and the pride of life, is not of the Father, but is of the world." What do think "all that is in the world" means?

—Tom Palmer

JUNE 8
MOTIVATION
FOR SEPARATION

Scripture Reading—2 Corinthians 6:16-7:1

Biblical separation is motivated not by **pleasing men** but by **pleasing God**. A godly Christian must carefully and prayerfully establish biblical standards of separation. Determining "what" standards will be, however, is not enough; we must determine "why" the standards are necessary. I fear that we often focus on the "what" and neglect to consider the "why." Motivation is essential because it determines the spirit we will display.

Jesus said, "And he that sent me is with me: the Father hath not left me alone; for I do always those things that please him" (John 8:29), speaking of the Heavenly Father. Paul wrote the following challenge to the Thessalonians: "As ye have received of us how ye ought to walk and to please God, so ye would abound more and more" (1 Thess. 4:1b). Paul challenged Timothy with this thought: "Study to shew thyself approved unto God" (2 Tim. 2:15a).

When pleasing God becomes our priority, the fear and the praise of man are not even factors. Separation is no longer aggravating or intimidating because we are driven by a passion to please our God. It is a blessing to say, "Dear God, what else can I do to please You?" when His pleasure motivates our hearts. It is a miserable experience to supposedly "do right" just to keep everybody happy. By the way, we can't do that anyhow; so why try?

Unfortunately, a desire to impress men has sometimes motivated our standards of separation. That desire has occasionally become a spirit of superiority over those who do not have the same standards. We need to remember that pride in any form is still an abomination to God, and God hates it (Prov. 6:16-17, 16:5). God is pleased not when we think we're better than others but when we're more like Him.

SHARE YOUR HEART: Ask each family member to share a reason he desires to please God. Discuss how you feel when you know God is pleased.

—*Tom Palmer*

JUNE 9
BASIS FOR
SEPARATION

Scripture Reading—Romans 12:2a
"And be not conformed to this world: but be ye transformed."

Biblical separation is not the result of being **conformed** to a standard but by being **transformed** by truth. When we apply truth, it has life-changing results. In 1 Thessalonians 2:13, Paul praised the Lord because the believers who received the Word of God "received it not as the word of men, but as it is in truth, the word of God, which effectually worketh also in you that believe."

Often we have heard the famous list of all the things we can and can't do if we want to be spiritual. By the way, this list provides good preaching material and produces lots of "amens" at big preaching conferences. Yet my observation is that we have a generation of Christians who can check off items on this list but have no concept of obedience "from the heart" (Rom. 6:17).

Separation does not begin with a list but with a heart decision to let the truth of God's Word bring about change. We must be willing to know the truth about ourselves, the truth about God, and the truth about what must change for us to be more like Him.

Living by a list of rules is why so many young people turn away from their upbringing to go their own way. For their first 18 years, they lived by the Christian school handbook, the church worker's policies, and their parents' "Top Ten Rules My Kids Will Never Break." If the teen ever had the courage to ask why, the simple answer was, "Because I told you so!"

For this reason, I fear many Christian teens do what they are told without ever learning Bible truths from God Himself. Though they conform outwardly, they do not experience a changed heart. When they sense the freedom to break out of the mold they've been squeezed into, they're gone!

DISCUSSION: According to 1 John 2:3-4, how do we prove that we know God?

—Tom Palmer

JUNE 10
DESIRE FOR SEPARATION

Scripture Reading—1 Corinthians 9:27
"But I keep under my body, and bring it into subjection: lest that by any means, when I have preached to others, I myself should be a castaway."

Biblical separation is not following standards *to make us* godly but establishing standards *because we are seeking* to be godly. Biblical separation is a great privilege because it allows us to identify with our God. We don't "have to" live a godly life; we "get to" live a godly life. We are talking about the difference between obligation and opportunity.

When cadets enter West Point, they are overwhelmed by the strictness of this institution. Those who adhere to the rigid guidelines eventually wear the uniform of the U.S. Army with pride. You can't make it too tough on them! They are willing, and they want to do anything they can to pursue their goal of becoming a part of "The Long Gray Line." To each soldier, it is a privilege and an honor to follow in the heritage of Robert E. Lee, Douglas MacArthur, or Dwight D. Eisenhower. Those who simply follow the rules because they have to never experience anything but a miserable existence. They are relieved to get out when their time is up. What a waste of time!

Paul's words to Timothy were as follows: "Exercise thyself rather unto godliness. . . . godliness is profitable unto all things" (1 Tim. 4:7b-8). A major part of any conditioning program is an attitude of "I want to." It works that way with a ball team, and it works that way with God's team.

Godliness is "Godlikeness." Godliness begins with a desire for more of the reality of God in our lives. What a blessing to become more like the One whose presence we desire in our lives. Taking steps to live a Godlike life ought not to be frustrating or intimidating. Rather, we will experience great blessing as godliness becomes a reality.

APPLICATION: Ask the children to briefly explain who they want to be like when they grow up. Ask them to explain why.

—Tom Palmer

JUNE 11
ATTITUDE
OF SEPARATION

Scripture Reading—Ephesians 4:11-16

Biblical separation means having not only **a right position** but also **a right disposition.** We are simply talking about a right attitude. Unfortunately, too often the attitude of the so-called "fightin' fundamentalist" has been that of a "cranky conservative" or a "sassy separatist." These attitudes are usually driven by a spirit of pride that assumes our position to be better than that of those who are less conservative or separated.

Ephesians 4 is a passage of Scripture that talks about "perfecting of the saints" and "edifying of the body of Christ" (v. 12). The emphasis of verse 13 is on becoming "a perfect man, unto the measure of the stature of the fulness of Christ." Talking about the reality of godliness—there it is. Verse 15 gives us the key. "But speaking the truth in love, may grow up into him in all things, which is the head, even Christ."

Separatists are known for their stand upon the truth, but sadly they often forget the part about "in love." Their actions are right, but their attitudes are wrong! A critical, judgmental, and condemning attitude often has a negative effect upon the pursuit of godliness. A loving attitude communicates a desire to help others attain the level of godliness God desires for them. We must take a separated position, but we cannot act like we are mad about it.

We need not fear or fight over biblical separation. Moody said, "It is a great deal better to live a holy life than to talk about it. Lighthouses do not ring bells and fire cannon to call attention to their shining—they just shine." Pascal said, "The serene, silent beauty of a holy life is the most powerful influence in the world, next to the might of the Spirit of God." A godless world wants to see the reality of God being lived out in the lives of those who claim to know Him.

PRAYER TIME: Ask God to make your home a holy place where He is on display.

—Tom Palmer

JUNE 12
DON'T BE
A MESS!

Scripture Reading—Titus 2:11-15

While speaking at a junior camp retreat, I stepped onto the platform wearing a cowboy hat, a western shirt, jeans, a fancy belt buckle, and boots. Carrying a lasso, I walked around as if I were bowlegged and called out, "Howdy y'all! What am I?"

"A cowboy!" the kids responded.

When I asked them how they knew who I was, they described my actions, outfit, words, and, of course, the fact that I walked like I'd been sitting in the saddle too long.

I stepped out of sight momentarily and returned wearing a baseball hat, a Phillies shirt, and baseball shoes. Carrying a baseball and glove, I crouched like a batter. "Play ball!" I yelled. "What am I?"

They said I was a baseball player and described each item that identified me as a baseball player. Again, I left the platform.

When I returned the third time, I wore both hats. I also wore a cowboy boot on one foot and a baseball shoe on the other. I carried a lasso in one hand and a baseball bat in the other. I strolled and crouched as before and called out, "Howdy y'all, let's play ball!" Again I asked, "What am I?"

Without hesitation, one junior camper called out, "A mess!"

The room erupted with laughter, but my point had been made.

Something doesn't make sense when a Christian tries to be worldly and godly. No one can be like the world and like God at the same time. There must be an obvious distinction.

The time has come for godly families to be different from the world around them. Our actions, appearances, attitudes, and even our walk and talk must show the world we are different. Otherwise, we'll just be a mess!

DISCUSSION: James 4:4 says, "Ye adulterers and adulteresses, know ye not that the friendship of the world is enmity with God? whosoever therefore will be a friend of the world is the enemy of God." According to this verse, who is the "friend of the world"?

—Tom Palmer

JUNE 13
THE TEN COMMANDMENTS
Scripture Reading—Exodus 19:16-25

We're all familiar with storms—the dark clouds, the wind, the lightning, and the thunder. Sometimes storms can be pretty scary. The children of Israel experienced some of these storms after leaving Egypt. They wandered in the wilderness for three months and camped in the desert at the foot of Mount Sinai. God had brought the people here to give them His commandments. Moses went up to the mountain, and the people remained below, awaiting his return. Moses had warned them not to go near the mountain (v. 23), which was now covered by a cloud. Thunder rumbled, lightning flashed, and the people trembled (v. 16). God was speaking.

God gave the Ten Commandments to the children of Israel and promised blessing and happiness if they obeyed. The commandments, intended for us as well, bring blessing when we obey them. But like the children of Israel, we cannot obey the law perfectly. God gave us the law to be our schoolmaster—to point us to the way of true salvation found in Jesus Christ (Gal. 3:24). Neither doing good works nor keeping the commandments can give us hope of eternal life. We find salvation only by trusting in the blood of Jesus Christ. He is the Way, the Truth, and the Life.

We can organize the Ten Commandments into two groups. The first four commandments address our relationship with God, and the last six instruct us in our relationships with others. In Matthew 22:37-40, Jesus summarized the Ten Commandments when He said that "the first and great commandment" is to "love the Lord thy God with all thy heart, and with all thy soul, and with all thy mind. . . . And the second is like unto it, Thou shalt love thy neighbour as thyself." The Ten Commandments are for our good—to point us to Christ.

DO THIS NOW: See if you can list the Ten Commandments from memory. Make a chart of the commandments to have as a visual reference over the next few days.

—*Debbie Vaughan*

JUNE 14
THE FIRST
COMMANDMENT
Scripture Reading—Exodus 20:1-3

It was a long, busy day. The day got off to a bad start when Billy overslept. He rushed to get his chores done and to get ready for school. He didn't have enough time for his devotions. *I'll have them later*, he thought.

Now it was almost bedtime, and he still hadn't read his Bible. He had a choice to make—to read the last chapter in the new book he'd gotten for his birthday or to read his Bible. What would he choose?

The first commandment we read about in Exodus 20 deals with Billy's dilemma. In His first commandment to the children of Israel, God said, "Thou shalt have no other gods before me" (v. 3). The children of Israel were familiar with idols and with false gods. They had lived 400 years in Egypt, a pagan society where worshiping false gods was something everyone did. The Egyptians lived in fear of their gods, and they had a different god for everything.

God gave His people a commandment: He wanted them to have no other gods except Him. A jealous God, He demanded their full allegiance and love. They were to worship Him and Him alone.

Today, especially in Christian homes, we tend to think that we serve no other gods. Maybe the children of Israel felt the same way. But do we *really* put God first? Is He really number one to us?

Sometimes, it's a good thing to ask ourselves if there is anything—or anyone—in our lives that means more to us than God. If God asked us to give something or someone up, could we obey Him? Would we obey Him? When God is first, we can trust Him with every part of our lives, knowing that He is sufficient for every need we will ever have. "Thou shalt have no other gods before me" (v. 3).

SONG TIME: Sing "Seek Ye First" by Karen Lafferty.

—Debbie Vaughan

JUNE 15
THE SECOND
COMMANDMENT
Scripture Reading—Exodus 20:4-6

Billy watched people enter the big church. Peering inside, he saw people bowing before a statue. The statue wasn't scary looking; in fact, it seemed to have a kind face. Were the people doing something wrong when they bowed down to the statue? Maybe it was better to go to this church than not to go to church at all. God's second commandment answers Billy's question.

God told the children of Israel, "Thou shalt not make unto thee any graven image, or any likeness of any thing that is in heaven above, or that is in the earth beneath, or that is in the water under the earth" (v. 4).

Man makes a "graven image" from wood, stone, or metal. Often it resembles something God created, or it may even represent God Himself. God instructs us not to bow down to or to worship anything or anyone but Him.

Psalm 115:5-7 describes idols the heathen made with their own hands. "They [these idols] have mouths, but they speak not: eyes have they, but they see not: They have ears, but they hear not: noses have they, but they smell not: They have hands, but they handle not: feet have they, but they walk not: neither speak they through their throat."

There is only one true, living God. Jehovah God is the only One worthy of our worship. How good it is to know that God has eyes that see us all the time! He has ears that hear us when we call upon Him. He knows all things and takes care of us in every situation.

We Christians need to take the good news of the Gospel to those caught up in religions that promote the worship of false gods. Their eyes are blinded. They need to hear of the one true God who provided a way for them to be saved.

MEDITATION: List Bible examples of those who worshiped false gods. Note how idol worship brought destruction to their lives.

—Debbie Vaughan

JUNE 16
THE THIRD
COMMANDMENT

Scripture Reading—Exodus 20:7
"Thou shalt not take the name of the Lord thy God in vain; for the Lord
will not hold him guiltless that taketh his name in vain."

While visiting his friend Bobby, Billy heard Bobby's brother, Jake, take God's name in vain when he accidentally hit his finger. What Jake said didn't seem to bother Bobby, but Billy knew it was wrong no matter what had happened.

God's third commandment to the children of Israel is not to take God's name in vain. To take something "in vain" is to use it in a way that has no value or importance. The Jewish people had a high regard for someone's name, and God's name was no different. It was not to be spoken lightly.

Today people generally see nothing wrong with using God's name in a light and irreverent way. You don't need to be out in public long before you hear people use God's name disrespectfully. The most common abuse is saying God's name as a curse word or a swear word. People often use God's name to show surprise or to draw attention to themselves. Even Christians sometimes take God's name in vain when they refer to Him in a casual way. These are all improper ways to use God's name.

The Bible lists many names for God. The most familiar ones are "God the Father," "God the Son," "Jesus," and "God the Holy Spirit." We should use utmost care, respect, and reverence when we talk about God. To say God's name when telling someone the good news of the Gospel is a wonderful way to use God's name. But to use His name as an exclamation as if there was nothing special about it is wrong and displeasing to God.

We must ask God to guard out mouths each day so our words are pleasing to Him. Make sure that you show only the utmost respect and reverence for God's name.

EXERCISE: Search the Bible for different names of God and explore their meanings. Discuss how the various names reveal different aspects of God's character.

—Debbie Vaughan

JUNE 17
THE FOURTH COMMANDMENT

Scripture Reading—Exodus 20:8-11

Billy's little league baseball team had made it to the championship game. He loved playing baseball, and seeing his team make it to the championship was like a dream come true. Then Billy learned that the final game was on Sunday, and he'd have to miss church to participate. This might be his only chance to play in a championship game, and his team had a good chance of winning. What should Billy do?

In the fourth commandment, God told the children of Israel to "remember the sabbath day, to keep it holy" (v. 8). The word *sabbath* comes from the Hebrew word meaning "to stop or to rest from work." God told the people to set apart a special day each week for rest and worship. "For in six days the Lord made heaven and earth . . . and rested the seventh day" (v. 11a).

We live in a busy world. To many, Sunday is a day when they don't have to go to work or school, so they catch up on work at home or activities they enjoy. Too often, they leave God out of their day. Even many Christians go to Sunday morning church and spend the rest of their day working. But we need time to rest and to meditate on our God.

In days gone by, Sundays were special days for worship and family. Today many forget about God and family on the day God wants us to set aside. "Sunday *is* my day of rest," they say. "I'll sleep in and rest." But they forget the second part of the commandment calling for worship.

Others work so hard on Sunday, getting ready to teach or preparing meals, that they get no rest and forget the first part of the commandment. Leaving out either part—rest or worship—is breaking the commandment. Our bodies need the rest, and we also need the time of worship for our spiritual well-being. "Remember the sabbath day, to keep it holy" (v. 8).

SONG TIME: Sing "Brethren, We Have Met to Worship."

—Debbie Vaughan

The Fifth Commandment
Scripture Reading—Exodus 20:12

B illy's mother told him he couldn't have friends over to play if she or his dad wasn't home. One Saturday morning, his parents went to do some errands. While they were gone, Bob, Billy's best friend, called. He wanted to come over and show Billy his new game. Billy knew he wasn't supposed to have friends over, but he thought having Bob over for just a few minutes would be okay. Bob would be gone before Billy's mom and dad would return, and no one would ever know. Was Billy doing the right thing?

In the fifth commandment, God says we should honor our father and mother. To honor someone is to show great respect for him, to value him. Think of all the things your parents do for you: They provide for your needs. They protect you from danger. They teach you many important things. Parents, gifts from God, deserve our honor.

One way we can show honor is to obey our parents. Obedience is doing what we are told to do completely as soon as we are told and with the right attitude. When we obey this way, we are honoring our parents.

Another way to show honor is to be kind to our parents. Look for ways to be kind to your parents. It might be a simple, "I love you." It could be a helping hand when they're tired. Look for ways to show honor through kindness.

Showing parents respect is another way to honor them. We should use great care when we talk to and about our parents. Our words should always show great respect. When people hear us talk about our parents, they should sense respect and honor.

The second part of the verse tells us that if we honor our parents, we have the promise of long life. The New Testament says this is the first commandment with promise—the promise of blessing if we honor our father and mother. Parents are a special gift from God.

EXERCISE: Take time to list how your parents are special to you.

—*Debbie Vaughan*

JUNE 19
THE SIXTH COMMANDMENT

Scripture Reading— Exodus 20:13
"Thou shalt not kill."

The sixth commandment stirs a lot of questions. Some believe no one should go hunting. Others use this commandment to say capital punishment is wrong. The word for *kill* here means murder, which is taking someone's life in an unlawful way. God tells us that murder is wrong.

Because man was created in God's image, all men are important to God. We should never let anything drive us to murder. The Bible gives us examples of people who committed murder, and God punished them for their sin. Cain, the first murderer in the Bible, was first filled with hatred for his brother, Abel. That hatred drove him to murder. God condemns murder, the unlawful taking of life.

The Bible describes another kind of murder in 1 John 3:15. "Whosoever hateth his brother is a murderer: and ye know that no murderer hath eternal life abiding in him." God says that hating others is the same as murdering them in our hearts.

People sometimes do mean things to us. If we're not careful, we can become unforgiving in our feelings. If we do not deal with an unforgiving spirit, we can become bitter and filled with hate. When we hate someone, God views our hate as murder.

Sometimes people get angry. They let their emotions get carried away, and they say unkind things. They might even say, "I hate you." When this happens, they have committed murder in their hearts. We need to be careful of our words. Spoken words are difficult to retrieve, and we can do great damage through angry words.

God tells us to love others. When our hearts are filled with love, they cannot be filled with hatred. In God's eyes, hatred is the same as murder; and we should eliminate it from our lives. "Thou shalt not kill" (Ex. 20:13).

SONG TIME: Sing "Jesus Loves the Little Children." Discuss how God views life as precious.

—Debbie Vaughan

JUNE 20
THE SEVENTH COMMANDMENT

Scripture Reading—Exodus 20:14
"Thou shalt not commit adultery."

After creating the world, God made Eve to be Adam's helper and companion (Gen. 2:18-25). No longer alone, Adam had someone to help him as he tended the garden. He had someone to love and to care for. God created marriage, and everything He created was good.

In His seventh commandment, God tells us that committing adultery is wrong. Marriage is supposed to be for life. After being joined together in marriage, a husband or wife shouldn't have wrong thoughts toward someone else's spouse. People sometimes think, *I wish I could be married to that person instead.* They let their thoughts wander and begin entertaining wrong thoughts.

Learning to control our thoughts is important. As children, we should learn to think right thoughts and to keep our minds pure. That way, controlling our thoughts will be easier after we are married. Philippians 4:8 tells us to think on good things.

God wants homes to be happy places where family members love and serve each other. Think of what you can do to make your home a happier place. Learning to serve and love others now will make it easier for you someday when you have a family of your own. Pray about whom God would want you to marry someday. Ask God to prepare your heart. Then when He brings you and your future spouse together, you will have the marriage He intends you to have.

First Corinthians 13 tells us how love behaves. "Charity [love] suffereth long, and is kind; charity envieth not; charity vaunteth not itself, is not puffed up, doth not behave itself unseemly, seeketh not her own, is not easily provoked, thinketh no evil" (vv. 4-5). Love bears all things, believes all things, hopes all things, and does not fail. When we are thinking the right thoughts and loving as 1 Corinthians 13 instructs us, having wrong thoughts about someone else's wife or husband is difficult.

SONG TIME: Sing "A Christian Home."

—Debbie Vaughan

JUNE 21
THE EIGHTH COMMANDMENT

Scripture Reading—Exodus 20:15
"Thou shalt not steal."

Playing at his friend's house, Billy saw some money lying on a table. He'd been saving his money to buy a new baseball glove and was two dollars short. No one was around. If he took just a couple dollars, who would ever know? What should Billy do?

In His eighth commandment, God tell us not to steal. Stealing is taking or keeping something that belongs to someone else. When you think about stealing, perhaps a bank robber or a criminal comes to mind. Sometimes we don't consider that stealing involves much more than bank robbers and criminals.

People sometimes steal in ways they don't consider to be stealing. Someone shoplifts from a store; we would call that stealing. But what about someone who samples fruit on the way to the supermarket checkout? How does he pay for fruit he's already eaten? What if a store clerk miscounts our change and gives us too much? Is keeping the extra change stealing? If a clerk overcharged us, we would certainly let him know. But what if the mistake was in our favor?

Maybe when the clerk was scanning our merchandise, he missed an item. *It's his fault he missed it,* we think. *I'm paying enough already.* Maybe we're going for a walk and pass a neighbor's apple tree. We notice that the tree is crammed with ripe apples that would taste so good. Would the neighbors miss the apples if we took just a few for ourselves? Should we ask for permission first?

Have you considered that cheating in a game is a form of stealing? When we cheat, we rob the other person of the chance to win. When we consider the correct way to treat others, we will not be tempted to take things from them.

God tells us, "Thou shalt not steal."

DISCUSSION TIME: What are some other ways people steal without calling their activity "stealing"?

—Debbie Vaughan

JUNE 22
THE EIGHTH COMMANDMENT— PART 2

Scripture Reading—Exodus 20:15
"Thou shalt not steal."

We know stealing is taking something that doesn't belong to us. Robbers, for example, take things from others. But what about stealing from God? Immediately, we think of tithing. Tithing is giving 10 percent of our income to God. Preachers often exhort us to give our tithe and not to rob God. What other ways can we steal from God—ways we would never call "stealing"?

"God should get the best part of our day, not the leftovers."

When we don't give God the glory that is due Him—is that stealing from Him? We should praise God daily and give Him "the glory due unto His name" (Ps. 29:2). Do we take credit for what God should get the credit for? Luke 19:40 tell us that if we don't praise God, the rocks will cry out to Him. If He is worthy of our praise, are we praising Him?

Do we give of our time to God? God should get the best part of our day, not the leftovers. Psalm 143:8a says, "Cause me to hear thy lovingkindness in the morning." Robert Murray M'Cheyne said, "I never see the face of man until I have seen the face of God." It is easy, living in our world, to get caught up in the "hurry and scurry" of the day. We have all said, "If I just had more time. There aren't enough hours in the day."

The truth is, if we had more time, we'd fill it up and still want more. Everyone has the same amount of time in a day; it's how we use our time that makes the difference. Are we investing our time in things that will count for eternity? Or are we caught up in the urgent? Ask yourself, "In a week from now, will this possession or activity be important? Will it be important tomorrow?" The day is easier to face if we've first spent time with God.

ACTION POINT: List other ways people steal from God.

—*Debbie Vaughan*

JUNE 23
THE NINTH COMMANDMENT

Scripture Reading—Exodus 20:16
"Thou shalt not bear false witness
against thy neighbour."

B illy's parents were out doing errands when his friend called and asked if he could come over to play. Billy knew his parents didn't want him to have friends over when they weren't there, but he thought nobody would know. Besides, his friend would be gone before his parents came back.

While playing, they accidentally broke a vase. When Billy's mom returned and asked him about her broken vase, he said he didn't know anything about it. Perhaps the dog had knocked the vase over and broken it, he said.

In the ninth commandment, God tells us to speak the truth. Jesus said, "I am the way, the truth, and the life" (John 14:6). According to Proverbs 6:17, one of the seven abominations to God is a lying tongue. God hates lies.

A lie is something we say or do to trick or deceive others. God always wants us to speak the truth. Sometimes people lie, thinking they are helping or protecting someone; but lying is never right. It is never right to do wrong.

Others think, *If I'm always supposed to tell the truth, I need to speak my mind. If I think someone is ugly, I should tell him so.* No, those words would be unkind. We need to think of others and speak only kind words. Just because we think something unkind doesn't mean we have to say it. At the same time, we shouldn't say untrue things to flatter others.

People expect us to tell the truth. If we lie to them, they will distrust what we say. Remember the story of the boy who cried "Wolf!" when there was no wolf? When the wolf came, no one listened to the boy's cries for help. One of the greatest virtues others can know us for is honesty.

Ask God to set a guard on your tongue so you speak only true and honest words.

ACTION POINT: List people in the Bible who lied. What consequences did they suffer because of their lies?

—Debbie Vaughan

The Ninth Commandment— Part 2

Scripture Reading—Exodus 20:16
"Thou shalt not bear false witness against thy neighbour."

God hates lying and wants us always to speak the truth. If we know lying is an abomination to God, why do we lie? People usually lie for two reasons. First, they want to avoid getting in trouble. Second, they want to gain an advantage.

No one likes to be punished. Man's natural tendency is to cover up. We do something wrong and lie instead of facing the consequences. The problem is that we usually need to tell a second lie to cover up the first. Before we know it, we're so covered up in lies that we don't know the truth anymore.

Doing the right thing means facing up to what we've done and dealing with the consequences. To live under a lie is a terrible way to live. Many of us heard when we were children—or we've told our own children—that telling a lie to cover up a wrong will get us into more trouble than the wrong thing we did. When we lie about our bad actions, we've committed two wrongs.

People also lie to gain an advantage. They boast or exaggerate about themselves to look better in the eyes of others. "I caught a fish that was 12 inches long," they say, knowing the fish was only eight inches long. Others tells lies about someone to make him look bad so they will look better. Some people make promises to others, well knowing they won't keep their promise. They want others to think well of them, so they make a commitment but fail to deliver.

If we love others as ourselves, we will always speak the truth in love. In Matthew 22:39b, Jesus commanded, "Thou shalt love thy neighbour as thyself."

BIBLE READING: Psalm 15:1-3a says, "Lord, who shall abide in thy tabernacle? . . . He that . . . speaketh the truth in his heart. He that backbiteth not with his tongue, nor doeth evil to his neighbour." In these verses, what does God say about truth?

—Debbie Vaughan

JUNE 25
The Tenth Commandment

Scripture Reading—Exodus 20:17

"Thou shalt not covet thy neighbour's house, thou shalt not covet thy neighbour's wife, nor his manservant, nor his maidservant, nor his ox, nor his ass, nor any thing that is thy neighbour's."

Billy's friend had gotten a new watch for his birthday. Billy loved the watch. One day, Billy saw his friend take the watch off and lay it on a shelf. His friend forgot where he had put the watch, but Billy remembered. If his friend didn't find the watch, Billy wondered if he could keep it for himself.

The tenth commandment deals with sinful desires. What does it mean to covet? To covet is to desire something that belongs to someone else. Maybe your friend buys a new car. It's a nice car, and you'd like to have a car like that, too. There's nothing wrong with that desire; but when you lose all peace of mind because you must have something, you are coveting. When you want something so badly that you're willing to do anything to get it, you are coveting.

God warns us against covetousness because this wrong desire can lead us to break some of the other nine commandments. Often we're not interested in a certain possession until one of our friends gets it. God warns us not to look at another man's possessions and to covet them.

How do we deal with covetousness? The answer lies in contentment. Learn to be content with what you have. Be thankful for the blessings God has bestowed upon you and do not compare your possessions to those of others. Be happy for others when God gives them nice things but don't set your heart on things that belong to someone else.

Someone who is discontent and is always wanting more is a miserable person. He gets one thing, but it's never enough. The Old Testament tells the story of King Ahab and his desire to possess Naboth's vineyard (see 1 Kings 21). His covetousness led to lies and murder. God tells us to be content and not to covet.

SONG TIME: Sing "Count Your Blessings."

—Debbie Vaughan

JUNE 26
KEEPING THE COMMANDMENTS
Scripture Reading—John 14:15
"If ye love me, keep my commandments."

How many of the Ten Commandments are broken in the following story? Billy was going outside to play when his mom told him to return in time to finish his homework before dinner. Billy met some of his friends at the corner lot for a ballgame.

When someone hit John's ball into the weeds, everyone looked for it. Billy saw the ball but decided not to say anything. When John asked if anyone had seen his ball, everyone said no, even Billy. Billy decided he'd get the ball later and keep it for himself. After all, John had lots of balls; and Billy had lost his only one.

When Billy looked at his watch, he realized he was late. He'd never finish his homework before dinner. Returning home, he went right to work; but his mom called him to dinner before he was finished. When she asked Billy if he'd finished his homework, he said yes.

After dinner, Billy went to his room to read his Bible but decided to work on his homework instead. *It's okay to skip my Bible reading just this once*, he thought.

How easy it is to break God's commandments! Jesus said we should "love the Lord thy God with all thy heart, and with all thy soul, and with all thy mind. . . . Thou shalt love thy neighbour as thyself" (Matt. 22:37, 39). When we concentrate on loving and knowing God, we will *want* to live pleasing to Him. When we love our neighbor as ourselves, we will want to treat him only in a loving way and want only what is best for him.

Keeping the law is not the way of salvation, but it does point us to Christ, who is "the way, the truth, and the life" (John 14:6). Through Christ we come to the Father. When we sin, we should confess our sins. God is "faithful and just to forgive us our sins, and to cleanse us from all unrighteousness" (1 John 1:9).

DO THIS NOW: List the Ten Commandments.

—Debbie Vaughan

JUNE 27
KEEP EVERYONE WORKING
Scripture Reading—Nehemiah 4:6b
"For the people had a mind to work."

Someone who wants to run well in a marathon must practice every day for years. Someone who wants a good harvest must put his hand to the plow until the job is done. If we desire to acquire wisdom, the Bible says we must search "for her as for hid treasures" (Prov. 2:4). We can accomplish these tasks only through plain old hard work.

An entire culture has come to believe that others are responsible to take care of their needs. While many are unable to care for themselves by no fault of their own, others lack the character to work. Each day someone gives little effort, possesses minimal initiative, and lacks personal motivation. Proverbs 18:9 says, "He also that is slothful in his work is brother to him that is a great waster." There is no escape from poor character; once unleashed, it spreads to every area of our lives. At the end of the day, we should exemplify hard work. If we do, we'll achieve more than we ever thought possible. We'll see great success and experience God's blessings.

Some effectively argue that poor work habits are either corrected or cemented at home. Romans 12:11 says, "Not slothful in business; fervent in spirit; serving the Lord." We should work until the job is done, finish tasks on time, do tasks right the first time, avoid procrastination, show initiative, cheerfully serve when others ask us to help, and demonstrate a commendable reputation.

This work ethic should begin at home and continue throughout life. We can accomplish many things if we have a "mind to work." Let's shed the tendencies of laziness and mediocrity, replacing these bad habits with an exceptional, responsible work ethic that will lead to individual achievement, productivity, and family success.

ASSIGNMENT: Read Nehemiah 1-4 and develop an appreciation for a good work ethic.

—Jeff Kahl

JUNE 28
RULING IN RIGHTEOUSNESS

Scripture Reading—Proverbs 29:2
"When the righteous are in authority,
the people rejoice:
but when the wicked beareth rule,
the people mourn."

William Penn, a Quaker preacher, was given a large piece of land between New York and Maryland in 1681. After receiving the property, he wrote, "My God that hath given it [the land] to me . . . will, I believe, bless and make it the seed of a nation." Penn believed Christian character was the basis of good government. In 1682, he wrote the Frame of Government for the colony he had established on the land. In the document, he described what he believed was the purpose of laws. He said laws were to "preserve true Christian and civil liberty in opposition to all unchristian licentious and unjust practices, whereby God may have his due, Caesar his due, and the people their due."

Pennsylvania, like many early colonies, had been established on a foundation of righteousness. Men like William Penn believed God was to be the ruler of the land even above any president, lawmaker, or judge.

A careful study of the original 13 colonies of the United States reveals similar Christian dominance in the founding of each colony. The joint statement of the New England Confederation of 1643 states, "We all came into these parts of America with one and the same end and aim, namely, to advance the kingdom of our Lord Jesus Christ, and to enjoy the liberties of the Gospel in purity with peace." Truly, these settlers believed that God and His ways needed to be the foundation of a great nation. To ignore or to leave God out was—and still is—the greatest mistake any civilization can make. Let us not be guilty of leaving God out.

ACTION POINT: Take time to study various pieces of American currency. Note the similar phrase on each.

—Tom Palmer

Source: Mark A. Beliles and Stephen K. McDowell, *America's Providential History* (Charlottesville, VA: Providence Foundation, 1989), pp. 90, 91.

JUNE 29
AN INDIAN BECOMES A BLESSING
Scripture Reading—Psalm 146

In December of 1620, 102 Pilgrims arrived on the shores of America near Cape Cod. For 66 days, they had lived in an area no bigger than a volleyball court aboard the *Mayflower*. Had they arrived several years earlier, no doubt they would have been wiped out by the Patuxet Indians. However, in 1617, a smallpox epidemic had wiped out the whole tribe except for one Indian named Squanto.

In 1605, an English explorer had captured Squanto and taken him to England. During his nine years there, he learned English. After returning to New England with Captain John Smith, one of the original founders of Jamestown, he was captured again and sold as a slave in Spain. Some local friars rescued him and introduced him to Christianity. Squanto returned home in 1619 to discover that his tribe had been destroyed by smallpox. In the spring of 1621, he joined the Pilgrims, determining to help them survive in the place where his tribe no longer existed.

Squanto taught the Pilgrims how to hunt deer, to catch fish, to trap beaver, and to plant corn and other vegetables. He also introduced the Pilgrims to the tribe of the Wampanoag Indians, the tribe that later joined them for the first Thanksgiving celebration. He even helped secure a peace treaty that lasted more than 50 years. In the words of colonist William Bradford, "Squanto . . . was a special instrument sent of God for their good beyond their expectation."

Things didn't go well for Squanto during his early years, yet God's hand is so evident. Though half of the Pilgrims died during their first year at Plymouth, half survived no doubt in part because of this special Indian God had prepared to assist them. Truly the Pilgrims had much to be thankful for, especially for an Indian named Squanto.

APPLICATION: Discuss how God turned bad into good for Squanto. Can you think of a young man in the Bible who had a similar experience?

—Tom Palmer

Source: Mark A. Beliles and Stephen K. McDowell, *America's Providential History* (Charlottesville, VA: Providence Foundation, 1989), pp. 73, 74.

JUNE 30
THE BEST TEXT IN SCHOOL
Scripture Reading—Psalm 119:1-8

In 1690, a book titled *The New England Primer* was published in Boston. The early Pilgrims and Puritans believed the Word of God needed to be a major part of their children's education. The *Primer*, often called the "Little Bible of New England," was one of the most influential textbooks in the history of American education. This three-by-five-inch, 88-page book was the school textbook of America during the late 1600's and throughout much of the 1700's. More than three million copies of this book were printed.

The Primer used simple verse to teach the alphabet while imparting the wisdom of God's Word in its sayings. In Old English, some words are spelled differently. See if you can read the following sayings:

In **Adam's** Fall, We finned all.

Thy Life to mend, This **Book** attend.

The **Cat** doth play, And after flay.

A **Dog** will bite, a Thief at Night.

An **Eagle's** flight, Is out of fight.

The idle **Fool**, Is whipt at School.

As runs the **Glafs**, Man's life doth pafs.

My Book and **Heart**, Shall never part.

Job feels the rod, Yet bleffes God.

These phrases are from a page in the *Primer*. Each phrase had a picture and a key word beginning the next letter of the alphabet. Each phrase also taught a special lesson. Did you notice the different word spellings?

Though its writing is unusual to us, this book clearly demonstrates that Christian character and values were part of the foundation of education in early America. Early Americans believed their children could never live right without the wisdom of the Bible.

ACTION POINT: Using the letters of the alphabet, create some catchy, little phrases that teach wisdom.

—*Tom Palmer*

Source: Mark A. Beliles and Stephen K. McDowell, *America's Providential History* (Charlottesville, VA: Providence Foundation, 1989), pp. 105, 106.

JULY 1
WHEN THE COMMANDER
IN CHIEF PRAYS

Scripture Reading—Matthew 6:8
*"Be not ye therefore like unto them: for your Father knoweth
what things ye have need of, before ye ask him."*

When most folks hear the name "George Washington," they think of a
great military general or of our first president. Yet the fact that George
Washington was a man of prayer is also noteworthy. In London in 1779, General Knox wrote, "He [George Washington] regularly attends divine service in
his tent every morning and evening, and seems very fervent in his prayers."

One story is a testimony of answered prayer in Washington's life. During
the horrible winter at Valley Forge in 1777-78, Washington faced a crisis; his
men were starving to death. Doubtless the general took this need to the Lord.
Bruce Lancaster relates the following account of answered prayer:

One foggy morning the soldiers noticed the Schuylkill River seemed
to be boiling. The disturbance was caused by thousands and thousands of shad which were making their way upstream in an unusually
early migration. With pitchforks and shovels, the men plunged into
the water, throwing the fish onto the banks. Lee's dragoons rode their
horses into the stream to keep the shad from swimming out of reach.
Suddenly and wonderfully there was plenty of food for the army.

In 1982, the late President Ronald Reagan said, "The most sublime picture in American history is of George Washington on his knees in the snow at
Valley Forge. That image personifies people who know that it is not enough
to depend on our own courage and goodness; we must also seek help from
God, our Father and Preserver." A nation will be blessed by a leader who recognizes his dependence on God.

PRAYER TIME: Pray that our president will acknowledge his dependence on
God in prayer.

—Tom Palmer

Source: Mark A. Beliles and Stephen K. McDowell, *America's Providential History*
(Charlottesville, VA: Providence Foundation, 1989), p. 157.

JULY 2
PRAYER AND
THE WAR OF INDEPENDENCE

Scripture Reading—Psalm 80:14
"Return, we beseech thee, O God of hosts: look down from heaven,
and behold, and visit this vine."

During the War of American Independence, England repeatedly tried to gain stronger control over the 13 colonies. On June 12, 1775, England announced that the colonies could be placed under martial law. In response, the Continental Congress set aside July 20th as a day of prayer. They determined to appeal to the "Great Governor of the World" as they called Him, who "frequently influences the minds of men to serve the wise and gracious purposes of His providential government." They appealed to Christians of all denominations "to assemble for public . . . humiliation, fasting, and prayer."

On July 20th, the entire Congress went as a group to the church of Jacob Duche to hear his message on Psalm 80:14 (you may want to read the verse again).

Only a few months before, Patrick Henry had made his famous speech to the delegates of the Virginia Convention and said the following:

An appeal to arms and to the God of hosts is all that is left us! The millions of people armed in the holy cause of liberty . . . are invincible by any force which our enemy can send against us. Besides, sir, we shall not fight our battles alone. There is a just God who presides over the destinies of nations; and He will raise up friends to fight our battles for us.

Henry closed his speech with the famous quote, "Give me liberty, or give me death!" Those powerful words inspired the colonists not only to fight for liberty but also to seek God in prayer.

HYMN TIME: Find "God of Our Fathers" in a hymnbook. Read through the words or sing them as a family.

—*Tom Palmer*

Source: Mark A. Beliles and Stephen K. McDowell, *America's Providential History* (Charlottesville, VA: Providence Foundation, 1989), pp. 142, 143.

JULY 3
STORMING TO VICTORY
Scripture Reading—Psalm 147:18
"He sendeth out his word, and melteth them: he causeth his wind to blow, and the waters flow."

Students of American history know that the Battle of Yorktown in October of 1781 ended the War of American Independence. What they may not know is that God allowed a storm to be a significant factor in that final victory for the American forces.

British General Cornwallis had stationed his troops at Yorktown, Virginia. General George Washington had begun moving his troops from New York to Yorktown. Simultaneously, a French fleet defeated a British fleet that was heading to Yorktown to reinforce Cornwallis's forces.

Realizing that support would not be coming, Cornwallis decided to retreat across the York River. At 10 p.m. on October 17, he loaded his troops into 15 large boats. Only a few of the boats had landed on the other side when an amazing event occurred.

Cornwallis recorded the event in his own words: "But at this moment, the weather, from being moderate and calm, changed to a violent storm of wind and rain, and drove all the boats, some of which had troops on board, down the river." This event divided Cornwallis's forces, preventing him from taking a stand against Washington's army. Later that day, Cornwallis surrendered to Washington, ending the war.

The Continental Congress responded to the surrender with these words: "Resolved, that Congress will, at two o'clock this day, go in procession to the Dutch Lutheran Church, and return thanks to Almighty God, for crowning the allied arms of the United States and France, with success, by the surrender of the Earl of Cornwallis."

Truly, our great God can do great things, even through the power of a storm.

ACTION POINT: Review Exodus 14. This passage records an occasion when God used His power to win another victory.

—Tom Palmer

Source: Mark A. Beliles and Stephen K. McDowell, *America's Providential History* (Charlottesville, VA: Providence Foundation, 1989), pp. 166, 167.

JULY 4
SO HELP ME GOD

Scripture Reading—Proverbs 14:34
"Righteousness exalteth a nation:
but sin is a reproach to any people."

In 1789, George Washington became the first president of the United States. While taking the oath, Washington placed his hand on a Bible opened to Deuteronomy 28. This chapter records a list of blessings and curses to a nation, based on its faithfulness to the principles of God's Word. Completing the oath, Washington added, "So help me God." Every president since Washington has repeated these last four words in an appeal to God.

Washington gave his inaugural address to Congress. They followed Washington's taking of the oath with their own resolution of April 29. "After the oath shall be administered to the President . . . the Speaker and the members of the House of Representatives, will accompany him to St. Paul's Chapel, to hear divine service performed by the chaplains."

During his inaugural address, Washington said, "No people can be bound to acknowledge and adore the Invisible Hand which conducts the affairs of men more than the people of the United States. Every step by which they have advanced to the character of an independent nation seems to have been distinguished by some token of providential agency." Washington recognized that God's hand was upon him and upon the new nation.

To leave God out of history is to make a great mistake. God is the God of history, and a careful study of history reveals God's control of the affairs of men.

Doubtless our nation has forgotten its spiritual roots. If our nation turned back to God, however, it would discover that God truly blesses a nation that can say, "In God We Trust."

PRAYER TIME: Spend some time in prayer. Tell God how desperately our nation needs His help.

—Tom Palmer

Source: Mark A. Beliles and Stephen K. McDowell, *America's Providential History* (Charlottesville, VA: Providence Foundation, 1989), pp. 174, 175.

JULY 5
PEOPLE WHO ARE "IN THE KNOW"

Scripture Reading
Daniel 11:32—*"And such as do wickedly against the covenant shall he corrupt by flatteries: but the people that do know their God shall be strong, and do exploits."*
Jeremiah 9:24a—*"But let him that glorieth glory in this, that he understandeth and knoweth me [God]."*

Imagine the cruelty of taking a native from the Amazon jungle rainforests and abandoning him in New York City without first teaching him English or anything about the culture. Yet consider how cruel the average person is to himself by going through life without knowing anything about the God who created the universe and keeps it working.

People who don't know anything about God stumble through life with no real sense of direction and with no understanding of their surroundings— much like the jungle native in Times Square. But the Word of God makes many promises to those who *do* know God.

On a subject as immense as God, where do we begin? An adult once observed a little boy who was drawing a picture. When the curious adult asked the boy what he was drawing, the boy replied, "A picture of God."

"But I thought no one knew what God looked like."

The boy smiled. "Oh, they will when I'm finished."

Knowing God isn't as simple as looking at a drawing. It's more like viewing a mountain rising before us and realizing that we'll need to climb it. The climb will require time and effort. Such a pursuit will demand a lifetime.

Knowing the true and living God is a prize worth any effort and any length of time. God said in Jeremiah 9:24, "But let him that glorieth glory in this, that he understandeth and knoweth me, that I am the Lord which exercise lovingkindness, judgment, and righteousness, in the earth: for in these things I delight, saith the Lord."

TABLE TALK: Why do you think it's important to know God? What are some practical ways you can get to know Him better today?

—*T.P. Johnston, Jr.*

JULY 6
MAGNIFICENT
OBSESSION

Scripture Reading—John 17:3
"And this is life eternal,
that they might know thee
the only true God, and Jesus Christ,
whom thou hast sent."

Years ago, a book titled *Magnificent Obsession* by Lloyd Douglas detailed the story of a drunken, immoral young man. His sinful, reckless actions led to a car accident that blinded a young woman. Overcome with remorse, the man not only changed his ways but also vowed to become a surgeon and to restore her sight. That goal became his "magnificent obsession."

Knowing God is the greatest undertaking anyone could imagine. What's amazing is that our God, the Creator of the universe, wants us to have a close relationship with Him. He wants us to know Him, and He rewards those who diligently seek to know Him. "For the eyes of the Lord run to and fro throughout the whole earth, to shew himself strong in the behalf of them whose heart is perfect toward him" (2 Chron. 16:9a).

God is seeking people to bless as they come to know Him. Why should we study God? God says He's the most important thing we can know, but we must know Him on His terms.

Sadly, the common view of God no more resembles Him than the dim flickering of a candle resembles the noonday sun. God has but to speak worlds into existence. He can destroy cities with His breath. He can set a bush on fire without consuming it. He can part the waters of the sea. He can rain dew on a fleece and keep the ground dry. Conversely, He can rain dew on the ground and keep the fleece dry. He can make shadows retreat on a sundial and cause the sun to stand still. He can put sinews upon bones and flesh upon sinews. He can breathe into man the breath of life. He can transform a valley of dry bones into a mighty army. He can calm the tempestuous sea.

TABLE TALK: What's your obsession? What most captivates your attention?

—*T.P. Johnston, Jr.*

JULY 7
WRONG ASSUMPTIONS
ABOUT GOD

Scripture Reading—Isaiah 55:8-9
"For my thoughts are not your thoughts,
neither are your ways my ways, saith the Lord. For as the heavens are
higher than the earth, so are my ways higher than your ways,
and my thoughts than your thoughts."

After feeding his horse, the farmer went into the field to feed his wild birds. While scattering seed, he heard a noise behind him and turned. A deer viciously attacked him, cutting him severely with its antlers and feet. Seriously wounded, the farmer crawled to his pickup truck. Just as he jumped inside, the deer attacked again, ramming its antlers into the truck body. The farmer experienced a long hospital stay and extended recovery.

Family and friends were shocked. The farmer's family had raised the deer and bottle-fed it as a fawn; they'd even allowed the deer in their home. The attack was the last thing anyone would have expected. But true to its nature, the deer felt threatened and attacked.

Just as the farmer and his friends misunderstood the deer, people often misinterpret the true nature of God. Some see Him as a cruel tyrant, watching and waiting for humans to make a mistake so He can go after them. Others see God as a syrupy-sweet grandfatherly type who spoils us when we convince Him to do so. Perhaps if we give a big offering, attend church regularly, or pray using the right words, God will come through. Still others see God as a bigger, better human than we are—some sort of superhero.

God is none of these things. Fortunately for all of us, God has chosen to reveal Himself to us so we can know something of what He is really like. He has revealed Himself primarily in two ways—through His Word, the Bible; and through His Son, the Lord Jesus Christ.

TABLE TALK: Discuss ways family members imagine God is like. Are these ways true and correct?

—T.P. Johnston, Jr.

JULY 8
NONE
LIKE HIM

Scripture Reading—1 Samuel 2:2
"There is none holy as the Lord: for there is none beside thee:
neither is there any rock like our God."

Describing our God can be challenging because we have no adequate way or words to do so. God Himself poses the question in Isaiah 46:5. "To whom will ye liken me, and make me equal, and compare me, that we may be like?"

In order to have an intimate walk with God, to be people who know their God, we need to know foundational truths about God's nature—what God is like. The place to begin is God's Word. The Bible reveals God as totally distinct and above His creation. In other words, God isn't like us—He's not a bigger us. Also, God is above us—He is far better than us in every way. These truths pose the challenge in our getting to know what God is like. He's not like anything we know! Therefore, whatever ideas we may naturally have about God are probably wrong. We must depend on the Scriptures and on God's Son to give us the truth.

When faced with life's difficult circumstances, we may ask, "Why would God let something like that happen?" Part of the explanation is that He doesn't think like we do. His thoughts are so much higher and better than ours.

Responding to a tragedy, people sometimes remark, "I just don't think a loving God would do that." Yet no one has the right to make that statement. What we think about what God does doesn't matter. God is God, and God does what He does, and what He does is always loving. This fact is true whether our minds can comprehend it.

We must learn to adjust our thinking to God's thinking. We must be committed to knowing Him as He really is, not as we *think* He is or how we *wish* Him to be. He has the right to be God.

TABLE TALK: Ask family members to list ways the Bible describes God.

—*T.P. Johnston, Jr*

JULY 9
A CONSUMING FIRE

Scripture Reading—Psalm 68:35

"O God, thou art terrible out of thy holy places: the God of Israel is he that giveth strength and power unto his people. Blessed be God."

What is God really like? The Scriptures give us several "God is" statements—God is love, God is light, God is a Spirit, and God is truth. Interestingly, we find one especially striking "God is" statement: God is holy, holy, holy. The word *holy* means set apart. Bible preachers and teachers sometimes present God's holiness and love as contrasting aspects of His character, but this understanding is incorrect. God's love is an expression of His holiness, not an opposite characteristic.

The Bible illustrates this truth through a symbol or picture. God often uses fire, for example, as a picture of His holiness. Three times the Bible says, "God is a consuming fire." God reveals Himself as a God that man cannot approach except by God's invitation and on His own terms.

In the Bible, those who offended God's holiness frequently died as a result. Uzzah touched the Ark of the Covenant, Nadab and Abihu offered strange fire on God's altar, Ananias and Sapphira lied to the Holy Spirit. The Bible often depicts God's fire of holiness destroying His enemies in judgment.

The Bible uses the symbol of fire to depict not only God's holiness but also His love. Upon the ordination of Aaron and his sons to God's priesthood, after they offered their sacrifice, God's fire consumed the sacrifice, demonstrating God's loving acceptance and pleasure at their offering. God repeated this symbol of fire at the dedication of Solomon's Temple and at Elijah's contest with the false prophets of Baal. When the children of Israel were caught between the Red Sea and the Egyptian army, God surrounded and protected them with a pillar of fire. God's love issues from His holiness.

TABLE TALK: Discuss other ways God's love expresses His holiness.

—T.P. Johnston, Jr.

JULY 10
THE PURIFYING FIRE

Scripture Reading—Job 23:10
"But he knoweth the way that I take:
when he hath tried me,
I shall come forth as gold."

God is up to something! He has an agenda and a motive for everything He brings our way as Christians. Can you guess what that motive is? Pause and see if anyone in your family has an idea.

Fire is a fitting emblem of God's holiness and of His love for His people because of how fire affects various substances. Fire reveals the true value of whatever it touches. If an object is flammable, fire will destroy it. But if an object is a valuable metal, such as gold, fire will not harm it. Fire will only burn away the contaminants and purify the base metal.

The fire of God's holiness demands purity and righteousness. His love, which expresses His holy demand, provides the means of purification. The ultimate purifier was the holy fire of God's wrath. God poured His wrath on His only begotten Son, the Lord Jesus Christ, when He became sin for us and paid for our sins by shedding His blood on the cross.

God also uses the purifying fire of trials, difficulties, disappointments, heartaches, and troubles to burn away impurities in our character so others will see the gold of Himself shining within us. In 1 Peter 4:12, the apostle Peter says, "Beloved, think it not strange concerning the fiery trial which is to try you, as though some strange thing happened unto you." James tells us to count such trials as "joy" (James 1:2). Of course, trials and hardships are hardly enjoyable, but God desires the result of those trials—the pure gold of the character of Jesus Himself.

What is God's motive? He was so delighted with His Son that He wants more sons just like Him.

TABLE TALK: What is God doing in your life right now to burn away impurities and to make you more like Jesus?

—*T.P. Johnston, Jr.*

THE REFINER'S FIRE

Scripture Reading—Malachi 3:3

"And he shall sit as a refiner and purifier of silver: and he shall purify the sons of Levi, and purge them as gold and silver, that they may offer unto the Lord an offering in righteousness."

Years ago in Dublin, Ireland, several ladies met for Bible study. As they studied the Book of Malachi, they came to chapter three, verse three. Deciding that knowing more about the process of silver refining would enhance their understanding, they chose a lady to visit a local silversmith, to make observations, to ask questions, and to report back to the group.

Visiting a silversmith, the lady noticed that he sat close to the vat that held the melted silver ore. She watched him skim off the waste and discard it. "Is it true that you sit by during the refining process?" she asked.

"Yes ma'am," he replied. "You see, the whole process must be very closely attended, for if the silver is heated even slightly too hot, it will all be ruined."

She asked a few more questions, made notes, thanked the silversmith, and prepared to leave. As she grasped the doorknob on her way out, the silversmith called across the room, "Oh, and don't forget to tell them this. I know that the purifying process is complete when I can see my reflection in the silver!"

God's holy nature cannot tolerate anything impure. He not only requires the removal of sin, which takes place only through Christ's blood, but also wants us to bear a positive likeness to the Lord Jesus. He wants to purify our lives so we will reflect His image back to Him.

What's encouraging to know is that during the painful purification process, the Lord sits by, carefully watching as our lives are melted down by fiery trials and hardships. He lovingly makes sure the fire doesn't become one degree hotter than necessary for God to see His reflection in us.

TABLE TALK: Thank the Lord for His "sitting by" during your refining trials.

—*T.P. Johnston, Jr.*

JULY 12
ANTICIPATE TRIALS

God led the children of Israel out of Egypt by the glory cloud. Soon they were at Marah (which means "bitterness"). No, it wasn't Moses' inability to follow directions that had brought them to this place. It was God who had led them to the bitter waters of Marah for the purpose of trying them, and the children of Israel failed miserably. They murmured and complained. Only days earlier, they were praising God with loud voices; and now they were lifting their voices against God and His man. Moses found himself in charge of three million gripers!

Sooner or later, God leads all of His children to bitter places to see if they will pass the test. It's not a matter of "if" but "when" trials will come. These trials are really blessings in disguise, and they are disguised so well that we would never consider them beneficial until they are passed.

Growing in Christlikeness is never cheap. It comes with a price tag. Alexander McClaren said, "The pathway of spiritual progress will be marked by the bloody footprints of wounded self-love." Affliction is God's way of deposing self. We should view adversity, trials, and temptations as opportunities to dethrone the "old man."

We may have no choice concerning the bitter circumstances that come our way, but we sure have a choice in how we respond to these trials. The bitter waters of Marah were made sweet by divine provision. The Lord told Moses to cut down the tree and cast it into the waters. When he did, the waters were healed. When we find ourselves drinking from a bitter fountain, our answer is also found in a tree. The cross of Christ has the amazing ability to heal the debilitating effects of bitter circumstances. Healing is never far off when we can look beyond the situation and remember the mighty atoning work of Calvary.

CONSIDER: Think about the trials Jesus went through. How did He handle difficulties? What can we learn from Him about handling trials?

—*Harold Vaughan*

JULY 13
BENEATH THE CLAY

Scripture Reading—1 Peter 1:7a
"That the trial of your faith,
being much more precious
than of gold."

In Bangkok, Thailand, in the mid-20th century, the government decided to build a large highway through a village. But in the path of the planned road sat a Buddhist monastery with a little chapel. The government had to relocate the monastery—including a heavy, 11-foot clay statue of Buddha—to another place. Using a crane, the government workers moved the monastery in sections.

When the workers transported the statue of Buddha to the new location and began to lower it into place, the clay on the statue began crumbling and falling off. The people were afraid because this religious symbol was precious to them, and they didn't want it destroyed. Yet the more the workers tried to place the statue, the more it fell apart. Eventually, all the clay fell off. Suddenly, the workers stared in amazement, realizing the statue was pure gold underneath. Before the statue was moved, people estimated it was worth about $50,000. Today, that golden Buddha is worth millions, and hundreds of thousands visit the site annually.

Things aren't always as they appear. Beneath the clay exterior, problems are solid gold. There is untold value in the trials God allows and designs for His people. Paul said the trying of our faith is "more precious than of gold" (1 Pet. 1:7).

You may be living a clay-pot existence. The trials you are going through are the means God is using to chip away the clay. Beneath the surface lies untold wealth. This is why we should welcome trials and not despise them. The benefits that emerge can be the source of untold value to many, many people.

FOOD FOR THOUGHT: Read Hebrews 12:5-7. It tells us not to despise training, discipline, and correction from the Lord. Can you recall a difficult trial in your family or in the Bible that proved to be beneficial?

—Harold Vaughan

JULY 14
THE BENEFITS OF CONFLICT
Scripture Reading—1 John 2:13b
"I write unto you, young men, because ye have overcome the wicked one."

When conflict comes, it can be a stepping stone or sinking sand. Hardships will move us closer to or farther away from God. Calamity can be a step forward or a slide backward. Nothing in life can harm us unless we allow ourselves to develop a bad attitude.

Conflict develops our integrity. Abraham Lincoln said, "Rivers follow the line of least resistance; that's why they're so crooked." A person who has no challenges becomes flabby. An athlete disciplines himself to get in shape. Because physical fitness has so many barriers, competitors are forced to work at it. Those who desire to excel in sports must pay a price to get in shape. The rigorous terrain of the spiritual landscape provides an excellent obstacle course for us as Christian soldiers. Life isn't always easy.

God wants us to be victorious. Overcomers view obstacles as opportunities. God gives us barriers not to destroy us but to develop us. Let's recall how the devil mercilessly attacked Job. His home, health, and herds were all destroyed. In her despair, his wife even turned against him. Yet in all this, Job didn't curse or charge God foolishly. He held his tongue. Job learned things about himself he couldn't have learned any other way. He was blessed more after the calamity than before.

"Forasmuch then as Christ hath suffered for us in the flesh, arm yourselves likewise with the same mind: for he that hath suffered in the flesh hath ceased from sin" (1 Pet. 4:1). God can use affliction to purge our hearts. Suffering has a way of causing us to concentrate on things that are really important.

There's no such thing as a saint who hasn't suffered. Let's not buy into the notion that God's people are immune from sorrow. Rather, we must understand that trouble can develop our integrity.

THOUGHT: "There can be no victory where there is no combat." —Richard Sibbes

—Harold Vaughan

JULY 15
DETERMINATION
VERSUS DESPONDENCY

Jesus said John the Baptist was the greatest human ever born, yet we find him sitting in prison in despair near the end of his life. He sent word to Christ and asked, "Art thou he [the Messiah] that should come, or do we look for another?" (Matt. 11:3b). If the "greatest" could get disheartened, we can also. Jesus sent him a reassuring, faith-building word.

Another great man in the Bible was Elijah. He had called down fire, slain the prophets of Baal, controlled the weather conditions, and seen miracles. Yet we find him sitting under a juniper tree, praying to die. These examples demonstrate that even the strongest and most godly people are subject to despondency on occasion. George Whitfield said, "The best of men are men at best."

Discouraging events happen to everyone, but we can determine ahead of time to avoid what John Bunyan called the "Slough of Despond." Do you remember in *Pilgrim's Progress* when Christian fell into the swamp?

A young Oriental student decided to mock his elderly teacher. The boy caught a small bird and cupped it in his hands behind his back. He approached the sage with this plan in mind: He would ask the old man what he had in his hand. If the teacher answered correctly, the boy would ask the teacher if the bird was dead or alive. If the old man said "alive," the boy would crush the bird. Should the teacher say "dead," the boy would release the bird.

Approaching his instructor, the student asked, "What do I have in my hand, old man?"

The teacher responded, "A bird, my son."

"Is he alive or dead, old man?"

"The answer to that question, my son, is in your hands."

Disappointments happen to all of us. How we choose to respond is our choice. Determination or despondency: the decision is in our hands.

SONG TIME: As a family, sing "I Have Decided to Follow Jesus."

—Harold Vaughan

JULY 16
GOD'S PURPOSE
IN TRIALS

Scripture Reading—James 1:2-3
"My brethren, count it all joy when ye fall into divers temptations; knowing this, that the trying of your faith worketh patience."

What's this? Consider it pure joy when we fall into all sorts of trials? No, this isn't a misprint! The words *divers temptations* refer to numerous trials. God tells us to rejoice when we're tested. To put it another way, we should face our ordeal with a smile!

Alexander McClaren said, "Every affliction comes with a message from the heart of God." Maybe you or your father has done wood crafting. When a cabinet maker wants to join two boards together, he puts glue on each piece of wood. Then he positions clamps on the planks to hold them in place. The clamps provide the needed pressure until the glue sets. Once the bond is set, the cabinet maker can remove the clamps because they're no longer needed. The union is set, and no external pressure is required.

The purpose of adversity is to bind our will to God's. As we respond properly under pressure, the Lord often "removes the clamps." God is committed for our will to be fused with His. Remember how Jesus prayed, "Not my will, but thine, be done" (Luke 22:42b).

We are maturing spiritually when our desires are identical to God's. Perhaps we remember that old song "Farther Along" (by J.R. Baxter and W.B. Stevens). The first line goes like this:

Tempted and tried will oft make you wonder,

Why it should be this all the day long.

The chorus finishes the song with the following words:

Cheer up my brother.

Live in the sunshine.

We'll understand it all by and by.

It's not our place to figure out *why* things happen. Our responsibility is to "count it all joy" in the midst of problems.

SCRIPTURE: Read James 1:2-3 aloud together three times.

—Harold Vaughan

JULY 17
MORE THAN CONQUERORS

Scripture Reading—Romans 8:37b
"We are more than conquerors
through him that loved us."

Circumstances influence us, but they don't shape us. Our reaction to our situation, not the circumstances, makes us what we are. Have we heard people say, "I'm getting along very well under the circumstances"? The problem is that they are "under" the load, but life is much more pleasant on top! It has been said, "Circumstances are like a mattress: when we are on top, we rest in comfort; but when underneath, we are smothered." God says we are more than champions in any circumstance!

India is known for its millions of Hindus. Religious festivals are frequent in that country. In some of these celebrations, Hindus load a big wagon, called a "Juggernaut," with idols. These chariots are pulled through the streets, and worshipers bow before this idolatrous procession. Some fanatical Hindus get so caught up in the ceremony that they throw themselves under the heavy wagon. The tremendous weight of the wagon smashes and kills them. Others hop on the wagon and are transported down the street. Some are *crushed* while others are *carried* by the same vehicle.

Circumstances are like the Juggernaut. If we're underneath circumstances, we get crushed. But if we're on top, the Juggernaut carries us farther down the road.

God has provided triumphant living for each of His children. He has called us to victory He has already bestowed upon us. Our text says, "We are more than conquerors..." It does not say we *will be* victorious. It says we *are* (present tense) conquerors. Spiritual growth is living out what we already are. If God says we are conquerors, we should act like it. We should dare to believe God!

THOUGHT: God wants us to be victors, not victims; to grow, not to grovel; to soar, not to sink; to overcome, not to be overwhelmed.

—Harold Vaughan

JULY 18
PASSING
THE TEST

Scripture Reading—1 Corinthians 10:13

Mathematics demands that a student master elementary concepts before learning how to solve more complex problems. The whole educational process is built on the idea that we must pass the test before moving on to new information. Before a high school student graduates, it's imperative that he makes the grade.

In God's Bible school, it's certain we will be tested. God places all of His children in trying circumstances sometimes. These tests are "common to man." That means we're not the first to find ourselves in a tight place. Watchman Nee said, "You will never learn anything new about God except through adversity." Trials are God's way of making us grow up. Often it's the furnace of affliction that accelerates our growth in grace.

God is grooming a bride for His Son. The Bible refers to us as the bride of Christ. The bride is without spot, wrinkle, and blemish. That means the Lord has a lot of work to do in order to make the bride ready for His Son. Adversity is the divine sandpaper God uses to smooth out the saints. Temptations, trials, and tribulations are the means God uses to grow us up.

"Beloved, think it not strange concerning the fiery trial which is to try you, as though some strange thing happened unto you: But rejoice, inasmuch as ye are partakers of Christ's sufferings; that, when his glory shall be revealed, ye may be glad also with exceeding joy" (1 Pet. 4:12-13). We must remember two truths about adversity. God permits it and limits it. It's neither unusual nor strange; it's to be expected and even welcomed. Hardships are part of the curriculum in Hallelujah Academy or God's Bible School.

It is said that most men are "born crying, live complaining, and die disappointed." But God wants better from us! When difficulties come, we need to view them as tests. If we respond properly, we'll pass the test. If we fail, we need to take the test over!

ASSIGNMENT: Together, read 1 Corinthians 10:13 aloud five times in a row.

—Harold Vaughan

JULY 19
THE CRAB
COMES BACK

Scripture Reading
Matthew 7:7—*"Ask, and it shall be given you; seek, and ye shall find;*
knock, and it shall be opened unto you."
Philippians 4:6—*"Be careful for nothing; but in every thing*
by prayer and supplication with thanksgiving
let your requests be made known unto God."

Prayer requests from a child can seem childish, especially to adults who think they understand what prayer is all about. That's why the prayer of my four-year-old, Andrew, seemed childish to me when he prayed that we'd find the hermit crab. It was just a bedtime prayer, and I had almost forgotten that we'd lost a hermit crab three weeks before.

We'd gotten hermit crabs for Julie and Andrew since dogs and cats were not permitted in our rental property. Hermit crabs are quiet and fun to play with, and they don't eat much or smell bad.

Julie had been playing with her crab on the floor when the phone rang. After answering the phone, she returned to find her crab gone. I searched everywhere—under furniture, in the heater vents, and in every other place I thought a crab might hide. After three weeks, I figured the crab was gone forever. Then came the childlike prayer.

At 1 a.m., I went downstairs on a baby-bottle-warming assignment. When I reached the bottom of the stairs, I was about to kick what I thought was a toy out of the way when I saw the crab. Holding it in my hand, just hours after the bedtime prayer, I realized with amazement that childish prayers do matter to God. In the morning, our home buzzed with excitement when I shared the answer to prayer—the crab was back.

Does your family have a special prayer request? Let one of your children talk to God about it. The results may amaze you, too!

PRAYER TIME: Ask your family for pet prayer requests. Take them to the Lord.

—Tom Palmer

JULY 20
Anytime Prayers

Scripture Reading—Psalm 55:16-17
"As for me, I will call upon God;
and the Lord shall save me.
Evening, and morning, and at noon,
will I pray, and cry aloud:
and he shall hear my voice."

I can't say that I was trying to make an impression. I was simply doing what my family and I do nearly every time we get into our vehicle to go somewhere. For years, our family has habitually prayed before trips, asking God for safety and direction.

Later, a friend of one of my children who had been traveling with us spoke about my prayer. "It was like your dad just started talking to God," he said. No, we hadn't gotten on our knees or bowed our heads, and I certainly hadn't closed my eyes since I was driving. Yet there in our truck, we had talked to God.

Many Christian families routinely pray before meals or at bedtime, but why stop there? A typical day is filled with more opportunities to talk to God. We can talk to God when we get in the car, maybe asking a different family member to lead in prayer for each trip. It's good to pray before the family leaves for school or work.

We can pray during times of corrective discipline or decision making. Prayer also becomes special when someone is sick or fearful. We can also talk to God before going shopping or making a purchase. I have friends who close phone calls with family and friends in prayer.

Families who pray together—and pray often—will be blessed. One of the greatest blessings is the continual awareness of God's presence. Constant access to God in prayer makes God more real to young children, teens, even moms and dads. When is the next time your family will talk to God? Don't wait long—He's already listening.

PRAYER TIME: Pause right now to thank God for always listening when we pray.

—Tom Palmer

A Shopping List for God

Scripture Reading
Philippians 4:6-7—*"Be careful for nothing; but in every thing by*
prayer and supplication with thanksgiving
let your requests be made known unto God.
And the peace of God, which passeth all understanding,
shall keep your hearts and minds through Christ Jesus."
Psalm 119:10—*"With my whole heart have I sought thee:*
O let me not wander from thy commandments."

Almost every kitchen boasts a shopping list. It may be held to a refrigerator by a magnet or be attached to a tablet in the junk drawer. A shopping list is a simple tool that helps us to be organized and not to forget what we need the next time we go to the store. Nobody likes driving back to the store because we forgot one ingredient we needed to finish a recipe.

A family prayer list is similar to a shopping list. By keeping record of prayer needs, our family prayer time is more structured, and we are less likely to forget important prayer requests.

When our children were small, we used prayer lists that included pictures of people and places we could pray for. Once our children could read and write, we encouraged them to use a small prayer notebook divided into sections by prayer request topic. For example, our church, our nation, our school, unsaved people, and missionaries.

We prepare a family prayer list and display it near the dinner table so we can remember needs during the meal. A list is also a great place to record answers to prayer. A checkmark, the date, and a summary of the answered request serve as a constant reminder of the wonderful things God has done.

When you prepare your next shopping list, don't forget your little notebook. It will help you remember your requests when you talk to the God who can do anything.

ASSIGNMENT: As a family, choose 10 prayer needs. Write them down and pray through them once each day over the next week.

—Tom Palmer

JULY 22
PLEASE LEAVE
A MESSAGE

Scripture Reading—Psalm 66:16-20
"But verily God hath heard me;
he hath attended to the voice of my prayer.
Blessed be God, which hath not turned away my prayer,
nor his mercy from me" (vv. 19-20).

You dial the number, you wait, and the phone rings. *Click!* "We're sorry," a voice says, "but we're not able to come to the phone right now, but your call is important to us. Please leave your name, your number, and a short message; and we'll get back to you as soon as possible. B-e-e-e-e-p."

More than once, you've hung up in frustration. "I want to talk to a person, not a machine!" you exclaim.

If telephones are a miracle of modern communication, answering machines could be its menace. Yes, they serve a purpose. And sometimes leaving a message *is* sufficient for the moment. But when you want to talk to a real person, you won't be satisfied to leave a message and hope to hear from him or her later.

What a blessing to know that God doesn't have an answering machine! He's always accessible, always available. He doesn't sleep, He doesn't take days off, and He's never on vacation. You'll never get a busy signal because He's talking to someone else, and He'll never ignore you because He saw your name on caller ID.

Several years ago, while dealing with a runaway teen, I called the children's services office in my county. It was the middle of the day, and I got an answering machine. The voice told me that if I had an emergency, I could leave a message, and a case worker would get in touch with me soon. What a shame! No one was available when I needed help.

Do you need to talk to God? Go ahead and call. He's listening and wants to hear from you.

DISCUSSION: As a family, discuss times or situations when you are thankful you didn't need to leave God a message.

—Tom Palmer

JULY 23
DADDY,
I NEED YOU

Scripture Reading—Psalm 145:18-19
"The Lord is nigh unto all them that call upon him,
to all that call upon him in truth.
He will fulfil the desire of them that fear him:
he also will hear their cry,
and will save them."

Few things are more terrifying to a child than a big thunderstorm in the middle of the night. When the wind is roaring, the rain is pounding, the lightning is flashing, and the thunder is rumbling, most youngsters experience total panic. Parents are used to hearing the desperate cry. "Daddy! Daddy!"

Amazingly, most dads aren't even aware of the storm. A tornado could pick up the house and move it three blocks, and they wouldn't realize the change until morning. Yet that cry does something incredible.

Sitting on the edge of his bed, Dad asks himself, *Is it raining?* He heads down the hallway as the cries echo above the rumble of the rolling thunder. Entering the bedroom, Dad stumbles over a toy or two and sits on the edge of the bed. Intermittent flashes of lightning illumine a cowering figure on the bed. Dad's big hand grasps the shaking little hand under the sheet. "It's okay," he whispers. "I'm here now."

And yes. Everything's now wonderfully okay. The child's breathing returns to normal. The shaking and crying cease. Peaceful rest returns though the storm continues. Dad's presence brings a sense of peace even during the most frightful times of life.

So it is with our Heavenly Father. Peace is not produced by the absence of trouble; rather, it is produced by the presence of God when His children experience trouble. Prayer brings a peaceful calm because prayer reminds us that God is with us and will keep us safe. What a blessing to know that when we call, our Heavenly Father is right there.

ACTION POINT: Ask family members to share an occasion when they were afraid. What helped them deal with their fear?

—*Tom Palmer*

JULY 24
GOD DID IT

Scripture Reading
Jeremiah 33:3—*"Call unto me, and I will answer thee,*
and shew thee great and mighty things,
which thou knowest not."
1 Samuel 12:24—*"Only fear the Lord, and serve him in truth*
with all your heart: for consider how great things
he hath done for you."

My son, Andrew, was a preschool-age boy when I invited him to join me on one of my special walks. Occasionally, I went to a secluded place to read, study, and pray. I told him to bring his little blue New Testament so we could read the Bible together out on the big rock. After I parked the van, we walked a short distance to the rocky ledge.

After we climbed up on a large rock and got situated, Andrew noticed that his New Testament was missing. I suggested that he pray and ask the Lord to help us find it. He prayed, and we shared a good time together.

Later, as we headed back to the road, I began praying. I asked God to show my boy that He was real by answering his prayer. We retraced our path and kicked leaves and sticks out of the way, hoping the Testament would appear. There was no sign of it anywhere.

When we reached the road, our van came into view. Andrew lagged behind as I walked the road's shoulder. Both of us were still looking, and I was still praying; but now my prayer was more intense.

As we made our way over a slight rise just before reaching the van, I saw the blue Bible. But I didn't say a word; I just walked right on by. Seconds later, I heard Andrew's outburst of excitement. In essence, his response was, "God did it!" And yes, God had. He loves to answer the prayers of His children—and of our children—when they ask.

DO THIS NOW: Recall a specific occasion when God answered a special prayer request for your family. How many details can you remember?

—*Tom Palmer*

JULY 25
HOW DOES GOD ANSWER PRAYER?

Scripture Reading—1 John 5:14-15

"And this is the confidence that we have in him, that, if we ask any thing according to his will, he heareth us: And if we know that he hear us, whatsoever we ask, we know that we have the petitions that we desired of him."

No study of prayer would be complete without some consideration of the *way* God answers prayer. We must thoroughly understand not only our part in asking but also God's part in answering. When we pray, God may choose to respond in one of the following ways:

1. A Definite Way—God may do what we request of Him. Often our specific request will get a specific answer.

2. A Denied Way—God may choose to say "no." In His sovereignty, He may know that our request would not be good for us if He granted it.

3. A Delayed Way—God may ask us to wait. He may answer the request but only when His timing is best for us.

4. A Different Way—God may have something in His plan other than what we desire. He may answer but not in the way we thought He would.

We often assume that answered prayer means God does exactly what we want, but prayer involves the yielding of our wills to God's. In other words, we ask God for what we want but follow up by asking God for what *He* wants. By recognizing that God is God, we acknowledge that He has our approval of anything He chooses to do. This attitude allows us to pray with thanksgiving (Phil. 4:6; Col. 4:2) for the answer God will give according to His will.

God delights to answer the prayers of His children. We must, however, allow Him the freedom to answer as He chooses without becoming frustrated, impatient, or even angry. This attitude provides the blessing of answered prayer.

THANKSGIVING: Thank God for the work He is doing in answer to prayer as He cares for the needs of your family.

—*Tom Palmer*

JULY 26
TRUE WORSHIP
Scripture Reading—Genesis 22:1-12

Is your family concerned about what's happening these days in the name of worship? I am, and I believe we have reason to be concerned. Many connect worship only to a church experience; they have no concept of worship beyond going to church on Sunday. They don't understand that true worship involves a heart attitude toward God as God. As born-again Christians, we should experience worship every day of our lives, no matter where we are or what we're doing.

Within the human heart, God has created an inborn need to worship. God created us this way so we would find our greatest satisfaction in Him. Unfortunately, sin defiled our nature and separated us from God. We began worshiping the things God created rather than God Himself (see Rom. 1:19-25).

Confused about worship, many Christians and churches are suffering a *worship crisis,* which has expressed itself in several ways. Some churches have returned to more formal, traditional forms of worship. Others have rejected anything formal or traditional and have chosen a contemporary style with worship leaders, worship teams, and worship bands. Some have rejected style altogether and have turned to activities, programs, and entertainment—all in an attempt to rediscover worship!

In the story of Abraham and Isaac (Gen. 22), we find the first mention of "worship" in the Bible. "And Abraham said unto his young men, Abide ye here with the ass; and I and the lad will go yonder and worship, and come back again to you" (v. 5). When Abraham took Isaac to the mountain to sacrifice him to the Lord, we see one of the best examples of *true worship* in Scripture. This story illustrates that *true worship is giving back to God what's rightfully His.* Isaac belonged to God, and Abraham simply gave him back as God had requested (v. 2). Hopefully, this story will help you grasp the meaning of *true worship* in a more helpful, practical way.

ACTION POINT: What's your family's understanding of "true worship"? Allow each member to share his thoughts.

—*Jack Palmer*

JULY 27
WHY DO WE WORSHIP?

Scripture Reading—Psalm 95:6
*"O come, **let us worship and bow down**:*
let us kneel before the Lord our maker"
(emphasis added).

There's nothing as frustrating as doing something and not knowing why we're doing it, but a lot of things in life are like that. Many folks go through life knowing they need to worship but not having a clue why. Is it any wonder worship is frustrating to so many?

God has placed the need to worship in every human heart, and that's why man is different from every other part of God's creation. God created man to worship Him. How tragic that sin destroyed our ability to worship God apart from God's saving grace!

Even with a defiled human nature, man desires to worship. He just doesn't always know who, how, or why. That's why many unsaved people worship animals, birds, trees, mountains, spirits, and idols.

Why do we Bible-believing Christians worship God? The best answer is because *worship is God's command!* Psalm 95:6 and many other verses make that truth clear. According to Psalm 95, we worship God for the following reasons:

1. Because He is *our Savior* (v. 1)
2. Because He is *so great* (v. 3)
3. Because He is *above all gods* (v. 3)
4. Because He is *all-powerful* (v. 4)
5. Because He is *our Creator* (v. 6)
6. Because He is *our God* (v. 7)

As Christians, it's essential that we develop a heart for worship in our families. We need not only to teach them that they must worship God but also to help them understand why. Only as we recognize the value of true worship will it become a vital part of family life.

ACTION POINT: What are some reasons worshiping God is essential for your family?

—Jack Palmer

HOW DO WE WORSHIP?

Scripture Reading—John 4:19-24
"God is a Spirit: and they that worship him
*must worship him **in spirit and in truth**" (v. 24, emphasis added).*

As the congregation entered the church auditorium, they not only found their seats but also found friends for "fellowship" before the service began. They were loud, and their laughter rang through the auditorium. Anyone listening would have heard conversations about the weather, sports, hobbies, yard-sale bargains, and school activities.

The organ began playing, but that only meant people needed to talk louder to be heard. The music was intended to encourage quiet meditation in preparation for worship. Unfortunately, no one seemed to be paying any attention.

The service began with halfhearted singing. To liven things up, the pastor told a joke. Everyone roared with approval as he began to get "in the spirit." Next came endless announcements and comments about meaningless activities planned to "keep folks busy." And on it went . . .

Nine-year-old Bobby turned to his father. "Daddy, is this really how we worship God?"

His dad sat in stunned silence, having no idea how to answer such a loaded question. In fact, he'd never thought about the question before. Perhaps he needed to take a serious look at the whole matter of worship before he could give a proper answer to his son.

How would you answer Bobby's question? Your answer needs to be based on the truth of God's Word. A good place to start is today's verse. We must worship God "in spirit" (from the heart) and "in truth" (according to God's Word). The implication is that worship must come from a heart of genuine sincerity toward God. Worship shouldn't be trivial; it should be a life-changing experience intended to deepen our walk with God and to bring us to a more intimate relationship with Him.

ACTION POINT: Request family members to ask questions about worship. Find biblical answers to their questions.

—Jack Palmer

WORSHIPING GOD
Scripture Reading—Revelation 22:1-9

It's alarming to observe how easily people worship the wrong things. No, most Christians would never dream of worshiping an idol, a tree, or an animal like heathen people do. But many worship their beautiful, new church building. They worship their loving, caring pastor or someone special to them. Some even worship a Christian organization. They allow someone—or something—to take God's place in their worship. The simple truth is that *anything that takes God's place is an idol!*

When God gave Moses the Ten Commandments on Mount Sinai, He said, "I am the Lord thy God, which have brought thee out of the land of Egypt, out of the house of bondage. *Thou shalt have no other gods before me*" (Ex. 20:2-3, emphasis added).

In today's Scripture reading, we read about the apostle John who wrote the Book of Revelation. In the reading, we find a valuable, interesting principle about worship. The Angel of God revealed to John the great things he should write. John was so overwhelmed with the experience that he fell at the angel's feet to worship him (v. 8). The angel said John must not worship him but "*worship God*" (v. 9, emphasis added) and only God. Though the angel was a heaven-sent being from God, he was not an object of worship. So important is this truth that it's God's last statement in the Bible about worship.

Is God our focus in worship? Any worship without God at the center is false worship. It may stir our emotions and make us feel good. It may make us want to do better and try harder. It may even draw us closer to others. But if God isn't the object of our worship, that "worship" contributes nothing of eternal value to your lives. It's nothing more than "wood, hay, [and] stubble" (1 Cor. 3:12).

ACTION POINT: Is your family allowing anything to take God's place as the object of your worship? If so, confess your worship of that object, remove it, and make God the center of your worship experience.

—*Jack Palmer*

JULY 30
WHAT IS WORSHIP?—PART 1

Scripture Reading—Psalm 105:3-4
*"Glory ye in his holy name: let the heart of them rejoice that **seek the Lord.** **Seek the Lord,** and his strength: **seek his face** evermore"*
(emphasis added).

We can't bake a delicious cake unless we find the proper ingredients, measure properly, mix properly, and bake at the proper temperature for the proper length of time. If we try to create a cake another way, we'll probably produce a "flop."

So it is with worship. Proper worship has many dimensions. Most essential is the fact that genuine worship must be *God-centered.*

What many churches consider to be "worship" is disturbing. In many cases, this worship is shallow and meaningless or a dull, boring routine. It's going through the motions with no purpose or results. In other situations, "worship" means laughter, jokes, foolishness, and fun. "No one's going to accuse our church of being dull and boring," some say. "We're here to have a good time!"

Others consider a good worship experience to be filled with emotional manipulation that stirs good feelings. "You have to make people feel good," they say, "or they won't come back!" The loud and exciting atmosphere works people up and draws big crowds. There's no substance or depth, but that's okay. "You have to give people what they want."

A heart that truly *seeks God* is at the core of worship that pleases Him and rewards His people. This kind of worship begins in the *heart*, is carried on in the *home*, and culminates in the *church* where God's people meet.

Do you have a heart that *seeks God?* If so, you are a true God-worshiper. As a family, is *seeking God* the goal of your family worship? When you go to church, are you *seeking God* and what He has for your family? If so, you won't be disappointed. God says, "And ye shall *seek me, and find me,* when ye shall search for me with all your heart" (Jer. 29:13, emphasis added). Genuine worship is *seeking God.*

ACTION POINT: Evaluate your family's worship experience. Is God central to all you consider worship?

—*Jack Palmer*

JULY 31
WHAT IS WORSHIP?—PART 2
Scripture Reading—Psalm 105:1-5

Psalm 105:1-5 teaches wonderful truths about worship. We have seen that our worship must be God-centered; anything else is false worship. Worship is our heart's response to God as God. Therefore, important elements should be part of our worship experience. The psalmist defines some of them for us.

1. **Giving thanks to God (v. 1)**
   A true heart of worship continually overflows with praise and thanksgiving for all God has done. We must never get tired of telling God, "Thank you!" God's heart rejoices when His people are generous with their thanksgiving.

2. **Praying (v. 1)**
   Worshiping properly is impossible without communion with God in prayer. Prayer may be in private, as a family, or in public; but prayer always characterizes true worship.

3. **Testifying to others (v. 1)**
   Telling others what God has done for you is giving glory to God for His blessings in your life. Our testimony should be the public expression of our appreciation for God's goodness.

4. **Singing unto the Lord (v. 2)**
   A worshiping heart is a singing heart. When God saved you, He put a new song in your mouth (Ps. 40:3). Often when folks sing in church, they never think of the words they're singing. You can sing all the hymns and never worship, but you can't worship without singing from your heart.

5. **Witnessing for the Lord (v. 2)**
   Our witness is telling others about Jesus Christ and His saving grace. The most wonderful thing God ever did for you was your salvation. Let others know He can do the same for them.

ACTION POINT: Check up on your worship by using these five expressions of true worship.

—Jack Palmer

WHAT IS WORSHIP?—PART 3
Scripture Reading—Psalm 105:1-5

Psalm 105 lists important elements God is looking for in our worship.

1. Rejoicing in God (v. 3)

True worship is always characterized by great rejoicing. Worshiping God should be a joyous experience.

2. Seeking God (vv. 3-4)

We looked at this aspect more closely in a previous devotional.

3. Remembering what God has done (v. 5)

Forgetfulness is spiritually dangerous. Psalm 106:7, 13, and 21 tell us that forgetfulness is the first step toward spiritual poverty ("leanness . . . [of] their soul," v. 15). Faithfully remembering what God has done draws our hearts into worship.

4. Giving God glory (v. 3)

For God's child, everything should be an opportunity to glorify God (1 Cor. 10:31). It doesn't matter where you are or what you're doing. You can worship God by giving Him the glory.

Have you considered what God wants most in your worship? You can give Him your time, your tithes, your talents, and your treasures and still not give what pleases Him most. The best expression of true worship is when you give *yourself.*

One Sunday at the mission church, the pastor preached to the Indians about the importance of giving oneself to God, based on Romans 12:1-2. God spoke to the Indian chief's heart. Going to the altar, he said, "Chief give knife and bow to God," and sat down. The pastor continued to preach. Again, the chief came forward. This time, he said, "Chief give pony to God," and sat down. As the message ended, God showed the chief what He really wanted. Returning to the altar again, he said, "Chief give self to God." That day, the chief learned the meaning of worship that pleases God.

When God saved you, He gave you all of Himself. The question is, does God have all of you?

ACTION POINT: Is God Lord of all, or isn't He? Only you can decide!

—Jack Palmer

LET'S BE A BARNEY
Scripture Reading—Acts 11:19-26

The Book of Acts tells an inspiring story of a man named Barnabas who made his reputation from his deep commitment to the ministry of encouragement. His given name was Joses, but those who knew him well nicknamed him "Barnabas," which means son of consolation or encouragement.

Once, my car battery died in a Wal-Mart parking lot. I was surely grateful for the man who used jumper cables to start my car. I was soon back on the road. Many people find their spiritual lives stalled and need their "spiritual jumper cables" to infuse strength into their weakened condition.

Acts 11:24 details the following characteristics necessary for being a "Barney."

1. **Barnabas Was an Honorable Man.**
He was probably converted on the day of Pentecost, and God made him a "good man." We are not born "good"; we must be born again to become good.

2. **Barnabas Was a Holy Man.**
He was full of the Holy Ghost and living under His control (Eph. 5:18). God gave us the Holy Spirit to make us holy saints.

3. **Barnabas Was a Hopeful Man.**
He was full of the Holy Spirit and faith. Only spiritually confident and courageous people can inspire courage in others.

4. **Barnabas Was a Helpful Man.**
He was a soul-winner and helped men come to Christ so that "much people was added unto the Lord" (Acts 11:24).

Only spiritually converted, controlled, and confident people can challenge others to walk in victory. One of the most consistent Christians I knew in Bible college was also one of the most exciting, dynamic people I've ever met. He was worth imitating. Is that true of you?

THOUGHT: More people fail because they lack encouragement than for any other reason.

—*Tom Farrell*

AUGUST 3
LET'S BE A BARNEY
Scripture Reading—Acts 4:36-37

No, the Barney we're discussing is neither Barney Fife from Mayberry nor the purple dinosaur named Barney. We're taking a close look at the biblical character Barnabas, whom his friends so named because he was a spiritual spark plug. Having viewed his **character** from Acts 11:24, we'll now focus on his **conduct**.

The Holy Spirit gives us at least five spiritual snapshots of the impact of encouragement from the life of Barnabas. First, in Acts 4:36-37, Barnabas encouraged others by his **contribution**. Persecution had come to the early church, but believers were thriving because of the spirit of unity and sharing. Barnabas, a Levite, sold a piece of property on the wealthy island of Cypress and gave all the profits to the church. This voluntary and sacrificial act of love, no doubt, blessed many.

One sure way to encourage others is to give to them financially. Luke 6:38 reminds us to "give, and it shall be given unto you." One of my college professors challenged us to give a "flying five"—to be an encouragement to fellow students financially. A "flying five" was an anonymous five-dollar gift sent to their post office box or slid under their door. More than one student rejoiced because of the generosity of others. Yes, the "flying five" brightened the day of many. If we adjust for inflation, we'd better make today's "flying five" a "twirling twenty."

First John 3:17 reminds us, "But whoso hath this world's good, and seeth his brother have need, and shutteth up his bowels of compassion from him, how dwelleth the love of God in him?" Don't be a getter but a giver. Whose spirit could you lift today by investing in him financially? Invest in eternity by contributing a gift of love to someone in need. You will be glad you did, and so will he.

THOUGHT: You are not living until you are giving.

—*Tom Farrell*

AUGUST 4
LET'S BE A BARNEY
Scripture Reading—Acts 9:26-31

These days, encouraging words are like priceless jewels. They're pretty hard to find, aren't they? Praise the Lord for Barnabas who heartened people not only by his works but also by his words! He was a man both of **contribution** and **commendation.**

The majority of the Christian world looked at the recently converted Saul with suspicion. When he tried to fellowship and minister with the rest the saints, "they were all afraid of him, and believed not that he was a disciple" (v. 26). Of course, their fear was understandable since this Christ-hater had "made havock of the church" (Acts 8:3) by imprisoning or slaughtering God's people.

The believers resisted him, "but Barnabas took him, and brought him to the apostles" (Acts 9:27). He verified Saul's testimony and conversion and championed his cause. From a human standpoint, if not for Barney, we might never have been privileged to meet Paul. When someone's name is mentioned in your presence, do you speak well or ill of him? Barnabas was highly respected, and Saul was heavily resisted. But because Barnabas spoke well of Saul, the church received him.

Missionary Robert Moffat was the Barney of his day. He listened to an aspiring young preacher attempt one of his first sermons. After a few minutes of his poorly delivered message, the young man sat down, frustrated and dejected. As the congregation departed, the young man wondered if God had truly called him to preach. Just then, Robert Moffat placed a comforting hand on the young man's shoulder and spoke these challenging and comforting words. "Young man, you have the potential to be a great and wonderful servant of the Lord." Those words encouraged the young man, who went on to be a mighty missionary for God in Africa. Today the world still remembers the life of David Livingstone.

THOUGHT: Don't be a Christian cannibal who "bites and devours" others. Encourage others every chance you get.

—*Tom Farrell*

AUGUST 5
LET'S BE A BARNEY
Scripture Reading—Acts 11:19-24

The birth of a baby is always a time of family celebration. So, too, should be the birth of a new believer into the family of God. The Book of Acts records many new births, and chapter 11 tells of a great number of Grecians at Antioch who believed and turned to the Lord. When this news reached the church at Jerusalem, "they sent forth Barnabas, that he should go as far as Antioch" (v. 22).

Apparently questioning the validity of these conversions, these Jewish believers sent Barnabas to check them out. When "Mr. Encouragement" arrived on the scene, he "had seen the grace of God, was glad, and exhorted them all, that with purpose of heart they would cleave unto the Lord" (v. 23). The word *glad* means cheerful, excited, or happy. Yes, Barnabas encouraged the new converts by celebrating their newfound faith. He was thrilled that they had been born again and exhorted or continually encouraged and invoked them to cleave and to remain loyal to the Lord Jesus. His visible and verbal **celebration** challenged the new believers to grow and to go for God.

Romans 12:15 reminds us to "rejoice with them that do rejoice." Are you jealous or jubilant because of another believer's success? Sometimes pastors, evangelists, and missionaries become critical because of another believer's fruitfulness. While sitting in a preachers' meeting years ago, one brother reported on the harvest of souls coming to Christ in another pastor's ministry. Upon hearing the news, one of the preachers responded, "Well, he must be compromising somewhere. There just aren't many people coming to Christ these days."

That's certainly not the spirit in heaven. "Likewise, I say unto you, there is joy in the presence of the angels of God over one sinner that repenteth" (Luke 15:10). Let's learn to rejoice in the salvation of a sinner who comes to Christ, whether in our ministry or in someone else's.

THOUGHT: It's not hard to "rejoice with them that do rejoice" if we first "weep with them that weep" (Rom. 12:15).

—Tom Farrell

AUGUST 6
LET'S BE A BARNEY
Scripture Reading—Acts 11:25-26

Proverbs 13:10 warns, "Only by pride cometh contention: but with the well advised is wisdom." Barnabas was not only an encourager but also a wise encourager. Antioch was ablaze with the power of God, and many Gentiles were being converted. The new disciples were growing and glowing in their faith so much that they had been branded "Christians" or followers of Christ. Barnabas knew that discipling these eager believers was too big a job for him to handle alone. His solution was to solicit Saul's assistance.

Barney was no glory boy; God's cause was bigger than his. Off to Tarsus he went to diligently seek Saul. We must remember that Saul's old cohorts, the Pharisees, hated and hunted him. Also, the church had not totally accepted him, so friends were at a premium. Imagine how Saul must have rejoiced when Barnabas appeared and announced that he had a wonderful ministry opportunity for Saul in Antioch. Barnabas' ministry of encouragement was marked by **cooperation**.

Selfish people work alone for their glory; humble people involve others for God's glory. In Ecclesiastes 4:9, Solomon declared, "Two are better than one; because they have a good reward for their labour." Exercising, dieting, studying, and ministering are all easier when we have a partner. Barnabas wanted to encourage both the disciples and the disciplees. He was looking for a spiritual win-win situation.

Years ago, my father involved me in the team effort of soul-winning. The effort certainly didn't need my youthful and inexperienced help, but often he took me with him on his witnessing adventures. His team spirit not only involved me but also instructed and inspired me so today I have a soul-winner's heart. Whom could you help and encourage today by involving him in your project? Do you know a Saul who has the potential to be a Paul if someone would give him the opportunity?

THOUGHT: If your cause is "the cause," you will experience contention. But if God's cause is "the cause," you will experience cooperation.

—*Tom Farrell*

AUGUST 7
LET'S BE A BARNEY
Scripture Reading—Acts 13:45-52

In our last episode of the life of the encourager, we saw Barnabas involving Saul in ministry through cooperation. In Acts 13, Barney blessed the life of Saul even further through the ministry of **condescension**. It is important to remember that Barnabas had been saved longer than Saul, was more highly respected, and held a higher position. But status meant nothing to Barney, and service meant everything. He humbled himself to honor his friend, Saul.

A quick survey of this evangelistic team reveals that Barnabas is always named before Saul in the Scriptures (see Acts 11:25; 12:25; 13:2, 7). Part way through Acts 13, Saul—then called Paul—began to take leadership of the team. In verse 46, the order changes to "Paul and Barnabas" and remains that way throughout the Book of Acts. Barnabas was a curtain puller so Paul could take center stage and be the chief preacher. Barney fulfilled Romans 12:10. "Be kindly affectioned one to another with brotherly love; in honour preferring one another." One of his greatest joys was Paul's success.

Someone once asked Leonard Bernstein, the famous conductor, which orchestral instrument was the hardest to play. "Second fiddle!" he replied. "Everybody wants to play first-chair violin, but it is hard to find someone who will play second chair." Barnabas loved not only pulling people up but also pushing them forward.

Philippians 2:3 admonishes us, "Let nothing be done through strife or vainglory; but in lowliness of mind let each esteem other better than themselves." One commentator says *lowliness of mind* means to be "carpet minded." The Lord Jesus demonstrated the spirit of condescension by laying down His life on the cross so we could step up to the kingdom of heaven. Are you willing to esteem, elevate, and encourage others so they can succeed for the glory of God? Are you willing to step back so others can step up? Are you willing to be walked over so others can walk on?

THOUGHT: God honors those who humble themselves. See 1 Peter 5:6.

—Tom Farrell

AUGUST 8
LET'S BE A BARNEY
Scripture Reading—Acts 15:35-41

This is the last in our series of snapshots of Barnabas, God's spiritual spark plug. Our final focus on this honorable, holy, hopeful, and helpful man magnifies his spirit of **compassion**. Jude 22 announces, "And of some have compassion, making a difference." Compassion sure made a difference in the life of John Mark.

Acts 15 records the only heated argument between Barnabas and Paul. This debate centered on Barnabas' nephew, John Mark. Mark had previously traveled in the missionary ministry with this spiritual dynamic duo but had "departed from them from Pamphylia, and went not with them to the work" (v. 38). The word *depart* means Mark not only quit the ministry but also may have apostatized and quit the faith for a while. While Barnabas "determined" that Mark would go with them on the coming journey (v. 37), Paul determined that he would not (v. 38).

Barnabas believed Mark needed a second chance, but Paul believed Mark couldn't be trusted. The debate probably sounded like this.

"Barnabas, the boy's a loser."

"No, Paul, he's a learner."

"Look, Barney. Mark has problems, and we have a mission to accomplish."

"I know he's had problems, but he also has potential, and he's part of our mission."

The disagreement ended in two mission teams. Paul and Silas headed for Syria, and Barnabas and Mark went to Cyprus. Interestingly, Paul later admitted that Barney had been right, and his compassion in the life of John Mark paid eternal dividends. He wrote in 2 Timothy 4:11, "Take Mark, and bring him with thee: for he is profitable to me for the ministry." The missionary Paul had originally seen as a pitiful loser had become a profitable leader.

Thank God for the Barneys in my life who gave me a second chance. To whom do you need to extend a second chance today?

THOUGHT: Everyone can have one ministry. It's the ministry of encouragement!

—Tom Farrell

AUGUST 9
THREE BIG QUESTIONS

Scripture Reading—Revelation 4:1-3, 9-11

Three questions often haunt the minds of human beings.

1. Where did I come from?

2. Why am I here?

3. Where am I going?

To Bible-believing Christians, the first and third questions aren't problems. We know where we came from. "In the beginning God created" (Gen. 1:1a). That verse settles it in spite of what past evolutionists and modern educators would tell us. We also know where we're going. Second Corinthians 5:8 tells us that "to be absent from the body" is "to be present with the Lord." The moment this life ends, a new life begins—"and so shall we ever be with the Lord" (1 Thess. 4:17b).

The second question, however, is more difficult to answer, even for some Bible-believing Christians. The answer is found in today's Scripture reading, which paints a beautiful picture of the 24 elders worshiping God. In their worship, they state, "For thy pleasure they are and were created" (Rev. 4:11b). We were created to bring pleasure to our God. This is His purpose for our existence. To miss His purpose is to miss our purpose for living. God's approval must be the highest priority in life.

Several other places in Scripture bring this truth out. In Proverbs 16:4a, we read, "The Lord hath made all things for himself." Again, in Romans 11:36, the Bible says, "For of him, and through him, and to him, are all things: to whom be glory for ever. Amen." In other words, life is all about God. To leave God out means to ignore the most important part. Those who have no place for God will struggle to find a reason for living for something other than themselves.

PRAYER TIME: Pause as a family to thank God that He's *your* God. Also read Psalm 86:8-10 as a good reminder.

—*Tom Palmer*

AUGUST 10
HE PLEASED
NOT HIMSELF

Scripture Reading
Romans 15:3—*"For even Christ pleased not himself; but, as it is written, The reproaches of them that reproached thee fell on me."*
1 John 3:22—*"And whatsoever we ask, we receive of him, because we keep his commandments, and do those things that are pleasing in his sight."*

The Scriptures contain certain "unexplainables" no human being will ever truly comprehend. Certainly one of them is the combination of humanity and deity we find in Jesus Christ. Though He was God, Jesus gave us a tremendous example of how believers ought to live.

As a man, Jesus lived to please God, His Heavenly Father. The words of the Father Himself make this truth clear. At Jesus' baptism, the Father said, "This is my beloved Son, in whom I am well pleased" (Matt. 3:17b). In Matthew 17:5, the Father repeated that statement on the Mount of Transfiguration. While Jesus was here on earth, He lived with His Father's total approval. His attitudes, actions, words, and thoughts made His Father happy. As a child, a teenager, and then an adult, He sought His Father's pleasure.

When I was a high school basketball player, I fouled out of the fourth quarter of a key game. Disgusted, I started for the bench and looked into the stands for my father, seeking his approval. He wasn't smiling, and I knew he wasn't pleased. We lost the game, and I didn't play well. Worse, I disappointed someone I really wanted to please. For me, my father's smile, whether present or absent, was the indicator of how well I had done.

Would the way you are living now bring a smile to your Heavenly Father's face? Would anything about your life cause Him to frown? These simple questions have a special way of telling us whether the Father is pleased.

EXERCISE: Play a game. Ask your children to name activities they do sometimes. Without speaking, Dad should smile or frown to let them know whether he is pleased.

—*Tom Palmer*

AUGUST 11
ADDING TO YOUR PRAYER LIST

Scripture Reading—Colossians 1:9-12

The Bible contains excellent prayer lists we can include in our prayer times (Ps. 51; Eph. 3:14-21). One of those lists is in Colossians 1. A unique request in verse 10 is worth noting: "That ye might walk worthy of the Lord unto all pleasing, being fruitful in every good work, and increasing in the knowledge of God." In this simple prayer, we can ask God for help to live a life pleasing to Him.

If you've been to a prayer meeting lately, you know that most believers limit their prayer requests to physical or material needs. There's certainly nothing wrong with these requests; the Bible tells us to "let your requests be made known unto God" (Phil 4:6). But imagine if a teen or an adult raised his hand and said, "Please pray for me. I have displeased my God, and I want to please him more." That prayer request would certainly differ from typical requests about surgery and car repairs. Yet it's a biblical prayer and certainly one God loves to hear and to answer.

If it's true that we "have not, because . . . [we] ask not" (James 4:2)—and it's certainly true—maybe we would do well to add this request to our list. Often the added dimension of spiritual prayer requests can be a great blessing. No Christian can please God in and of himself; the assistance of God is necessary. God loves to answer prayers we pray according to His will, and certainly pleasing God is according to God's will.

Next time you go to a prayer meeting, consider making requests based on spiritual needs. God will create a new dimension of prayer when you let God know how desperately you need Him.

PRAY FOR ONE ANOTHER: Ask each family member to list an area where he desires to please God more. Ask a family member to pray specifically for these areas of need. God is there to hear and to answer.

—*Tom Palmer*

AUGUST 12
SOME THINGS TAKE TIME

Scripture Reading—Philippians 2:13
"For it is God which worketh in you both to will
and to do of his good pleasure."

Most people are inclined to get what they want when they want it. Toddlers, teens, and even grownups rarely want to wait for anything.

Modern technology has made patience even less attractive. An ATM makes money available 24/7. A microwave cooks a meal in minutes. Cell phones and fax machines enable us to communicate information anytime. Of course, we like all these conveniences because they make life easier—or at least they're supposed to.

The problem is that we assume spiritual maturity works the same way. Just insert your card, punch in the numbers, press a button and—WOW!—God is smiling with approval. We must understand, however, that in the age of the instantaneous, the development of a life that pleases God takes time.

Note two key thoughts in our verse for today. "To will" describes what God desires. "To do" speaks of what God does. This verse clearly indicates that God has not only a definite purpose for each life but also a definite plan. We must allow God to develop His plan so He ultimately achieves His purpose.

In high school, I received a button to wear on my shirt. On the button were the following letters:

P B P G I N F W M Y

If someone asked me what the letters meant, my answer was, "Please be patient. God is not finished with me yet." The button was a simple reminder that God is taking whatever time is necessary to develop His plan in my life. The finished product will prove that the time at the drawing board and on the work bench was worth it.

EXERCISE: Make a bag of microwave popcorn. While your family is eating the popcorn, ask each family member to share a spiritual lesson God is teaching him.

—Tom Palmer

AUGUST 13
GUIDELINES
FOR GOD-PLEASERS

Scripture Reading—1 Thessalonians 4:1
"Furthermore then we beseech you, brethren,
and exhort you by the Lord Jesus,
that as ye have received of us how ye ought to walk
and to please God, so ye would abound more and more."

Those who live to please God must make tough choices. When they decide to say "yes" to pleasing God, they must also decide to say "no" to certain things. Note the following choices we must make to please God:

1. **God-pleasers are not self-pleasers.** Romans 8:8 says, "So then they that are in the flesh cannot please God." The flesh, as the Bible calls it, is self-centered and desires only what will satisfy itself. Yet those things that please the flesh are often displeasing to God.

2. **God-pleasers are not men-pleasers.** In 1 Thessalonians 2:4, we read, "But as we were allowed of God to be put in trust with the gospel, even so we speak; not as pleasing men, but God, which trieth our hearts." In Galatians 1:10, Paul said, "For do I now persuade men, or God? or do I seek to please men? for if I yet pleased men, I should not be the servant of Christ." Attempting to please others, we can easily offend or bring shame to our God.

3. **God-pleasers are not world-pleasers.** While instructing Timothy, Paul wrote, "No man that warreth entangleth himself with the affairs of this life; that he may please him who hath chosen him to be a soldier" (2 Tim. 2:4). The world system leaves God out of everything, but this philosophy doesn't work for those who seek to please God.

Changes begin with choices. Not all choices are easy to make, but they are necessary. A God-pleaser will make the right choices so nothing can rob him of the pleasure of his God.

APPLICATION: Read Proverbs 29:25 and John 12:43. Note ways people can influence the choices we make.

—*Tom Palmer*

AUGUST 14
GOD'S HANDBOOK
FOR LIFE

Scripture Reading—2 Timothy 2:15, 3:14-17

Whether we're a new student, employee, or member, handbooks are a blessing. In handbooks, we learn what others expect of us. We discover lists of what we can and can't do and find explanations of the benefits we can enjoy. We read standards of conduct and appearance we must follow. We also read about penalties if we fail to live up to expectations.

Did you know that God has prepared a handbook for us? It's the book from which you read the Scripture reading a moment ago. The Bible, of course, is God's handbook for living. According to the Scripture reading, the Bible is "profitable" in the following ways:

1. For Doctrine—It teaches us what *is* right.

2. For Reproof—It teaches us what is *not* right.

3. For Correction—It teaches us how to *make* things right.

4. For Instruction—It teaches us how to *keep* things right.

What a blessing the Bible is! God has given us a book to teach us how to live. God has not only told us to please Him but also explained how. Those who would live to please God must be students of the Word. When we have a question about life, we should go to God's handbook for the answer. When we have a problem, we should reach for God's handbook. When we are confused, we should read God's handbook. Second Timothy 2:15 says, "Study to shew thyself approved unto God, a workman that needeth not to be ashamed, rightly dividing the word of truth."

On February 22, 1947, the late missionary Jim Elliot wrote the following to his father: "My grades came through this week and were as expected, lower than last semester. However I make not apologies and admit I've let them drag a bit for study of the Bible, in which I seek the degree, 'A.U.G.,' approved unto God."

ASSIGNMENT: Gather all the Bibles in your home and count how many copies you have. Sing "The B-I-B-L-E" together.

—Tom Palmer

AUGUST 15
THE ULTIMATE
TEST

Scripture Reading—John 8:29
"And he that sent me is with me:
the Father hath not left me alone;
for I do always those things that please him."

Read the Scripture reading again. See if you can find the most important word. Here's a hint: The word starts with the letter *a*. You got it! It's the word *always*. First, let's be sure we understand that the Lord Jesus is speaking here. Now let's read the verse again but leave out the word *always*. Lots of us could say what Jesus did if we left out this keyword. Of course, we do things that please God. But when Jesus used the word *always*, He said something we ought to say but usually can't.

When we determine to live in a God-pleasing way, we must ask one question to evaluate everything in our lives. The question is, "Is God pleased?" You may have your own opinion, and others may give you their thoughts. The world will try to push its ideas down your throat. Yet we must determine what God wants and do it!

George Mueller wrote, "There was a day when I died, utterly died, died to George Mueller, his opinions, his preferences, tastes and will—died to the world, its approval or censure—died to the approval or blame even of my brethren and friends. Since then I have studied only to show myself approved unto God." This man understood that pleasing God was all that mattered, and he determined to obey no matter what.

Hebrews 11:5 tells us about Enoch, a man who walked with God. "He had this testimony, that he pleased God" (v. 5b). What a testimony and example for us to follow! May we live in such a way that others will say of us someday, "He [or she] pleased God."

THINK ABOUT IT: How would you like others to remember your life? List several ideas.

—Tom Palmer

AUGUST 16
TURNING THE HEART
BACK TO GOD

Scripture Reading—1 Kings 18:1, 36-39

Leonard Ravenhill, the great evangelist, said, "I know why we do not have revival in America. It is very simple. We are content without it." He also said, "Our country is in more need of revival now than it has ever been."

First Kings 18 describes three key elements of a revival sent from God. Verse one says, "And it came to pass after many days, that the *word of the Lord* came to Elijah in the third year, saying, Go, shew thyself unto Ahab" (emphasis added). The first element of revival is *hearing* the Word of God. After many days of silence, God spoke to Elijah; and Elijah listened.

Verse two describes the second element of revival. "And Elijah went to shew himself unto Ahab." After hearing the word of God, Elijah *heeded* that word. Responding to the voice of God, he went to see Ahab.

The first two elements of revival are hearing and heeding the Word of God. We find the final element of revival in verses 36b-37. "Elijah the prophet came near, and said, Lord God of Abraham, Isaac, and of Israel, let it be known this day that thou art God in Israel, and that I am thy servant, and that I have done all these things at thy word. Hear me, O Lord, hear me, that this people may know that thou art the Lord God, and that thou hast turned their heart back again." Elijah had a word with God in *prayer*. After Elijah's prayer with God, we read in verses 38-39 that "the fire of the Lord fell" and that "the people . . . fell on their faces" and acknowledged the Lord as God.

When we combine the hearing of God's Word and the heeding of the commands given in Scripture to the vital element of prayer, we will experience *power* from God. Acts 4:31a says, "And when they had *prayed*, the place was shaken" (emphasis added).

PRAYER: "Lord, send revival fire to everyone under our roof."

—Robert Booth

AUGUST 17
SERVING IN THE FAMILY

Scripture Reading—Galatians 5:13

"For, brethren, ye have been called unto liberty; only use not liberty for an occasion to the flesh, but by love serve one another."

It's God's plan that every home be a close home. This closeness doesn't happen by accident but by design. One way to experience relational intimacy is to practice the "one another" commands in the Bible. These are practical, measurable expressions of our concern for others.

One such command is in our text—"Serve one another." Jesus served His disciples by doing tasks that were often menial, mundane, and humbling. He washed their dirty feet (John 13:4-5) because He loved them and wanted to serve them. His ministry to them met a need and is an example to us; we should serve others in small, practical ways. In John 13:14, Jesus said, "If I then, your Lord and Master, have washed your feet; ye also ought to wash one another's feet."

Ultimately, we serve because we are servants of Christ, and we serve Him by serving others. This truth is especially so in the family. Loving service is that which takes initiative. We don't need to be told; we're looking for opportunities to serve those whom we love. In so doing, we are serving the Lord Jesus.

Don't just do your assigned chores. Be a servant by picking up trash in the yard, bringing in the mail or the paper, washing the car, cleaning your room, mowing the yard, starting your homework, ironing clothes, doing laundry, vacuuming, dusting, cleaning the bathroom, or washing dishes—all without being asked. That is the heart of service.

At graduation, a well-known Bible college presents graduates not only with a diploma but also with a small towel to remind them of their spiritual responsibility to "wash feet" in loving service. Serve those in your home—even in the smallest, humbling, and unspectacular of tasks.

ASSIGNMENT: What are specific ways you can voluntarily serve your family members?

—Rick Johnson

AUGUST 18
LEADERSHIP IS SERVICE
Scripture Reading—Luke 22:25-27

What does servanthood look like in a Christian family? The primary way is when *the leader serves first.* Corporate America typically has a pyramid of service that places those to be served at the top and those who serve under the leader. This model is unbiblical. Jesus said, "He that is greatest among you, let him be as the younger; and he that is chief, as he that doth serve" (Luke 22:26b). In God's economy, serving begins at the top.

"Leadership is not a position to be enjoyed but a responsibility to be employed."

God gives us authority to use for the benefit of those whom we serve. Therefore, the best servant in the family ought to be the father, and the choicest servant among siblings ought to be the eldest child. Leadership is not a position to be enjoyed but a responsibility to be employed. We express this responsibility through serving first—a truth plainly taught in Scripture. (See Rom. 15:1-2; 2 Cor. 12:15; and 1 Thess. 2:7-8.) The leader serves first.

The second way a leader serves is *by putting himself last.* See that the needs of others are met first. Put yourself last intentionally. Don't fight for the first or best place. Seek the lowest place. The flesh cries out against this because of fear that you will be left out if you don't fend for yourself.

Jesus taught, "When thou art bidden of any man to a wedding, sit not down in the highest room. . . . But when thou art bidden, go and sit down in the lowest room" (Luke 14:8a, 10a). The more we practice this attitude of servanthood in our families, the less stress we will experience in the home environment. When everyone is trying to meet needs, a bulk of work isn't left for one person. Zig Ziglar said, "There's no traffic jam on the second mile." Leaders rise to the top through their willingness to serve.

ASSIGNMENT: In your home, how can you serve first? How can you put yourself last?

—*Rick Johnson*

AUGUST 19
BENEFITS OF SERVING IN THE HOME
Scripture Reading—Acts 20:35

A family that focuses on serving each other experiences two special blessings. Both are crucial to a meaningful home. First, *service brings joy to a family.* The greatest joy we receive is found in serving. This joy is infectious.

In Acts 20:35, Paul focused on those who were weak—even laboring to help provide for their needs. He was not a taker, but a giver. We find the greatest joy not in receiving but in giving. "If ye know these things, happy are ye if ye do them" (John 13:17).

Conversely, selfishness brings misery and unhappiness to a family. The atmosphere in your home will be transformed when each person is eager to serve others.

When we were on vacation, my son, Jake, bought me a key chain with his own money; the key chain was engraved with the word *Dad.* His act of service brought joy to my heart and to his. The greatest joy always goes to the giver, not to the receiver. Someone once said, "Receivers eat well, but givers sleep well."

A second blessing service brings to a family is the *reduction of conflicts and argumentation.* The Bible records conflicts Jesus' disciples experienced because of their desire to be served rather than to serve (Mark 10:35-41; Luke 22:21-24).

When we scheme to get first place, the best, and the most, the home becomes a place of competition and rivalry. When it doesn't matter which part of the pie we get, there is no conflict or argument; the source of the argument has been removed. One of God's ways to remove conflict in the home is to foster a spirit of servanthood in the heart of each family member.

It's hard to believe that those involved in a divorce suit were once married! Usually those involved in a divorce have regressed from a desire to serve the other person to expecting the other person to meet his or her needs. It has been said, "If you treat your wife like a thoroughbred, she won't turn out to be a nag."

DISCUSSION: How can we serve one another in our homes?

—*Rick Johnson*

AUGUST 20
Hindrances to Serving in Your Family—Part 1
Scripture Reading—John 13:3-6

One reason we fail to experience lasting change in our lives is that we often deal with a problem's symptoms rather than its root issue. True repentance deals with the cause—not just being sorry about painful results. Leadership problems in the home stem from failing to serve biblically.

Some fail to serve because of insecurity. Jesus willingly served the disciples because He had centered His life in accomplishing His Father's will, not in having His own needs met. True security comes from centering our lives on the Heavenly Father's plan. If we center our lives on temporal values, we will always be insecure; however, if our lives are centered on eternal values (God, His Word, and His kingdom), we will be secure because these values don't change.

Position-conscious people are not servants. They are more concerned about image, status, and reputation. It's obvious that Peter hadn't yet learned the lesson of true servanthood from the Lord. When Jesus came to wash Peter's feet, Peter resisted (13:6-8). His response conveyed the idea of "Lord, leaders don't wash feet! Servants wash feet." What was unspoken was his attitude—"Lord, I'm one of the leaders of this group, and others are supposed to wash our feet." His insecurity and image-consciousness hindered his willingness to serve.

Others fail to serve because of personal pride. Arrogance makes us believe we deserve better. Washing feet—hard and demeaning work—was the task of a lowly servant.

A true servant is willing to do the most undesirable tasks in the home. Elisha wasn't looking for a position but for an opportunity to be a blessing to Elijah, his leader. He provided water to wash Elijah's hands (2 Kings 3:11). If we are true servants, we won't hesitate to put on the garment of a humble servant (1 Pet. 5:5) and to do a task we may consider to be beneath us.

DISCUSS: What responsibilities in your home do you consider to be beneath you? What is keeping you from serving your family members?

—*Rick Johnson*

AUGUST 21
HINDRANCES TO SERVING IN YOUR FAMILY—PART 2
Scripture Reading—Ephesians 4:31-32

It's difficult to serve those with whom we've suffered an offense. Rather than seeing them blessed and desiring to help them, we want them to pay for their wrongdoing. A personal offense we haven't properly dealt with leads to bitterness. A bitter person isn't necessarily filled with hate and anger; he's consumed with harbored hurt. Bitterness is the result of being disappointed with someone. It causes us to turn inward and to become so absorbed with our own pain and hurt that we can't see the needs of others.

Sometimes children become bitter toward their parents. A biblical example is the prodigal son's brother. He became bitter toward his father because of his father's goodness toward his undeserving brother. Note the bitterness in his words—"And he answering said to his father, Lo, these many years do I serve thee, neither transgressed I at any time thy commandment: and yet thou never gavest me a kid, that I might make merry with my friends" (Luke 15:29). He was so wounded that he refused to celebrate his brother's return with the rest of his family.

The Bible also warns husbands not to become bitter toward their wives. "Husbands, love your wives, and be not bitter against them" (Col. 3:19). Of course, it's possible for a wife to become bitter toward her husband and for parents to become bitter toward their children.

The most likely place for bitterness to appear is in the family; because we spend most of our time in our homes, the possibilities of being wounded there are greater. The only solution for bitterness is a forgiving heart. Ephesians 4:32 says, "And be ye kind one to another, tenderhearted, forgiving one another, even as God for Christ's sake hath forgiven you."

Sometimes a hesitancy to serve is the fruit of a bitter heart. Bitterness blinds us to loving service and makes us selfish and sour.

ACTION POINT: Is there anyone to whom you need to offer forgiveness?

—*Rick Johnson*

AUGUST 22
HINDRANCES TO SERVING IN YOUR FAMILY—PART 3
Scripture Reading—Colossians 3:23-24

Most people deal with life from the standpoint of assets and liabilities. They measure everything by how it benefits them. Their mindset is one of *always being involved in a transaction.* This way of thinking is devastating to the development of a servant's heart. When we serve others, they may compensate us in three ways. Sometimes they won't give us anything for our service. Other times they may give us proper compensation or at least recognition for services rendered. And sometimes they'll give us far more than we ever dreamed.

"Keeping score" inhibits us from having a true servant's heart. The proper way to serve is to remember that we ultimately serve the Lord, as we see in Colossians 3:23-24 and in Ephesians 6:6-8. The wrong perspective will make us stingy and bitter when others don't properly compensate us.

God has promised to reward those who realize their service is ultimately to Him. *Because we will rarely receive reward on this earth,* we can be tempted to think we are going to be left out of being compensated. If we fight and claw to ensure that we get our way, we probably will. But our efforts will reap a temporal reward versus an eternal one.

God promises to reward those who serve with a willing spirit, and His reward will exceed our imaginations. "By faith Moses, when he was come to years, refused to be called the son of Pharaoh's daughter; choosing rather to suffer affliction with the people of God, than to enjoy the pleasures of sin for a season; esteeming the reproach of Christ greater riches than the treasures in Egypt: *for he had respect unto the recompence of the reward*" (Heb. 11:24-26, emphasis added). God will abundantly reward us when we have a servant's heart.

DISCUSS: Are you willing to serve even when you don't receive the recognition you feel you deserve?

—*Rick Johnson*

AUGUST 23
HINDRANCES TO SERVING IN YOUR FAMILY—PART 4
Scripture Reading—Luke 17:7-10

Someone wisely said, "Expectations destroy relationships." *A servant fulfills his duty faithfully without expectation of reward or praise* (see Luke 17:7-10). When our expectations don't come to pass, the result is disappointment; and serving becomes drudgery.

What expectations have you placed on your family? I would encourage you to place higher expectations on yourself. The business community has a motto that ought to be in our homes: *underpromise and overdeliver.* Go the second mile in serving your family and watch what happens. Usually we expect family members to go the second mile in meeting our needs. When our expectations aren't met, the natural result is bitterness.

Be the type of person who has a reputation for serving his family. Phebe had the reputation of being a servant in her local church. "I commend unto you Phebe our sister, which is a servant of the church which is at Cenchrea: That ye receive her in the Lord, as becometh saints, and that ye assist her in whatsoever business she hath need of you: for she hath been a succourer of many, and of myself also" (Rom. 16:1-2). She so faithfully evidenced a servant's heart that others knew her by it.

Paul's attitude was that he was a servant of all. "For though I be free from all men, yet have I made myself servant unto all, that I might gain the more" (1 Cor. 9:19). He wasn't seeking others to serve him; he was committed to serving those around him.

Are you willing to see yourself as a servant—to your spouse, to your children, to your parents, to your brothers and sisters? Change your expectations from your family serving you to your serving them.

DISCUSS: Are you a giver or a taker in your family? If your family took a poll and rated each family member according to his servant's attitude, how would you rate? Which family member has the reputation of being the best servant? Why did you select him?

—Rick Johnson

AUGUST 24
GOD'S FORMULA FOR SUCCESS

Scripture Reading—Nehemiah 8:1-12
Observe how God's people respond
to His Word as a result of revival.

God brought Nehemiah back to Jerusalem to supervise the rebuilding of the wall of that great city. The people were in reproach and great affliction. "The wall of Jerusalem also is broken down, and the gates thereof are burned with fire" (Neh. 1:3b). It was a sad situation. In the process, they not only rebuilt the wall in a miraculous 52 days against unbelievable opposition (Neh. 6:15) but also experienced a genuine revival. One of the most obvious indications of revival is an intensified hunger for God's Word.

Chapter 8 tells how this moving of God was evident. First, they **requested** the Word of God (v. 1). Second, they **read** God's Word (v. 3a). Third, they **received** the Word of God (v. 3b). Fourth, they **responded** to God's Word (vv. 5-6, 9). Finally, they **rejoiced** in God's Word (v. 12). Because God was doing a reviving work, the Scriptures became a priority to them.

What place does God's Word have in your home? Most Christian families have lots of Bibles, but many fail to prioritize what God says. Your family needs to be **founded on** God's Word. It must be your final and absolute authority for everything. You also need to be **grounded in** the Word of God. You must teach it to your family daily to provide a solid, biblical foundation for them—one that can weather the most severe storms in life. And your family must also be **bounded by** the Word of God.

Let God's Word set your family's spiritual boundaries. Never forget, God's Word does not merely contain God's formula for success; it *is* God's formula. Jeremiah 15:16 says, "Thy words were found, and I did eat them; and thy word was unto me the joy and rejoicing of mine heart: for I am called by thy name, O Lord God of hosts."

APPLICATION: Discuss ways you and your family can make God's Word your priority. How can God's Word help you be successful?

—*Jack Palmer*

AUGUST 25
GOD'S FORMULA FOR SUCCESS—PART 2

Scripture Reading—Joshua 1:1-9
Give special attention to verses seven and eight,
noting what God said to Joshua about success.

Have you ever met someone who wanted to be a failure? I never have. We all want to succeed in what we do. Failure hurts; it's also part of being human. We all fail sometimes due to a lack of preparation, a bad decision we've made, the wrong influence of friends, or ignorance. Whatever the reason, we didn't want our efforts to turn out that way. That's why we need to know what God says about success.

As God prepared Joshua to lead the children of Israel into the Promised Land, He told him four times to be strong and courageous (Josh. 1:6, 7, 9, 18). His assignment was not going to be easy. Certainly Joshua wanted to be successful, and God shared his desire. God told Joshua what he needed to know so he wouldn't fail.

In Joshua 1:7-8, the Word of God is central. Twice God says, "Observe to do." Knowing what God says isn't enough; the key to success is *doing* what He says. Obedience is the first step toward success.

God warned Joshua about the danger of distractions when He said, "Turn not from it [the law] to the right hand or to the left" (v. 7). How easy it is for the things of the world to turn us away from God's Word. A biblical focus is essential for success.

God then commanded him to "meditate therein day and night" (v. 8). Scriptural meditation is indispensable for success. God's Word must condition your thinking.

If you desire to be spiritually successful, you, too, must follow God's plan. Remember, people in the world have a different standard by which they measure success. They look at your bank account. But when God determines success, He looks at your heart. What does He see?

TALK ABOUT IT: As a family, discuss the three things God said to Joshua and determine whether you are following God's plan for success. If not, make whatever adjustments are necessary.

—Jack Palmer

AUGUST 26
GOD'S FORMULA FOR SUCCESS—PART 3

Scripture Reading—Psalm 1:1-6
Compare the blessed man
to the unrighteous man.

Every Christian desires God's blessing in his life. Every Christian couple longs for the blessing of God on their marriage. Every Christian parent pleads with God for His blessing on his children. Yes, the blessing of God is important to us, and we all desire to experience it.

However, we need to realize that God's blessing is often conditional. God has certain requirements before He will extend His blessing. But never forget that every blessing of God is because of His grace. Someone has said that "grace is God giving us what we could never deserve." Even if God requires certain things and we faithfully meet those requirements, it's still because of His amazing grace that He would ever bless us. What a glorious God we serve!

Psalm 1:1-3 lists three conditions of God's blessing: **separated from the world** (v. 1), **saturated with the Word** (v. 2), and (3) **situated by the waters** (v. 3). In speaking of God's blessing, we must keep in mind that success and blessing are synonymous.

Some folks never want to hear anything negative—like the man who came home after a bad day at work and told his wife he didn't want to hear any bad news. After thinking a moment, his wife said, "I have good news. Jimmy only broke one arm!" Psalm 1:1-3 lists both the negative and positive commands because that's where the power is.

Those who seek God's blessing must recognize and reject the "counsel of the ungodly" by comparing it to Scripture. Then they must "delight . . . in the law of the Lord; and in his law . . . meditate day and night." Verse 3 says, "Whatsoever he doeth shall prosper." That's success!

Again, we see that God's formula for success is His Word. Saturate your family with God's Word, and He will bless you with success.

ASSIGNMENT: Memorize Psalm 1:1-3 and let it saturate your family. Let it help you recognize and reject the "counsel of the ungodly."

—Jack Palmer

AUGUST 27
GOD'S FORMULA FOR SUCCESS—PART 4
Scripture Reading—Matthew 7:24-29

What are the differences between the wise man and the foolish man? We live in a world of foolishness. Whatever happened to wisdom? God calls "the wisdom of this world" foolishness (1 Cor. 3:19). Today's Scripture describes a wise man and a foolish man. One was successful, and one failed.

Verses 24 and 26 tell us they both heard the Word of God, and each was building a house. One house had a rock-solid foundation; the other was built on sand. Each responded to what God said. One obeyed; the other didn't. The same storms of life came upon both of them (vv. 25, 27). The result? The wise man weathered the storm, and the foolish man lost everything. What is the lesson of this parable? To be successful, we must build upon the rock-solid foundation of God's Word.

In a seacoast village in New England, a lighthouse stood on the rocks near the village. A storm hit, and the light in the lighthouse went out. The villagers were terrified to think of the ships that would know nothing of the dangerous rocks without the light. A volunteer stood on the rocks in the worst of the storm and waved a lantern to warn the ships. The next morning, after the storm had passed, the weather-beaten man returned to the village as a hero. Someone asked, "Weren't you afraid standing out there in the midst of the storm?"

He replied, "No!"

"Why not?"

He responded, "Because the rock never moved!"

Each family will face storms. Some will be mild, but others will be severe. When your family stands on the solid rock of God's Word, you can successfully weather the storm—and even be better afterwards. But families who face the storms with no foundation are often swept away, losing everything. The key is knowing what God says and doing it. That's wisdom, and that's success.

DISCUSSION: As a family, share together about "storms" you've faced. How did God's Word bring you through?

—Jack Palmer

AUGUST 28
GOD'S FORMULA FOR SUCCESS—PART 5

Scripture Reading—2 Timothy 3
Find the apostle Paul's advice to Timothy
about success in the "perilous times"
that characterize the last days.

Hard times are the greatest test of our Christian faith and when many of God's people fail. But faith is like muscle. To become strong, we must exercise it. According to Romans 10:17, God's Word gives us the ability to trust. "So then faith cometh by hearing, and hearing by the word of God." During difficult times, we must depend on the Bible to carry us through. Sometimes God's Word is all we will have. During those times, we will discover that God's Word is all we need.

Paul wrote two letters to young Timothy to prepare him for the "perilous times" he would face. In the third chapter of his second epistle, Paul gave him the secret. "But continue thou in the things which thou hast learned. . . . And that from a child thou hast known the holy scriptures" (2 Tim. 3:14a, 15a). Timothy's godly grandmother, Lois, and his godly mother, Eunice, had taught him God's Word. They had laid a solid, biblical foundation in his life. On this foundation everything stood. In verse 16, Paul reminds Timothy that the Bible is divinely inspired and "is profitable for doctrine [to teach us what's right], for reproof [to teach us what's wrong], for correction [to teach us how to get right], for instruction in righteousness [to teach us how to live right]."

Paul concludes the chapter by listing three ways God's Word blesses our lives. It enables us to be *spiritually mature, spiritually complete, and spiritually productive.* In other words, even in the worst of times, God's Word will accomplish God's purpose for His glory. If you have a solid foundation based on God's truth, you can be successful when others are failing. Again, we see that the Bible is God's formula for success.

BRINGING THE TRUTH HOME: As a family, how are you learning and growing through obedience to God's Word? Is the Bible ruling your lives?

—*Jack Palmer*

GOD'S FORMULA FOR SUCCESS—PART 6
Scripture Reading—Luke 6:47-49

Again, in this passage of Scripture, Jesus teaches the importance of a solid foundation. He indicates that those who hear what He says and obey His Word are laying a rock-solid foundation on which they can safely build. Whether life, marriage, family, ministry, or business, God's Word must be our foundation.

A family built a lovely new home and moved in. But their happiness was short-lived. After several months, a large crack appeared in the living room ceiling. The man of the house, assuming the crack was the builder's fault, called and asked him to return immediately and to fix the crack. The builder fixed the problem, and the ceiling looked as good as new.

The family was happy again but only for a few months. The ugly crack returned. The builder found the best "crack fixer" in town. The gentleman examined the crack and took a walk around the house, but he returned with bad news. "Sorry folks," he said, "but I can't fix your crack." Of course, the family wanted to know why. "The problem isn't your ceiling," he said. "It's your *foundation!*" Due to a bad foundation, the house had settled. The settling had caused the cracked ceiling.

Take a good look at your family. Do you see "cracks" in your ceilings? Many Christian families go to extremes, trying to fix "cracks" when they should be checking their family's foundation. If your family is building on the solid foundation of God's Word, you won't find any "cracks." However, if you're building on the sinking, shifting sands of this world, you're going to be in trouble.

How do you repair a faulty foundation? Go to the Bible, discover what God says, and follow His instructions. That's God's formula for success.

GET REAL AND GET RIGHT: Be willing to be honest with God and with others. Acknowledge any areas of your family life that aren't built solidly on God's Word. Confess your failure to God, accept His cleansing and forgiveness, and commit yourselves to build only on God's foundation, the Bible.

—Jack Palmer

GOD'S FORMULA FOR SUCCESS—PART 7

Scripture Reading—James 1:22-25
As you read this devotional, determine which words in the text are the most important.

A family bought a major appliance they'd never had before. They desperately tried to figure out how to install it and to make it work. No matter what they did, they were unsuccessful. They called neighbors and friends, trying to get help. Nothing worked. Finally, someone asked them if they had read the instruction manual that had come with the appliance. Guess what? They hadn't even looked at it! They followed the directions. Before long, the appliance was properly installed and working great. Isn't human nature something? Our approach is often, "If all else fails, read the directions."

God's Word is our instruction manual for life. Within its pages is everything we need to know to be successful Christians. We spend so much time trying to figure life out and making it work, but nothing helps. We struggle along, making mistakes and getting discouraged, until we're ready to quit. Then somebody asks us, "Are you studying your Bible?" And our answer is, "No." Somehow we think we can pull life off on our own. Then, if all else fails, we might read the directions, God's Word.

In today's Scripture, James indicates that our problem isn't information. We know what the Bible says. Our problem is application; we just don't do what God tells us. He pictures God's Word as a mirror that shows us how we look from God's perspective (vv. 22-25) and tells us what we need to do. If we're "doers of the word," God will bless us with success. But if we're "forgetful hearer[s]," we're only deceiving ourselves; and we will fail.

ACTION POINT: Has God been speaking to your heart about an area of truth? Have you failed to respond to Him in obedience? After today's lesson, what do you think you should do about your disobedience? Are you willing to obey God?

—Jack Palmer

AUGUST 31
Resting in God

Scripture Reading

Psalm 37:7—*"Rest in the Lord, and wait patiently for him:*
fret not thyself because of him who prospereth in his way,
because of the man who bringeth wicked devices to pass."
Psalm 16:8-9—*"I have set the Lord always before me: because he is at*
my right hand, I shall not be moved.
Therefore my heart is glad, and my glory rejoiceth:
my flesh also shall rest in hope."

One day, John went into the forest and became lost. Unable to find his way out, he spent the night in the woods. The forest was pitch black, and he heard all sorts of strange sounds. John started to get scared, but then he remembered Psalm 37:7a. "Rest in the Lord, and wait patiently for him." Remembering that verse, he trusted in the Lord and was able to rest in God. To rest, we must trust in God. In the physical sphere, rest is essential to our well-being. In the spiritual sphere, resting in God is also essential.

Turn to Exodus 33:14 and ask someone to read it. God wants his children to rest. We are the ones who need rest, and God is the one who provides it. Patience is an indicator of rest. When John became lost, he was able to stay calm and to find his way out. Some "saved adults" are unable to stay calm.

When a bear cub is in the den with his mother and an intruder is nearby, the cub is able to rest in the fact that his mother will protect him. Our lives should operate the same way. Whether in a spiritual or physical sense, we should know that God will keep us safe. We should rest in the fact that God knows everything and that whatever happens is for His best and for our good.

ACTION POINT: Sing the hymn "Jesus, I Am Resting, Resting."

—*Stephen Vaughan*

SEPTEMBER 1
THE BIBLE IS
THE WORD OF GOD

I was beside my wife when my daughter and my three sons were born. One of the first things out of my mouth to my daughter was, "Esther, see this book." Her eyes weren't yet able to focus. "This is the Bible, God's Word. Say it, Esther! 'Bible, Word of God!' Say it! 'Bible, Word of God!'"

When Andrew, Jonathan, and Aaron were born, I did the same thing. Hundreds of times. "'Bible, Word of God! Bible, Word of God.' Say it! Say it! Say it! 'Bible, Word of God!'"

Every time I go to the hospital to see a newborn, I say the same thing. "Bible, Word of God!" "Bible, Word of God!"

Why do I say this? One reason is because the Bible claims to be the Word of God. "All scripture is given by inspiration of God, and is profitable for doctrine, for reproof, for correction, for instruction in righteousness: that the man of God may be perfect, throughly furnished unto all good works" (2 Tim. 3:16-17).

Here are some important words to put in your vocabulary:

Inspired: This comes from a word that means "God-breathed." The Bible is the very breath of God!

Verbally Inspired: Every word of the Bible is God-breathed.

Plenary: This word means "all of it." We can't pick and choose which verses are God-breathed. Every word in the Bible is God-breathed.

Inerrant: The Bible is without error or contradiction.

Preserved: We believe God has kept His Word secure and without error since the day it was written.

Ok, here's a test. What do we mean when we say we believe in the verbal, plenary, inspired, inerrant, preserved Word of God?

ASSIGNMENT: Look up 2 Peter 1:21. It means that God's Word didn't come by man's decision to write it. Men wrote from God as the Holy Spirit moved and impelled them.

—*Craig M. Scott*

SEPTEMBER 2
THE WORD OF GOD—FULFILLED PROPHECY

A wealthy man told me, "I only believe in three things: the American Constitution, the dollar, and myself." I mentioned to him the instability of the Constitution and the dollar and said, "Sir, you believe in yourself. What happens when you die?"

He told me he'd reincarnate and come back to live as another being. "Let me ask you a question," I said.

"Okay, ask away. "

"Sir, on what do you base that? Where are the facts? How do you know you're right?"

Looking me square in the eye, he asked, "How do you know *you* are right?"

"I base what I believe on the Bible, God's Word," I said. Of course, right away the conversation went to questions like "What makes you think the Bible is the Word of God?" and "Why is the Bible more reliable than any other book?"

The Old Testament is filled with dozens of prophecies about Jesus Christ that were written hundreds of years before Christ was born. What's the chance they would come true?

Let's look at only eight of those prophecies. What are the odds that they would come true exactly as the prophets said?

Let's pile 50-cent pieces six feet high over the whole planet Earth. We'll put a black dot on one of them. Now let's blindfold you and take you up in a helicopter and fly around. When you give the word, we'll drop you out. When you land, you'll have one chance to pick up that marked 50-cent piece.

You say, "No way! Not a chance! Never in a lifetime." That's my point. But hear me! Not only did eight of the prophecies concerning Jesus come true. All the prophecies did! John 17:17b says, "Thy word is truth." Believe me, we can trust God's Word.

ASSIGNMENT: Written 700 years before Christ, the Book of Isaiah is full of prophecies concerning Jesus. Read Isaiah 52:13-53:12. You'll find several prophecies concerning Christ, all of which were fulfilled.

—*Craig M. Scott*

THE BIBLE IS UNIQUE

Sitting in an airport in London, England, I struck up a conversation with a well-dressed man, hoping to witness to him about Jesus. He seemed intelligent and had a lot of religious knowledge. After talking with him for a while, I learned that he was a religion professor in a well-known university. I also discovered that he had neither a personal relationship with Jesus Christ through the new birth nor a belief that the Bible was the Word of God.

This man's arrogant attitude bothered me. He was the kind of man who would have delighted in destroying a young believer's confidence in the Word of God.

We debated whether the Bible is God's Word and whether it has errors or contradictions. I mentioned to him that the Bible is a library of 66 books, written by more than 35 authors in a period of approximately 1,500 years on three continents. The authors of the Bible came from a cross-section of humanity: educated, uneducated, kings, fishermen, public officials, farmers, teachers, and physicians. The Bible covers several subjects: religion, history, law, science, poetry, drama, biography, and prophecy. Its various parts are as harmoniously united as the parts that make up the human body.

For 35 men from such different backgrounds to write on so many subjects over a period of approximately 1,500 years—and agree perfectly—is mathematically impossible. It's a miracle. It simply couldn't happen.

So how do we explain the Bible? Second Peter 1:21 says, "For the prophecy came not in old time by the will of man: but holy men of God spake as they were moved by the Holy Ghost."

"Well, we all know that there are hundreds of contradictions in the Bible," the professor said.

I replied, "Sir, I will give you $1,000 if you can show me one."

I never gave him $1,000.

ASSIGNMENT: Romans 15:4 says, "For whatsoever things were written aforetime were written for our learning, that we through patience and comfort of the scriptures might have hope." Read and discuss Acts 17:11; 2 Timothy 2:15, 3:16-17.

—*Craig M. Scott*

THE BIBLE IS UNIQUE IN ITS POWER

Voltaire, an ungodly 18th century philosopher, said that it took hundreds of years to build up Christianity but that he, one Frenchman, could destroy it in only 50 years. Taking his pen, he dipped it into the ink of unbelief and wrote against God and the Bible.

Twenty years after his death, the Geneva Bible Society bought his house and used it for Bible printing. The house later became the Paris headquarters of the British and Foreign Bible Society.

Hey, guess what? The Bible is still the bestseller. In contrast, an entire six-volume set of Voltaire's works was once sold for 90 cents. Just before he died, this noted atheist said, "I wish I had never been born!"

The Bible is powerful. Listen to what it says about itself:

A Devouring Fire: "I will make my words in thy mouth fire, and this people wood, and it shall devour them" (Jer. 5:14b).

A Fire and Hammer: "Is not my word like as a fire? saith the Lord; and like a hammer that breaketh the rock in pieces?" (Jer. 23:29).

A Saving Force: "It [God's Word] is the power of God unto salvation to every one that believeth; to the Jew first, and also to the Greek" (Rom. 1:16b).

A Defensive Weapon: "The sword of the Spirit . . . is the word of God" (Eph. 6:17b).

A Two-Edged Sword: "For the word of God is quick, and powerful, and sharper than any twoedged sword" (Heb. 4:12a).

A Purifier of Life: "Wherewithal shall a young man cleanse his way? by taking heed thereto according to thy word" (Ps. 119:9). "Now ye are clean through the word" (John 15:3a). "Sanctify them through thy truth: thy word is truth" (John 17:17). "Seeing ye have purified your souls in obeying the truth through the Spirit" (1 Pet. 1:22a).

If the Bible is so powerful, are you memorizing it? Are you reading it daily? Have you ever decided to put yourself under its authority?

PRAYER TIME: Praise the Lord for our God-breathed Book!

—*Craig M. Scott*

THE BIBLE—DIFFICULT TO UNDERSTAND?

Sam knows Sally only from a work relationship. Sally is getting married as soon as her fiancé, Cecil, gets back from Iraq. Listen to their conversation during a lunch break.

"So you got a letter, huh?" Sam asks.

"Yes!" Sally replies.

"Who wrote it?"

"My fiancé, Cecil! The one who loves me. The one with whom I'll spend the rest of my life."

"Oh really!"

"Yeeeeessss!"

"May I read it?"

"Of course! Here."

Sam reads, "Dear Sally, I'm here in Iraq and thought I'd take a couple minutes to write. Been thinking about you a lot. How are things going for you? Hope to return in a couple months. Love, Cecil."

Sam thinks, *Just a letter. How boring!* He returns the letter to Sally, who goes off by herself and slowly reads it again.

She reads, "Dear Sally (*Oh, my! He called me "dear." I'm dear to him.*), I'm here in Iraq. . . . Been thinking about you a lot (*Oh, how sweet! He's been thinking about me A LOT. He must really love me!*). How are things going for you? (*Oh, how sweet! He really cares about my life.*)

What was the difference between the two readers of this love letter? The difference is that **Sally has a personal relationship with the author!** This story illustrates the way some people approach the Bible. One man says, "Oh, how boring! You mean to tell me that you read that book every day?" The second man replies, "So it's boring, huh? Did you know that God's Word is His love letter to His family? That's what you get for reading someone else's mail!"

God's Word is God's love letter to His family! In order to appreciate and comprehend it, one must have a personal relationship with the Author!

READ AND DISCUSS: John 16:12-15; 1 Corinthians 2:9-14

—*Craig M. Scott*

SEPTEMBER 6
THE BIBLE—
LET'S STUDY IT!

A famous medical professor told his class, "Students, I have something very important to teach you today. I would like to teach you the importance of observation. Noticing details. Watching carefully. Seeing the little things."

He continued, "I would like to begin class with a simple illustration. In my left hand, I have a bowl filled with a liquid. The liquid looks harmless, but believe me—it is very powerful. It has very powerful bacteria in it. If the liquid gets in a cut or in a sore on your tongue, it will make you horribly sick for about three days."

He then taught his class the importance of looking at everything very carefully. At the conclusion of class, he returned to the bowl filled with the liquid containing the powerful bacteria.

"Now class, I want you to do what I do." He stuck his finger into the liquid and put his finger into his mouth. The class groaned!

He passed the bowl around, and everyone followed his example. He concluded, "Now here is the lesson. If you had been observing me properly, you would have seen me put my index finger into the bowl but put my pinky into my mouth. You all failed to observe carefully. You stuck your index finger into the bowl and then put it in your mouth.

"I have an announcement. Class will be canceled for the next three days. None of you will be able to get out of bed."

Observation! Noticing the small things. Seeing things as they really are. Seeing all the truth.

When we study the Bible, we notice every *the* and *and*. God inspired every little word. We notice who is speaking and to whom it is speaking. We notice the big words and the little words. Why? Every word is God-breathed. Second Peter 1:21b says, "Holy men of God spake as they were moved by the Holy Ghost."

BIBLE READING: Read these verses together aloud—Matthew 5:18; 2 Timothy 2:15.

—Craig M. Scott

SEPTEMBER 7
THE BIBLE—
LET'S MEDITATE UPON IT

A promise in the Scriptures is attached to a project. If you apply this project to your life, you will reach your full potential in whatever you do. If you will practice this project, God will give you success.

I found out about this principle in college. I was extremely busy. I was on the wrestling team, I worked a job, and I was president of my class. Plus, I was involved in other extracurricular activities. My grades were suffering.

I heard about this project and learned that if I made it a priority, my grades would go up. Plus God would bless in every area of my life.

I decided to dedicate one hour each day to this project. Prime time. As a result, God blessed every area of my life, including my grades. I discovered I could concentrate better. My listening skills improved! I didn't need to read my notes over and over again before tests. God blessed!

What was this project? "This book of the law shall not depart out of thy mouth; but thou shalt meditate therein day and night, that thou mayest observe to do according to all that is written therein: for then thou shalt make thy way prosperous, and then thou shalt have good success" (Josh. 1:8).

Meditation of the Word!

The project:

1. Memorize it. Every word! Quotable! Chapter at a time. Books at a time.
2. Visualize it. Climb inside each verse and properly interpret it. Look up the meaning of each word. Understand the context, grammar, history, and culture.
3. Apply it. Make it your own. Put your name in the verse. "For God so loved _____, that he gave his only begotten Son" (John 3:16a).
4. Worship with it. Pray it and sing it back to God. Many of the Psalms reflect David's internalizing the Word, praying it, and singing it back to God.

ASSIGNMENT: Pick a passage of Scripture for your meditation. Set aside time tomorrow to do your project.

—*Craig M. Scott*

SEPTEMBER 8
WHEN A CHILD WON'T OBEY

Scripture Reading—Deuteronomy 21:18-21

W e are in great danger when we treat anything God takes seriously in a casual manner. That's why we must consider our passage from Deuteronomy with much concern. God presented to His people a plan for dealing with a son who was stubborn, rebellious, and disobedient.

The key phrase is found in verse 18b—"when they have chastened him, [he] will not hearken unto them." God never commanded His people to stone a child who just disobeyed. Rather this punishment was reserved for a child who refused to change after he was properly disciplined.

We might assume that these child-stoning events were a regular occasion. I highly doubt it! In fact, I believe these events rarely occurred. In verse 21b, we read, "And all Israel shall hear, and fear." In Proverbs 16:6b, we read, "By the fear of the Lord men depart from evil." The stoning of a rebel was God's way of letting children know that He would not tolerate a rebellious attitude toward parents. If and when a child was put to death, his death served notice to all the children in the land that God would deal harshly with them if they didn't change.

Can you imagine this discussion among a group of teens? "What happened to him?" "Where is he?" "I think he was having a hard time getting along with his parents." "Probably a bad attitude." "Did you hear what they did? They stoned him." Something tells me that every teen listening would have gotten the message and would have been more serious about having a right attitude toward his parents.

Attitude is everything. If God suddenly required that we enforce this Old Testament Jewish law in our church youth groups, I wonder if we would find any empty chairs in teen Sunday school this week. Closer to home, I wonder if we would have any empty bedrooms in our houses. God doesn't look lightly on rebellion, and neither should we.

DISCUSSION: As a family, describe some ways you would identify an attitude of rebellion.

—Tom Palmer

The First Commandment with Promise

Scripture Reading—Exodus 20:12
"Honour thy father and thy mother:
that thy days may be long upon the land
which the Lord thy God giveth thee."

The first four of the Ten Commandments deal with our relationship with God. God knew that His people needed to keep Him first in every dimension of their lives. Commandment number five is significant because it focuses on the most important of all human relationships. The relationship someone has with his parents is such a high priority that it's second only to his relationship with God.

This commandment is so important that God backs it up with the promise of a life lived longer and better than that of one who dishonors his parents. It is important to remember that we aren't just talking about number of years here. God isn't just talking about adding years to your life but adding fullness of life to the years you live.

Why is this relationship with parents so important for a child? God places parents in children's lives to teach them how to get along with God. Where does a child first learn the difference between right and wrong? Where does a child first learn that he will receive rewards for doing right and consequences for doing wrong? Where does a child first learn how to obey? Is it not at home under the training of parents who know God and want their child to do the same? A child who cannot get along with his parents will have a difficult time getting along with God. To be even more blunt, a child who is not right with his parents will find it impossible to be right with God.

God did not make a mistake when He gave children their parents. No, in so doing, He was preparing them for a life of blessing that would come from knowing Him. Parents are God's special blessing to children.

BIBLE READING: Read Ephesians 6:2-3. Discuss some ways life will "be well" for children who honor their parents.

—Tom Palmer

SEPTEMBER 10
DON'T GET
PICKED APART!

Scripture Reading—Proverbs 30:17
"The eye that mocketh at his father, and despiseth to obey his mother,
the ravens of the valley shall pick it out,
and the young eagles shall eat it."

A friend of mine was hunting deer in Indiana and had harvested a deer. Because he was a significant distance from home, he dragged the deer to the hedgerow and walked home to get a four-wheeler so he could bring the deer home. Later, while returning to the hedgerow, he saw several buzzards fly away from the area near the deer.

Approaching the deer carcass, he noticed that in the short time he was gone the buzzards had picked one of the deer's eyeballs out of its socket. Interestingly, Proverbs uses a similarly grotesque picture to describe what can happen to a child who jokes about obeying his parents.

Big, old, black buzzards are smart. As scavengers, they feed on dead animals; however, they must confirm that the animal is dead before they can feed on it. It wouldn't be good to try to enjoy some venison steak from a deer that's just taking a nap! As the birds approach the carcass, they go to the head and pick at the animal's eyeball with the sharp point of their beaks. The eyeball is sensitive. If the animal is still alive, he will respond immediately. No response, of course, indicates that the animal is dead.

The writer of Proverbs presents a graphic and unpleasant picture of what can result for children who don't properly respond to their parents. How sad to see a young person miss out on much of God's blessing in life because he refused to cooperate with his mom and dad. Ephesians 6:1 says that children should obey their parents "in the Lord: for this is right."

ASSIGNMENT: See if you can recall Bible stories of young people who died prematurely because they rebelled against their parents. (Hint: Look in 1 Samuel 2 and 2 Samuel 18.)

—*Tom Palmer*

SEPTEMBER 11
RULES FOR
RAISING PARENTS

Scripture Reading—Proverbs 17:6
"Children's children are the crown of old men;
and the glory of children
are their fathers."

Here are two good rules children should follow to treat their parents well:

1. **Love them.** Years ago, I was driving home late at night from a preaching engagement. It was necessary for me to travel through a town where my parents were attending a week of meetings. I knew the motel where they were staying and pulled into the parking lot. Not knowing their room number, I drove around until I found their van. Their room was dark, so I knew they had already gone to bed. Parking, I wrote a note that said, "I am thankful for you, and I love you." After signing my name, I placed the note under one of their van's windshield wipers. I hope I never get so big that I stop telling my parents I love them. Sure I love them, but I want them to know it. Whether the end of a phone call, a birthday card, or just a "good night" when we stay with them, I plan to keep saying "I love you."

2. **Obey them.** "Obedience is doing exactly what I am told, when I am told to do it, with a right heart attitude." I learned that definition years ago, and I've never forgotten it. As I've grown older, I've continued to learn that partial obedience, postponed obedience, and pouting obedience are all disobedience. The first people a child learns to obey are his parents. This fact is crucial because he will be submitting in obedience to God-given authorities for the rest of his life. If he learns obedience at home, life will be much easier on the job, at school, or with the team. Parents aren't interested in other opinions or options; they simply desire obedience. Obedience is the key that opens every door of opportunity in life.

DO THIS NOW: When was the last time you said "I love you" to your parents? Determine to tell them at least once in the next 24 hours.

—Tom Palmer

SEPTEMBER 12
Rules for Raising Parents— Part 2

Scripture Reading—Proverbs 15:20
"A wise son maketh a glad father: but a foolish man despiseth his mother."

Here are two more rules for children to follow when they respond to their parents.

3. **Honor them.** When we honor someone, we place value upon him. Children may honor their parents in several ways. First, they must never allow conflicts to go unresolved. Few things can do more to strengthen relationships than the words, "I was wrong. I'm sorry. Please forgive me." Rather than allowing offenses to build up, children can quickly resolve them and strengthen relationships. Second, it's a blessing for children to go to their parents for counsel. Children reach a point when they no longer directly obey their parents because God has given them a home of their own. Yet parents remain a wonderful God-given source of counsel based on their own experience and on their walk with God.

4. **Appreciate them.** A spirit of gratitude has a wonderful way of making home a pleasant place. Children should learn to appreciate all Mom and Dad do for them. A fine meal, clean clothes, laundered sheets, and a packed lunch are blessings they must not take for granted. Older children must learn to appreciate things like tuition payments and the use of the car. Once we are ungrateful, it doesn't take long before we begin to take things for granted. We will treat carelessly anything we take for granted. Unfortunately, children often assume they deserve all they get. They may even become upset or mad if the meal is different or the car is unavailable. How foolish! Children should let their parents know they are appreciated. Gratefulness on their part will make parents increasingly grateful for their children. Colossians 3:15 says, "And let the peace of God rule in your hearts . . . and be ye thankful."

ASSIGNMENT: Choose a special way to say "thanks" to Mom and Dad. (This works for grownups, too.) A note, a gift, or even a hug will work just fine.

—Tom Palmer

SEPTEMBER 13
DON'T SAY "NO" TO RULES

Scripture Reading
Proverbs 1:8—*"My son, hear the instruction of thy father,*
and forsake not the law of thy mother."
Proverbs 3:1-2—*"My son, forget not my law;*
but let thine heart keep my commandments:
For length of days, and long life, and peace,
shall they add to thee."

Several years ago, I clipped a newspaper article with the headline "Teen study: Rules lower use of drugs." This Associated Press article said the following in several interesting quotes: "Parents who impose strict rules on their teenagers have a better chance of raising drug-free children, but most set few guidelines or none at all." "The study [done by the National Center on Addiction and Substance Abuse] shows that teenagers who live in highly structured households are at a low risk of abusing drugs."

One of the great heartbreaks of modern society is when teens abuse drugs. Teens are ruining their lives because they have adopted an out-of-control lifestyle that supposedly liberates them to do as they wish. But the Bible is clear that rules (or "laws" as Proverbs says) help eliminate trouble for young people. Rules produce a system of controls. This system protects lives from destructive tendencies that seek to control.

Children and teenagers have a tendency to resist when parents establish and enforce rules. The Bible clearly says, however, that by following rules, young people have the promise not only of a longer life but also of a peaceful life. Rules are not designed to hurt, harm, or hinder, but rather to help. Young people who understand the importance of rules will enjoy much freedom in growing up to be all that God desires.

God knew what He was talking about when He allowed parents to establish rules. Young person, as you grow older, you will have to make the choice to say "no" to drugs; but never allow yourself to be guilty of saying "no" to rules.

ACTION POINT: Discuss what life would be like if you could drive a car for 24 hours without any stop signs.

—*Tom Palmer*

SEPTEMBER 14
BACK TO THE WOODSHED

Scripture Reading
Proverbs 22:15—*"Foolishness is bound in the heart of a child;*
but the rod of correction shall drive it far from him."
Proverbs 23:13-14—*"Withhold not correction from the child:*
for if thou beatest him with the rod, he shall not die.
Thou shalt beat him with the rod, and shalt deliver his soul from hell."

Boys and girls dread hearing one quote. It's the statement a loving dad makes just before he delivers a good spanking to a child who has done wrong. The statement goes something like this: "This is going to hurt me far more than it's going to hurt you." Most children find that statement hard to believe and are inclined to think that if Dad would just forget the whole idea of punishment, he wouldn't get hurt.

That statement is hard to comprehend, I know, until you become a father. Suddenly, you realize that disciplining a child is painful. A truly godly parent will discipline not out of pleasure but out of love. Motivated by love, that parent is willing, if necessary, to bring pain for the purpose of change in the child's life.

Back in the good old days, people commonly talked about going to the woodshed. When they did so, they referred to a time of discipline, punishment, and correction. Maybe that's part of the problem in America. Because of electricity and oil furnaces, most homes no longer have a woodshed. More seriously, most homes no longer have the proper form of loving discipline to make wrongs right.

A wise parent recognizes the responsibility God has given him to correct his children. On the other hand, children must acknowledge God's plan and purpose in discipline—to keep them from growing up loving to do wrong. Discipline isn't easy for a parent or a child, but the results typically prove that when parents administer it properly, it will be for the better.

APPLICATION: Take time to read Hebrews 12:5-11. Note the benefits of chastisement when the recipient handles it properly.

—*Tom Palmer*

SEPTEMBER 15
GOD'S HOME ADDRESS

Scripture Reading—Psalm 22:3
"But thou art holy, O thou that inhabitest the praises of Israel."

Businesses need our home address to deliver items we order online. Visitors need to know our home location when we invite them over for dinner. Our home is where we live; it's our abiding place.

Praise is God's home address. David said God "inhabitest the praises of Israel." That means God dwells in praise. In heaven, there is an unceasing stream of praise to the Lamb in the midst of the throne. Praise is God's home element. It's the atmosphere in which God resides.

Why do Christians sing? One reason we sing is because God is attracted to praise. To put it another way, God shows up and dwells in the midst of praise. He inhabits praise. God's presence is precious, and we can entertain Him as our guest anytime we choose to praise Him!

The Book of Revelation refers to Jesus as the Lamb at least 27 times. The elders fall down before the Lamb and sing, "Worthy is the Lamb." The saints are made white by the blood of the Lamb. Redeemed sinners and the heavenly hosts give blessing, honor, and glory to the Lamb. Throughout the entire book, we find reference upon reference concerning praise directed to the Lamb of God. Praise is the language of heaven. In heaven, they worship the Lamb, and we should do the same on earth! A countless multitude of God's people will be praising Him throughout all eternity. Praise is where God lives both now and in eternity. You can get ready for heaven by praising God here on earth!

A.W. Tozer said, "God dwells in the heart where praise is." The Lord inhabits praise wherever He finds it. What is heaven's dress code? Scripture says to put on "the garment of praise for the spirit of heaviness." (Isa. 61:3). Whenever we feel like God is far away, we should start praising the Lord from our hearts. We will find that He inhabits praise.

DO THIS NOW: See how many references to the "Lamb" you can find in Revelation.

—Harold Vaughan

SEPTEMBER 16
IT GETS BETTER
UP HIGHER!

Two ladies went to church visitation, one of whom was wealthy. Robed in furs, she drove a luxury car and had the best of everything. Assigned to visit a poor part of town, she and her partner pulled in the parking lot of a run-down apartment building on the wrong side of the tracks. The grass hadn't been cut, and the shrubs hadn't been trimmed. Broken toys littered the ground, and graffiti covered the building.

The wealthy woman was horrified by the terrible living conditions. She said to her visitation partner, "How can anyone live in a place like this?"

The partner had previously visited the lady who lived in a third-floor apartment. She said to the wealthy woman, "It gets better up higher."

Getting out of the car, they approached the steps. The sidewalks were dirty, and trash lay everywhere. Appalled, the wealthy woman said, "How can anyone live in a place like this?"

Again, her partner replied, "It gets better up higher."

They climbed steps to the third floor. The handrail was falling off, and filth covered the stairwell. Disgusted, the wealthy woman repeated, "How can anyone stand to live in a place like this?"

Her partner said, "It gets better up higher."

When they knocked on the door, a little, old lady let them in. The apartment was dark, dingy, and dirty. When they sat down, the old lady thanked them for coming and talked about how good God is and about how beautiful heaven is going to be.

The wealthy woman didn't hear a word she said; all she thought about were the terrible living conditions of this dear, old saint. Shocked and dismayed, she couldn't hold her revulsion in any longer. She blurted out, "How can you stand to live in a place like this?"

The old woman replied, "It gets better up higher!"

REJOICE: Heaven is a glorious place filled with praise to the Lamb of God.

—Harold Vaughan

SEPTEMBER 17
PRAISE IS THE PROPER
RESPONSE TO GOD

Scripture Reading—Psalm 9:1-2

The word *praise* literally means "to hold out the hand." Praise is bestowing approval and worship upon a superior being. David said, "I will sing praise to thy name, O thou most High" (Ps. 9:2b).

Isaiah saw the Lord "high and lifted up" (Isa. 6:1). Daniel said the "*most High* ruleth in the kingdom of men" (Dan. 4:17, 25, 32; emphasis added). Hebrews tells us that Melchisedec was "priest of the *most high* God" (7:1, emphasis added). Isaiah refers to God as the "*high and lofty One* that inhabiteth eternity" (Isa. 57:15, emphasis added). Before we have a proper response to God, we must first have a proper view of God. Praise is the result of seeing God in His exalted position as the most High.

The Old Testament priests had a regulated procedure for approaching the Lord in the tabernacle. Under the old covenant, God was meticulous about how His priests came before Him. He spent seven chapters (243 verses) detailing His prescribed worship in the tabernacle but described the creation of the universe in only 31 verses. Approaching Almighty God isn't a light matter. It's a time for recognition, respect, and reverence.

"And he appointed certain of the Levites to . . . *praise* the Lord God of Israel" (1 Chron. 16:4, emphasis added). These men were dedicated to one thing—singing praise to the Lord. They were to boast about God in joyful song.

Praise is boasting about Jesus. It's giving God the glory due unto His name. The natural outflow of viewing God properly is unbridled praise. We have many reasons to praise the Lord—because He commands us to, because He answers prayer, because He does so many good things for us. But the main reason is because of who He is! The Most High God deserves our highest praise; and when we see Him in His elevated position, our proper response is praise.

PRAISE THE LORD: Sing a song that expresses praise to God.

—Harold Vaughan

SEPTEMBER 18
PRAISE THERAPY
Scripture Reading—Psalm 150:1-6

Those with physical injuries need physical therapy. Those who have other problems are sometimes treated with "color therapy" or "aromatherapy." But God's Word offers another kind of therapy—praise therapy.

Because God made us, we owe our existence to Him. We should praise the Lord because He is worthy of our praise; He is God! One of the Puritans said, "In prayer we sound like men, but in praise we sound like angels." The entire angelic host is continually praising the Lamb in the midst of the throne. Praise is the language of heaven.

Praise is not so much therapy as it is our obligation and privilege. Appropriate praise, however, brings great benefits. Praise is for God, but it brings great blessing to our hearts. Sometimes we need to put on "the garment of praise for the spirit of heaviness" (Isa. 61:3). When we feel down in the dumps, we should rehearse and praise the Lord for His goodness, mercy, holiness, love, longsuffering, and kindness. We should express our appreciation to the Lord in verbal praise. We will find that praise not only exalts God but also elevates the praiser.

We should praise God every time we feel like it. Other times, we should praise God *until* we do feel like it. We shouldn't let our emotions control us. Character means we do right whether we feel like it or not. We should do right because it is right until doing right becomes a natural part of our lives. As we do our duty, our feelings will eventually catch up. "Every thing that hath breath [should] praise the Lord" (Ps. 150:6)—and that includes you and me!

APPLICATION: According to Psalm 150, for how many things should we praise the Lord? Do you remember which instruments this psalm said should be used in praise?

—Harold Vaughan

SEPTEMBER 19
PRAISING:
THE SECRET OF VICTORY
Scripture Reading—Acts 16:20-34

Paul and Silas were severely beaten and cast in prison for preaching the Gospel. How did they respond? "And at midnight Paul and Silas prayed, and sang praises unto God: and the prisoners heard them" (Acts 16:25). Amazing, isn't it? Rather than complaining, they were praising the Lord in jail!

The secret of victory is not praying but praising. Those who praise are people who believe God. They look beyond what they can see on a human level and look to the divine level. Circumstances may be difficult in the short run, but praising can lift us out of our pit. God sent an earthquake and opened the prison doors for Paul and Silas. The bands holding them were loosed. The prison keeper and his entire household came to the Lord that night.

Paul and Silas knew God had their situation under control. Second Peter 1:3 says God "according as his divine power hath given unto us all things that pertain unto life and godliness, through the knowledge of him that hath called us to glory and virtue." That means God has already provided everything we need in this life. There are no accidents in the Christian journey. Praise is never out of season! In fact, praising is the way God has designed for us to confront difficulties. When we praise the Lord in adversity, we demonstrate that we actively believe God. Perhaps we know that powerful little chorus:

It's amazing what praising can do, Hallelujah, Hallelujah.
It's amazing what praising can do. Hallelujah!
I don't worry when things go wrong; Jesus fills my heart with a song.
It's amazing what praising can do, Hallelujah!

The key to triumphant living is learning to live a life of praise. Don't underestimate this valuable resource. Psalm 7:17 says, "I will praise the Lord according to his righteousness: and will sing praise to the name of the Lord most high."

SONG TIME: Sing a couple of your favorite choruses or songs of praise.

—*Harold Vaughan*

WHOLEHEARTED PRAISE
Scripture Reading—Psalm 9:1a
"I will praise thee, O Lord, with my whole heart."

Praise calls for full concentration of all our faculties. David determined to praise the Lord with his whole heart.

Acceptable praise is more than just mouthing words. True praise comes from the depths of our souls. It's something that involves our entire being, our *whole heart*. Halfheartedness has no place in the Christian life. Ecclesiastes says, "Whatsoever thy hand findeth to do, do it with thy might" (9:10a). In other words, when we do something, we should put all of our energies in it. We should be enthusiastic! If our faces look like a reprint of the Book of Lamentations, we need a facelift. Going through the motions isn't enough. We need to put our strength, mind, and soul into it. We should praise the Lord with our *whole heart*.

The Bible says much about the heart of man. It describes a hard heart, a fainting heart, a stirred heart, a merry heart, a trembling heart, a tender heart, and a perfect heart. Our heart is the seat of our affections. "For where your treasure is, there will your heart be also" (Matt. 6:21). We become preoccupied with things that are valuable to us and invest in them. We meditate about concerns that are important to us. Whatever we treasure is precious to us.

Worship is good because it interrupts our preoccupation with self! God desires full-blown praise from the depths of our souls.

Songs and hymns of praise are joyful celebrations of God's goodness. Fanny Crosby wrote the following hymn of praise:

Praise Him! praise Him! Jesus, our blessed Redeemer!
Sing, O earth, His wonderful love proclaim!
Hail Him! hail Him! highest archangels in glory;
Strength and honor give to His holy name!
Like a shepherd, Jesus will guard His children,
In His arms He carries them all day long.

SONG TIME: Sing this great hymn of praise to the Lord with all your heart.

—Harold Vaughan

SEPTEMBER 21
WITNESSING THROUGH PRAISE

Scripture Reading—Psalm 107:2a
"Let the redeemed of the Lord say so."

When we speak in church and tell how God is working in our lives, we call this "sharing a testimony." If we said the same thing to lost people, we would call it "witnessing." Our testimony is a powerful, evangelistic tool. Not everyone can preach a sermon, but everyone can share a testimony. One of the most powerful weapons in our evangelistic arsenal is our personal testimony.

We can use our testimony to gain a hearing for the Gospel. Jesus told the woman at the well to return home and to tell the people what had happened to her. She told the townspeople to come and see the man who told her everything she had done. Everybody came to hear Jesus because of her testimony.

In Mark 5, we read about a man dwelling in the tombs. He was so fierce and full of evil spirits that people were afraid of him. Jesus cast the demons out of this man, and he wanted to follow the Lord. But Jesus said to him, "Go home to thy friends, and tell them how great things the Lord hath done for thee, and hath had compassion on thee" (v. 19b). People marveled when they heard this man's testimony.

Praise is simply bragging about what we appreciate. Robert Murray M'Cheyne said, "Give unlimited credit to God." I was preaching in a church where the pastor told me about a 92-year-old man who went downtown every week to pass out Gospel tracts. If God has done something for us, we should *broadcast it.*

C.T. Studd was a wealthy man who sold everything he had so he could be a missionary to China, India, and Africa. He once said, "Some wish to live within the sound of a church or chapel bell. I want to run a rescue shop within a yard of hell." God can use our praise to shine the light on the path of unsaved people.

SPEAK UP FOR GOD: Seize every opportunity to brag on Jesus and on what He has done for you!

—Harold Vaughan

SEPTEMBER 22
TIME TO WISE UP!

Scripture Reading—Proverbs 2:4
"If thou seekest her as silver, and searchest for her
as for hid treasures."

Treasure hunters have my full admiration. They trek through jungles unlocking the secrets of ancient maps, searching for sunken treasure, and unearthing past civilizations one grain of sand at a time. I think it's clearly evident that all of us have some treasure hunting naturally built into us. We all like to find money on the sidewalk, and we all enjoy finding a good deal at our favorite store. Many of us hunt for houses, cars, jobs, and freebies regularly. Of course, everyone takes his treasure-hunting hobby to varying levels; but let's face it: all of us enjoy treasure hunting to some degree.

Every day people look for that long-forgotten heirloom or search for a one-of-a-kind trinket from an out-of-the-way antique shop. Some treasures are found in obvious places like attics or safety deposit boxes. But some people find surprises hidden between walls, tucked in secret compartments, or buried under 100-year-old trees. You never know where you'll find treasure!

To be successful treasure hunters, we must possess certain qualities. We must have unusual stamina, plenty of perspiration, and unbridled enthusiasm. The art of treasure hunting has little to do with luck but everything to do with preparation and patience.

The same is true for spiritual treasure. If we want spiritual maturity, we must search "for her as for hid treasures" (Prov. 2:4). We must take the time to hunt for those truths that make our lives "approved unto God, a workman that needeth not to be ashamed" (2 Tim. 2:15). The heavenly treasure of wisdom is just a shovel throw away from the one who earnestly searches for it. Are you looking for heavenly treasure? Are you studying the Bible? Some men are fortunate enough to find gold, but God said that all who search diligently can find wisdom. Hurry up! There's enough treasure for you, too!

GO TO THE WORD: Read Proverbs 2 and discover the spiritual treasure it contains for you.

—Jeff Kahl

SEPTEMBER 23
FACING
THE FUTURE

Scripture Reading—Proverbs 27:1
"Boast not thyself of to morrow; *for thou knowest not*
what a day may bring forth" (emphasis added).
Also read Matthew 6:25-34.

There's a lot about the future we cannot know, but we do know that the future is unpredictable. We may not know what the future holds, but we know who holds the future. If God knows the future and if we're trusting Him, we can face tomorrow courageously. Missionary William Carey correctly said, "The future is as bright as the promises of God." If we can count on anything, we can count on God's promises. They will not fail us! My sister-in-law used to say, "The future is looking gloriously dark." Remember, life has to get worse before it gets better; and for Christians, *the best is yet to come.*

In Matthew 6:25-34, in His Sermon on the Mount, Jesus addressed worry. Many things people worry about spring from uncertainties about the future. When Jesus says, "Take therefore no thought for the morrow: for the morrow shall take thought for the things of itself" (v. 34a), He doesn't imply that we shouldn't think seriously about important matters. He simply tells us not to be overcome by worry or anxiety about the future. We cannot change anything about tomorrow by worrying about it, but worrying will change us.

If God takes care of birds (v. 26) and flowers (v. 28), surely He will take care of us. Food and clothing, the material things of life, are what the unsaved are concerned about. As Christians, we must look beyond the temporal and focus on the eternal through our relationship with God. If we concentrate on kingdom issues and on living godly lives, God will take care of our needs (v. 33). Our future is secure because we're secure in Him.

MEDITATION: As you consider your future as a Christian family, what concerns could worry you? What can you do to prevent anxiety about those concerns?

—Jack Palmer

SEPTEMBER 24
FACING THE FUTURE
REQUIRES GREAT COURAGE
Scripture Reading—James 4:13-15

One thing we cannot do is stop the hands of time. Time continually moves forward. Do you ever wish you could freeze time right where it is? Have you ever wished to capture a special event so you could hold on to it? That's why people take pictures and make home videos. We don't want certain events or experiences to get away from us. We'd rather not move on to the uncertainties of tomorrow.

The fact is, there's a future we all must face. For some, the future may be longer than others. When facing the future, we must be mindful of *the will of God.*

Facing the future requires great courage. The future can be overwhelming and frightening because we don't know what's out there. But where do we find the courage? In Isaiah 41:10, we read, "Fear thou not; for I am with thee: be not dismayed; for I am thy God: I will strengthen thee; yea, I will help thee; yea, I will uphold thee with the right hand of my righteousness." Within this wonderful verse, God lists three blessings we can claim when we need courage.

1. The Presence of God
2. The Person of God
3. The Promises of God

"Fear thou not" is a command based on the fact that God is with us—"for I am with thee." "Be not dismayed" means don't become discouraged at the prospect of trouble. The reason? "For I am thy God." When God is personally involved in our future, we know our future is in the best of hands. God promises to give us strength and to help us as He holds us up with His strong right hand. Nothing is so big that God cannot carry it. When we claim His presence, His person, and His promises, we find all the courage we need to face anything the future brings our way.

DISCUSSION: From today's Scripture reading, what is the most valuable lesson you've learned about the future? Share your thoughts with each other.

—Jack Palmer

SEPTEMBER 25
FACING THE FUTURE
DEMANDS GREAT COMMITMENT

Scripture Reading—Colossians 3:23-24
*"And whatsoever ye do, **do it heartily, as to the Lord**, and not unto men; knowing that of the Lord ye shall receive the reward of the inheritance: **for ye serve the Lord Christ**" (emphasis added).*

One of the most important qualities of a Christian is commitment. Commitment is the measure of our determination. It's our refusal to be distracted, discouraged, or defeated. It's knowing that everything I do must be done "heartily, as to the Lord, and not unto men" (Col. 3:23). But many of God's people seem to know little or nothing about real commitment.

In the spring of 1821, when the city of Indianapolis, Indiana, was in its infancy, Jeremiah Johnson fell in love with a local maiden named Rachel Reagin. Since there was no legal organization in the city, Jeremiah realized that a trip of 60 miles to Connersville, Indiana, was necessary to secure a marriage license. His father couldn't spare him a horse from the plow team, but so great was Jeremiah's love for Rachel that he traveled 120 miles round-trip through the unbroken wilderness barefoot.

Poor Jeremiah's delays weren't over. He waited six more weeks for a minister to arrive in Indianapolis to perform the city's first wedding. In his countrified English, he related, "I determined from the moment I seed her, to have her, or to die a-trying!" Isn't it amazing the sacrifice someone will make for the sake of love? Jeremiah's English might not have been the best, but he sure knew something about commitment.

Commitment is the test of true love, whether commitment to God, to His Word, to godly living, to your marriage, to your family, to your church, to your witness, or to just plain faithfulness. Sure, the future is uncertain, but commitment can carry you forward with confidence, knowing you are following the course God has planned for you. A lack of commitment results in insecurity. As you face the future, *be committed!*

APPLICATION: Discuss your family's commitment to God, to His Word, and to each other.

—Jack Palmer

SEPTEMBER 26
FACING THE FUTURE
WITH GREAT CONVICTION

Scripture Reading—2 Timothy 1:12
"For the which cause I also suffer these things:
*nevertheless I am not ashamed: for **I know whom I have believed**,*
and am persuaded that he is able
to keep that which I have committed
unto him against that day"
(emphasis added).

The apostle Paul faced an uncertain future. He was a prisoner of Rome because he had faithfully preached the Gospel (2 Tim. 1:8). He had suffered much for the sake of Christ, and apparently death was inevitable. In Acts 20:22-24, he spoke confidently about his future, knowing that in human terms the worst awaited him. "But none of these things move me, neither count I my life dear unto myself, so that I might finish my course with joy" (v. 24a). How could he, not knowing what was ahead of him, be so courageous? He was a man of great conviction.

Sure of his salvation, he knew God had called him to preach the Gospel. He knew he was in the center of God's will. He knew that no matter what happened to him, God was in control. He knew nothing could touch him without God's permission. He knew he was on his way to heaven when he died, and he based everything on his convictions.

Conviction is what we believe based on God's Word. A conviction is something we are willing to live or to die for. It's knowing what we believe and why we believe it. When we believe right, we will live right. Convictions are the anchor of our souls against the storms of life. Someone once said, "He who stands for nothing will usually fall for anything."

Preferences change, but convictions don't. Patrick Henry said, "Give me liberty or give me death." When you have the kind of conviction he had, you can face the future victoriously. Build strong convictions because everything in your life will stand upon them.

ACTION POINT: Talk together about your family convictions. Be sure you are basing them on Scripture.

—*Jack Palmer*

SEPTEMBER 27
GREAT CONCENTRATION ON FACING THE FUTURE

Scripture Reading—Acts 2:46-47

"And they, continuing daily with one accord in the temple, and breaking bread from house to house, did eat their meat with gladness and single-ness of heart, praising God, and having favour with all the people. And the Lord added to the church daily such as should be saved" (emphasis added).

He who aims at nothing will certainly hit it! Many challenges in life require great concentration. That's especially true in the sports world—hitting a golf ball straight down the middle of the fairway, shooting a jump shot into the basket at 20 feet, kicking a field goal through the uprights at 35 yards.

A colony of ants lived in a golf course sand trap. A golfer hit a ball into the trap. When he tried to hit the ball out of the sand, he missed several tries and destroyed many ants in the process. One ant said to another, "If we're going to get out of here alive, we better get on the ball!" That fellow didn't know much about concentration.

Concentration requires intense focus. The early church had that kind of focus and did everything with "singleness of heart" (v. 46). Christian families need that kind of focus to face the future's uncertainties.

Peter lost his concentration. In Matthew 14, we read that Jesus invited Peter to walk on the water with Him. Peter was doing great until he took his eyes off the Lord and focused on the storm. Immediately, he began to sink. "Lord, save me!" he cried. Jesus rescued him but also rebuked him for his lack of faith (v. 31).

As you face future unknowns, you must maintain an intense focus on the Lord, on His Word, and on prayer. If you take your eyes off Him, your faith will falter; and you, too, will sink under the "waves" that threaten to wash over you.

APPLICATION: What potential "storms" do you anticipate facing in your future? How can you prepare so you will not lose your concentration? What can you do to maintain your focus?

—*Jack Palmer*

SEPTEMBER 28
OUR CONFIDENCE
FOR THE FUTURE
Scripture Reading—Psalms 42-43

So many face life without hope. No wonder most suicides occur among teens and young adults. As they consider life with all of its uncertainties, they conclude that there's no reason to go on. This hopelessness is not limited to the unsaved. Many professing Christians struggle, too. What a sad commentary on life!

As you read Psalms 42 and 43, you hear the cry of one who is desperate for God. There is no better place to be than in desperation for God. Many in humanly hopeless and helpless situations have discovered their only hope in God. Romans 15:13 describes Him as the "God of hope." Apart from God, there is no hope. That's why the psalmist wrote, "Hope . . . in God" (Ps. 42:5, 11; 43:5). Don't look for hope in government, in the judicial system, in education, in money, in military strength, or in any of man's solutions. You won't find it.

In 1982, I was asked to preach my dear mother's funeral service. My mother had been a godly woman who served the Lord at my father's side for many years. As I pondered her life and asked the Lord what I should preach, He directed me to 1 Corinthians 13, the great love chapter. I was especially drawn to verse 13—"And now abideth faith, *hope*, charity, these three; but the greatest of these is charity" (emphasis added).

I concluded my message by saying, "It was faith that gave Mother courage, *it was hope that gave Mother confidence*, and it was love that made Mother complete." Events like burying three of her children could have caused her to conclude that life was hopeless. But her confidence didn't rest in the unpredictable circumstances of life; it rested in her God. Therefore, she was able to face the future confidently for more than 81 years. She was an inspiration to all of us.

DISCUSSION: As a family, talk about seemingly hopeless difficulties you may face. Reaffirm your confidence in God as you face the future.

—*Jack Palmer*

SEPTEMBER 29
WE KNOW WHO
HOLDS THE FUTURE
Scripture Reading—Psalms 78:1-8

Earlier this week, we read, "We may not know what the future holds, but we know who holds the future." What a wonderful encouragement that truth is! In Psalm 78:7, we discover that one of the most important values we will ever pass on to our children and grandchildren is "that they might set their hope in God." If we can successfully teach them to hope in God, we have given them something priceless. We've given them what they need to face the future.

Some years ago, Stuart Hamblen wrote a great song about facing the future. The chorus goes like this:

Known only to Him, are the great hidden secrets;
I'll fear not the darkness when my flame shall dim;
I know not what the future holds, but I know who holds the future,
It's a secret known only to Him.

Yes, the future holds many secrets we cannot know until we get there. But we need not fear the darkness. Remember what Adoniram Judson said. "Our future is as bright as the promises of God!" Don't get caught sitting on the premises or leaning over the precipice when you should be *standing on the promises!*

The best way to communicate confidence in God to the next generation is to live it before them every day. No one watches us more closely than our family members. They want to see if we will face life's uncertainties with confidence. If they see us in despair, their hope will be diminished. But if they observe that our hope is in God, they'll know where to find hope for their future.

The greatest test of our confidence is when we've exhausted every human resource. That's when God's at His best. Remember, He's not our last hope; He's our *only* hope!

ASSIGNMENT: Choose Bible verses that give hope to your family as they face the future.

—*Jack Palmer*

VALUABLE TREASURE FOUND IN AN UNLIKELY PLACE

In 1988, during a clearance sale of unclaimed property, a man bought a painting for $1,000. Though the painting was in poor condition, he thought it might be worth as much as $1,500. Securing the painting to the roof of his van, he drove it to Christie's Auction House in New York City, where collectibles are sold. He told an attendant there that he would accept as little as $1,500 for his find.

When the resident expert saw the painting, he realized with surprise that it was a fabulous work by Dosso Dossi, one of the better Italian Renaissance painters. Called *Allegory of Fortune* and commissioned and painted around 1530, the painting had disappeared during the 19th century. But now it was found.

The painting went to auction on January 11, 1989. Though sellers expected to sell the painting for $600,000 to $800,000, a London dealer bought it for $4 million! Later, the Paul Getty Museum purchased the painting, though it was in need of repair. One leg of the male figure had been punctured in several places, and the painting was so damaged and dirty that many of its details were lost.

The painting's restoration was a three-year project, including an extensive study. The restorer said, "It was a slow, tedious process—really mind-boggling." But her work paid off. The original, warm gray background that emerged lends to the picture a haunting, atmospheric tone.

She repaired holes, filled in cracks, restored losses of paint, and gave the painting a coat of varnish. The result is dramatic, but museum visitors see only the impact of the finished work.

God's work is a "salvage business." Through grace, He saves, sets apart, and uses saved sinners to rescue those who are perishing. Our witness can result in the salvation of those who will bring many to Christ.

THOUGHT: Everyone will spend eternity either in heaven or in hell. What could more valuable than an eternal soul?

—Harold Vaughan

OCTOBER 1
HOW DOES YOUR
FAITH HOLD UP?—FAITH
Scripture Reading—Hebrews 10:35-39

Just wondering—did you happen to check the strength of the chair you're sitting on right now? Did it cross your mind to see if the chair could handle the weight of your body? You may think it's ridiculous to ask such a silly thing. After all, you just sat down. In fact, if you're a teen, you probably either "flopped yourself" down or "collapsed yourself" into the seat. No big deal, right? We do it all the time.

"Your faith will be as strong as the seat on which you choose to sit."

Finding a seat is no big deal as long as the chair holds you up. Sitting down is simple until you find yourself on your back in a pile of splintered lumber! Like sitting, faith is also a simple matter. The part of faith that is so critical, however, isn't the "sitting" part but the choosing the "seat" part.

The seat part of your faith is what you're trusting. Your faith will be as strong as the seat on which you choose to sit. A strong faith comes from trusting something or someone who is strong enough to hold you. A weak faith is the result of trusting something or someone who will fail you.

What are you trusting in? In other words, what are you depending on to hold you? It's a great blessing to have faith in God because you're placing your trust in Someone who cannot and will not fail you. You can trust Him for salvation, for protection, for direction, and for everything else you may need in your life.

Faith in God is a great foundation on which to build your life. Depending on God is the key to providing stability and strength in your life. Your confidence is not in yourself but in a great God who will not let you down (like the chair that wasn't made for someone your size).

DISCUSSION: What are several things we could depend on that would fail us?

—Tom Palmer

OCTOBER 2
GENUINE IS FOR REAL—
VIRTUE

Scripture Reading—Philippians 1:9-21

Let's imagine that you are going gift shopping in an ancient market. Your mother's birthday is only days away, and you decide to purchase a lovely piece of pottery as a special gift for her. After visiting several merchants' displays, you hold in your hand what you believe is your piece of choice. It's a vase—dainty, delicate, and beautifully decorated. What makes the vase more appealing is the price. It's within the limits of your coin collection.

Suddenly, another shopper steps to your side, inquires about the vase, and asks if he can look at it. You agree. Stepping near the window where brilliant rays of sunlight shine through, he lifts the vase, seemingly allowing sunlight to shine through the pottery.

"Do you see that dark spot?" he asks. He repositions the piece to allow you a careful look. "It's wax the merchant used to fill a crack in the pottery, hiding a flaw so that it wouldn't be noticeable." You realize that you've given your approval to a vase that's actually damaged.

The vase was not excellent or sincere. To be sincere literally means to be tested by the sunlight, revealing that something is genuine and authentic. Philippians 1:10 says, "That ye may approve things that are excellent; that ye may be sincere and without offence till the day of Christ."

Is your Christianity genuine? Does it prove to be authentic even when tested? God's desire is for excellence—giving our best so we might have God's best. Don't ever settle for cheapness because you will always get a bad deal. Unfortunately, much of modern Christianity has become just a cheap imitation of the real thing. In other words, it's generic. Virtue, an uncommon word in everyday language, implies a spirit of excellence in all that we do for God. Nothing less than excellence will do.

DISCUSSION: How would you describe a hypocrite? Would you want to be one?

—*Tom Palmer*

OCTOBER 3
GET TO KNOW GOD—
KNOWLEDGE

Scripture Reading—Colossians 1:1-12

You've heard the statement, "It's not *what* you know that matters; it's *who* you know." Knowing the right person can make the difference when you're looking for a job or trying to buy a car. Similarly, who you know determines where you'll spend eternity. Unfortunately, the world is full of people who think knowing the right things will give them eternal life. They fail to understand that knowing the right person is what produces eternal life. Eternal life is based on a personal relationship with God.

In John 17:3, Jesus said, "And this is life eternal, that they might know thee the only true God, and Jesus Christ, whom thou hast sent." First John 5:11 says, "And this is the record, that God hath given to us eternal life, and this life is in his Son." Christianity is uniquely different because of the fact that it's based not on a religion but on a relationship. When someone is born again, he begins a relationship with the God of the universe. That relationship provides the basis for fellowship with the same God of the universe.

So how does a child of God get to know his God better? The answer is found in one word—communication. First, God talks to us through His Word. We talk to God through prayer. We'll never be able to learn about someone if we don't communicate with him. Meaningful communication allows us to enjoy the relationship as we get to know God better. Without good communication, any relationship will become meaningless.

As a young man, the late missionary Jim Elliot prayed that his life would be "an exhibit of the value of knowing God." He understood the value of a relationship and the fellowship that would allow him to know his God better. To build a lasting relationship with God, nothing compares to time in God's presence.

THINK ABOUT IT: Would it be possible to introduce a friend to someone you have never met and didn't know personally?

—*Tom Palmer*

OCTOBER 4
WHEN THE MOUSE GETS CAUGHT—
TEMPERANCE
Scripture Reading—Genesis 39:1-12

T'was the night before Christmas, when all through the house not a creature was stirring but a fat, little mouse. Suddenly, the fat little mouse said, "I think that is the aroma of Eater Dan Extra Crunch Peanut Butter that I smell." The fat, little mouse began to follow his twitching nose until, oh my, there it was: a little scoop of Eater Dan, delicately smeared on a small metal-looking platter, placed upon a wooden platform. "This could be a trap," thought the little mouse, "and I have heard that they can really ruin your day, but who cares. A little bit can't hurt." Without hesitation, the mouse took a little mouse bite—SNAP! BANG! BOING! And so ends the story of Mighty Foolish Mouse.

Sounds a bit childish, doesn't it? However, "a little bit can't hurt" is probably the last thing a mouse thinks before taking that fatal bite. It's also the last thing to cross the minds of most people just before they yield to a sensual, sinful temptation. You see, a little bit may not only hurt you but also kill you. Just ask the little mouse.

Few words in the English language are more difficult to learn than the simple word "no." The word may not have seven syllables or a three-line definition, but it's a word we often forget when we need it most. Saying "no" occurs when a Christian recognizes the presence of God and chooses to resist temptation with the help of the Lord.

When temptation knocks at the door of your life, depend on the Holy Spirit to enable you to refuse. The choice determines whether you will be victimized or victorious. As the anti-drug slogan says, "Just Say No!" The simple word "no" may keep you out of a trap that could cause much harm. It's a word you need to know not only how to spell but also how to use!

APPLICATION: What's an area where temptation is difficult for you to overcome?

—Tom Palmer

OCTOBER 5
GOD WILL BE ON TIME— PATIENCE
Scripture Reading—James 1:1-8

Modern culture has done a great job of creating a "hurry up" society and of programming people to want what they want when they want it. The 24/7 ATM, the 10-minute oil change, and the fast-food value meal have convinced us that we can always get what we want without having to wait long. No doubt technology has produced many timesaving devices, but time-savers and shortcuts aren't always the best—especially when we deal with spirituality!

God isn't limited by time. He doesn't experience stress because of deadlines. When God builds a life, He's interested in the ultimate goal, not in getting a job done as quickly as possible. Take Moses for example. He spent two-thirds of his life preparing for the work God had for him to do. It may seem strange to spend 80 years getting ready and then starting when you're an old man. Yet that was God's plan.

God enrolled Moses in the "School of Hard Knocks," put him in the classroom of experience, and used loneliness, failure, and discouragement as teachers. Yes, he faced tests, as does anyone in a learning experience. Yet after 80 years, Moses graduated with degrees in meekness, faithfulness, and courage. No wonder he was such an effective leader for God.

Have you been hoping that God would hurry up and make things happen in your life? Maybe you face a decision you need to make or a prayer God hasn't answered or a trial that never seems to end. Pause and thank God that in His time, He will accomplish His purpose; and you will be blessed for it. In light of eternity, the blessing is worth waiting for. Ecclesiastes 3:11 says that God "hath made every thing beautiful in his time."

PRAYER TIME: List an area where you sense God hasn't moved as quickly as you'd hoped. Tell God about it and ask Him to make you patient.

—*Tom Palmer*

OCTOBER 6
BECOMING LIKE GOD—
GODLINESS
Scripture Reading—1 Timothy 4:7-16

"What do you want to be when you grow up?" That's one of my favorite questions to ask young people. A variety of answers indicates that young people do occasionally think about their future. Sometimes they give me typical answers—you know, a teacher, a nurse, a lawyer, or a fireman. Other times they give me sophisticated answers—a marine biologist, a forensic pathologist, or maybe even president of the United States. Of course, some give me the classic, "I don't know."

When we're finished having a good laugh, I always say something like this: "The truth is that in reality none of us really know, do we? However, you need to know that right now you're becoming what you will be for the rest of your life." Sobering thought, isn't it? You may not know your vocation or occupation 10 years from now, but today you are developing into the person you will be for the rest of your life! That's where godliness comes in.

Godliness is Godlikeness. In other words, in my life I'm seeking to become more like God. Attitudes, values, priorities, thoughts, habits, and lifestyles must be consistent with God's character. God develops that character as we spend time with God, learn more about God, communicate with God, and, of course, yield to the Holy Spirit, who is working to shape us into a Godlike people. Godly people live in such a way that God is pleased with their lives.

When I was a high school basketball player, I would watch my father's face even when I was on the court. His smile told me he was pleased. When God looks at you, does He smile or frown? Though you can't see His face now, your answer will reveal whether godliness is becoming part of your life.

THINK ABOUT IT: What part of my life would God most like to change? Am I willing to allow Him to do it?

—*Tom Palmer*

NOT GETTING EVEN— BROTHERLY KINDNESS

Scripture Reading—Colossians 3:12-17

As a young person, I remember hearing, "Do unto others before they do unto you and split!" That seemed to be the attitude of those who were just plain obnoxious. Another statement was, "I'll be good to you if you will be good to me." Those words express the attitude of those who wanted everybody to be fair with everybody else. One other statement went like this: "I'll get even with you. Just wait and see!" This statement reflects the attitude of those who live for revenge. Unfortunately, many self-centered people demonstrate vengeful feelings toward others. Romans 12:19 says, "Dearly beloved, avenge not yourselves, but rather give place unto wrath: for it is written, Vengeance is mine; I will repay, saith the Lord." In our dog-eat-dog world, we need to learn about the way Jesus treated others.

Jesus was mistreated during His life here on earth. He was rejected, threatened, hated, and ultimately crucified. Yet never once did He seek to get even with His enemies. Rather, He loved them, prayed for them, and even died for them.

When the mob went to the Garden of Gethsemane to arrest Him, He refused to fight. In the midst of unfairness and injustice, Jesus refused to retaliate. Peter grabbed a sword and tried to behead a member of the mob, but Jesus restored the ear on the head Peter had tried to cut off. Jesus refused to retaliate against those who had fought against Him throughout His earthly ministry. He could have evened the score easily, but He understood His mission to save them.

Jesus' example shows us what being kind means. Like Him, we must learn to do good—to go out of our way to help and to minister to those around us. When people see an attitude of kindness, they'll see the reality of Christ being lived through our lives.

APPLICATION: When was the last time someone hurt or offended you? How should you respond to him?

—Tom Palmer

I LOVE YOU—CHARITY
Scripture Reading—1 Corinthians 13

How would you define the word *love?* First John 4:7-8 says, "Beloved, let us love one another: for love is of God; and every one that loveth is born of God, and knoweth God. He that loveth not knoweth not God; for God is love." To truly understand love, we must understand God's kind of love. Genuine love is God's kind of love.

A boy sat in the doctor's office and listened intently to the doctor's explanation. The boy's sister was dying of a terminal illness. A blood transfusion was the only hope, the doctor said, if her life was to be spared. He explained that the sister had a rare blood type that was hard to match. A blood test revealed that the boy had the needed blood type to save his sister's life. After thinking it through for a moment, the boy agreed to give blood with hopes of saving his sister's life.

Bravely, the boy climbed onto the table and allowed the nurse to insert a needle into his arm so she could collect the blood. The nurse noticed tears in the boy's eyes. "Are you in pain?" she asked.

"No."

"Then what's wrong?"

Tears flowed down his cheeks. "When do I die?"

"Die?" the nurse said. "You're not going to die. We're just collecting a small amount of blood to help your sister. You'll be fine."

Genuine love is selflessly giving of ourselves to meet the needs of someone else. That's what the boy did, and it's also what God did. God didn't just tell the world of His love; He proved it. When we show this love, we clearly demonstrate God's love—that's real love! It's one thing to say, "I love you." It's another to prove it. Self-sacrifice is the proof of genuine love—God's kind of love for us.

EXERCISE: Give an example of how you could show God's love to someone today.

—*Tom Palmer*

OCTOBER 9
CHRISTIAN JOY

Many who scream like Comanches at a Saturday night ball game sit like wooden Indians in church on Sunday morning! No doubt many suffer from a lack of Christian joy.

Augustine said, "The Christian should be a walking 'alleluia' from the top of his head to the bottom of his feet." Excited beyond belief, David danced before the Lord when the Ark returned to Jerusalem. But when he made a spectacle of himself, his wife despised him and was smitten with barrenness. Long-faced critics are always smitten with barrenness. We don't measure our spirituality by the length of our faces!

David was a man after God's own heart. Though he had known seasons of unspeakable joy, he lost his joy. What caused David to lose his joy? Sin is the great joy-robber. David committed serious sins, and he was miserable until he repented. Likewise, committed Christians may lose their joy in the Lord because of sin.

Psalm 51 is the prayer of a man who strayed from God. Going from dancing to dust, David poured out his heart to the Lord, acknowledged his wrongdoing, and pleaded for mercy. *"Restore unto me the joy of thy salvation; and uphold me with thy free spirit"* (Ps. 51:12, emphasis added).

God wants His people to rejoice in Him. Many of the most effective saints were people who learned to find their greatest delight in God Himself. These were ones who learned the secret of getting their souls happy in God. Preoccupation with the Lord, rather than self, is the key to everlasting joy.

Mary said, "My soul doth magnify the Lord, and my spirit hath *rejoiced in God* my Saviour" (Luke 1:46b-47, emphasis added). She rejoiced in God her Savior. How is your soul? Are you rejoicing in the Lord? Are you happy in Jesus?

SCRIPTURE READING: Read Psalm 51. Notice the suffering David endured because of his sin. He paid a high price for his low living! Has sin caused you to lose the joy of your salvation? You, too, can have your joy restored.

—*Harold Vaughan*

OCTOBER 10
ON EARTH
AS IT IS IN HEAVEN

Heaven is a place of unbridled praise. The Book of Revelation describes the redeemed multitudes singing praise to the Lamb in the midst of the throne. Heaven is all about celebrating Jesus, the Lamb of God. Every tribe and nation will be represented in this everlasting festival. The elders, angels, seraphim, and entire host of heaven will join in joyfully worshiping the Lord Jesus. Every worship service here is choir practice for eternity. If joy is the serious business of heaven, maybe we should make it our business on earth!

Life on earth isn't a picnic, but true joy glows in the dark. The heart of the prophet Jeremiah, known as "the weeping prophet," was broken because of the sad state of his nation. He had his share of heartbreak and sorrow, but he said, "Thy words were found, and I did eat them; and thy word was unto me the joy and rejoicing of mine heart" (Jer. 15:16a). Here is a man who took in God's words, and those words brought great rejoicing to his soul. David said God's judgments are sweeter "than honey and the honeycomb" (Ps. 19:10). He took pleasure and delight in God's Word. Godly men throughout history have learned to feed on God's words. These words have brought tremendous joy and rejoicing.

The Bible is a not only a *sword to cut* and a *rod to chasten* but also *bread to feed*, *water to quench*, a *light to lead*, and a *source to bring joy*! The Bible is God-breathed. It's the mind and heart of God in written form. God has not abandoned us to figure out life on our own. He has spoken directly to us through His book.

Do you know the chorus "The B-I-B-L-E. Yes, that's the book for me"? Sing it together now. Heaven is rejoicing tonight, and we can, too.

PRAYER: "Lord, let us be joyful on earth like it is in heaven. Thank You for Your Word, which is the source of joy. Amen."

—Harold Vaughan

OCTOBER 11
PRAY
WITHOUT CEASING

Scripture Reading—1 Thessalonians 5:17

Years ago, I flew home after preaching in a distant city. Normally, my wife and children would be waiting for me at the airport, but they weren't there. As I made my way to baggage claim, I reasoned they would be waiting for me there. But still my family was absent. I wondered if traffic had held them up. After waiting and watching, I decided to call and to see if I could reach them, but the phone wasn't working.

"As soldiers in an army must stay in touch with their superiors, we must stay in touch with God."

All kinds of wild thoughts ran through my mind. I imagined my family had an accident or that something terrible had happened. Lack of communication is the birth of distortion. Finally, I contacted them and discovered that 11 inches of rain had fallen that day; they couldn't get to the airport because of flooded roads. My heart was relieved to learn they were safe. When we're out of touch, everything gets distorted.

As soldiers in an army must stay in touch with their superiors, we must stay in touch with God. Military people must keep connected with headquarters, and we must stay on speaking terms with Jesus! We must keep on praying. We must speak with God regularly.

The psalmist said, "Seven times a day do I praise thee because of thy righteous judgments" (Ps. 119:164). This man set aside times throughout the day to express praise to the Lord. Nothing is more important than staying in tune with God.

POINTS TO PONDER: Have you prayed "without ceasing" today? Are you "in touch" with your Heavenly Father? Like the psalmist, will you purpose to set aside times throughout the day to talk to God? Discuss today's Scripture reading and ask each family member to pray about his prayer life.

—Harold Vaughan

OCTOBER 12
REJOICE!

Scripture Reading—1 Thessalonians 5:16
"Rejoice evermore."

Have you noticed how many times the words *joy* and *rejoicing* are mentioned in the Bible? Philippians 4:4 says, "Rejoice in the Lord alway: and again I say, Rejoice." The word *rejoice* means to be full of cheer. Rejoice *evermore* means we should rejoice at all times. Our rejoicing doesn't depend on how we feel. Neither does it depend on circumstances. Joy is the fruit of being filled with the Holy Spirit (Gal. 5:22).

It's interesting that God commands us to rejoice. Many commands tell us what *not* to do, but this command tells us what *to* do—REJOICE! Praise the Lord for this positive command.

The Bible tells us that being under the influence of alcohol is sin (Eph. 5:18). Also sinful is not being under the control of the Holy Spirit. The command to rejoice depends on our obeying the command to be filled with the Holy Spirit.

Someone has counted more than 550 references to joy and rejoicing in the Bible. The large number of references concerning rejoicing indicates that God wants His people to be joyful. Of all people, we have countless reasons to be joyful. We are too blessed to be depressed.

It's both normal and natural for humans to desire happiness. There is a season to laugh and a season to cry. In Ecclesiastes, the preacher said there's a season for everything. God want us to rejoice in Him; happiness is a choice. We don't need to wait around for our emotions to kick in. By an act of our will, we can choose to rejoice *now*. Make a habit of rejoicing; become a chronic rejoicer.

QUESTIONS: Have you been rejoicing in the Lord today? If not, bow your head and confess your lack of rejoicing. Are you filled with the Holy Spirit right now? You can become empty of sin and self and become full of God's Spirit, if you will. Talk through your struggles, pray over these matters, and begin rejoicing.

—Harold Vaughan

OCTOBER 13
THANKSGIVING

Scripture Reading
1 Thessalonians 5:18— *"In every thing give thanks: for this is the will of God in Christ Jesus concerning you."*
Hebrews 13:15— *"By him therefore let us offer the sacrifice of praise to God continually, that is, the fruit of our lips giving thanks to his name."*

The Bible says to "give thanks." Giving thanks—how we express our gratitude to God—is verbal appreciation expressed in words. It's an activity God tells us to practice.

How much prayer time did you devote to thanking God today? Have you told Him that you appreciate Him and His numberless benefits? "Every good gift and every perfect gift is from above, and cometh down from the Father of lights, with whom is no variableness, neither shadow of turning" (James 1:17). Because God is the source of all gifts we have received, He deserves to be thanked.

The Bible also says to give thanks "in every thing," not just for the good things. Giving thanks for our blessings seems natural, but how often do we neglect to give thanks "in every thing"? We don't thank God because everything is good; we thank Him because *He* is good! If we learn to respond with an attitude of gratitude, we will discover that "all things work together for good to them that love God, to them who are the called according to his purpose" (Rom. 8:28).

Matthew Henry said, "Thanksgiving is good, but thanksliving is better. Thanksgiving can be heard, but thanksliving can be seen." Grateful people are pleasant to be around. We can train ourselves to be thankful!

Count your blessings,
Name them one by one;
Count your blessings,
See what God has done.

APPLICATION: Ask each family member to list five things he's grateful for. You may want to ask members to write their lists on paper. Then ask each person to share his list. Go to God in prayer and rehearse your blessings. Don't rush! Be deliberate and reflect on God's goodness to you.

—Harold Vaughan

OCTOBER 14
HE KNOWS ALL ABOUT YOU
Scripture Reading—Isaiah 40:13-14
"Who hath directed the Spirit of the Lord, or being his counsellor hath taught him? With whom took he counsel, and who instructed him, and taught him in the path of judgment, and taught him knowledge, and shewed to him the way of understanding?"

A wealthy grandfather was having hearing problems. After years of his family's pleading with him, he saw a hearing specialist. Fitted with a powerful state-of-the-art hearing aid, he returned to the specialist several weeks later for a follow-up. "How do you like the hearing aid?" the specialist asked.

The grandfather smiled. "Oh, it's a wonderful thing."

"I guess your family is really pleased that you can hear again."

Sheepishly, the grandfather replied, "Actually, I haven't told my family yet. I've had so much fun listening to their conversations without them knowing that I can hear. In fact, since I got this hearing aid, I've changed my will five times."

We all behave according to what we think others know about us. Knowledge is a vital part of all relationships. But unlike man's limited knowledge, God's knowledge is complete. Theologians say God is omniscient. The word *omniscient* comes from two words meaning "all" and "knowledge."

Indeed, our God knows all about everything and everybody! No one ever taught God anything, and He never learns anything. He's never been a student, and His knowledge is complete and timeless. In fact, all knowledge comes from Him.

God's knowledge is different from ours. Our capacity for knowledge is limited. We quickly learn that the more we know, the more we discover there is to know. It's humbling to consider that the God who knows everything about us still loves us. Though He possesses limitless knowledge, the Scriptures declare that He thinks about us!

SELAH: Would you be embarrassed about anything in your life if you looked the Lord in the eye, realizing that He knew all about it?

—T.P. Johnston, Jr.

OCTOBER 15
In the Know in the Here and Now

Scripture Reading—Acts 15:18
"Known unto God are all his works
from the beginning of the world."

Important in our understanding of how much God knows is the fact that His knowledge is in the eternal present. Our knowledge is based on past experiences. We know how to sit in a chair because we learned to do so. We can talk because we learned a language and know how to communicate with it.

Not so with God. He never has to flip back into the past to consider anything. When God's attention is focused on you, He never has to stop and think, *Now, let's see. When does he or she live in relation to when Abraham lived?* God doesn't need to run through a mental checklist to figure things out.

Whatever you are going through right now is just as much in the present in God's mind as what Abraham did several thousand years ago. God knows the end in the beginning; His knowledge is timeless. According to Revelation 7, John the apostle has already seen those of us who are saved gathered around God's throne. But we're not even there yet! Yes, even the future is present tense with our God.

It's awesome to meditate on the vastness of God's knowledge. Though His knowledge of us is unlimited, it's also personal. He's not a God who created everything and left it to run on its own. He is personally and intimately involved with His creation and with each of us, His creatures. He is personally, presently, and consciously aware of everything going on in your life and in mine. These are the perfections of God's knowledge. His knowledge is perfect in that it's complete and all-inclusive—it's eternally present tense.

SELAH: Did you know that God sees what's going on in your heart right now? His desire is for you to acknowledge to Him what He already knows. Is there something you need to talk to Him about today?

—T.P. Johnston, Jr.

OCTOBER 16
HE'S HERE, HE'S THERE, HE'S EVERYWHERE

Scripture Reading—Psalm 139:7-10

"Whither shall I go from thy spirit? or whither shall I flee from thy presence? If I ascend up into heaven, thou art there: if I make my bed in hell, behold, thou art there. If I take the wings of the morning, and dwell in the uttermost parts of the sea; even there shall thy hand lead me, and thy right hand shall hold me."

God is everywhere. A story about a burglar illustrates this reality. Having broken into a house, a burglar was ransacking as he pleased. He was certain no one was home, but soon he heard the words, "Jesus is watching you!"

Shaken by those words, the burglar was relieved to discover that the speaker was only a parrot. He continued with his stealing. Several more times, he heard the parrot squawk, "Jesus is watching you! Jesus is watching you!"

Each time the parrot said those words, the burglar became more unnerved. Just as he finished with the last room, however, he heard, "Jesus is watching you!" followed by, "Sic 'em, Jesus!" The burglar turned to face the family's Doberman as the dog lunged at him.

The point is, the doctrine of God's omnipresence (being everywhere at once) isn't just theology; it's stark reality! How often do we pray, "Lord, be with us"? Those are wasted words because God is always with us. Though we know that truth, how easily we go about our business as if He wasn't there. The truth of God's omnipresence makes some people nervous when they stop and think it through.

If we know the Lord and are walking with Him, the glorious truth of His being everywhere at once is a source of great joy and comfort. It means He's capable of having a personal relationship with each of us. He never needs to leave me to be with you.

SELAH: Discuss practical differences the truth of God's omnipresence should make in our lives.

—T.P. Johnston, Jr.

OCTOBER 17
THE DIFFERENCE
HE MAKES

Scripture Reading—Psalm 139:11-12
"If I say, Surely the darkness shall cover me;
even the night shall be light about me.
Yea, the darkness hideth not from thee;
but the night shineth as the day:
the darkness and the light
are both alike to thee."

Daniel in the lions' den (found in Daniel 6) is a familiar, yet fascinating story. In terms of his public life and service, Daniel's political enemies could find nothing by which to accuse him. They managed to get a new law on the books that said no one could pray to anyone but the king of the land. Ever faithful to his God, Daniel continued to pray regularly despite the new law. His commitment landed him in the lions' den, and God allowed His man to be placed in the darkness of the den. An interesting fact, as noted in Daniel 6:17, is that Daniel was thrown into a pit that was sealed by a stone. Daniel was literally in darkness.

The king had grown to respect Daniel and to appreciate his service. After Daniel was thrown into the lions' den, the Scriptures tell us that the king went back to his palace and spent a sleepless night (v. 18). Here sat the king of the land in his palace, yet he was too upset to sleep. By contrast, Daniel sat in a dark pit, surrounded by hungry lions; and he was perfectly fine!

What made the difference, of course, was the awareness of God's presence. No wonder the psalmist exclaimed, "Surely the darkness shall cover me; even the night shall be light about me" (Ps. 139:11b). God did not spare Daniel from the lions' den or from the darkness of the situation. Yet God, by His presence, can bring light into any situation.

SELAH: Recall a time when a family member experienced the peace of God's presence in a difficult situation. Thank God for His ever-present reality!

—*T.P. Johnston, Jr.*

OCTOBER 18
POWER UNDER CONTROL

Scripture Reading

Psalm 62:11—"God hath spoken once; twice have I heard this;
that power belongeth unto God."
Psalm 147:5—"Great is our Lord, and of great power:
his understanding is infinite."
Jeremiah 32:17—"Ah Lord God! behold, thou hast made the heaven
and the earth by thy great power and stretched out arm,
and there is nothing too hard for thee."

Knowing that a Sunday school class had been studying the power of God, a pastor stopped a boy on his way out of class. "Son, if you can tell me something God can do," he said, "I'll give you an apple." The little fellow, understanding more than the pastor bargained for, replied, "Pastor, if you can tell me something God *can't* do, I'll give you a whole box of apples!"

Perhaps the greatest power man has harnessed is nuclear power. Atomic power is capable of generating electricity or of being used in a bomb to destroy millions. Yet even more dramatic than nuclear and atomic power are the forces of nature. Frequently, we hear about the destructive power of volcanoes, earthquakes, hurricanes, tornadoes, floods, and wildfires. Yet none of these forces even begin to compare to the unlimited, infinite power of God.

Omnipotence—having all power—means more than an out-of-control forest fire or avalanche. God's omnipotence includes the choice of His will to use His power to reflect His glory and to accomplish His purposes. God can use that power any way He chooses because He is God; but thankfully for us, God chooses to use it only in wise and good ways.

People tend to shy away from God's omnipotence because such power demands our obedience. If God truly has all power and all authority, we should fear and obey Him.

SELAH: Have you acknowledged God's complete authority over your life? Have you submitted your mind and reasoning to God's holy Word?

—T.P. Johnston, Jr.

OCTOBER 19
NOTHING
IS IMPOSSIBLE

Scripture Reading—Jeremiah 32:27
"Behold, I am the Lord, the God of all flesh:
is there any thing too hard for me?"

A church youth worker listened patiently as a child recited Jeremiah 32:17. The boy didn't say the verse quite right, but he certainly got the point across. "Oh, my God!" the boy said. "Behold, You made heaven. You made earth, and there ain't nothing You can't do."

While the boy's memorization wasn't word-perfect, he seemed to understand God's omnipotence. The power of God has a practical result—it adds the impossible to the equation of life.

Perhaps the greatest example of God's demonstrating His omnipotence is the familiar Christmas story. When the angel Gabriel announced to the virgin Mary that she was going to bear a son, she reacted as expected. In essence, she said, "That's impossible! I'm not married. How could that be?"

The angel told Mary that her cousin Elizabeth was also with child. Mary knew Elizabeth was too old to have a baby. The angel responded simply, "For with God nothing shall be impossible" (Luke 1:37).

God did the impossible and brought His own Son into the world as a baby, born of a virgin, conceived of the Holy Spirit. Because of God's power, the impossible is a regular aspect of the Christian's life.

God also has the ability to create out of nothing. He causes change to take place, and He can create something new out of something old. Spiritually speaking, He creates a new man out of an old, sinful man. According to 2 Corinthians 5:17, he makes us new creatures in Christ Jesus. The verse continues: "Old things are passed away; behold, all things are become new." God is able to put a new man in a suit without unbuttoning the coat! This transformation is perhaps the greatest feat of God's power!

SELAH: Have you personally experienced the life-changing, nothing-is-impossible power of God in your life through Jesus Christ?

—*T.P. Johnston, Jr.*

OCTOBER 20
THREE OMNIS
AND YOU

Scripture Reading—Ephesians 3:19-21
"And to know the love of Christ, which passeth knowledge,
that ye might be filled with all the fulness of God.
Now unto him that is able to do exceeding abundantly above all that we
ask or think, according to the power that worketh in us,
unto him be glory in the church by Christ Jesus throughout all ages,
world without end. Amen."

Do you believe I can lift a ton (2,000 pounds)? No matter how big or strong-looking I might be, you probably doubt I could succeed. But it's true; I can. Take me to the moon, and you're welcome to take all the pictures you'd like of me lifting a ton! We can do things in a weightless environment that we can't do on earth.

Our finite minds try to reject things we don't understand and can't comprehend, but God is unlimited. We have seen that He is unlimited in His knowledge, unlimited in His presence, and unlimited in His power.

How do birds know to migrate when winter is coming? In Job 39, the Scriptures tell us that God's knowledge and wisdom make this migration possible. He takes note when one sparrow falls to the ground. While His greatness extends to life's impossibilities, it also extends to everyday life.

God must have a good laugh when men flex their power muscles, spout off their proud knowledge, and pretend they're really something by traveling a few thousand miles into space! To those who are willing to humble themselves, recognizing that we really aren't much, God makes His all-sufficiency available. His unbounded knowledge can provide wisdom for daily life choices as Christ is made wisdom unto us. His immeasurable presence can strengthen and comfort us in the midst of life's darkest tests. His absolute power can transform our hearts and lives, making us into the very image of His perfect Son, the Lord Jesus Christ.

SELAH: Discuss with your family how you can appropriate the "omnis" of God.

—T.P. Johnston, Jr.

OCTOBER 21
LIVING IN PERILOUS TIMES

Scripture Reading—2 Timothy 3:1
*"This know also, that in the last days **perilous times** shall come"*
(emphasis added).

If you spend any time reading the newspaper or watching TV news, you're aware of the **perilous times** in which we're living. We see conflict and war between nations. Natural disasters have devastated parts of our country and regions of the world. Our society is a moral cesspool, and the Church is quickly slipping into apostasy. But God's Word assures us that the world has to get worse before it will get better. For the child of God—no matter what happens—the best is yet to come.

But in the meantime, what are we to do as Christian families? Must we cave in to the pressures of a world that has gone crazy? Or does God have an answer? We cannot afford to look to the "experts" of our day. Many claim to have the answer, but the problem is that they don't know the real questions! Without a doubt, we must get our direction from God's Word.

During this week's devotional times, we'll consider how to protect our families from the flood tide of evil that threatens to destroy us. Every Christian parent has the God-given responsibility to stand between his family and anything that threatens to harm them—whether physical, mental, emotional, social, or spiritual.

A pioneer family arrived in a frontier town looking for a place to call home. The father, who was driving the covered wagon, asked a man on the street how many saloons were in the town.

"Four!" the man replied enthusiastically.

Slapping the horses with the reins, the father yelled, "Git up!"

The man cried, "Where ya goin', mister?"

The father hollered back, "I have three sons in this wagon, and I won't raise them in a town with four saloons." And away they went.

That dad knew something about protecting his family from evil!

BIBLE READING: Read Genesis 6 and see how Noah protected his family.

—Jack Palmer

OCTOBER 22
NOAH: WHAT KIND OF MAN WAS HE?

Scripture Reading—Genesis 6:8
*"But **Noah found grace** in the eyes of the Lord"*
(emphasis added).

When studying the story of Noah and the building of the ark, we must determine what kind of man he was and why God chose him for such an unbelievable task. Genesis 6:5 says, "And God saw that the wickedness of man was great in the earth, and that every imagination of the thoughts of his heart was only evil continually." That verse sounds a lot like the days in which we're living. In the midst of all the wickedness, "Noah found grace." Why?

Verse 9 says, "These are the generations of Noah: Noah was a *just man* and *perfect* in his generations, and Noah *walked with God*" (emphasis added). When God says that Noah was "just," it means he was right with God. As wicked as mankind was, Noah was the one man who had a right relationship with God. By describing him as "perfect," the Bible doesn't mean he was sinless. The record of Scripture makes that fact clear (see Gen. 9:20-24). What Scripture means is that Noah sought to please God in his generations. Then Genesis 6:9 says, he "walked with God." These words indicate that Noah lived close to God in his daily life. Verse 22 adds, "Thus did Noah; according to all that God commanded him, *so did he*" (emphasis added). He obeyed God.

This is the kind of man God wants to lead today's families—a saved man who is right with God, who lives to please God, who lives close to God, and who is obedient to God.

Sir, if we were to ask your family what kind of a man you are, what would they say? I trust they would say what God said about Noah. Being your family's spiritual leader means being your family's spiritual protector. What an awesome privilege and responsibility God has entrusted to us as dads!

ACTION POINT: Tomorrow, we will find out why Noah did what he did. In preparation, read Hebrews 11:7.

—Jack Palmer

OCTOBER 23
WHY DID
HE DO IT?

Scripture Reading—Genesis 6:14, 22
"Make thee an ark of gopher wood; rooms shalt thou make in the ark,
and shalt pitch it within and without with pitch. . . .
Thus did Noah; according to all
that God commanded him, so did he"
(emphasis added).

God gave Noah an overwhelming job when He commanded him to build the ark. The ark was 300 cubits (450 ft.) long, 50 cubits (75 ft.) wide, and 30 cubits (45 ft.) high. Imagine building something so huge! Researchers have estimated that the ark would have weighed 44,000 tons. Why did Noah do it?

Yesterday, we studied Noah's character and discovered that he lived to please God. Therefore, he obeyed God's command to build the ark. Anyone who desires to please the Lord must be living a life of obedience. Hebrews 11:7a records that Noah also built the ark because of (1) **his faith**, (2) **his fear of God**, and (3) **his family**. "By *faith* Noah, being warned of God of things not seen as yet, moved with *fear*, prepared an ark to the saving of *his house*" (emphasis added).

When God said He would destroy the earth with a great flood (Gen. 6:17), Noah believed Him. Because he feared God (knew he was accountable to God for everything), he obeyed Him. Because he saw his family as his most precious earthly possession, he worked many years to provide the ark for their protection from the flood.

From Noah, we learn the importance of doing whatever is necessary to protect our families from the flood tide of evil that threatens to destroy them. Parents must be willing to make radical decisions and to take drastic steps to ensure their families are safe and secure. May God help us to be as committed as Noah was.

ACTION POINT: List and discuss specific ways you are protecting your family. Share with them the reasons.

—*Jack Palmer*

OCTOBER 24
No Place to the Devil!

Scripture Reading—Ephesians 4:27
"Neither give place to the devil."

Noah built an ark for the protection of his family. As a result, when God sent the flood, Noah's family was spared when other families drowned. How can we provide an ark of safety for our families while so many around us are being destroyed? For the rest of the week, we will look at four ways God's Word instructs us to do so.

In today's verse, we find the first step—"Neither give place to the devil." Satan, our enemy, has one thing in mind for Christian families—to destroy them at any cost. *He'll never do that to our family*, you may think. But plenty of Christian families have thought that way only to discover they were wrong. They gave Satan an opportunity and suffered the consequences.

Second Corinthians 2:11 says, "Lest Satan should get an advantage of us: for we are not ignorant of his devices." The Bible tells us how he works so we can prepare our defenses. Genesis 3 and 4 provide five cautions so we won't give him the advantage he wants.

1. Beware of his **disguise** (v. 1).
2. Beware of his **deception** (vv. 4-5).
3. He will seek to **defile** (v. 7).
4. He **divides** (v. 8).
5. But his greatest goal is to **destroy** (4:8). He's never content with anything less than destruction.

Prayerfully consider these important steps. "*Submit yourselves therefore to God.* Resist the devil, and he will flee from you" (James 4:7, emphasis added). Being totally submitted to God is where you begin. "Whom resist *stedfast in the faith*" (1 Pet. 5:9a, emphasis added). The next step is a steadfast, unwavering faith—totally dependent on God. "Put on the whole armour of God, that ye may be able to *stand against the wiles of the devil*" (Eph. 6:11, emphasis added).

DISCUSSION: As a family, discuss ways you can better defend yourselves against Satan's attacks.

—Jack Palmer

OCTOBER 25
NO FELLOWSHIP WITH DARKNESS!

Scripture Reading—Ephesians 5:8, 11
"For ye were sometimes darkness, but now are ye light in the Lord:
*walk as children of light. . . . And have **no fellowship with the***
***unfruitful works of darkness**, but rather reprove them"*
(emphasis added).

L ight and darkness are opposites. The Bible describes our spiritual condition before we were saved as "spiritual darkness." But when we accepted Christ as Savior, we moved from the darkness into "spiritual light." One of the great dangers threatening the Christian family is having continual "fellowship" with the unprofitable things from which we were saved.

To the born-again Christian, fellowship is precious and describes our love for one another in the Lord. It means closeness, enjoyment, pleasure, and satisfaction. God says we should have no fellowship with the "darkness" He saved us from.

When we enter a dark room, the first thing we find is the light switch. As soon as we touch it, light floods the room, and the darkness is gone. Light and darkness cannot exist together. Light overcomes darkness. That's what the word *reprove* means.

Yesterday, we learned that the devil wants to *destroy* our families. Today's lesson is that the works of darkness will *defile* your family. When a Christian family constantly returns to the things of the old life from which Christ saved them, they will experience the contaminating effects of sin.

One of the most convenient ways a Christian family can fellowship with darkness is through the TV, which brings the worst darkness into the middle of family life. Because of TV, many Christian families not only tolerate but also accept drinking, swearing, indecency, perversion, violence, and a whole lot more. Computers, music, dress, reading, toys, and entertainment are other readily accessible ways darkness invades our homes. Yes, this is radical, but so is protecting our precious families from evil!

APPLICATION: Today, make a commitment to protect your family from the defiling effects of spiritual darkness and to take a strong stand against them.

—Jack Palmer

OCTOBER 26
No Conformity
to the World!

Scripture Reading—Romans 12:1-2
"I beseech you therefore, brethren, by the mercies of God,
that ye present your bodies a living sacrifice,
holy, acceptable unto God, which is your reasonable service.
*And **be not conformed to this world:***
but be ye transformed by the renewing of your mind,
that ye may prove what is that good, and acceptable,
and perfect, will of God"
(emphasis added).

As we address the importance of protecting our families from the over-whelming flood of evil that threatens our destruction, we must consider the influence of the world on the Christian home. Satan wants to *destroy us,* the powers of darkness want to *defile us,* and today we see that the world wants to *conform us*—to make us like they are. To *conform* means to be *"squeezed into a mold."* The world is putting pressure on the Christian family in an attempt to squeeze us into its mold.

Many Christian families measure their spirituality by how far they stay away from the world. But the world is always changing and moving farther from God. Unfortunately, as the world moves, so do those families—just so they maintain their distance. Before long, they are right where the world was not long ago. The true measure of our spiritual lives should never be how far we stay from the world but *how close we are living to God.* As the world moves away from God, we should live closer to Him. Therein is our protection.

The world seeks to conform us because it knows if it can destroy our distinctiveness as Christians, it has destroyed our effectiveness. What do we offer the world if we're just like it? We must not think, talk, act, or look like the world if we want to be effective for Christ in the world.

ACTION POINT: Read and discuss the following verses with your family— 2 Corinthians 6:17; James 1:27, 4:4; and 1 John 2:15-17, 5:19. What is God saying about the world?

—Jack Palmer

OCTOBER 27
No Catering to the Flesh!

Scripture Reading—Romans 13:14
"But put ye on the Lord Jesus Christ,
*and **make not provision for the flesh**,*
to fulfil the lusts thereof"
(emphasis added).

We build an "ark" of protection for our families so we can rise above the flood tide of evil that threatens to destroy us. Like Noah, we must be willing to go to any extreme against evil. We've already looked at the devil, the darkness, and the world, and at how compelling their influences are on the Christian family. What we're considering today is what we always have with us—*the flesh*. Wherever we go, we take our biggest problem right along with us, and the flesh wants to *control us*.

The flesh is the part of us that always asserts itself against our spiritual nature. The flesh and the Spirit are forever at war (Gal. 5:17). Because of our flesh, we say and do unkind things to others. Because of our flesh, we are jealous, resentful, and bitter toward others. Because of our flesh, we crave satisfaction from pleasures that are morally wrong. The flesh causes rebellion, but Galatians 5:16b provides the solution. "Walk in the Spirit, and ye shall not fulfil the lust of the flesh." Ephesians 5:18 commands us to "be filled with the Spirit." First Thessalonians 5:19 says, "Quench not the Spirit," and Ephesians 4:30a says, "And grieve not the holy Spirit of God." Our only protection against catering to the flesh and being controlled by it is to live each day in the power of God's Spirit.

If you're a gardener, you understand that you will harvest whatever you plant. That's the principle Galatians 6:7-8 teaches. Before you finish your family worship, read those verses and see what God is saying about sowing and reaping and about the flesh and the Spirit. Though we continually battle the flesh, we will always find our victory in Jesus Christ (Rom. 7:24-25).

ASSIGNMENT: Read Galatians 5:19-23. Compare the works of the flesh to the fruit of the Spirit.

—*Jack Palmer*

OCTOBER 28
LEARN TO CONTROL
YOUR EMOTIONS

Scripture Reading—Proverbs 16:32
"He that is slow to anger is better than the mighty;
and he that ruleth his spirit than he that taketh a city."

I love a good war story in which soldiers, against all odds, defeat a superior enemy or defend some faraway outpost. Historians have documented soldiers who narrowly cheated death, cleverly escaped from prison, and helped their fallen comrades to safety.

Proverbs 16:32 says that those who control their anger are stronger than the general who captures a city. For citizens to properly defend their city, they must build reinforced walls that can resist the strongest and cleverest of enemies. As history records, victorious armies break down walls by every possible means. They ram them, burn them, climb them, and blow them up. Sometimes days, weeks, even months pass before an army can destroy the walls. But destroying walls was the key! Those who could break down the walls could destroy the city.

What does it take to destroy you? Satan is always devising new schemes to attack, to wound, and to defeat besieged believers. He wants to break us down, too. Walls we build in our lives are the greatest defense against our enemies. Having self-control that prevents emotions from getting out of control is a great wall. Yet many Christians are easily angered.

Good soldiers are disciplined during war. When pressures come, they are confident their walls will not tumble down. Good families must exhibit the same discipline amid the stresses of life. We must have strong walls to be successful in life.

People disappointments, unfulfilled expectations, and failures visit the best of Christians; but we must never yield to the vice of anger.

APPLICATION: If you have an anger problem in the home, confess it now. Proverbs 16:32 says that we should be "slow to anger." Resolve anger quickly before the enemy finds your weakness.

—Jeff Kahl

OCTOBER 29
A PURE LIFE

Scripture Reading—1 Timothy 4:12
"Let no man despise thy youth;
but be thou an example of the believers,
*in word, in conversation, in charity, in spirit, in faith, in **purity***
(emphasis added).

One of the most valuable assets we have is our testimony. "A good name is rather to be chosen than . . . silver and gold" (Prov. 22:1). We must guard our witness.

Never have there been more opportunities for impurity than today. Neither has there been a greater resource for purity than what is available to us today. The same Holy Spirit who empowered the apostle Paul will empower us. Never forget that the Holy Spirit is a "holy" spirit. When He fills our lives, we can be holy, too. Living purely in an impure world requires God's mighty power.

Joseph refused the temptations of Potiphar's wife because he had predetermined that he wouldn't sin against God. We must make up our minds ahead of time that we're going to live clean lives.

God calls us to purity of thought, language, and life. Notice these straightforward Scriptures:

"Keep thyself pure" (1 Tim. 5:22b).

"Flee . . . youthful lusts" (2 Tim. 2:22a).

"Intreat. . . . the younger as sisters, with all purity" (1 Tim. 5:1-2).

In the area of purity, it's a good thing for young people to write down their personal standards. They should be specific about things they will avoid and also write down characteristics of the person they would consider as a potential mate. Having these guidelines will protect their purity and testimony.

VERSE TO CONSIDER: "But as he which hath called you is holy, so be ye holy in all manner of conversation; because it is written, Be ye holy; for I am holy" (1 Pet. 1:15-16).

—Harold Vaughan

An Excellent Spirit

Scripture Reading—1 Timothy 4:12
"Let no man despise thy youth;
but be thou an example of the believers,
*in word, in conversation, in charity, in **spirit**, in faith, in purity"*
(emphasis added).

What does being an example in "spirit" mean? The word *spirit* refers to one's mental disposition or attitude. Proverbs 17:27 says, "He that hath knowledge spareth his words: and a man of understanding is of an *excellent spirit*" (emphasis added). Because Daniel had an excellent spirit, the king put him in charge of the kingdom (Dan. 6:3). Someone who has an excellent spirit is positive, humble, and joyful.

Everybody is enthusiastic at times—some for 30 minutes, some for 30 days. But the man who's enthusiastic for 30 years is the man who is a success at life! Positive people are pleasant to be around. Because they're upbeat and optimistic, they achieve more.

Micah 6:8 says, "He hath shewed thee, O man, what is good; and what doth the Lord require of thee, but to do justly, and to love mercy, and to *walk humbly* with thy God?" (emphasis added). Pride is the first thing to enter a man and the last thing to go. God is attracted to those who possess a humble spirit. A prideful spirit not only repels God but is also repulsive to others.

Jesus said, "These things have I spoken unto you, that my joy might remain in you, and that your joy might be full" (John 15:11). The Lord desires His children to experience fullness of joy. We can develop a joyful spirit.

Those who have an excellent spirit are happier and more productive. We can discipline our minds to think properly.

Sow an action, reap a habit.
Sow a habit, reap a character.
Sow a character, reap a destiny.
—Samuel Smiles

An *excellent spirit* brings blessing both to God and to man. Choose to be positive, humble, and joyful.

THOUGHT: The pinnacle of man's greatness is the height of his own character.

—Harold Vaughan

OCTOBER 31
BE AN EXAMPLE

Scripture Reading—1 Timothy 4:12
"Let no man despise thy youth;
*but be thou an **example** of the believers,*
in word, in conversation, in charity, in spirit, in faith, in purity"
(emphasis added).

This verse says we shouldn't let anyone look down on us because of our age. Also, we should never act in a way that causes others to reject us because of our immature actions. Youth doesn't have to be a limitation. George Washington was a colonel at age 22, Napoleon commanded the Italian army at age 25, and Josiah was only eight years old when he became king in Jerusalem.

Men don't despise an acorn because it's not an oak. Nor do they look down on an orange blossom because it has no fruit. Youth is a time when we can excel by living an honorable life.

Paul told Timothy to be an "example." That meant he was to be a pattern or model for others to follow. Albert Schweitzer said, "Example is not the main thing in influencing others. It is the only thing." Your life can provide an example for others to follow.

We've all seen concrete birdbaths and statues. They are formed by pouring liquid concrete into a form, a pattern that provides shape and design. A pattern is what Paul meant when he said, "Be ye followers of me, even as I also am of Christ" (1 Cor. 11:1). In other words, we should pattern our lives after God. An ounce of example is worth a pound of advice. A heart for God is the greatest incentive for a Christlike life. Everyone tries to be like someone. To be like Jesus is a blessed possibility! A Spirit-filled life empowers us to be a worthy example to other believers.

It has been said, "You are only young once, but you can stay immature indefinitely." We can bless others' lives by living the Christ life.

SING A SONG: Sing all stanzas of the hymn "O to Be Like Thee."

—Harold Vaughan

NOVEMBER 1
BEHAVING

Scripture Reading—1 Timothy 4:12
"Let no man despise thy youth;
but be thou an example of the believers,
in word, in **conversation***, in charity, in spirit, in faith, in purity"*
(emphasis added).

It has been said that your talk talks, and your walk talks; but your walk talks louder than your talk talks! The word *conversation* refers to behavior or manner of life. The way we conduct ourselves speaks volumes. Our lives can tear down what our words build up. "Dead flies cause the ointment of the apothecary to send forth a stinking savour: so doth a little folly him that is in reputation for wisdom and honour" (Ecc. 10:1). We lose respect for those who engage in foolish behavior. People judge us by the way we behave. Notice these verses:

"But if I tarry long, that thou mayest know how thou oughtest to *behave* thyself in the house of God, which is the church of the living God" (1 Tim. 3:15a, emphasis added).

"But as he which hath called you is holy, so be ye holy in all manner of *conversation*" (1 Pet. 1:15, emphasis added).

"Having your *conversation* honest among the Gentiles: that, whereas they speak against you as evildoers, they may by your good works, which they shall behold, glorify God in the day of visitation" (1 Pet. 2:12, emphasis added).

"Let your light so shine before men, that they may see your *good works*, and glorify your Father which is in heaven" (Matt. 5:16, emphasis added).

"And Jesus increased in wisdom and stature, and *in favour with God and man*" (Luke 2:52, emphasis added).

Jesus conducted Himself in such a way that He won the favor of those who observed Him. Those who knew Him best respected Him the most. Your life should complement the Gospel.

FAMILY TIME: Behavior at home, at church, and in the world is important to God. Talk about ways your family can exemplify good behavior.

—Harold Vaughan

NOVEMBER 2
Example in Word

Scripture Reading—1 Timothy 4:12
"Let no man despise thy youth;
but be thou an example of the believers,
*in **word**, in conversation, in charity, in spirit, in faith, in purity"*
(emphasis added).

1. Think before you speak.

When I was in the first grade, the second-graders performed a play. They dressed up like animals and acted out their parts. Sitting there, I thought the play was probably the worst performance I'd ever witnessed.

Later that day, I told a second-grader how I felt about the play. I didn't intend to be rude or hateful; I was simple giving my opinion. Offended, he told his teacher what I had said. His teacher told my teacher, and I got in trouble! That day, I began learning to think before I spoke. I discovered that I don't need to say every thought that enters my head. My tongue is in a wet place and can easily slip!

2. Say what you mean and mean what you say.

Three men were eating dinner at a restaurant. The waiter asked, "What will you have for dessert?" The first diner said, "Nothing for me." The second said, "I'm stuffed." The third replied, "Couldn't eat another bite." When the waiter told them dessert came with the meal, the first diner said, "Ice cream." The second said, "Pecan pie." The third responded, "Chocolate layer cake."

Telling the truth is important. We should let our communication be honest and forthright.

3. Speak the truth in love.

Jesus was full of grace and truth, and the people "wondered at the gracious words which proceeded out of his mouth" (Luke 4:22). What we say is important, but how we say it is equally important. Our tone can either strengthen or weaken our influence.

Most of man's sins are by his tongue. God has provided supernatural power to control our tongues and to speak helpful words.

BIBLE STUDY: Turn to Ephesians 4:29-32. Read, discuss, and apply these verses about our speech.

—*Harold Vaughan*

NOVEMBER 3
Examples in Love
Scripture Reading—1 Timothy 4:12
"Let no man despise thy youth;
but be thou an example of the believers,
*in word, in conversation, in **charity**, in spirit, in faith, in purity"*
(emphasis added).

Of all virtues, God says love is superior to the rest. First Corinthians 13 is known as the "love chapter." It speaks about faith and hope but says love excels them both.

Fear, reward, and guilt are factors that provoke others to action. Of all things that motivate us, love is by far the greatest. A young missionary who had surrendered to go to China was asked, "Are you going to China because you have such a great love for the Chinese people?" She replied, "I have no love at all in my heart for the Chinese people, but I have a great love for the Lord Jesus; and He has a great love for the Chinese people." It was her love for Christ that inspired that young person to leave home and family for a strange land. Faith makes all things possible, but love makes all things easy.

Love goes beyond feelings. It would have been more comfortable for that young missionary to stay in her own country with what she was familiar with. Godly love involves sacrifice. It's giving of ourselves for someone else's benefit. Paul said, "And I will very gladly spend and be spent for you; though the more abundantly I love you, the less I be loved" (2 Cor. 12:15). Paul exhausted himself serving those who did not appreciate him. The love of God constrained him to invest his life on their behalf.

Jesus Christ is the greatest example of love. "Greater love hath no man than this, that a man lay down his life for his friends" (John 15:13). God so loved the world that He gave His Son to die in the sinner's place.

You've heard the saying, "People don't care how much you know until they know how much you care."

SCRIPTURE: Read 1 Corinthians 13 and discover the characteristics of *agape* love.

—Harold Vaughan

NOVEMBER 4
FAITH

Scripture Reading—1 Timothy 4:12
"Let no man despise thy youth;
but be thou an example of the believers,
*in word, in conversation, in charity, in spirit, in **faith**, in purity"*
(emphasis added).

A Christian is someone who makes believing in God easy. His life mirrors the Lord Jesus. Exemplifying faith means being a living illustration of what we say we believe. We not only believe in God, but we actually believe God.

A group of scientists in Scotland offered a young boy lots of money if he would allow himself to be lowered by rope over a steep cliff into a mountain gorge. The boy was poor and wanted the money, but when he looked down into the 200-foot chasm, he said, "No." After more persuasion, he said, "I will go if my father holds the rope." He knew he could trust his father; he had confidence in him. He exercised his will and allowed his father to lower him into the chasm.

Living by faith means we have perfect confidence in God. We don't look to self or to others; we look to One much greater than ourselves. When the pilot of a Boeing 747 fires up his engines and races down the runway, he has perfect confidence in the law of aerodynamics. He believes the giant plane will lift off the ground, but he doesn't trust himself to perform that act. He trusts in something more powerful.

Those who live by faith know how to trust God for provision, protection, and direction. They rest in Him for every need. Walking by faith means looking beyond what we can see to what can be. We launch out with full assurance in our Heavenly Father. If that young boy hadn't placed his trust in his dad, he wouldn't have attempted that feat. Had he not trusted, he wouldn't have succeeded. If we don't believe, we won't try. And if we don't try, we won't succeed.

THOUGHT: A good example is the best sermon.

—Harold Vaughan

I'll Be Your Friend

Scripture Reading—Romans 12:10
"Be kindly affectioned one to another with brotherly love;
in honour preferring one another."

Sunday school isn't usually where we expect to take a test. Yet every Sunday school class takes a test whenever a visitor enters the classroom. How do you think your class would do?

1. Into the junior department walks a new "bus kid." He's wearing shoes with no laces and a coat with no zipper. He still has jelly on his face from the piece of toast he ate for breakfast.

2. Into the teen department strolls a 17-year-old guy who is 6 feet, 3 inches tall and weighs 270 pounds. He wears braces and stutters when he talks.

3. Into the adult department wanders an old man with a backpack. He hasn't shaved or had his hair cut for a long time, and he smells like he hasn't been in a bathtub for a while either.

Now class, are you going to pass the test?

When most of us arrive at our Sunday school class, we find a seat with someone we know or like. It's easy to be friendly with someone who's friendly to us. But who will be friendly to those "new and not-very-nice guys"? Will anyone offer them a seat? Will someone talk to them? Will anyone give them a Bible to use? This is a tough test!

In our Scripture reading, Paul says kindness and love are two ways to make others feel special. When we "prefer" someone in "honour," we tell him that he is important and that we care about him. If anyone should treat others with kindness, it should be the Christian. After all, we were "not-very-nice guys" when Jesus reached out to us in love and gave His life to let us know how important we were to Him. Those who visit your Sunday school class and feel special will come back again—and they just might stay.

ACTION POINT: This Sunday, find someone in your Sunday school class who usually sits alone. Be that person's friend.

—Tom Palmer

NOVEMBER 6
LOVING LIKE GOD LOVES
Scripture Reading—1 John 4:7-11

Our Scripture reading says that "God is love" (v. 8). In a world that promotes a distorted view of love, we must seek to understand God's love to fully grasp how to "love one another" (v. 7, 11). God's love provides a perfect pattern for us to follow in loving each other.

1. God's love is **unconditional.** God doesn't love only those who are lovely or lovable. "But God commendeth his love toward us . . . while we were yet sinners" (Rom. 5:8a). A sinless God demonstrated perfect love for sinners, not because they loved God but because they needed God.

2. God's love is **unselfish.** The proof of God's love is that He is a giving God. John 3:16a says, "For God so loved the world, that he gave." God didn't merely tell the world He loved it; rather, He proved His love. It might be said that you can give without loving, but you will never love without giving.

3. God's love is **unending.** There is no such thing as short-time love from God. People often love as long as someone is loving them back. Romans 8:38-39 tells us nothing can "separate us from the love of God" (v. 39). God keeps loving no matter the response from those He loves.

A relationship that pleases God will demonstrate God's kind of love. When we love like God loves, His love becomes the bond that holds the friendship together. This is the kind of friendship that provides a lifelong blessing. As you develop friendships, ask these important questions. "What kind of friend am I?" "Have I learned to demonstrate God's love to those I claim are my friends?" God's love is a wonderful blessing, and your love will be a great blessing, too, if you love like God loves.

PRAY: Pause in prayer to thank God for His love. Ask Him to teach you how to love like He loves.

—*Tom Palmer*

NOVEMBER 7
Be a Friend to Have a Friend

Scripture Reading—Proverbs 18:24
"A man that hath friends must shew himself friendly:
and there is a friend that sticketh closer than a brother."

Everyone likes to have friends. Friends are a special blessing from the Lord. Without good friends, we will be lonely, miserable, and unhappy. Genuine friendships, however, do not just happen. They take effort not only to get started but also to continue throughout life.

When we look at God's loving example, we see that "we love him, because he first loved us" (1 John 4:19). God first loved us and initiated the relationship we now enjoy as His children. In response, we love Him in return.

When we apply this concept to friendships, a simple truth stands out: In order to have a friend, we must be a friend. As Proverbs says, we must show ourselves friendly. It also says that "a friend loveth at all times" (17:17). Change often challenges families, putting them in a new neighborhood, school, or church. Many of us tend to become isolated as we wait for others to reach out to us. If others don't befriend us, we can become resentful toward people we don't even know.

The key is friendliness. Friendliness can quickly bridge the gap and create great friendships that will be a source of blessing for many. Friendliness means to take an interest in others, particularly in those who are lonely and need a friend.

A smile, a greeting, a kind word, or an act of kindness can connect friends who will enjoy each other for years to come. Let's face it—at one time, even best friends didn't know each other. Somebody had to make the first move. In the end, both believers were blessed. Why not become a friendly person? You'll soon discover that you have many special friends.

BE A BLESSING: Choose someone who needs a friend. The next time you see that person, seek to be a friend by being friendly.

—*Tom Palmer*

DON'T RUN WITH A SKUNK

Scripture Reading
1 Corinthians 15:33—"Be not deceived: evil communications corrupt good manners."
Amos 3:3—"Can two walk together, except they be agreed?"

Whether we like it or not, we usually become like those with whom we spend our time. The influence of companions can impact our lives greatly.

Sixth grade was a really tough year for me. My family had moved to the area several months earlier, and I began sixth grade in a new school with a classroom of students who had been together their whole lives. They all knew each other, but nobody knew me.

I decided to make a move. Five boys who had banded together called themselves "The Vikings." They were big, bold, and bad (or at least as much as sixth-graders can be). I started hanging around them, talking like them, and acting like them. Not long after, they took me in. Before long, I was also big, bold, and bad (or at least I thought so). Unfortunately, I was soon getting in trouble with them, too. Their influence had impacted me negatively.

Someone once said that you can't run with a skunk and smell like a rose! That's the truth—and the warning—our Scripture reading teaches. "Evil communications" means those with whom we communicate—in other words, our companions. "Good manners" means the rules we live by or our moral standards for living.

Tragically, bad people can ruin good things in our lives. Many young people have made the mistake of choosing wrong friends and have paid dearly for their decision. The skunks they chose to run with turned them into rascals who rejected authority and convictions, even God Himself.

What kind of person do you want to be? Your answer depends on what kind of people you choose to be with. Before long, you may be just like them.

EXERCISE: Make a list of good qualities you would seek in those who would make good friends.

—Tom Palmer

THE BLESSING OF A GOOD FRIEND
Scripture Reading—1 Samuel 18:1-9

David needed a good friend. King Saul, who was jealous because of David's victory over Goliath, had threatened his life. Several times, Saul had also tried to kill David (18:11, 19:10), and he had told his servants to kill David if they could (19:1, 11). Needless to say, David's life was in jeopardy, and turmoil ruled the circumstances of his life.

During those desperate days, God gave David a faithful companion and friend named Jonathan. The twist in the story is that Jonathan was Saul's son. In fact, his friendship with David put Jonathan's life at risk; his father didn't want anyone assisting David. During this time, however, these two young men were drawn together to support, protect, and encourage each other.

In our Scripture reading, we read that "the soul of Jonathan was knit with the soul of David" (v. 1). These men shared with each other in such a way that they became a part of each other's lives. The Bible tells us that they loved each other as they loved their own lives.

David's friendship with Jonathan became a great blessing for both of them. Verse 14 says that "the Lord was with him [David]," but humanly speaking, David was alone much of the time. Yet during those times of great seclusion, Jonathan was there as David's friend. Together, they were able to go on, living their own lives but also living for the person they called their friend.

If you have a good friend, thank the Lord for that person. Friends are a gift from God, a blessing God has brought into your life for your benefit. You will be amazed to see how your God—and your friend—will be there for you during the most difficult times of life.

EXERCISE: Proverbs 17:17 says, "A friend loveth at all times, and a brother is born for adversity." Note when a true friend will be there for you.

—*Tom Palmer*

NOVEMBER 10
BECOMING A BLESSING TO YOUR FRIEND
Scripture Reading—1 Samuel 20:35-42

David and Jonathan's friendship is a classic demonstration of how two friends can be a blessing to each other. These two men knew not only how to gain a friend but also how to maintain a friendship. Several truths are particularly worth noting.

First, note the level of commitment these men demonstrated. In chapter 18 (v. 3) and again in chapter 20 (v. 42), we read that David and Jonathan made a covenant. Their covenant was an agreement that they would stay true to each other forever. Their relationship also included giving and sharing. In 1 Samuel 18:4, Jonathan gave David several garments as well as his valuable weapons.

In 1 Samuel 19:2, we read about Jonathan's willingness to protect his friend from harm and danger at the hand of his father, Saul. As a true friend, Jonathan dreaded the thought of his friend losing his life.

In 1 Samuel 19:7, we read that David and Jonathan were open and honest. Because of their desire to be transparent, they kept few secrets.

According to 1 Samuel 20, David and Jonathan also prayed together (vv. 11-15). Together, they sought the Lord's direction and protection in their dire situation. As men of God, they joined together and sought to know God's will.

Finally, the key thought comes in 1 Samuel 20:42. In the name of the Lord, they said, "The Lord be between me and thee, and between my seed and thy seed for ever."

What drew these men together as friends was that the Lord was at the center of their friendship. As each friend initially sought to draw closer to God, the result was that they drew closer to each other. In the Lord, they blessed each other. Friendship isn't just finding a good friend but being a good friend.

PRAY: Ask each family member to pray for someone he considers to be a special personal friend.

—Tom Palmer

NOVEMBER 11
CRACK THE CLIQUE
Scripture Reading—James 2:1-10

You can spell it two ways. Whether you spell it "c-l-i-c-k" or "c-l-i-q-u-e," we're talking about something that can have a damaging impact on friendships. No, I'm not talking about an irritating noise but a group of people who isolate themselves from others and don't let others in. These groups don't officially incorporate, and they don't advertise themselves as a clique. Yet they are real—something you'll discover if you try to crack their clique.

When choosing those with whom we'll associate, we can easily select those we like or those who are most like us. That was the problem with the believers to whom James was writing. The first verse of our Scripture reading tells us these people displayed "respect" of persons; in other words, they showed partiality and favoritism. They allowed qualities like personal appearance and economic status to determine their friends. In so doing, they became "judges of evil thoughts" (v. 4). They "commit[ted] sin" (v. 9) and were "transgressors" of the law (v. 9). In God's eyes, the problem was serious.

The Christian life has no room for discrimination. Race, ethnic background, physical condition, financial status, and educational experience should never be the basis for relationships. We do nothing wrong by enjoying people with whom we have things in common, but the problem occurs when we reject or ignore those with whom we have nothing in common.

The time has come to begin a campaign in our churches, schools, and youth groups to eliminate cliques or "clicks," depending on your choice of spelling. This campaign will occur only when we are willing to let the "royal law" rule our lives. Jesus' command to love others is second only to the command to love God with all our hearts (Matt. 22:37-40).

EXERCISE: Ask each family member to prepare a copy of the "royal law" to display in his room.

—Tom Palmer

HOW GREAT THOU ART!

Scripture Reading

Psalm 95:3—*"For the Lord is **a great God**, and **a great King** above all gods" (emphasis added).*

Titus 2:13—*"Looking for that blessed hope, and the glorious appearing of the great God and our Saviour Jesus Christ."*

One of my favorite hymns is "How Great Thou Art." In this wonderful song, the writer exalts God for the many ways He has demonstrated His greatness. Some of the words are,

> Oh, Lord my God, when I in awesome wonder,
> Consider all the worlds Thy hands have made.
> I see the stars, I hear the rolling thunder,
> Thy power throughout the universe displayed.
> Then sings my soul, my Savior God to Thee.
> How great Thou art!

Another song exalts God this way,

> Our God's a great God, and worthy to be praised!
> Our God's a great God, oh praise His holy name!
> He made the world so great, He keeps me by His grace,
> And soon I'll see His face,
> Our God's so great!

When our children were small, we had a table grace we prayed before our meals.

> God is great, and God is good,
> And we thank Him for our food.
> By His hand we are all fed,
> Give us, Lord, our daily bread.
> In Jesus' name, amen.

Yes, we can seek to acknowledge the greatness of our God in many ways. But it's easy to sing songs and to say words that speak of God's greatness without experiencing that greatness. We can see the best proof of God's greatness in a life He has changed. When Isaiah experienced God in all of His greatness and glory (Isa. 6), his whole life was transformed.

POINT TO PONDER: How is God's greatness evident in your life, in your marriage, or in your family?

—*Jack Palmer*

NOVEMBER 13
GOD'S GREATNESS IN HIS WORD

Scripture Reading—Psalm 95
As you read this chapter each day,
make it part of your family life
as you meditate on God's promises.

Everywhere we look in this world God created, we see His greatness. No wonder the psalmist wrote, "The fool hath said in his heart, There is no God" (Ps. 14:1a, 53:1a). Someone is utterly foolish to think that our world evolved into existence. It's as crazy as thinking we could take the separate parts of a watch, shake them up in a box, open the box, and discover a beautiful, accurate timepiece. We need more faith to believe that God didn't create this world than that He did.

Though this world is a wonderful testimony to God's greatness, we need to base our faith on something more permanent. The Bible tells us, "Heaven and earth shall pass away, but my words shall not pass away" (Matt. 24:35; Mark 13:31; Luke 21:33). This world is only temporary; God's Word is eternal. Therefore, the testimony of Scripture is our greatest authority for understanding God's greatness.

The following are wonderful Bible verses (with emphasis added) for meditating on the greatness of our God: "O Lord my God, thou art *very great*" (Ps. 104:1). "And Ezra blessed the Lord, the *great God*. And all the people answered, Amen, Amen" (Neh. 8:6a). "Looking for that blessed hope, and the glorious appearing of the *great God* and our Saviour Jesus Christ" (Titus 2:13). "Wherefore, *thou art great*, O Lord God" (2 Sam. 7:22a). "For *thou art great*, and doest wondrous things: thou art God alone" (Ps. 86:10). "Oh Lord; *thou art great*, and thy name is great in might" (Jer. 10:6b).

It's wonderful to see God's greatness in the world but more wonderful to see it so clearly described in His Word.

ACTION POINT: Read the verses listed above again. They will make God's greatness more real to you and to your family.

—Jack Palmer

NOVEMBER 14
GOD IS GREAT
IN HIS PERSON
Scripture Reading—Psalm 95

Once one of my sons and I went to a local park because he had issues regarding God's existence we needed to talk about. It was a dreary, overcast day. Clouds hung low, and the sun was absent. As we talked, he asked me how I could believe in a God I couldn't see. As an airplane passed overhead, I said, "There's no airplane up there."

"Yes, there is," he said. "I hear it."

"But how can you believe there's an airplane up there when you can't see it?"

"Because I hear the motor."

His answer was all I needed to explain the fact that we can believe in a God we can't see because we observe the evidence of His existence everywhere we look. I talked to him about the importance of basing faith on the truth of God's Word and on the wonders of creation. That's all the evidence we need! Hebrews 11:1 says, "Now faith is the substance of things hoped for, the *evidence of things not seen*" (emphasis added). By faith, we believe in God's existence and in what He's like. Our talk helped my son understand the person of God.

Verse 3 of today's Scripture says, "For the Lord is a great God, and a great King *above all gods*" (emphasis added). When God spoke to Moses from the burning bush and sent him back to Egypt to deliver His people from bondage, Moses asked what he should say when the people asked who had sent him. "And God said unto Moses, I AM THAT I AM: and he said, Thus shalt thou say unto the children of Israel, I AM hath sent me unto you" (Ex. 3:14). In that statement, God declares Himself to be the eternally existing God; or, as the psalmist put it, "From everlasting to everlasting, *thou art God*" (Ps. 90:2b, emphasis added).

APPLICATION: Share evidences that help you believe God is *great in His person* even though you can't see Him.

—*Jack Palmer*

NOVEMBER 15
GOD IS GREAT
IN HIS PRESENCE

Scripture Reading—Psalm 95
Give special attention to verse 2.

Though much has changed in the 21st century, children still love to play "hide and seek." It's fun to close our eyes, count to 50 while our friends go and hide, and look for them. That game is as old as time itself. In the Garden of Eden, Adam and Eve played the first game of hide and seek when they tried to hide from God. Before they sinned, they enjoyed sweet fellowship with God. But after they sinned, their perfect innocence was gone. They feared God's presence and hid from Him, covering themselves with fig leaves. To their surprise, they discovered they couldn't escape from God's presence (Gen. 3:1-13).

The Book of Jonah describes someone else who tried to flee from God's presence. God told Jonah to go to Nineveh and to preach against their wickedness. "But Jonah rose up to flee unto Tarshish *from the presence of the Lord*" (Jonah 1:3a, emphasis added). He boarded a ship to Tarshish, thinking he'd escaped God—only to discover he was wrong. God is great in His presence. No matter where we go, He's there. Have you ever tried to play hide and seek with God?

Psalm 139 offers tremendous verses about God's presence. David asks, "Whither shall I go from thy spirit? or whither shall *I flee from thy presence?*" (v. 7, emphasis added). He enumerates the many places people go in their attempt to avoid God (vv. 7-12). His conclusion? It's impossible!

Practicing the presence of God is key to a successful Christian life. If we understand that God is with us everywhere we go, this truth should have a life-changing impact on our lives. Hagar, Sarah's handmaid, said in Genesis 16:13, "Thou God seest me." That's a powerful truth to remember.

DO THIS NOW: Read Psalm 139 and discuss the dangers of playing hide and seek with God.

—*Jack Palmer*

NOVEMBER 16
GOD IS GREAT IN HIS POWER

Scripture Reading—Psalm 95
Give special attention to verses 4-6.

Years ago, we purchased a modular home for our lot. The foundation was built, the house arrived, and a special crew came to set the house on its foundation. The house came in two pieces, 68 by 14 feet each. We wondered how the workers were going to move those sections from the trailers to the foundation. A huge crane arrived, and workers attached cables to each section. Our stomachs were in our throats as the crane lifted the house onto its foundation with ease. We sighed in relief! Because the crane was so powerful, the job wasn't a problem.

In the Book of Jeremiah we read, "Thou hast made the heaven and the earth by thy *great power.* . . . Behold, I am the Lord, the God of all flesh: is there any thing too hard for me?" (32:17, 27; emphasis added). We often encounter life situations that are too big for us. We can't imagine how we'll ever get through them. That's when we need to remember that our *God is great in His power* and to allow Him to do for us what we cannot do for ourselves.

A missionary offered a native man a ride in the back of his truck. The man was carrying a load of firewood on his shoulders. Accepting the offer, the man climbed into the back. When the missionary looked in the mirror, he noticed the native still carried the wood on his shoulders. Stopping the truck, the missionary asked him to put his load down.

The man replied, "No, you have been kind to give me a ride, but I wouldn't think of asking you to carry my wood, too." Dear friends, the good news is that when God carries you, He carries your load, too. And He does so because *He is so great in His power.*

APPLICATION: Discuss Scripture passages that describe God's demonstrating His great power. Encourage your family to see that nothing is too big for God to handle.

—*Jack Palmer*

NOVEMBER 17
GOD IS GREAT
IN HIS PROVISION

Scripture Reading—Psalm 95
Give special attention to verse 7.

In John 10:11, Jesus describes Himself as the "good shepherd." According to His teachings, the shepherd must *protect* his sheep and *provide* for their needs. One of the greatest promises in God's Word is in Philippians 4:19. "But my God shall *supply all your need* according to his riches in glory by Christ Jesus" (emphasis added). In today's Scripture reading, we read, "For he is our God; and we are the people of His pasture, and the *sheep* of His hand" (v. 7a, emphasis added). In Psalm 23:1, David wrote, "The Lord is *my shepherd*; I shall not want" (emphasis added). Our God is in the need-meeting business!

My dad, Dr. George Palmer, became a pastor in the early 20th century. God blessed him and my mother with eight children. In the early years, they lived on a meager salary and often had no money and nothing to eat. Mother brought the family to the table so Dad could pray for the meal God *was going* to provide. A man of great faith, Dad loved to tell about times when he was praying and someone brought food for the family. He would pray again, giving thanks for the food God *did provide*, and Mom would prepare the meal. Was he merely presumptuous of God? Absolutely not! He believed with all his heart that God was *great in His provision* and would be true to His Word. With that kind of faith, no wonder God gave him a worldwide ministry.

Do you have faith to take God at His Word? Hebrews 11:1 reminds us, "Now faith is the substance of things hoped for, the evidence of things not seen." Real faith thanks God for His provision even before He provides. God allows us to experience special needs so we can experience His great provision.

COUNT THE COST: Allow God to test your faith with a special need so you can experience His great provision. You may need to wait awhile because God is never in a hurry, but He's always on time.

—Jack Palmer

GOD IS GREAT IN HIS PROMISES

Scripture Reading—Psalm 95
Give special attention to verse 11.

Parents must learn the value of being true to their promises. If they promise a bicycle, they had better be prepared to fulfill that promise. If they promise a spanking, they must fulfill that promise, too. Most promises are made sincerely, but some are foolish. That's why we must be careful about making promises.

God's Word is a book of promises. When God promises blessing, He blesses. When He promises judgment, He judges, as we see in verses 10-11 of our text. God is always true to what He promises. If God promises something, you can count on Him to follow through. Second Peter 1:4a says, "Whereby are given unto us exceeding great and precious *promises*" (emphasis added). Second Corinthians 1:20 is another good reminder of God's promises. "For all the *promises of God* in him are yea, and in him Amen, unto the glory of God by us" (emphasis added). Too many of God's people are sitting on the premises or leaning over the precipice when they should be *standing on the promises.*

I heard about some folks who agreed to do a job for a fellow for a certain amount of money. It was a difficult project. Finished, they went to the homeowner to collect their pay. Would you believe it? He looked them right in the eye and said he wasn't going to pay them what he'd agreed. That poor fellow knew nothing about keeping a promise. Though it was hard for the Christians to accept his broken promise, they trusted the Lord and learned a valuable lesson. People can break promises and think nothing of it, but God will never break His promises.

ACTION POINT: Have you made promises to God or others that you haven't kept? If so, be willing to ask forgiveness and to make a commitment to be true to your word. If you made a promise you can't possibly fulfill, ask to be relieved of that promise. That's how to maintain a clear conscience.

—Jack Palmer

NOVEMBER 19
CLEAR CONSCIENCE—
SIN

God called King David "a man after mine own heart" (Acts 13:22). David had a special relationship with God and "behaved himself wisely" (1 Sam. 18:5). God used him to rebuild the nation of Israel after King Saul destroyed and divided it. David was a successful and spiritual man.

When David was older, he decided not to go to battle with his army and stayed home. His sinful relationship with a woman named Bathsheba devastated his personal relationship with God. As a result of David's sin, he lost his joy, his kingdom suffered, and his family was never the same.

We never sin and get away with it. Moses told the children of Israel, "Be sure your sin will find you out" (Num. 32:23b).

What is sin? Sin is anything that violates God's Word and will. The word *sin* comes from an archery term. It means to miss the target and to hit the wrong target. When I sin, I miss the target of God's holiness as spelled out in the Word of God. I hit a target that is against God's Word and will.

The most miserable person in the world is a Christian who harbors unconfessed sin in his life. Sin hinders our relationship with God because God is holy and hates sin. Sin causes us to lose our joy and devastates our lives.

David described his misery in Psalm 32:3-4. "When I kept silence, my bones waxed old through my roaring all the day long. For day and night thy hand was heavy upon me: my moisture is turned into the drought of summer. Selah."

APPLICATION: Read Psalm 51 and discuss how David dealt with his sin.

Psalm 51:2—"Wash me . . . and cleanse me from my sin."
Psalm 51:3—"For I acknowledge my transgressions: and my sin is ever before me."
Psalm 51:10—"Create in me a clean heart, O God; and renew a right spirit within me."

—*Craig M. Scott*

NOVEMBER 20
BUT I FEEL SO GUILTY!

Have you ever experienced a guilty conscience? Have you felt so guilty that you lay awake at night thinking about it? You lost your joy, and you wanted to crawl into a hole and forget about everything and everyone.

What happened to you? You suffered from a guilty or violated conscience. You did something wrong, and your conscience—God's alarm system—blared inside you like a fire alarm.

How do we get a clear conscience? How did King David get a clear conscience? Notice what he prayed to God. "Purge me with hyssop, and I shall be clean: wash me, and I shall be whiter than snow. Make me to hear joy and gladness. . . . Create in me a clean heart, O God; and renew a right spirit within me. . . . Restore unto me the joy of thy salvation; and uphold me with thy free spirit" (Ps. 51:7-8a, 10, 12).

What caused David to lose his joy and gladness? What caused him to have a dirty heart and a bad spirit? One thing—sin. He had disobeyed God. He had sinned with Bathsheba and had not properly dealt with his sin before God.

Now, after a year of suffering with a guilty conscience, David took the proper steps to gain a clear conscience. Notice what he prayed. "For I acknowledge my transgressions" (Ps. 51:3a). David called sin what it is; he was honest before God. "Against thee, thee only, have I sinned, and done this evil in thy sight" (v. 4a).

David knew that the one he had offended the most was God. He wanted to make sure things were right between him and God. "If we confess our sins, he is faithful and just to forgive us our sins, and to cleanse us from all unrighteousness" (1 John 1:9).

1. What must I do when I sin?
2. What is God's response to my confession?

ASSIGNMENT: Read and discuss the following verses: Psalm 51:3-12; 1 John 1:9.

—*Craig M. Scott*

NOVEMBER 21
CLEAR CONSCIENCE—
VICTORY OVER SIN

"I just can't get victory over this sin in my life! I try and try and try and keep falling. What is wrong with me?"

Two men in the Bible allowed something to happen in their lives that caused great damage to their relationship with God and with others. They were once spiritual leaders in the church, but something devastated their spiritual lives. The apostle Paul says they "made shipwreck" in regard to their faith.

Their names were Hymenaeus and Alexander. In relation to their faith, they allowed their consciences to be violated. The apostle Paul says he had to kick them out of the church. See what God says about them in 1 Timothy 1:19-20. "Holding faith, and a good conscience; which some having put away concerning faith have made shipwreck: Of whom is Hymenaeus and Alexander; whom I have delivered unto Satan, that they may learn not to blaspheme."

I don't know what happened. Maybe they became bitter because of something that happened or toward someone who hurt them. Perhaps they became involved in some kind of sin and never made it right with God. Whatever the case, we know they failed to clear their consciences before God and others. As a result, they "made shipwreck" of their faith. Their relationship with God was devastated.

Having a clear conscience means we know that no unconfessed sin is hindering our relationship with God. No one can point a finger at us and accuse us of a wrongdoing we have not made right.

What can we learn from these two men? We learn that if we allow sin to go unconfessed in our lives, we will make shipwreck of our faith. We learn that we can't have victory in our lives until we have a clear conscience.

ASSIGNMENT: Acts 24:16 says, "And herein do I exercise myself, to have always a conscience void of offence toward God, and toward men." What does God say in this verse about a clear conscience? Look up 1 John 1:9 to see how to get a clear conscience.

—*Craig M. Scott*

A Clear Conscience—
Ready to Speak Out for Christ!

A young lady said to me, "Pastor, I've recently gotten my life right with God, and I really want to do right! I want to go back to my friends and take a stand for Christ."

"That's tremendous!" I said. "I'll pray that you'll be able to do so."

Hanging her head, she said sadly, "I want to take a stand, but I can't. Whenever I get ready to say something about the Lord, I feel like my mouth is taped shut. I can't speak." I asked her to explain.

"The moment I start to say something about the Lord," she said, "something inside of me says 'Don't talk yet! Wait 'til they've observed your life for a few months. If you say something now, they'll think you're a hypocrite.' Pastor, what can I do?"

She expressed what many Christians feel after they've made things right with God. They feel so guilty that they can't speak out for the Lord.

What would you say to this young lady?

Here's what I told her. "Have you considered that the reason you don't have the freedom in your spirit to speak out for the Lord is because you've been a bad testimony to your friends? Consider clearing your conscience with them. Let them know that you've been a bad example and that you've recently made it right with the Lord and want to make it right with them. Then ask them for their forgiveness for not being the kind of Christian you needed to be."

In 1 Peter 3:15, God tells us to "be ready always to give an answer to every man." We need to be ready to take a stand for what the Word of God says.

Why do we fail to read verse 16a? "Having a good conscience." Here's the thought: If we want to take a stand for Christ, we must have a good conscience.

READ AND DISCUSS: Acts 24:16

—*Craig M. Scott*

NOVEMBER 23
CLEAR CONSCIENCE—
LEAVE YOUR GIFT AT THE ALTAR

In Old Testament times, an Israelite brought his gift of sacrifice to the court of the Israelites. He waited with his gift at the rails of the altar separating the place where he stood from the place where the priests stood in a separate courtyard. He waited until the moment when the priest approached the Israelite with outstretched hands to receive the sacrifice.

At that moment, about to present himself to the priest and to God, asking for forgiveness and mercy, if the Israelite remembered that a brother had something against him, he left his gift at the altar and made things right with his brother. Then he returned to the court of the Israelites and presented his sacrifice to the priest.

Jesus teaches the importance of restoring relationships in Matthew 5:23-24. "Therefore if thou bring thy gift to the altar, and there rememberest that thy brother hath ought against thee; leave there thy gift before the altar, and go thy way; first be reconciled to thy brother, and then come and offer thy gift."

In the early church, believers followed the common practice of resolving offenses and disputes with brothers and sisters in the Lord before partaking of the Lord's Supper.

On one occasion, I remember being challenged to ask God if there was anyone in my life, past or present, that I had offended. I bowed my head and asked God to reveal these people to me. Immediately, four people came to mind. I promised God that I would do everything within my power to seek forgiveness from those individuals. Within days, God brought me in contact with each one of those people.

Words cannot express the joy and freedom that came to my spirit when I made things right with them.

ASSIGNMENT: Look up and discuss Acts 24:16. Can you think of anyone in your past you've offended and with whom you've not made things right?

—*Craig M. Scott*

CLEAR CONSCIENCE—
SHORT SIN ACCOUNTS

"Don't sweat the small stuff!" Does this statement accurately describe how we should handle issues with God and with others?

Does God ever tell us only to be concerned about "big" sins? No, He doesn't! Every sin, whether big or small, is an offense to our holy God. That's why we must keep short sin accounts with Him.

Every time we sin, we must apply 1 John 1:9. "If we confess our sins, he is faithful and just to forgive us our sins, and to cleanse us from all unrighteousness."

Notice the little word *sins*. Separate sins! Little and big sins!

If I'm going to have a clear conscience before God and others, I must learn to confess every sin, whether big or small. Sins of attitude. Sins of action. I need to keep short sin accounts with God!

Acts 24:16 is so important for us to understand. "And herein do I exercise myself, to have always a conscience void of offence toward God, and toward men."

We must confess "little sins." Like making a rude, cutting remark to someone. Like being disrespectful to an authority figure. Like lying, stealing, or cheating. Every one of these sins is big to God. To have freedom of spirit in our relationship with God, we must maintain a clear conscience.

A teen guy came up to me one day. "Pastor, I need to ask your forgiveness for chewing gum."

I thought, *Good night. Why ask forgiveness for chewing gum?*

He explained that someone had donated new carpet for our bus and requested that the teens not eat candy or chew gum on the bus. I made this a rule. This young man didn't think chewing gum was a sin, but the issue was that he'd disobeyed his authority. In so doing, he'd disobeyed God.

APPLICATION: How about you? Are you concerned about the "little sins" as well as the "big ones"? Ask God to point out any unconfessed sins in your life.

—*Craig M. Scott*

NOVEMBER 25
CLEAR CONSCIENCE—
TAKE THE PROPER STEPS

The day when I asked God to reveal anyone I had offended was a life-changing day for me. As God revealed those people, I went to them one by one and asked them to forgive me for my offenses.

After completing the task, I sensed a freshness and a freedom in my relationship with God I'd been lacking. An indescribable freshness and joy came to my life and ministry.

I then made a commitment to maintain short sin accounts with God and with others. I didn't want anything to hinder my relationship with God or with others and realized that maintaining a clear conscience was hard work. As Paul says, it takes "exercise" (Acts 24:16).

As I sought a clear conscience before God and man, God challenged me with three steps.

1. I made a list of those from whom I needed to seek forgiveness. I listed them in order of importance. The most important one was God, then family, then authority figures, then friends.

2. The scope of my confession was only as big as the scope of my offense. What do I mean? If I offended one person, I went only to that one person. If I offended others, I went to them. If I offended a group of people, I went to the group. If my offense was only toward God, then I went to God alone!

3. I needed to have a sincere, humble, and repentant attitude. I couldn't say something like, "I'm sorry for my part. Are you sorry for yours?" Or "I'm sorry IF I was wrong." No! I had to say, "I was wrong when I _____. I'm sorry! Will you forgive me?"

Why do you think God tells us not to "let . . . the sun go down upon . . . [our] wrath" (Eph. 4:26)?

READ AND DISCUSS: Acts 24:16 says, "And herein do I exercise myself, to have always a conscience void of offence toward God, and toward men." Discuss this verse as well as 1 Timothy 1:18-20 and Hebrews 5:11-14.

—*Craig M. Scott*

ATTITUDE

"There is little difference in people, but that little difference makes a big difference. The little difference is attitude." —Clement Stone

A turtle gets nowhere until it sticks its neck out.

A tea kettle is up to its neck in hot water, but it still sings.

A kite rises *against* the wind, not *with* it.

Adversity is the refiner's fire that burns the impurities from our souls. Everybody encounters difficulties, but few approach their problems with a proper outlook. What happens *to* you is not nearly as important as *how* you respond. You can learn to maintain a good viewpoint regardless of what happens.

Attitude is an inward feeling expressed by your behavior. People can often detect your attitude, even if you don't speak a word. The most important decision you make each morning is what kind of attitude you will have during the day.

David was discouraged when he penned, "Why art thou cast down, O my soul? and why art thou disquieted in me?" (Ps. 42:5a). He asked himself, "Why am I discouraged? Why am I so restless?" David spoke to his own soul.

People often think that talking to themselves is a bad sign. But on occasion, we need to look ourselves square in the face and talk to ourselves. David said, "Why art thou cast down, O my soul? . . . hope thou in God: for I shall yet praise him for the help of his countenance" (Ps. 42:5).

If we wouldn't think of sitting around all day and listening to trash talk on TV, then we should stop listening to trash talk coming out of our souls! "Nobody cares about me." "So and so was ugly to me, so I'll be ugly to him!" "Nobody knows all the trouble I've known." We must put a stop to garbage self-talk. When we start feeling sorry for ourselves, we should preach to our own souls. We should stop listening to ourselves and start talking to ourselves like David did.

CONSIDER THIS: Talk about the importance of attitude.

—Harold Vaughan

NOVEMBER 27
CONTENTMENT
IN CHRIST

Scripture Reading—Philippians 4:11-13

"Not that I speak in respect of want: for I have learned, in whatsoever state I am, therewith to be content. I know both how to be abased, and I know how to abound. . . . I can do all things through Christ which strengtheneth me."

I met Ida Brinkman at a church in Ohio. She was carried into the sanctuary with various equipment, including a respirator. Ida and her paraphernalia took up a lot of space.

Preaching that evening, I glanced down where Ida was lying. Her radiant countenance arrested my attention. She had an angelic glow about her.

After the service, I introduced myself. After small talk, I asked Ida why she was bedridden. Forty-nine years earlier, she'd contracted polio; and the disease had left her paralyzed. Unable to help herself, she'd required others' assistance. For 49 years, her husband had taken care of her until he passed away. When I met her, she was living in a nursing home.

I asked Ida how she kept a good attitude in spite of her difficulties. "I try not to look at my circumstances," she replied. "I look to Jesus."

After visiting with Ida, I prayed, *Lord, if Ida can make it, so can I!* What an inspiration to meet people like Ida who find peace and contentment in spite of difficult circumstances! A senior citizen once told me, "I have so many blessings in my life. I have no right to fret over what I've been denied."

The apostle Paul learned to be content. Whether hungry or full, in prison or in a palace, in a riot or in a revival, Paul trained himself to be satisfied. Notice that he "learned . . . to be content." Having experienced so many difficulties, Paul conditioned himself to take things in stride. Learning to be content is one of life's most valuable lessons.

BRINGING IT HOME: List some of the trials Paul endured. How do you think he learned to be content when he faced so many difficulties?

—Harold Vaughan

NOVEMBER 28
EXCITEMENT IN
THE EARLY CHURCH

Evangelist D.L. Moody was preaching in England when his songleader told him things weren't going well. Moody replied, "Before you can have a big fire, you must have a little fire." We should never despise the day of small things because *big* things can result from modest beginnings. If we fan the spark, it can become a flame!

The early church was pregnant with joy. We read they ate their "meat with gladness and singleness of heart" (Acts 2:46). Those who were saved "gladly received his [God's] word" (v. 41). The healed lame man walked, leaped, and praised God (3:8). Those early days were jam-packed with excitement!

In Acts 12, when Peter was thrown into prison for preaching the Gospel, "prayer was made without ceasing of the church unto God for him" (v. 5). The angel of the Lord led Peter through the prison doors, which miraculously opened, and Peter walked out a free man. Immediately, he headed for the house where believers were praying. When Peter knocked at the door, a girl named Rhoda became so excited when she heard his voice that she forgot to let him in. She "opened not . . . for gladness" (v. 14). God answered the believers' prayers, and they were thrilled.

God had mercy on the Gentiles (non-Jews), and there was great persecution. How did God's people respond? "And the disciples were filled with joy, and with the Holy Ghost" (Acts 13:52). Some of them were even put to death for Christ's sake.

Two signs of God's immediate presence are conviction and celebration. An overwhelming sense of the fear of the Lord fell on them when Ananias and Sapphira were struck dead for lying. Yet they had unspeakable joy because "in thy [His] presence is fulness of joy" (Ps. 16:11).

People are attracted to fire. Fire breeds excitement, and the fire of God is the most electrifying thing on earth.

PRAYER TIME: Read these verses about joy in the Book of Acts (2:28; 8:8; 13:52; 15:3). Ask the Lord to send revival fire to your home and church.

—Harold Vaughan

HAPPINESS

A king was so unhappy that he dispatched one of his men to find a happy man. "When you find the happy man," the king ordered, "purchase his shirt and bring it back to me so that I might wear it and also be happy." For years, the king's man traveled and searched, but he couldn't find a happy man. Finally, when he was walking in the poorer section of one of the most impoverished counties, he heard a man singing at the top of his lungs. Following the sound, he found a man plowing a field.

"Are you happy?" the king's man asked.

"I have never known a day of unhappiness in my life," the plowman replied.

The king's representative explained the purpose of his mission and asked the plowman for his shirt. The plowman laughed uproariously. "Why, man, I don't have a shirt!"

Happiness isn't obtained by acquiring someone's shirts, toys, money, or anything else he may possess. Happiness is a byproduct of gratitude; grateful people are cheerful people. Instead of complaining about what you lack, thank God for what you have. Consider the following poem:

I had the blues because I had no shoes,

Until upon the street I met a man who had no feet.

No man ever found joy by acquiring material gain. Jesus said, "Take heed, and beware of covetousness: for a man's life consisteth not in the abundance of the things which he possesseth" (Luke 12:15b).

Whenever you feel what Ron Hamilton calls the "poochie lip disease" coming on, look at all the benefits God has given to you. Don't develop what one lady called a case of "ingrown eyeballs." At all costs, don't fall into a trap of self-pity. Genuine concern for others comes naturally as you take interest in them.

ACTION POINT: Perhaps an elderly neighbor could use a hand or a friendly visit. Go out of your way to encourage someone who would benefit from your cheerful spirit.

—*Harold Vaughan*

NOVEMBER 30
OTHERS

Scripture Reading—Philippians 2:3
"Let nothing be done through strife or vainglory;
but in lowliness of mind let each esteem other
better than themselves."

The happiest people are those who have learned the blessing that comes from ministering to others. John Haggai said, "No man who is interested in others has time to worry about his own problems." The Bible tells us to esteem others better than ourselves (Phil. 2:3).

By all means, we should use common sense in our efforts to assist others. We shouldn't be like a certain Cub Scout who had his own idea about assisting others. One night during a pack meeting, the scoutmaster asked those who had done their good deed for the day to lift their hands. Everyone except one scout lifted his hands.

"Johnny, go do your good deed for the day," the scoutmaster barked, "and don't come back until you've done it!"

Johnny was gone for about 20 minutes. When he returned, his clothes were in shreds, his hair disheveled. His face was cut and bleeding.

"Johnny, what have you been doing?" the scoutmaster asked.

"I did my good deed for the day, sir," Johnny replied.

"What was that?"

"I helped an old lady across the street, sir."

"Well, how did you get in that condition?"

"She didn't want to go."

Plenty of folks have needs and would appreciate a helping hand. We should assist others at the point of their greatest need. Let me suggest we do something specific for someone every day. Doing good deeds with no thought of remuneration is good medicine.

PROJECT: Drop a line of appreciation to your child's teacher, to your pastor, to your friend, or to someone who has contributed to the life of your family. Thankfulness is always appropriate.

—Harold Vaughan

DECEMBER 1
PUTTING YOUR BEST FOOT FORWARD

Scripture Reading—Proverbs 18:24
"A man that hath friends must shew himself friendly: and there is a friend that sticketh closer than a brother."

Your attitude is your best friend or your worst enemy. Your attitude toward others will affect their attitude toward you, and the way you relate to others will affect how they relate to you. The way you present yourself will impact the way others interact with you.

Forgetting it was garbage-pickup day, a housewife ran after the garbage truck with a trash bag in each hand. She wasn't wearing makeup or her false teeth, and she'd left her wig on the dresser. With her bathrobe flapping in the wind, she shouted to the garbage man, "Am I too late? Am I too late?"

The garbage man yelled back, "Go ahead and jump on. We've got plenty of room."

How you treat others will affect how they treat you! Your attitude will either draw people or repel them. What's most likely to determine your success or failure is your disposition, your attitude. Your mindset is more important than your education, skills, assets, failures, or past. God never consults your past to determine your future, but your attitude has a definite bearing on your destiny.

What happens to you is not as important as *how you think* about what happens to you. And what happens *to* you isn't as important as what happens *in* you. Each morning, you have a choice: a good attitude or a bad attitude.

Everybody likes to be around upbeat people. The Bible says that a man who wants friends needs to be friendly (Prov. 18:24). You can endear yourself to others by showing an interest in them. Your positive outlook will inspire others to look on the sunny side of life.

CONSIDER: List those you enjoy having in your company. Can you name the qualities these people possess that make them pleasant to be around?

—Harold Vaughan

DECEMBER 2
YOUR ATTITUDE
IS YOUR CHOICE

Scripture Reading—Psalm 9:2a
"I will be glad and rejoice in thee."

A small, 92-year-old woman was well-poised and fully dressed by eight o'clock each morning. Though she was legally blind, her hair was always combed and her makeup perfectly applied. When her husband of 70 years passed away, she moved to a nursing home. On the day of the move, she patiently waited in the lobby for many hours. She smiled when a nurse said her room was ready. As she maneuvered her walker to the elevator, the nurse gave her a visual description of her tiny room.

"I love it," the old lady replied with the enthusiasm of an eight-year-old who'd just received a new toy.

"But Mrs. Jones, you haven't seen the room yet," the nurse replied.

"That doesn't have anything to do with it," Mrs. Jones replied. "Happiness is something you decide on ahead of time. Whether I like my room or not doesn't depend on how the furniture is arranged. It's how I arrange my mind. I have already decided to love it."

Wow, what a tremendous attitude! We may not be able to do anything about *where* we are, but we can do something about *how* we are! We may be unable to control our circumstances, but we can control our attitude.

Attitude is a little thing that goes a long way! We have little choice about many things in life, but we can adopt the attitude of contentment. Being glad is a personal decision. We should stop whining and start shining; we're too blessed to be depressed.

"I will be glad" means we can determine to choose gladness over gloominess. If a 92-year-old could choose happiness, we can, too! David said, "I will be glad." Will you say those words, too?

POINTS TO PONDER: Have you had a positive attitude today? Do you need to seek forgiveness from God or from family members for a bad attitude? Never forget that your attitude is your choice.

—Harold Vaughan

DECEMBER 3
LEARN TO LOVE

Scripture Reading—1 John 3:18
"My little children,
let us not love in word, neither in tongue;
but in deed and in truth."

You may have mastered many languages or earned degrees from highly praised educational institutions. You may be a notable philanthropist who has given your goods to worthy causes. But 1 Corinthians 13 says that if you don't possess love, you've missed the primary purpose of life.

While you may be proud of your diploma or confident in your business skills, life isn't measured by brain power or bank accounts alone. While personal discipline may have garnered significant human praise, love is what draws God's attention.

Some people may demonstrate ultimate loyalty and die a martyr's death. Some may have the ability to understand and skillfully articulate the Scriptures. Others may seemingly move mountains by the strength of their faith. This is quite a group of people. Who wouldn't place them in some human hall of fame? Yet 1 Corinthians 13 says that though we may die for a just cause or graduate summa cum laude or move mountains by our faith, we possess nothing of lasting value if we do not possess love. Can anything be of more value to you than this principle of love? You may pursue medals, degrees, and material possessions; but the one who catches love gets God's applause.

We may accomplish many good things in life, but we must succeed at love most of all. Yes, we should know how to read, to write, and to work. But most importantly, we should know how to love God, our neighbors, our family, and our friends. When biblically applied, love brings greater value to all academic, spiritual, relational, and vocational pursuits. Arguably, it is the most important quality we could ever possess.

DO THIS NOW: Read 1 Corinthians 13. Tell everyone in your family that you love him.

—*Jeff Kahl*

DECEMBER 4
DOES JESUS CARE?
Scripture Reading—Matthew 9:18-26

Matthew 9 is a chapter filled with faith. In verse two, Jesus healed a man sick of the palsy when He saw the faith of those who brought him. In verse 22, Jesus said to the woman with the issue of blood, "Thy faith hath made thee whole." In verse 29b, Jesus said to the blind men, "According to your faith be it unto you." Immediately their eyes were opened. Another man in this chapter showed great faith, though his faith is never mentioned. We could describe his faith as interrupted faith.

This man came to Jesus because his daughter had died. Doubtless grief and sorrow overwhelmed him as he said to Jesus, "Come and lay thy hand upon her, and she shall live" (v. 18b). Others in this chapter were ill, yet they were alive. Jesus responded by following the man, but was quickly interrupted.

A woman—sick but alive—sought Jesus' attention. We see the most difficult part of this passage in the words, "But Jesus turned him about" (v. 22a). The father's natural reaction could have been, "But Jesus, what about me? Don't you care?" However, this father's faith apparently never wavered. Eventually Jesus honored a father's faith and brought his daughter back to life.

When I was an assistant pastor, I went to the hospital one day to visit two of our church couples on the maternity floor. One couple was rejoicing in the birth of a new son. Several doors down, the other couple was mourning the loss of a baby.

Moving from the first room to the second, I realized that I would need to assure the second family of God's care. God had not forsaken them but was with them in their sorrow. Circumstances were different, but the promise was the same. God cared. Throughout Scripture, we find encouragement in the promise that God cares—regardless.

EXERCISE: Write 1 Peter 5:7 on signs and hang one in each family member's room.

—Tom Palmer

DECEMBER 5
ONLY A SHADOW

Scripture Reading—Psalm 23:4
"Yea, though I walk through the valley
of the shadow of death,
I will fear no evil:
for thou art with me;
thy rod and thy staff they comfort me."

Recently, I made myself appear bigger than I had ever appeared in my life. I stepped out of my second-floor office onto the deck at the back of our house. The valley was already engulfed in the darkness of night, but I had turned on the outside light beside the door. My figure cast a huge shadow across the lawn and field behind our house. The shadow was probably 150 feet long.

I tried several poses, then used my shadowy hand and began "grabbing" things like trees and the burning barrel. I covered the garden with only one hand. Then I realized something—the closer I moved to the light, the bigger the shadow became. I also realized that with the click of a light switch, my jumbo image was gone. Without a light, the shadow vanished.

David described the experience of death as passing through a valley where death creates a shadow. Notice that death doesn't create a blackout. First John 1:5b says, "God is light, and in him is no darkness at all." Repeated references, particularly in the Psalms, refer to light as it relates to God. I believe David was creating a picture of God who enlightens our lives. But death passes through, creating the appearance of a shadow for a while. God is still there. Indeed, we must move closer to Him. The shadow of death may grow bigger, but God remains close by.

For the most part, shadows cannot hurt us. Likewise, death may pass through our lives; but as we stay close to the Lord, the truth that He is near will comfort our lives.

DO THIS NOW: Turn off the lights and use a flashlight to create shadows. Discuss the true harmlessness of the images you make.

—Tom Palmer

DECEMBER 6
WHERE IS GOD IN THIS?

Scripture Reading—Job 23:1-10

It was a Friday night, and I was the trauma chaplain on call in our hospital emergency room. A 16-year-old young man had died in an automobile accident. His parents had come to the hospital, and I was with them in the private family waiting room. We were meeting with doctors, police officers, and the coroner. The young man's mother was seated on a chair in the corner, weeping quietly. I did something I often do in these situations. Getting down on one knee, I asked if I could pray with her.

She exploded out of her chair. Swinging her fist at my face, she yelled, "God didn't answer our prayer before. Why would He answer it now?" I literally had to duck out of the way to avoid being struck in the face.

Sometimes in life and in death, God doesn't seem to be present. "If God is so near," we may ask, "why does He seem so far away?" In our text, I believe Job was asking this question. "Oh that I knew where I might find him! that I might come even to his seat!" he cried in verse three. In verses eight and nine, he looked forward and backward and to the left and to the right. But still he couldn't find God. His comfort doesn't come until verse 10; he realizes that though he may not know where God is, God certainly knows where *he* is. "But he knoweth the way that I take: when he hath tried me, I shall come forth as gold."

We must remember that the presence of trouble in our lives doesn't mean the absence of God. God is ever-present, even in a hospital emergency room. Whether trouble in our life means a couple of stitches or a fatal accident, God knows all about it. We can take comfort in His presence.

PRAYER TIME: Pause as a family to thank God that He is always near, no matter where we may have to go in life.

—Tom Palmer

DECEMBER 7
TROUBLE IS GOD'S TOOL
Scripture Reading—2 Chronicles 14:8-12

You may not like what I'm about to say, but it's the truth. **Trouble is God's tool to teach us to trust**. I quickly add that I don't welcome trouble to my life any more than the next person, but my previous statement is the truth. I can't say that I have a "dose of trouble" on my prayer request list for me or my family, but again, what I said is a fact. God uses troubling experiences in our lives to teach us to trust Him more than we ever would have if the trouble had not come.

In our text, King Asa experienced the invasion of his comfort zone. An army of one million Ethiopians prepared for battle against Judah at a time when everything was going just the way a king would want. His kingdom was experiencing peace, prosperity, and power. But suddenly they were threatened by an overwhelming enemy.

Asa responded in verse 11 by acknowledging his total dependence on the great God he knew and served. Sure, he needed God, but now things were different. Maybe he'd become somewhat self-sufficient, maybe a bit independent. After all, life was perfect—or, at least, close to it. Now we find a king declaring that he's nothing and that God is everything. He was insufficient, but God was all-sufficient. He couldn't, but God could!

And, of course, isn't that just the way God wants us to live anyhow? A threatened attack brought a great king to his God to acknowledge that he needed God more than anything else. God simply used trouble to teach this king to trust Him.

I like the following thought: "When you come to the place where God is all you have, you will find that God is all you need." But to this thought we must add, "God will never be all you need until God is all you have." It's a wonderful blessing when God reminds us that we really need Him.

APPLICATION: What does 2 Corinthians 3:5 say about our sufficiency?

—*Tom Palmer*

DECEMBER 8
THE SUFFICIENCY
OF GOD'S GRACE

Scripture Reading—2 Corinthians 12:9
"And he said unto me,
My grace is sufficient for thee:
for my strength is made perfect in weakness.
Most gladly therefore will I rather glory in my infirmities,
that the power of Christ
may rest upon me."

Standing in the foyer of the church where I was preaching, I listened as a father told his story. With a lump in his throat and a tear in his eye, he told me about the horrible van crash involving his teen son and other members of his ball team. Everyone on board had been killed in the fiery crash when the van slid on icy roads and struck an oncoming bus. The father shared some of his intimate feelings, thoughts, and emotions. It was obvious that his heart was aching.

Finally, he related to me the process he was working through to deal with his grief. Through the whole account, I hardly said a word. When he appeared to be finished, I spoke in the form of a question. "Was God's grace truly sufficient?" This heavyhearted father answered my question with one word. By the tone in his voice, I knew he meant what he said. "Absolutely!"

During times of sorrow or suffering, God's greatest blessing is His grace. It doesn't come until it is needed, and it usually comes only to those who need it. I like to define the word *grace* as God's ambulance rushing to my assistance in time of need. What this dad was saying was that everything about God became real to him as God took him through this experience of human tragedy. Simply, he could not have made it without God. When you face your own tragedy, you too will find that God's grace will bring you through it. Will God's grace be sufficient? You can count on it—absolutely!

PRAYING FOR OTHERS: Remember a sorrowing friend or loved one in prayer, asking God to give him His grace.

—Tom Palmer

DECEMBER 9
TRIED BY FIRE

Scripture Reading—1 Peter 1:7
"That the trial of your faith,
being much more precious than of gold
that perisheth, though it be tried with fire,
might be found unto praise and honour
and glory at the appearing of Jesus Christ."

I remember the tour my brother and I took of the Corning Glass Plant in Corning, New York. Part of the tour included watching skilled craftsmen produce delicate, beautiful glassware. Sitting in bleacher-like seats, we watched these men in their work areas in front of us. Several craftsmen were busy at a number of large furnaces. The process began when a worker attached a "hunk" or "glob" of glass to the end of a long pole. The piece was usually rough and shapeless.

As a worker opened the furnace door, I could see the orange glow as he put the chunk of glass into the fire. After a few seconds, he pulled the pole out of the furnace and used a special tool to begin fashioning the glass. He repeated the process over and over. As my brother and I watched, a design became clearer each time the glass was heated and molded again. The process took time, it took fire, and it took skill. But when it was finished, the worthless-looking piece of glass was a masterpiece.

The tour concluded as a guide took us into a showroom where these masterpieces were on display. Needless to say, the prices made it impossible for me to buy a piece to take home to my mother. The guide pointed to one set and explained, "This is the same set President Reagan sent to Princess Diana and Prince Charles as a wedding present." Now the lesson was clear. **The painful process produces a priceless product.** Is the process painful in your life right now? Remember, God is making a masterpiece, a treasure all His own.

ACTION POINT: Read James 1:2-4. Note the kind of product God is seeking to prepare in our lives.

—Tom Palmer

DECEMBER 10
WORSHIPING OR WHINING

Scripture Reading—Job 1:13-19

Most of us think of a time of worship as something that occurs on Sunday morning in our churches. We assume that worship occurs in a God-centered atmosphere as we praise God.

But look at Job 1 and notice when Job worshiped God. Job experienced unending calamity and catastrophe, including the deaths of all of his children. Then we come to verse 20. "Then Job arose, and rent his mantle, and shaved his head, and fell down upon the ground, and worshipped." In verse 21b, he says, "The Lord gave, and the Lord hath taken away; blessed be the name of the Lord." Finally, verse 22 tells us, "In all this Job sinned not, nor charged God foolishly."

Explain Job's behavior if you will. You can't unless you understand Job's view of God. Worship is based on our response to the greatness and goodness of God. Job recognized that God is great and good. No matter what came into his life, it didn't change his God.

When crisis comes, it's easy to whine. "Why me?" seems to be the typical attitude of our self-made pity parties. Unfortunately, this response leads us to get angry and bitter at God as we blame Him for the difficulties in our lives.

No doubt Job had his struggles as time passed. This truth is clear as you read through the Book of Job. Still, he repented before God and again acknowledged how great and good God is (Job 42:1-6).

Worshiping God in a hospital bed or at a graveside isn't easy. Yet in times of the greatest suffering and sorrow, God wants to be glorified in our lives. He desires to be put on display in families that can accept the trials and the testings with determination to represent their God well. Your crisis can be either a worship service or a pity party—it's your choice.

PRAISE THE LORD: Pause to praise God for His goodness and greatness at all times.

—Tom Palmer

DECEMBER 11
BLESSED THROUGH BELIEVING

Scripture Reading—John 20:29
"Jesus saith unto him, Thomas, because thou hast seen me, thou hast believed: blessed are they that have not seen, and yet have believed."

Recall how skeptical Thomas was when the disciples told him they had seen the resurrected Christ? "The other disciples therefore said unto him, We have seen the Lord. But he said unto them, Except I shall see in his hands the print of the nails, and put my finger into the print of the nails, and thrust my hand into his side, I will not believe" (John 20:25).

Thomas was not alone in his doubts. Prior to His death, Jesus told the disciples He would be raised up on the third day. After Jesus' death, all the disciples were sad because their dreams had been dashed. The situation hadn't gone as they had hoped. They didn't understand that Jesus would rise again.

Peter and John ran to the tomb when they heard Jesus' body was gone. Later, Jesus appeared in the upper room where the disciples were huddled, fearing the Jews. But Thomas was not with them when Jesus came among them on that occasion.

Afterwards, Jesus came among them a second time. "Then saith he to Thomas, Reach hither thy finger, and behold my hands; and reach hither thy hand, and thrust it into my side: and be not faithless, but believing. And Thomas answered and said unto him, My Lord and my God. Jesus saith unto him, Thomas, because thou hast seen me, thou hast believed: blessed are they that have not seen, and yet have believed" (John 20:27-29).

Faith is the only doorway for God to enter the soul. Those who believe in Jesus are supremely blessed. How fortunate are those who find forgiveness for their sins by trusting in Christ's shed blood! Peace, joy, love, and eternal life are a few of the blessings that come through believing.

SONG TIME: Get your hymnbooks and sing all stanzas of "Blessed Assurance."

—*Harold Vaughan*

DECEMBER 12
BLESSING THE LORD

Scripture Reading—Psalm 34:1
"I will bless the Lord at all times:
his praise shall continually
be in my mouth."

I know many who "ask the blessing" at mealtimes. I've also listened to others ask God to bless their home, family, and friends. But rarely have I heard believers speak about blessing God, yet this activity is precisely what David was talking about. "I will bless the Lord at all times."

David *chose* to praise the Lord. He said, "I will," which indicates that his praise was voluntary. He wasn't forced into praise; he chose to "bless the Lord." In Psalm 55:17a, he said, "Evening, and morning, and at noon, will I pray." Prayer and praise are activities we decide on ahead of time. We choose how to spend our time. It's good to get in the habit of setting aside some time each morning to read our Bible, to praise, and to pray. Praise is something we plan to do. God has blessed us abundantly, and we can choose to "bless the Lord" with praise!

David's praise was *continual*. "His praise shall continually be in my mouth." This was not a haphazard, hit-or-miss, or random process. David purposed in his heart that he would regularly "bless the Lord." The word *bless* here refers to the future. He predetermined that he would repeatedly be a blessing to God.

God loves to be praised, and He appreciates being appreciated. Maybe this is one reason the Lord referred to David as a man after His own heart. No, David was not perfect, but he determined he would "bless the Lord at all times."

It's good to ask God's blessing for our food, and it's good to ask for God's blessing on our lives, our families, our friends, and even our enemies. But how much better it is to "bless the Lord!" Praise is simply bragging on Jesus! We can be like David and "bless the Lord at all times."

BLESS THE LORD: As a family, spend time expressing your appreciation to the Lord.

—*Harold Vaughan*

DECEMBER 13
BLESSING YOUR FAMILY

Scripture Reading—Genesis 49:28

"All these are the twelve tribes of Israel: and this is it that their father spake unto them, and blessed them; every one according to his blessing he blessed them."

Jewish culture understood the importance of blessing one's offspring. The blessing consisted of spoken words that bestowed affirmation upon the descendants. Blessings were positive statements spoken directly to the child. Godly fathers possessed a sense of destiny concerning their children. In Genesis, we find Jacob pronouncing verbal blessings on his sons.

Words have tremendous power and the potential to direct life. Jacob had specific blessings for each of his sons. Today's Scripture reading says he blessed each "according to his blessing." That means his bestowal of good fortune was according to the individual child.

All children crave their father's approval, acceptance, and attention. A smile is better than a frown, and wise parents give enough smiles to make the child want more. It's only natural that children desire to be blessed; blessed is the child whose father blesses him. Mom and Dad can instill security and confidence in a child's soul when they affirm their child.

Jacob gave these blessings near the time of his death. The family was called in to hear what their father had to say prior to his departure. I'm confident that Jacob spoke meaningful words to his children on many occasions.

We can speak blessings to our children, parents, and siblings *now*. Try these new words from this old song:

Speak your blessings,
Speak them one by one,
Speak your blessings,
See what they have done.
Speak your blessings,
Speak them one by one,
And it may surprise you all the good you've done!

DO THIS: Ask each family member to express one thing he appreciates about other family members.

—*Harold Vaughan*

DECEMBER 14
BLESSING YOUR ENEMIES

Scripture Reading—Matthew 5:44b
"Love your enemies, bless them that curse you,
do good to them that hate you, and pray for them
which despitefully use you, and persecute you."

Subjects in the kingdom of God live differently than those who belong to the kingdom of darkness. As God's people, we must obey our King. The rules in His kingdom seem strange when we compare them to the ways the world operates.

Jesus said to treat our enemies like our friends. We should love, bless, do good, and pray for our adversaries. No wonder God said, "For my thoughts are not your thoughts, neither are your ways my ways, saith the Lord" (Isa. 55:8). God's ways are totally foreign to man's natural way of thinking. We can do right even when we've done wrong. Just because someone treats us badly doesn't mean we have to return the favor! God's people have a power unknown to unsaved people.

What does "blessing our enemies" mean? The word *bless* means to speak well of or to praise. We don't curse back when we're cursed. We speak softly when others speak roughly to us. We treat people right when they treat us wrong.

We shouldn't ignore mistreatment or act like nothing happened. Jesus said to pray for those who falsely accuse us. When we are wronged, we shouldn't take the abuse sitting down. We should *kneel down* and pray for those who have mistreated us.

"How can I pray for my enemies?" you may ask. Ask God to save them. Ask God to bless them and use them. Ask the Lord to have mercy on them. Pray positive things for your adversaries.

When Jesus was crucified, He prayed, "Father, forgive them; for they know not what they do" (Luke 23:34). He prayed for those who had hung Him on the cross. Job prayed for the men who had attacked and accused him.

DISCUSSION: Read Job 42:10. Discuss what Job's "friends" said about him and how Job rose above the criticism and blessed them.

—Harold Vaughan

DECEMBER 15
COUNT YOUR BLESSINGS

Scripture Reading

Psalm 40:5—*"Many, O Lord my God, are thy wonderful works which thou hast done, and thy thoughts which are to us-ward: they cannot be reckoned up in order unto thee: if I would declare and speak of them, they are more than can be numbered."*
Psalm 78:4—*"We will not hide them from their children, shewing to the generation to come the praises of the Lord, and his strength, and his wonderful works that he hath done."*

Scientists tell us that billions of stars populate our universe. Most stars lie at such vast distances from earth that we can't see them. Because so many stars exist, counting them would be a futile exercise. Long before the claims of modern science, the Bible told us the stars were numberless.

Likewise, the benefits we receive from God are endless—"they are more than can be numbered." Take plenty of time to count your blessings but never spend a minute in worry. Concentrate on the positive things God has done for you. Learn to rehearse your blessings. The old song says the following:

Count your blessings,
Name them one by one;
Count your blessings,
See what God hath done;
Count your blessings,
Name them one by one;
Count your many blessings, see what God has done.

Let's focus on the good things God has provided for us. Review the following gifts from God: spiritual blessings, physical blessings, friendship blessings, financial blessings, family blessings, national peace, and many others. The list is never-ending.

COUNT YOUR BLESSINGS: As you consider your blessings, reflect on God's goodness. Ask each family member to list 10 things he is thankful for. After completing your lists, share your blessings with one another. After sharing, have a season of thanksgiving prayer.

—Harold Vaughan

DECEMBER 16
THE BLESSING OF
ADVERSITY

Scripture Reading—Romans 8:28
"And we know that all things work together for good
to them that love God, to them who are the called
according to his purpose."

Spurgeon, the great Baptist preacher of the last century, wrote about a young man who had broken his hip in an accident. The hip didn't heal properly, leaving the man crippled. Earnestly, the people prayed that God would restore this young man to health and strength.

Shortly after their intense, concerted intercession began, apparent tragedy struck. The young man fell and broke his hip again. Was this a tragedy? It would have been completely natural for the young man and for his intercessors to complain; his condition was apparently much worse.

Fortunately, many of the intercessors were wise, mature Christians who saw God's hand in the entire affair. They began praising God and thanking Him for the blessing. Now the hip was set properly. It wasn't long until the period of recovery under God's leadership did its perfect work. The young man walked with no limp whatsoever. The apparent tragedy turned out to be a blessing.

"All things" are not necessarily good and don't always turn out as we would desire. But "all things [do] work together for good to them that love God." Providence is the belief that God in His foresight allows things to happen that are unexplainable from a human standpoint. As we grow in the faith, we come to understand that all things serve a greater purpose and ultimately "work together for good." By responding with patience and faith, we often reap the unseen blessing sooner rather than later.

Instead of complaining and griping when difficulties and trials come, we should lay hold on Romans 8:28. We should believe the promise and thank God by faith that He designs all things with His best and our good in mind.

DO IT NOW: Turn in your Bibles to Romans 8:28. Repeat this verse aloud together five times.

—Harold Vaughan

DECEMBER 17
THE BLESSING OF REVIVAL

Scripture Reading—Psalm 85:6
"Wilt thou not revive us again:
that thy people may rejoice in thee?"

Will we pursue business as usual or the unusual business of revival? Some say the days of great revival are over. They say we are doomed to endtime lukewarmness, and we shouldn't get our hopes up. Throughout church history, there have been seasons of great spiritual upheaval. Miraculous revivals have occurred in various places and cultures. I'm not speculating on the prospects for national or international revival, but I believe you and I can be revived *now*.

Corporate revival is when the majority of a given church body is revitalized. Interpersonal revival is when a group of believers have an up-to-date encounter with God. But personal revival is when an individual meets God in a new way. Personal revival is available and attainable to any open, obedient, and optimistic (faith-filled) heart.

You can cultivate the presence of God. Each farmer cultivates his crops to enhance his harvest. He pulls or plows weeds. He pulls soil toward the stalk. He applies fertilizer to feed the roots. Friend, you can draw near to God, "and he will draw nigh to you" (James 4:8). That is God's promise to you. God will pour water on those who are thirsty and floods upon the dry ground. Are you thirsty for a fresh touch of grace? Are you longing for a visitation from heaven?

Set your face toward a sweeping spiritual revolution, and you will not be disappointed. A daughter once pleaded with her backslidden father, "Whatever it costs, go through with God!" Duncan Campbell went "through with God," and the Lord used him in the well-known Hebrides revival afterwards. It might cost you a lot to put something right, but it will cost you more to leave it wrong. *No* price is too great to pay for the blessing of revival.

PRAYER TIME: Read Psalm 85. Pray together as a family for a reviving work in your hearts, home, and church.

—Harold Vaughan

DECEMBER 18
I'M DREAMING OF A RIGHT CHRISTMAS...
Scripture Reading—Matthew 1:18-25

Down through the years, one of the most popular Christmas songs has been "I'm Dreaming of a White Christmas." A white Christmas is fine, but for Christian families, a *right Christmas* is much better.

Christmas means different things to different people. To some, it means celebration—parties, fun, and entertainment. To others, it means gifts—lots of shopping, spending, giving, and receiving.

Folks get weary trying to decide what to buy. Have you noticed how much time, work, and money go into Christmas decorations? Families sometimes go to ridiculous extremes trying to have the most impressively decorated house in the neighborhood.

And don't forget the bills that must be paid. Credit cards encourage people to spend money they don't have on things others don't need. Many never recover from overspending that goes on year after year at Christmas.

And what can we say about Santa, Rudolph, and Frosty?

Yes, Christmas is a wonderful time for families to get together. For some, it's the only time they see family members each year. But do these things really make a *right Christmas*?

No! The Bible tells us that a *right Christmas* is one we've centered on the coming of Jesus Christ into this world to become our Savior. Isn't it sad that in the midst of all the things that mean Christmas to so many, Jesus Christ is often the one who gets completely left out? It's so easy to get caught up in the wrong things. Not that they're bad in themselves, but they're so distracting—they leave no room for Jesus.

Christian families are not immune to distractions that crowd Jesus out. We've all heard that "Jesus is the reason for the season." As you prepare your family to observe Christmas, make sure it's a *right Christmas* because Christ is at the center of it.

ACTION POINT: As a family, discuss ways you can honor the Lord in every aspect of your Christmas observance.

—Jack Palmer

DECEMBER 19
BEHOLDING HIS GLORY

Scripture Reading
***Galatians 4:4-5**—"But when the fulness of the time was come, God sent forth his Son, made of a woman, made under the law, to redeem them that were under the law, that we might receive the adoption of sons."*

Gypsy Smith, the great evangelist of the early 20th century, was in his 80s when someone asked him why he was still so excited about his salvation. He answered, "I've never lost the wonder of it all!" He never got over the fact that as a young gypsy boy, he put his faith and trust in Jesus Christ and was gloriously saved.

One of the most serious problems about Christmas is that far too many have "lost the wonder of it all"! Just think, at the right moment in human history, Jesus Christ entered this world as a tiny, helpless baby in a humble manger in the city of Bethlehem.

Some seminary students once asked a great theologian, "What is the greatest theological truth you have ever discovered in all of your years of study?" He thought for a moment. "Jesus loves me, this I know," he said, "for the Bible tells me so." Oh, the wonder of it all, that Jesus came to be our Savior! Don't ever get over it.

How can we behold His glory?

1. His Virgin Birth
Isaiah 7:14; Matthew 1:23

2. His Virtuous Life—He was without sin.
John 18:38, 19:4-6; Hebrews 4:15

3. His Vicarious Death—He died for our sin, not for His own.
Romans 5:8; 1 Corinthians 15:3; 2 Corinthians 5:21

4. His Victorious Resurrection—The grave could not keep Him.
Matthew 28:6; John 20:25; 1 Corinthians 15:4

5. His Visible Return—Jesus is coming again!
John 14:3; Acts 1:11; 1 Thessalonians 4:16

ACTION POINT: During the Christmas season, take time to look up the above Scriptures and share them with your family. Behold His glory.

—Jack Palmer

DECEMBER 20
JESUS IS
THE REASON

Scripture Reading—Matthew 2:1-6; Micah 5:2

When the angel appeared to Joseph, announcing the details surrounding the birth of our Savior, he told Joseph to "call his name **Jesus**: for he shall save his people from their sins" (Matt. 1:21, emphasis added). The name "Jesus" was a sacred and heroic title to the Jewish people. It means "Savior" or "Jehovah is our salvation." God gave Jesus His name long before He was born. In His name, God declared the reason for His coming into this world—to be the Savior of all who would trust Him for their salvation.

When our children were born, we had no idea whether they would be boys or girls. We had no ultrasound to inform us ahead of time, so we chose a boy's and a girl's name. Then we would be ready when the time came. But that's all changed now due to technology. Today, parents can know the sex of their child months in advance and name their child long before he or she is born.

How interesting that, because Jesus was to be "God with us" (Matt. 1:23b), God planned every detail in advance of His arrival. Before creating the world, God determined that Jesus would be His lamb and die for our sins (Rev. 13:8). No wonder John declared to his followers, "Behold the Lamb of God, which taketh away the sin of the world" (John 1:29b).

As your family prepares for Christmas, make the Lord Jesus Christ your focus. Let Christmas be a time when you give more serious consideration to the reason for His coming. If your family is like most, this time of year is overflowing with things to do, places to go, presents to buy, and people to meet. In the midst of it all, don't forget what Christmas is meant to be—the celebration of Jesus' birth. He really is the reason!

ACTION POINT: As you plan your gifts to others, determine the best gift you can give to Jesus for His birthday. Ask each family member to share his ideas.

—Jack Palmer

DECEMBER 21
WHILE SHEPHERDS WATCHED THEIR FLOCKS

Scripture Reading—Luke 2:8-22

Picture yourself sitting on a peaceful Judean hillside on a beautiful, starry night, resting quietly beside a camp fire, and enjoying the solitude. Suddenly, an angel appears, and the sky is filled with God's glory. Are you scared? The shepherds were! That's why the first thing the angel said was, "Fear not: for, behold, I bring you good tidings of great joy, which shall be to all people. For unto you is born this day in the city of David a Saviour, which is Christ the Lord" (vv. 10b-11). He had come from God to make the greatest announcement the world had ever heard. Jesus Christ was born! How surprising that God chose these humble men with whom to share this wonderful news.

What kind of men were they?

1. **Faithful men (v. 8).** A shepherd could not leave his sheep no matter what happened. He was responsible for them.
2. **Humble men (v. 9).** Shepherds were considered a lower class of people.
3. **Special men (v. 10).** God chose them to receive His message. That made them very important.
4. **Seeking men (v. 15).** They were eager to find Jesus.
5. **Believing men (vv. 15-16).** They believed the message the angel had given them.
6. **Witnessing men (v. 17).** They went everywhere, telling what they had experienced.
7. **Joyful men (v. 20).** Their hearts overflowed with praise, and they glorified God that they had found Christ.

Are you glad God chose the shepherds to be the recipients of His announcement? We, too, should be like those shepherds. Everything they were, God wants us to be. The shepherds can teach us some great things. At this wonderful season of the year, as you celebrate Christ's birth, let the shepherds' lives be a good example and motivation to you and to your family to be all God wants you to be.

ACTION POINT: Study the characteristics of the shepherds. Use them to evaluate your family's attitude toward Christmas.

—*Jack Palmer*

DECEMBER 22
MARY, THE MOTHER
OF JESUS

Scripture Reading—Luke 1:26-38

Every aspect of the Christmas story is filled with awe and wonder. Centuries before Jesus was born, the prophet Isaiah wrote, "Therefore the Lord himself shall give you a sign; Behold, *a virgin shall conceive*, and bear a son, and shall call his name Immanuel" (Isa. 7:14, emphasis added). Mary was most likely an older teenager. She was "espoused" to a young man named Joseph. To be espoused was a more binding commitment to be married than a mere engagement. It was a legal transaction.

Mary was a virgin; she'd never been morally defiled. She and Joseph had a pure relationship in preparation for their marriage. During that time, God sent the angel Gabriel to tell her she was chosen to be Jesus' mother. What a shock that must have been!

She wondered how she could be pregnant when she had always kept herself morally pure. Gabriel explained that Jesus would not have a human father. His birth would be the result of God's power working in her life. After his explanation, she yielded herself to God's plan.

What was Mary like? First, she was pure (Luke 1:27). She was a virgin who had never been morally defiled. She was most likely pure in her thoughts, words, actions, and appearance. She had a clean heart before God and others. Second, she was trusting (vv. 37, 45). As incredible as the news of her pregnancy was, she chose to believe God and to leave the results to Him. Third, she was submissive (v. 38). She submitted herself to God's will though others may not have understood. Fourth, she was blessed (vv. 28, 30). Because she had kept herself pure, God blessed her. Finally, she glorified God (vv. 46-47). Her only desire was for God to be glorified in all that would happen.

ACTION POINT: What important lessons can we learn from Mary's life as we observe this Christmas?

—*Jack Palmer*

DECEMBER 23
THEN THERE WAS JOSEPH
Scripture Reading—Matthew 1:18-25

You read this Scripture a few days ago. As you read it today, pay attention to what it says about Joseph. Don't miss the great lessons God has for your family. If we think Mary had a hard time receiving word from Gabriel that she was to become a mother, how do you think Joseph felt when he heard the news? Mary was his sweetheart, and they were committed to marriage. We can only imagine what went through his mind. He assumed, as anyone would, that Mary had been unfaithful. What should he do?

While Joseph considered his responsibility, the angel of God appeared to him and answered his questions. The angel not only told Joseph what was happening but also gave clear instructions that he and Mary were to proceed with their marriage plans. He also told Joseph what to name the child.

We should take a closer look at Joseph and learn from his life. God wants us to emulate the following outstanding characteristics.

1. **A Humble Man.** Joseph was a carpenter (Matt. 13:55), a lowly profession. Joseph's role as a carpenter required humility to do such common work.

2. **A Just Man (Matt. 1:19).** Joseph was committed to doing right no matter how difficult it was. His conviction was, "It is always right to do right."

3. **A Loving Man (v. 19).** Though Joseph thought Mary had done wrong, he loved her enough not to shame her publicly. Had he been unloving, he would have wanted to hurt her.

4. **A Spiritual Man (v. 20).** Joseph lived close enough to God that He could speak to him.

5. **An Obedient Man (v. 24).** Joseph did what God told him to do without question.

6. **A Disciplined Man (v. 25).** Though Joseph had every right to enjoy the blessings of his marriage relationship with Mary, he refrained until after Jesus was born. What a beautiful picture of a godly man!

ACTION POINT: How does your family handle tough situations? Do you devise your own plan, or do you seek direction from God? Talk about it.

—Jack Palmer

YOU CAN BE A STAR
Scripture Reading—Matthew 2:1-12

Do you place a star on top of your Christmas tree? Many families do. Though we often associate the star with Christmas, Scripture records events associated with the star and the wise men that probably took place at least two years after Jesus' birth. Regardless, the star played a major role in guiding the wise men to Jesus. How long it took them to travel to Jesus from the East, we don't know. We can learn something from the star they followed.

Is anything more spectacular than standing under a beautiful, starry sky and realizing that God made every one of them, put them in their place, and keeps them there? Some stars are so far away that scientists measure their distance in thousands of *light years*. How vast is God's universe!

Have you ever wanted to be a star? I don't mean the stars in the sky but the kind we speak of when someone is outstanding in a particular area. Those folks are considered exceptional—the ones who are better than all the rest. Not everyone can be that kind of star.

You can be a star! Consider what the star mentioned in Matthew 2 teaches us.

1. God created it (Gen. 1:16), and He created you, too. Each star is God's unique creation, and so are you. God created stars to shine for Him; He created you to shine, too.

2. The star belonged to God (Matt. 2:2). Because God created the star, He decided what to do with it. Because God created you, you are also His to do with as He pleases (1 Cor. 6:19).

3. The star did not attract attention to itself (Matt. 2:9). The wise men were not drawn to the star itself; it simply directed them to Jesus. God didn't create you to draw attention to yourself. Your life should be a "signpost" to help seekers find the way.

4. The star pointed others to Jesus (v. 10). And that's why you're here, too.

ACTION POINT: Read Matthew 5:16. Discuss what letting "your light so shine before men" means.

—Jack Palmer

DECEMBER 25
IN CONTROL

Scripture Reading—Psalm 24:1
"The earth is the Lord's,
and the fulness thereof;
the world,
and they that dwell therein."

The word *sovereignty* should translate "relax" for believers in Christ. Yet relaxing is often our opposite reaction to the idea of God's sovereignty. If our response is anything but resting and relaxing because God's in control of all things, it's because we don't know Him very well, and He's probably not really on the throne of our lives.

As one person put it, "He is more like the light of a flickering candle than the blazing of the noonday sun." Most people decide God is simply too small. Looking at the attitudes, actions, fears, and the opinions people express, one would conclude that God isn't big enough to take care of our human problems. Observing the way we struggle, squirm, and try to manipulate situations to solve our problems, one would assume that we are on our own and that God really doesn't help His people.

What do we actually mean when we talk about the sovereignty of God? In essence, God's sovereignty involves the aspect of His character by which He exerts absolute rule and control over every aspect of His creation. One Christian thinker observed that "not a blade of grass moves without His notice and apart from His control."

In other words, everything that happens in our world occurs either because God directly causes it to or because He consciously allows it to take place. Nothing enters into history or even exists outside history that doesn't come under God's complete control.

The key to our understanding is the little word *His*. God is in control because this universe and all the beings in it—including us—belong to Him. He has the right. He made it all; He owns it all.

SELAH: As a family, read Psalm 135:5-7 together. Discuss the implications of God's sovereignty in your lives.

—T.P. Johnston, Jr.

DECEMBER 26
HE DID IT HIS WAY

Scripture Reading
Psalm 115:3—*"But our God is in the heavens:*
he hath done whatsoever he hath pleased."
Romans 11:36—*"For of him, and through him, and to him,*
are all things: to whom be glory for ever. Amen."

What would you think if I visited your home and, after looking around, began complaining about how you'd arranged your furniture in the living room? Beyond that, imagine that I chided you for buying a house with its design in the first place. Maybe I didn't like the way your pictures were hung on the walls, and I told you so. You would be hurt and insulted. You might feel as though I'd slapped you across the face. You probably wouldn't think much of me either.

Consider that this behavior is precisely how we treat God sometimes. You and I have no more right to complain about what God chooses to do or allow in our lives than I would to come into your home (which belongs to you) and to criticize your tastes and choices.

After we've created our first planet out of nothing, then perhaps we'll have the right to complain to God about the way He's doing things. Perhaps right now you're unhappy with God about something in your life. You're complaining about the way God has arranged the furniture in your life. You're complaining about where He's hung the pictures.

You have no right to do that. You may not like the way God does things, but He's sovereign. He owns you, and He formed you in your mother's womb. If you are a believer in Christ, He owns you twice. He created you and redeemed you.

SELAH: First Corinthians 6:19-20 says, "What? know ye not that your body is the temple of the Holy Ghost which is in you, which ye have of God, and ye are not your own? For ye are bought with a price: therefore glorify God in your body, and in your spirit, which are God's." Discuss how these verses might apply to griping in your home.

—*T.P. Johnston, Jr.*

DECEMBER 27
A GOOD AND MAD GOD

Scripture Reading—Nahum 1:2-8

I chuckle every time I recall the story of a little boy who sat beside his dad in church. The fiery preacher had a strong, loud voice. At one point in the sermon, the little fellow nudged his dad and said, "Boy, God's mad today!"

While this story is amusing, God's wrath is a serious and sobering subject and an unpopular subject. The idea of an angry, wrathful God just doesn't fit the "feel-good-about-God" image that's so in vogue today. What is God's wrath? It's the necessary, just, and righteous punishment for sin.

Just as we wouldn't think much of a police officer who stood by and watched a crime occur or of a fireman who complacently looked on while a house burned to the ground, so we must understand that God's wrath is an essential part of His being. Just as importantly, we must understand that God's wrath is an extension of His goodness!

God is a God of love and tender mercy. The Bible says He is slow to anger. But a part of God's goodness is His wrath against all that is not good. The wrath of God is an essential, integral part of our understanding of who He is and what He does. God could just look the other way and let anybody go to heaven without doing anything about sin, but what would that be? If God let anybody into heaven—and, of course, you know many think that's the case—do you know what we would have? It wouldn't be heaven. It would be this world all over again. It would be this life with all its sin and the problems sin produces. God wouldn't be a God of love if He did that. That wouldn't be heaven. At best, it would be just another Earth, and really it would be hell.

SELAH: Meditate on today's Scripture passage and on how there can be no real love or goodness apart from God's wrath.

—*T.P. Johnston, Jr.*

JUST LIKE YOU

Scripture Reading—Psalm 7:11
"God judgeth the righteous, and God is angry with the wicked every day."

What's your reaction when you see someone do something mean to someone else? How do you feel when you know someone has lied about your friend? When you hear reports about terrorists ruthlessly beheading innocent people for propaganda purposes, what's your gut reaction?

In all these instances, you probably experience anger. We like to call the response "righteous indignation." Scriptures are clear that being angry isn't wrong. In Ephesians 4:26a, God commands us, "Be ye angry, and sin not." Anger can easily become sin, but it's not sin in and of itself.

Have you considered why? We are made in the image and likeness of God. God, too, is angry when He sees injustice and unrighteousness. The Bible says that "God is angry with the wicked every day" (Ps. 7:11b). Being angry at wrong is part of God's being, part of His nature. Just so, our anger at injustice is a reflection of God's nature in our own being.

God's wrath against sin is essential. A famous evangelistic sermon titled "One More Night with the Frogs" details Moses' experience with the Egyptian Pharaoh. God brought His wrath upon the king of Egypt and his people in the form of various plagues. A plague of frogs was upon the land, and frogs were everywhere. When Moses asked Pharaoh if he was ready to repent, the king's response was interesting. In effect, he said, "One more night. I'll repent tomorrow."

God's wrath, while sure and certain, can be averted by one means. That means is recognizing our offense to a holy God and repenting of that wrong. Repentance turns God's wrath to God's mercy. The Scriptures are replete with examples. Is your life such an example?

SELAH: As a family, cite instances from the Bible when God displayed His wrath. Also give examples of how repentance spared His wrath.

—*T.P. Johnston, Jr.*

DECEMBER 29
PLAYING UNDER GOD'S SPRINKLER

Scripture Reading—Ephesians 1:4-6, 12-14

Everything God does, including acts of love toward us, brings glory to Himself. The whole purpose of our salvation is for the praise of God's glory. Ephesians 1:12 says, "That we should be to the praise of his glory, who first trusted in Christ." While this purpose may sound selfish, remember that we're not referring to a fellow human being. We're speaking of Almighty God. He is so marvelous that He deserves all glory, and getting that glory is consistent with His perfections.

Glorifying God brings several results. First, God loves us without our deserving it. God is free to love us because loving us is part of His glory and praise. He doesn't need us to earn or to deserve His love. Second, He can keep on loving us regardless of our response. Our response isn't essential because the goal of His love is His own glory.

How do we benefit from God's love? Imagine that you're watering your lawn one day. Several children begin playing under your sprinkler. Being the kindhearted person you are, you don't run them off because they're having such a delightful time. In fact, you're so kind that you prepare them a snack and share it with them. You help them experience even more enjoyment. They are grateful.

But consider this story. You didn't water your lawn so the children would have a good time. You had other reasons for watering your yard. Yet the youngsters enjoyed the watering, though their enjoyment wasn't your purpose. God is such a loving God that as He seeks to live out His glory, you and I enjoy the overflowing benefits of His being a holy, just, perfect, and loving God. His blessings are a beautiful byproduct. God's love is simply part of bringing glory to Himself, but you and I enjoy the benefit of playing in His sprinkler.

SELAH: Discuss practical implications of how God is able to love us.

—*T.P. Johnston, Jr.*

DECEMBER 30
OUR ENERGIZER GOD

Scripture Reading—Isaiah 40:28
"Hast thou not known?
hast thou not heard, that the everlasting God,
the Lord, the Creator of the ends of the earth, fainteth not,
neither is weary? there is no searching
of his understanding."

Surely everyone has smiled at the Energizer bunny commercials. He just keeps going . . . and going . . . and going. It's difficult to imagine anything going on forever and never needing a refill or recharge of its energy source.

The Bible teaches us that God is sufficient—He's perfectly complete within His own being. Understanding God can be difficult because we have nothing to compare Him to. He doesn't fit any formulas, and He defies all descriptions. He will never "fit" into a box or any packaging we devise. We can only comprehend in a limited way all the magnificent things God has revealed about Himself.

In contrast, we humans are insufficient. If we don't eat properly, if we fail to get adequate rest, we run down quickly. You and I need many things, including relationships with others. The Lord is so complete in Himself that all the relationships He has are completely voluntary on His part. None are necessary. If God had not reached out to us by giving us His Word and then His own Son, we would be eternally lost. He doesn't need us, but we desperately need Him.

That dependency makes our relationship with Him even more precious and important! Though God doesn't need us, He has chosen to include us in His plan. He has also given us the privilege of sharing His plan with others. He has given us the privilege of investing in His work and in becoming a part of His plan, though He doesn't need us. What an amazing God!

SELAH: Scripture says in God "we live, and move, and have our being" (Acts 17:28). As a family, discuss what would happen if God removed His all-sufficient hand from our lives for an instant.

—*T.P. Johnston, Jr.*

DECEMBER 31
THE ULTIMATE PURPOSE

Scripture Reading—John 17:3
"And this is life eternal, that they might know thee the only true God, and Jesus Christ, whom thou hast sent."

Philosophers have long discussed the ultimate questions of life. As Christians, we know that having eternal life is the most important goal imaginable. But what is eternal life?

In His conversation with His Heavenly Father, the Lord Jesus Christ prayed that God would reveal to us that eternal life is more than going to heaven when we die. Jesus makes it clear that eternal life is *knowing* God through Him!

God has made it possible for us to know Him before we go to heaven. The purpose of man and of life is to know the true and living God. That's why God allows us to be so needy and to experience the hardships, difficulties, sorrows, and trials of life—that we might look to Him and get to know Him.

Having knowledge of God—His holiness, glory, goodness, sufficiency, wisdom, grace, and love—demands a response. It can never remain merely academic or just something we're curious about. We must have a desire to know God and to respond to Him.

What response does God desire? He requires that we see ourselves as we are in the light of who He is. Seeing ourselves that way results in recognizing our desperate need for Him and reaching for Him. He is such a God that He will always respond when we do so. Reaching for God begins by realizing our need for His forgiveness and by placing our trust in Christ to save us from our sins. It continues when we learn to see His hand at work in every detail of life—the good and the difficult—and when we look to Him to meet our needs, to fulfill our lives, and to make us like His Son, the Lord Jesus Christ.

SELAH: Consider whether each family member has initially responded to God by trusting Christ as Savior. How is each family member doing in the area of looking to the Lord in every aspect of life?

—*T.P. Johnston, Jr.*

Check Out These Other **Helpful Resources**

FORGIVENESS: How to Get Along With Everybody All the Time!
by Harold Vaughan and T.P. Johnston

"In a world filled with so much hatred and misunderstanding, few subjects are as timely as forgiveness. And yet, few works of biblical accuracy have been written on this important subject. Vaughan and Johnston's book is the best, purest and most practical treatment of the subject I know. Everyone who has been forgiven should read this book to know how and why to forgive."
—Woodrow Kroll, *Back to the Bible*

"LORD, HELP ME NOT TO HAVE THESE EVIL THOUGHTS!"
by Harold Vaughan

Quite often Christians pray this prayer, but instead of the thoughts ceasing, they only intensify. Here's a practical guide to achieving a healthy thought life while engaged in mental warfare.

WHAT IT MEANS TO BE CRUCIFIED WITH CHRIST
by Harold Vaughan

What did Paul mean in Galatians 2:20: "I am crucified with Christ"? Here are twelve brief and readable chapters on the "exchanged life" along with many helpful charts and study guides.

THE NATURE OF A GOD-SENT REVIVAL
by Duncan Campbell

Will it be business as usual or the usual business of revival? This powerful booklet is packed with power from a man who saw spiritual awakening in his ministry. Thousands were converted when God stepped down from heaven in the Hebrides.

TIME WITH GOD
by Harold Vaughan

Would you like to read through the entire Bible in just one year? Are you interested in a tool that will assist you in organizing your Bible study? Do you desire to help your family develop the daily discipline of studying God's Word? If you answered "Yes" to any of the above questions, then *Time with God* is the answer. *Time with God* provides you with a reasonable reading schedule that will get you through the Scriptures in a single year. It also will assist you in contemplating the Word by furnishing space to record your thoughts each day. Accountability is another great benefit when the entire family is working through the *Time with God* diary. Whatever your age, you can begin studying to show yourself approved TODAY!

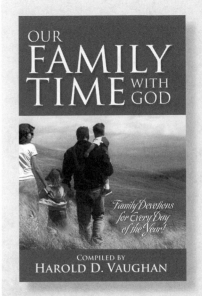

Quantity Discounts!

Christ Life Publications offers special discounts to persons, churches, and distributors who buy *Our Family Time with God* in bulk quantities. To obtain the current discount schedule, please contact us directly.

P.O. Box 399
Vinton, VA 24179

Website: **www.christlifemin.org**
E-mail: **info@christlifemin.org**
Phone: **(540) 890-6100**

MINISTRIES

Christ Life Ministries is committed to providing messages, materials, and ministries that will further revival, both personally and corporately, in the local church.

- Spiritual Life Crusades
- Prayer Advances
- Christ Life Publications

Visit our website

www.christlifemin.org

- Read thought-provoking articles.

- Learn about the Prayer Advances for men, ladies, students, and couples.

- Sign up for our online newsletter.

- Listen to audio sermons.

- Review publications and resources that will help you and your family.

- Learn more about Christ Life Ministries.

NOTES

NOTES